AF593382

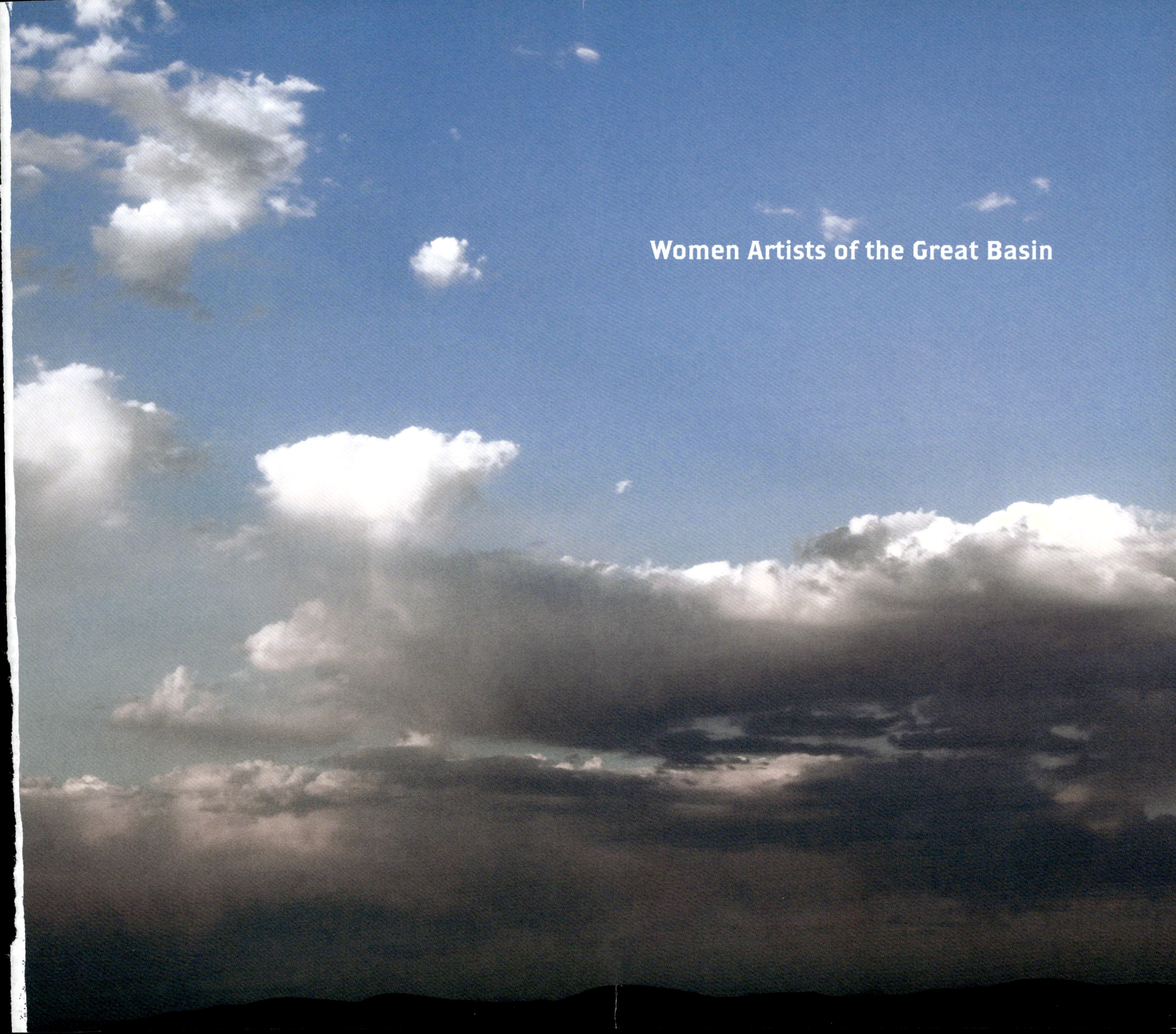
Women Artists of the Great Basin

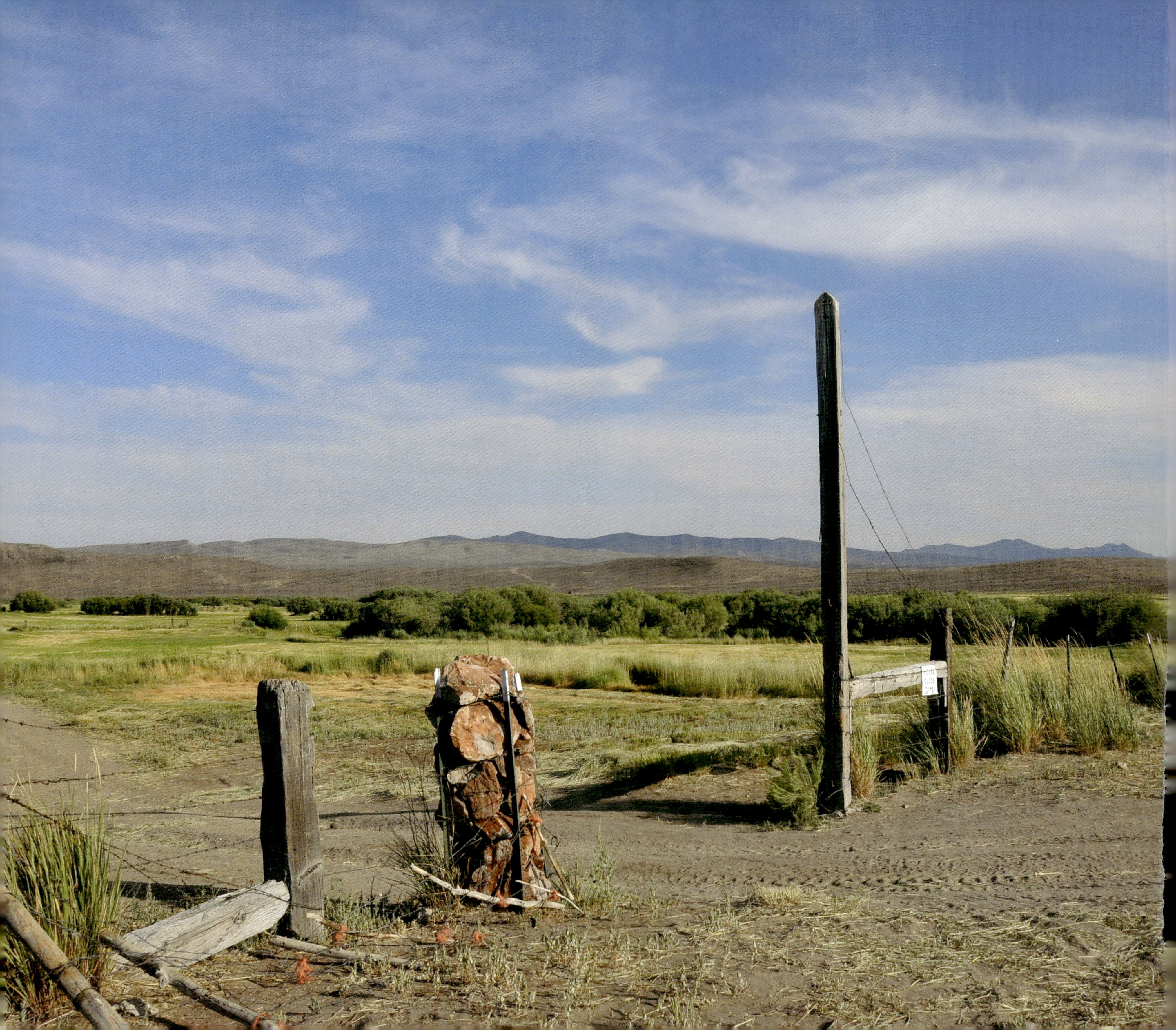

WOMEN ARTISTS OF THE GREAT BASIN

text by Mary Lee Fulkerson

with photographs by Susan E. Mantle

UNIVERSITY OF NEVADA PRESS | *Reno & Las Vegas*

University of Nevada Press | Reno, Nevada 89557 USA
www.unpress.nevada.edu

Cover landscape photo: Leaving Klamath Falls, Oregon, toward Susanville, California. Headed home.
Page i: Pink clouds over the mountains, Elko County, Nevada.
Frontispiece: Keddy Ranch, Elko County, Nevada.
Page v: Tuscarora Range.
Page vi: Patricia Wescott, *Wabuska Woman*. Mixed Media of railroad tie and spikes, old muffler cover, copper wire, metal strapping; 6 ft. 8 in. x 4 ft. An ode to East, one of the four directions.
Book and jacket design by Jinni Fontana

LIBRARY OF CONGRESS CATALOGING-IN-PUBLICATION DATA
Names: Fulkerson, Mary Lee, 1936– author. | Mantle, Susan E., 1948– photographer (expression)
Title: Women artists of the Great Basin / text by Mary Lee Fulkerson; photographs by Susan E. Mantle.
Description: Reno & Las Vegas : University of Nevada Press, 2017. | Includes bibliographical references and index.
Identifiers: LCCN 2016059985 (print) | LCCN 2017000218 (e-book) | ISBN 978-1-943859-37-5 (cloth : alk. paper) | ISBN 978-0-87417-656-8 (e-book)
Subjects: LCSH: Women sculptors—Great Basin—Biography. | Great Basin—Biography.
Classification: LCC NB236 .F85 2017 (print) | LCC NB236 (e-book) | DDC730.92/2 [B]—dc23
LC record available at https://lccn.loc.gov/2016059985

The paper used in this book meets the requirements of American National Standard for Information Sciences—Permanence of Paper for Printed Library Materials, ANSI/NISO Z 39.48-1992 (R 2002).

FIRST PRINTING

Printed in China by Four Colour Print Group, Louisville, Kentucky

I prescribe you this—
go to the desert
high or low,
cold or hammers of Hell

shed the clothes of care
strip down to the bones
step out brave
let the desert see you're unarmed
and only ask for time

to hear the song of sage
turn green leaves silver

laugh out loud
or sing
those sounds are welcome here

rest
sleep until you numb the earth
we all must have our time
and yours is now

—Linda Hussa, *"The Cure"*

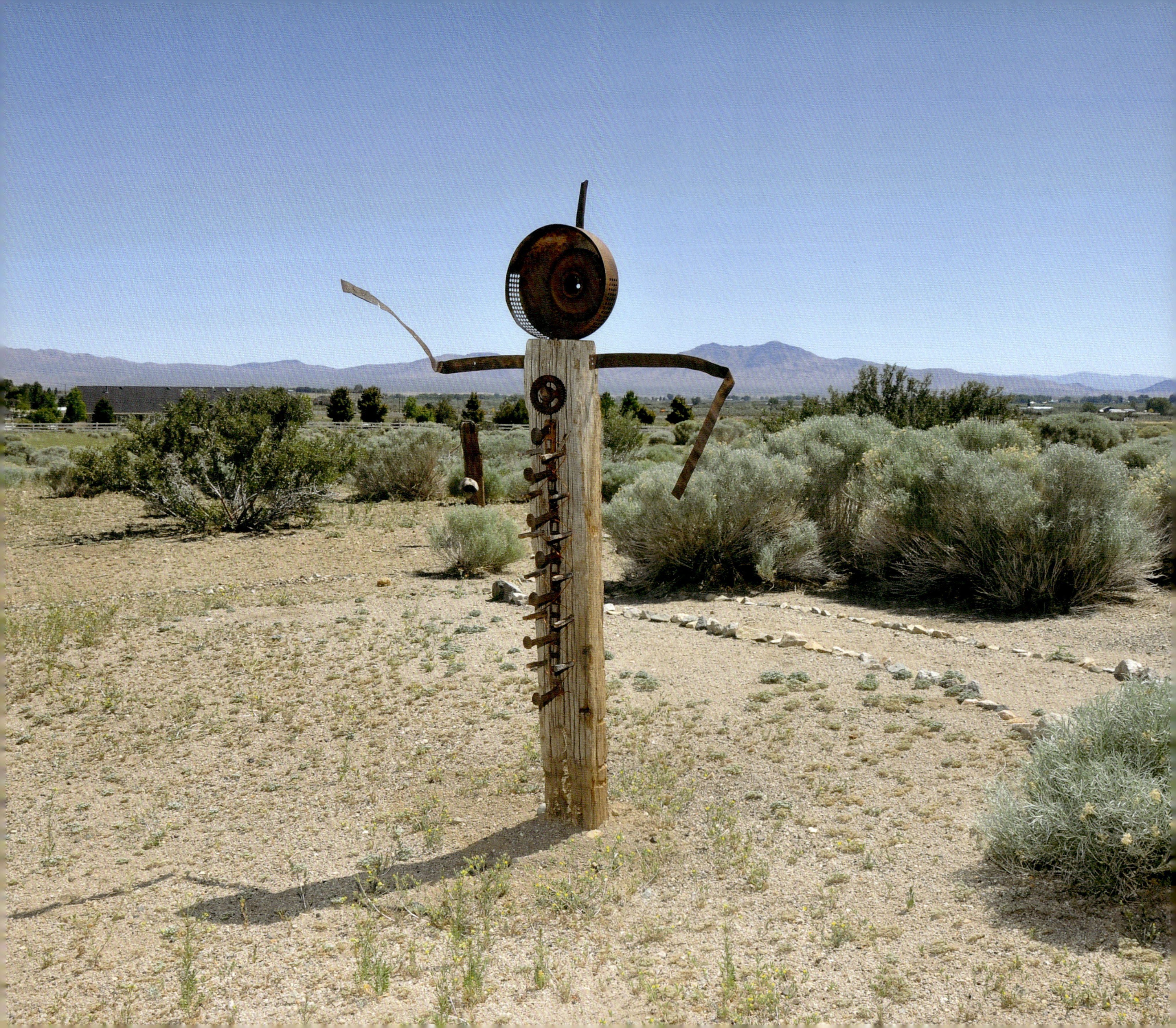

CONTENTS

List of Illustrations viii

Preface xi

MAPPING **3**

LANDING **11**

FIRING **15**

Carola Nan Roach • Born 1964 15
Kristen Frantzen Orr • Born 1951 19
Susan Glaser Church • Born 1952 23
Barbara Glynn Prodaniuk • Born 1954 31

BUILDING **37**

Elaine Jason • Born 1942 37
Danaë Bennett-Miller • Born 1959 40
Gretchen Ericson • Born 1965 46
Mimi Patrick • Born 1941 50

ADVOCATING **55**

Jann Haworth • Born 1942 55
Sarah Sweetwater • 1940–2015 60
Jean LaMarr • Born 1945 67
Joan Giannecchini • Born 1943 72

SPIRITING **79**

Rebecca Eagle • Born 1964 79
Tia L. Flores • Born 1960 83
Kay Minto • Born 1941 90
Patricia Wescott • Born 1947 95
Kathleen Curtis • Born 1941 100

STAGING **107**

Barbara Uriu • Born 1950 107
Gail Rappa • Born 1969 112
Jimmie Benedict • Born 1944 117
Jill Altmann • Born 1947 122
Jill Atkins • Born 1946 126

CHEERING **133**

Nancy Peppin • 1945–2015 133
Claudia Knous • Born 1946 137
Kathleen Weymouth Durham • Born 1943 141
Christine Shively-Benjamin • Born 1952 147

HONORING **153**

Joan Arrizabalaga • Born 1939 153
Pam Bowman • Born 1953 157
Demetrice P. Dalton • Born 1960 162

EXPLORING **169**

Rebekah Bogard • Born 1971 169
Sue Cotter • Born 1955 174
Elaine Parks • Born 1959 181

DREAMING **189**

About the Author 195
About the Photographer 196
Bibliography 197
Index 199

ILLUSTRATIONS

Sue Cotter, *Tangle of Language* x
Warm Springs Valley, where the desert meets the hills 1
Susan Glaser Church 2
Sarah Sweetwater in her garden 5
Rebecca Eagle and granddaughter, Monica 6
Kay Minto, Eagleville, California 8
Beowawe area, south of I-80 10

- Carola Nan Roach
  - Artist at work 14
  - *Furor Poeticus* 16
  - *The Big Screw* 18
- Kristen Frantzen Orr
  - Artist at work 20
  - *Autumn Honey* 21
  - *Strength and Beauty* 22
- Susan Glaser Church
  - Artist at work 24
  - *Mastectomy* 26
  - *Radiant* 27
- Barbara Glynn Prodaniuk
  - Artist at work 30
  - *Roller Derby Chicks* 32
  - *Rabbit Reliquary* 33
- Elaine Jason
  - Artist at work 36
  - *Never Always* 38
  - *Night Flight* 39
- Danaë Bennett-Miller
  - Artist at work 41
  - *Bueno: Homage to the Great Basin Buckaroo* 42
  - *Dancing for Flossie* 44
- Gretchen Ericson
  - Artist at work 47
  - *Pods* 48
  - Punctuation Series 49
- Mimi Patrick
  - Artist at work 51
  - *Untitled* 52
  - *Untitled* 53
- Jann Haworth
  - Artist at work 56
  - *Old Lady I* 58
  - *The Set, 1962* 59
- Sarah Sweetwater
  - Artist at work 61
  - *Maya* 62
  - *Labyrinth* 65
- Jean LaMarr
  - Artist at work 68
  - *Dolly Dingle's Friend* 69
  - *Washo Indian Woman and Papoose* 71
- Joan Giannecchini
  - Artist at work 73
  - *Square Holed Elder Brother* 74
  - *China Man* 76
- Rebecca Eagle
  - Artist at work 78
  - *Lake Tahoe* 81
  - *Lake Tahoe/Pyramid Lake* 82
- Tia L. Flores
  - Artist at work 84
  - *Papalotl, Monarch Butterfly Gourd* 86
  - *Imagine Peace* 89
- Kay Minto
  - Artist at work 91
  - *Walking the Dog* 93
  - *Nike of Mastectomy* 94

- Patricia Wescott
  - Artist working on *Wabuska Woman* 96
  - *Out of the Dark, Into the Light* 98
  - *Dragon Spine* 98
- Kathleen Curtis
  - Artist at work 101
  - Dancing figures swaying 102
  - *The Queen's Ride* 105
- Barbara Uriu
  - Artist at work 108
  - Japanese "Mon" bracelet and earrings 110
  - Gold pendant/brooch with stones 111
- Gail Rappa
  - Artist at work 113
  - *Moon Dreams,* pin/pendant 114
  - *Raven Finds Home*, shadow box concho belt 115
- Jimmie Benedict
  - Artist at work 118
  - *Triangle Vest* 120
  - *Reversible Swing Coat* 121
- Jill Altmann
  - Artist at work 123
  - *Washoe Bark Clothing* 124
  - *Origami Fold Jacket* 125
- Jill Atkins
  - Artist at work 127
  - *The Power of a Sunset at Tahoe,* Wedding Train series 128
  - *Ruby Mountains* 129
- Nancy Peppin
  - Artist at work 132
  - *Marie Twinkoinette* 134
  - *Cmdr. T. T. Kidd's Steam Subway Train* 135
- Claudia Knous
  - Artist at work 138
  - *Tendril Basket* 139
  - *Acrobat* 140
- Kathleen Weymouth Durham
  - Artist in storytelling, *Here Is Bobby Pin.* 142
  - *The Thirteen Icelandic Brothers Ready to Launch Their Pirate Ship* 144
  - *Getting Ready for the Million Mouse March* 146
- Christine Shively-Benjamin
  - Artist at work 148
  - *Altered Ego* 149
  - *Return to Me II* 150
- Joan Arrizabalaga
  - Artist at work, *Dead Man's Hand* 152
  - *Nevada Deer* 154
  - *Electricity Is Life* 156
- Pam Bowman
  - Artist at work, *Ebb and Wax* 159
  - One view of *Becoming* 160
  - Another view of *Becoming* 160
- Demetrice P. Dalton
  - Artist at work 163
  - *Untitled* 165
  - *The Bride* 167
- Rebekah Bogard
  - Artist at work 170
  - *Crush* 172
  - Scene from the *Heaven* installation 173
- Sue Cotter
  - Artist at work 175
  - *Testament of Beauty* 176
  - *Un Amor de Mexico* 179
- Elaine Parks
  - Artist at work, *Slip* 182
  - *Hercules* 184
  - *Night Sky Reversed* 185

Truck in landscape, Tuscarora 188
Wally Cuchine, Eureka, Nevada 192
Barbara Glynn Prodaniuk, *Untitled* 194

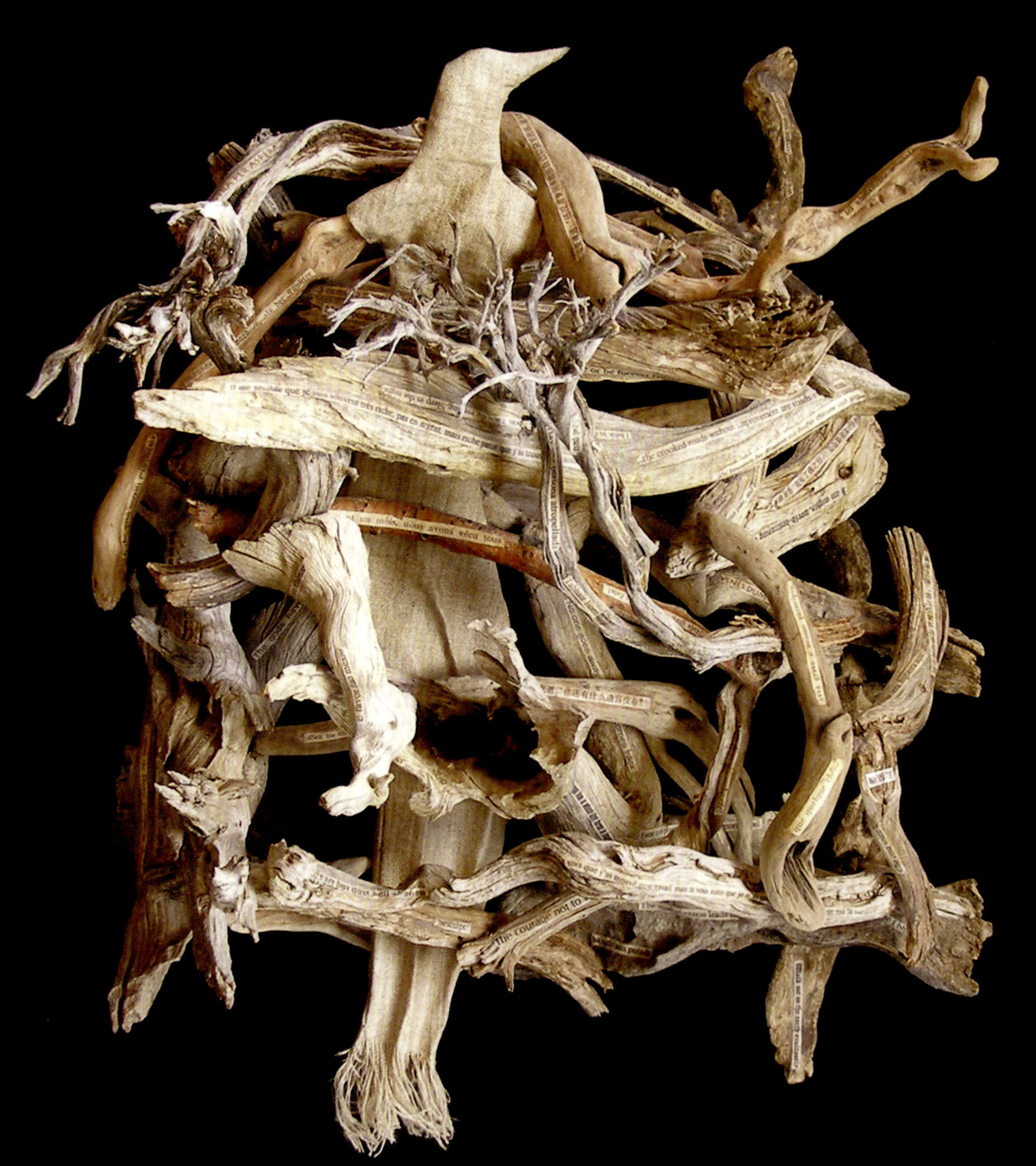

PREFACE

This is a book about women, art, and story, and those three potent topics have blended into powerful and authentic art, art that is cradled in the memories and experiences that women have mined and shaped over the years. In the coming pages you will discover art whose power lies in the memories and experiences these women have mined and shaped over the years. Their stories grew out of their lives like roots from a tree, and you will find lingering evidence of their journeys in the strength of their art. Each woman, as she moved along in her life's journey, seemed to seek something just out of the corner of her eye. And eventually she found it.

Living in the Great Basin has provided a certain cultural and/or geographical impact, which I call a *force,* that flows through their work. I should know: as a basket artist and fourth-generation Nevadan, my interest in Great Basin art is a lifelong journey that to date has yielded exhibitions, curation, documentation in national publications, and various other art-related scenarios.

As with many of the artists described here, my life activities determined the path I would take, and it wasn't always in a straight line. My father was a sawmill man, and when I wasn't running wild through the woods, climbing trees, and chewing on pine needles, I would watch a hewn log become a piece of sweet-smelling lumber. It was the memory of those fragrant boards that later turned me to willow, bark, and baskets.

In the 1970s I obtained a degree in art and sculpted baskets into undulating shapes, skinned them with paper, and painted them to represent Artemis, Mother Nature, or Wonder Woman. Sometimes they became story baskets that were encircled with legends and myths.

Soon my works appeared in books, galleries, museums, and corporate settings. One piece went to the White House. I organized and curated traveling shows, spoke at conferences, networked with professional women artists, formed the Great Basin Basketmakers and other organizations, and moderated tours, where I met artists throughout the Great Basin area.

My journey includes the publication, with photographer Kathleen Curtis, of *Weavers of Tradition and Beauty: Basketmakers of the Great Basin* (1995), which presents information on twentieth-century Native American basketry from the viewpoint of the weavers themselves. Their stories led to a discovery of a deep connection to the People of the sage and to the landscape into which they and their ancestors blended.

For nearly three decades my love and esteem for all artists of the Great Basin have grown. The variety and richness I discovered in the work of women artists scattered over the vast landscape inspired me to document their creations and stories. Because distance between the artists is so great, and with only a smattering of towns and cities, exhibition opportunities are few. But the art is jam-packed with originality.

This collection is not intended to be comprehensive. Instead, it showcases a range of women artists who are diverse in their methods and creative expression, and who treasure their individualism. Many of the women grew to

Sue Cotter, *Tangle of Language*. Mixed media; 20 x 16 x 15½ in.

prominence during the rise of women artists in the 1970s, while others represent succeeding generations.

I elected to focus on those who create sculpture in all its variations. What is sculpture? I redefined it. What exactly is "professional"? Not always what I thought. Media? Prepare for surprise and delight.

Photographer Susan Mantle and I traveled 4,500 miles around the four directions that spiked north, south, east, and west from our Reno home, spraying water on our faces in sizzling heat and snugging under heavy coats during freezing temperatures. We bumped across sage-dotted playas, cooled off near indescribably blue lakes, enjoyed picnics in the shade of piñon and juniper and lunches with the artists. We fell under the spell of sage, alfalfa fields, frontier towns, ranches, and a few lively cities.

Journeys in any form are opportunities to see something new. If you view them with an open mind, they can take on a shape and meaning that sometimes are only clear later. Our fieldwork indeed influenced us to cross new frontiers in interpreting the meaning of the word *art.*

As I planned our road trip to find the artists, my editor, Sara Vélez Mallea, advised me to consider my core values before beginning. I attempted to use that insightful advice to establish a tone of diversity in every area, from age to ethnicity to the character of work featured.

It was during the interview process that I found my aim. The aim, which I now realize is the essence this book, was to discover and communicate the rich stories of each artist's individual journey and how their stories influenced the raw vitality of their art. Their journey to fullness was actually their pilgrimage, and writing about them became mine.

You might say that I have been preparing to write this book all my life.

Many people across the Great Basin gave their support to our vision, beginning with our editor, Sara Vélez Mallea, whose advocacy and encouragement kept us going when challenges seemed too great to conquer. Next, great gratitude to the artists themselves, who gave so willingly of their time and resources.

We gained insights from Ann Wolfe, senior curator and deputy director, Nevada Museum of Art; Jeff Lambson, curator, Brigham Young University Museum of Art; Brianna Ostler and Jill Haacking, interns, Brigham Young University Museum of Art; Wally Cuchine, collector; Eugene Hattori, PhD, curator of anthropology, Nevada State Museum; Carolyn White, director, Department of Anthropology, University of Nevada, Reno; Catherine Fowler, PhD, professor emerita, University of Nevada, Reno; Katee Withee, graduate student, University of Nevada, Reno; Gene Quintana, art dealer and collector; Susan Shillinglaw, professor, San Jose State University; James McCormick, professor emeritus, University of Nevada, Reno; and *15 Bytes,* published by Artists of Utah.

Many thanks also to our moral and/or financial supporters. Without Carol Purroy's writing classes, this book would never have happened. Great thanks to her and the ever-encouraging Writers Unanimous group: Helen Stevens, Joyce Phillips, Vonda Novelly, Karin DeRocco, Audrey Cournia, Robin Winter, Celeste Leon, Betty Johnson, and Marie Edwards; the Surprise Valley Writers' Conference; Nevada Women's History Project; Truckee Meadows Community College Writers' Conference; Cathy Fulkerson; Jake and Marisa Fulkerson; Bob Fulkerson and Mike Perrier; Sheila Leslie; Vicki LoSasso; Mona Reno; Judy Topol; Meri Shadley; John Metzker; Loretta Terlizzi, Pam Russell; Janet and Michael Gilbert; Abigail Johnson; Sallie Moore; Andrea Duflon; Sarah Chvilicek; Carol Cooke, Patti Bernard; Susan Stewart; Janet Carter and Jerry Kumar. The late, great Chuck Fulkerson never wavered in his support. Nor did Elizabeth Mae Nedoff.

Warm Springs Valley, where the desert meets the hills.

Women Artists of the Great Basin

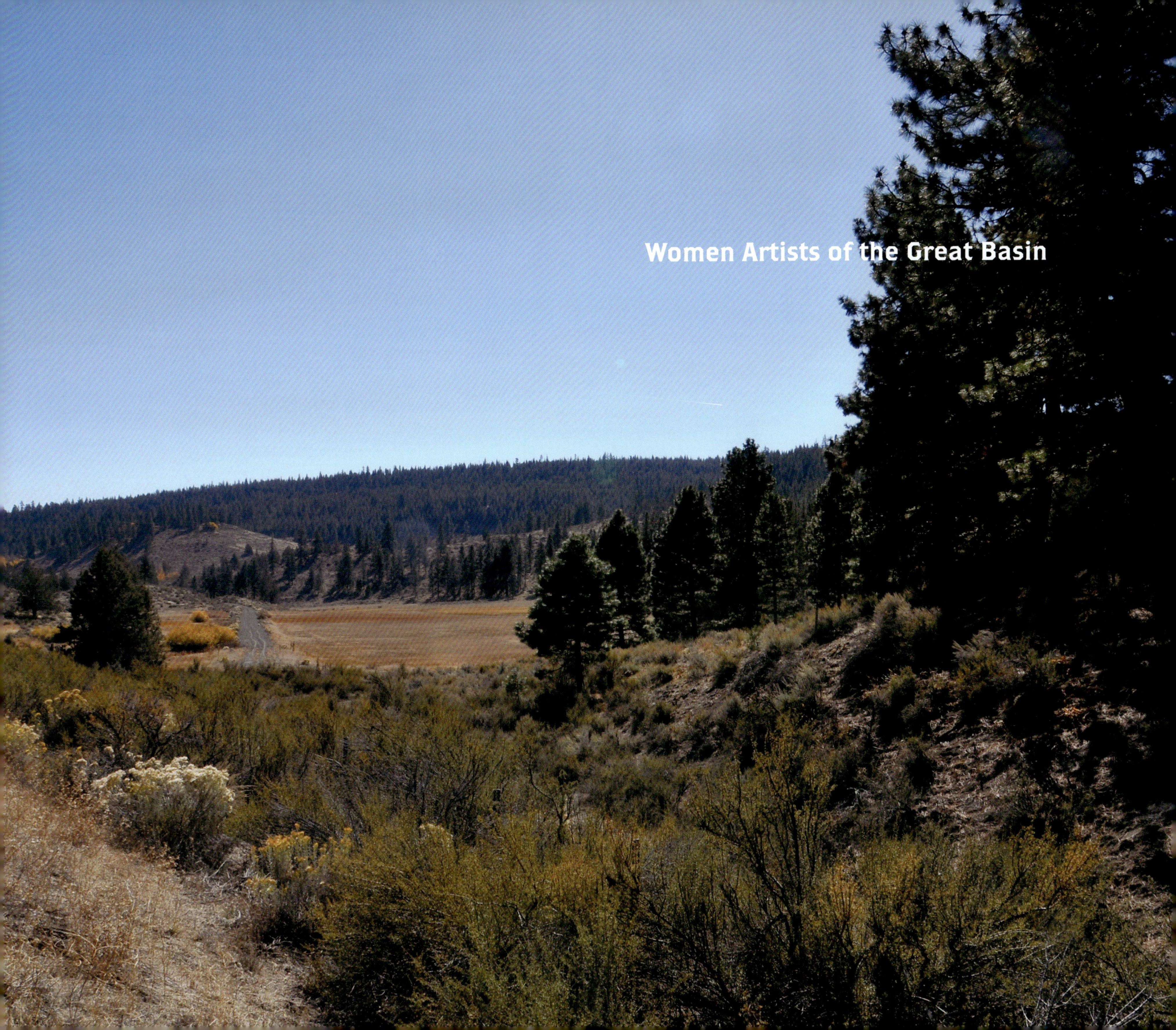

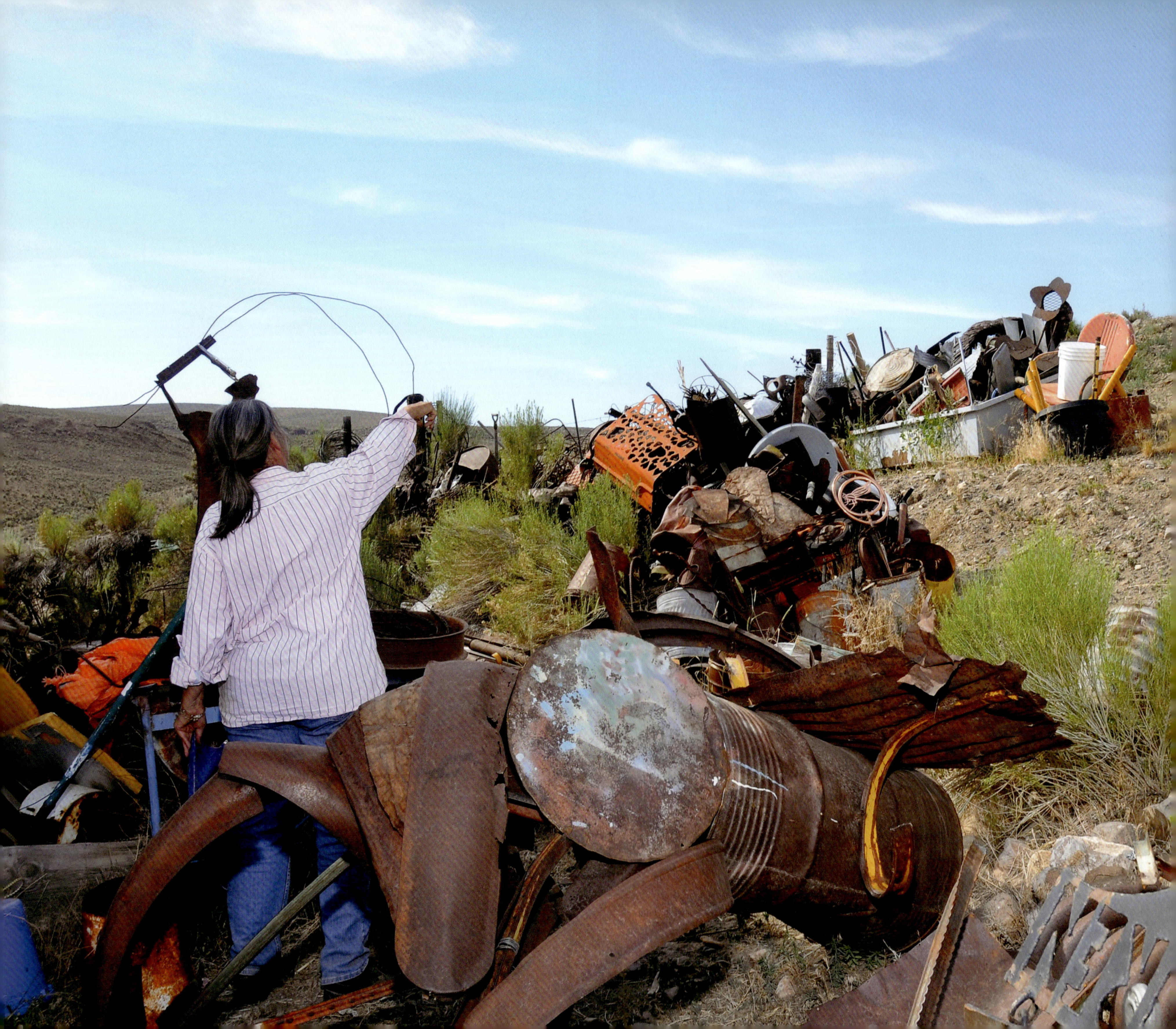

MAPPING

In Eleanor Munro's 1979 first-edition book, *Originals: American Women Artists,* she writes that she believed that because white European, male aesthetic values predominated for centuries, it was impossible, and will be so for a long time, to know what women's art might be. She concluded that the female voice was never lost: it simply was not listened to.

Munro's testimony had validity back in 1979 when *Originals* was first published, but a great deal has changed since then. Today, a wave of women's art has begun to paint the land with a giant brush, and nowhere have the winds of change been more evident than in the Great Basin, where a sense of freedom and rugged individualism has swept across the playas and through cities and towns. Photographer Susan Mantle and I present case studies of women artists who live and work in this land of wind and sky, sage and sand, neon and poker, and blazing sunsets. These artists have discovered their own frontiers of expression; today they're at the center of reshaping and retelling the Great Basin story.

This book presents a diversity of design and media as well as differences in cultural identities, education, and practice among the artists. And in spite of the dissimilarities, you will also find commonality. The works of art represent a variety of journeys, where edges and boundaries shift and become signposts to the realization that women artists follow diverse and converging trails along the Great Basin map.

Perhaps their sense of innovation emerged because they have little recorded history on which to dig and sift. Author Whitney Chadwick, in her book *Women, Art, and Society* (1990, 350), said women artists today "often find themselves negotiating a complex territory as they seek to locate themselves within a tradition where they've been historically discriminated against and which has been defined in male terms." Stylistically, the artists share little, and many create work outside the generally accepted imperatives of the art world. Some have exhibited worldwide, while others, whose work is equally important, don't buy into the standard rule that exhibition is required in order to be recognized as "real" artists. Working tools vary from welder's torch to needle and thread, and their communication technology ranges from Twitter to voice to paper and pen. But they have in common intensity and a generosity associated with hope, belief in beauty, and even healing. They are, without realizing it, challenging the current definitions of art, and their risk and reward are to venture outside the imposed art contexts. Their mentors were frequently mothers, aunts, and grandmothers who spun and wove wool, stitched samplers and clothing, and crafted beauty in their own homes. Many women artists today are rehabilitating the stitch-like mark, swaddling and wrapping, the techniques and materials of women's traditional art and work. Feminist art expands these sources to include what we learn from our own lived experiences as women. Author Rebecca Solnit mentioned this notion of the feminine influence in her book, *Men Explain Things to Me* (2014, 72–73).

Women Artists of the Great Basin is by no means a comprehensive survey. There are hundreds of excellent women

Susan Glaser Church examines sculpture possibilities.

(and men) artists who live and work in this region, but because of space limitations and a desire to present a logical flow, I mapped out a specific set of criteria.

First, geography. The majority of the artists live and work within the Great Basin; a few are at the western edges and beyond, but their work reflects the culture of this region. Barbara Prodaniuk lives in a land in-between, west of Verdi, Nevada, and east of California's Sierra Nevada range. Danaë Bennett-Miller's home is at the northern border, in the rural Oregon community of Tumalo. Elaine Jason, who now maintains a studio at Lake Tahoe, lived and produced her groundbreaking work in Reno for twenty-five years, and Kathleen Curtis, who lives near Auburn, California, has always drawn her inspiration from the land and mysticism of the Great Basin. The 1873 mining town of Tuscarora, home to Elaine Parks, Gail Rappa, and Joan Giannecchini, among others, is surrounded by the Great Basin but not in it, because the nearby Little Owyhee River flows into the Pacific Ocean, while Great Basin rivers flow inward.

This so-called wasteland resonates strongly, even spiritually with the artists. Joan Arrizabalaga's clay and fiber gaming sculptures are witty takes on the casino culture, while Nancy Peppin puts "all the colors of the Great Basin into . . . art—ultramarine blue, ochre, sage, burnt umber, lavender, Indian red." It's the light that moves Carola Nan Roach. Paiute-Shoshone artist Rebecca Eagle says this is "home to the ancient ones, and with every step so delicate, I remember the ground is sacred, and I give thanks to the Creator and Mother Earth." Jann Haworth says the Great Basin offers light and space. "You feel supported here. I have a sense of exuberance!" Barbara Prodaniuk developed what she calls "the mudcrack glaze" after being inspired by Pyramid Lake tufa formations. Pam Bowman echoes what many of the artists have expressed: "You just can't live here without being affected by it."

The next mapping point required that artists be female, be professional, take their work seriously, and work at it full time. After that, I narrowed the form of their art to the realm of three dimensions. Fourth, I sought a range of media. And finally, I wanted to tell their stories. Why them, I wondered? What series of events led them to their particular art?

MAPPING SCULPTURE

University of Nevada, Reno (UNR), professor of sculpture Robert Morrison once said jokingly, "Sculpture is something you back into while looking at a painting."[1] This way of thinking has been around for a long time, and is part of the reason as a former basket artist I decided to showcase the brilliant diversity of three-dimensional art. Attitudes toward sculpture have changed in the past thirty or so years as the result of influences from multicultural art/craft traditions. With outsider artists whose histories contain no bias about defining art standards, and with a resurgence of the work of the hand, possibilities loosened and sculpture leapt from its pedestal, found other spaces, fractured into many parts, and multiplied in a frenzy of disparate directions. And with the emergence of sound, performance, three-dimensional imaging, and social media, the entire definition of sculpture has expanded. For this reason, I've stretched the framework of my study to include wearable sculpture as well as storytelling and art activism.

MAPPING MEDIA AND TECHNIQUE

One of the critical parameters in any discussion of the arts of making—across the entire spectrum from craft to fine art—is material. What are some of the ways we do or do not recognize the significance of materials in discussions of art? What something is made of and how the material is employed affects the form, function, and perception of the finished piece.

Late-California clay sculptor Gillian Hodge said, "Artists who work in unnoble materials are opening the door to what art is, can be, and should be."[2] Hodge's was a

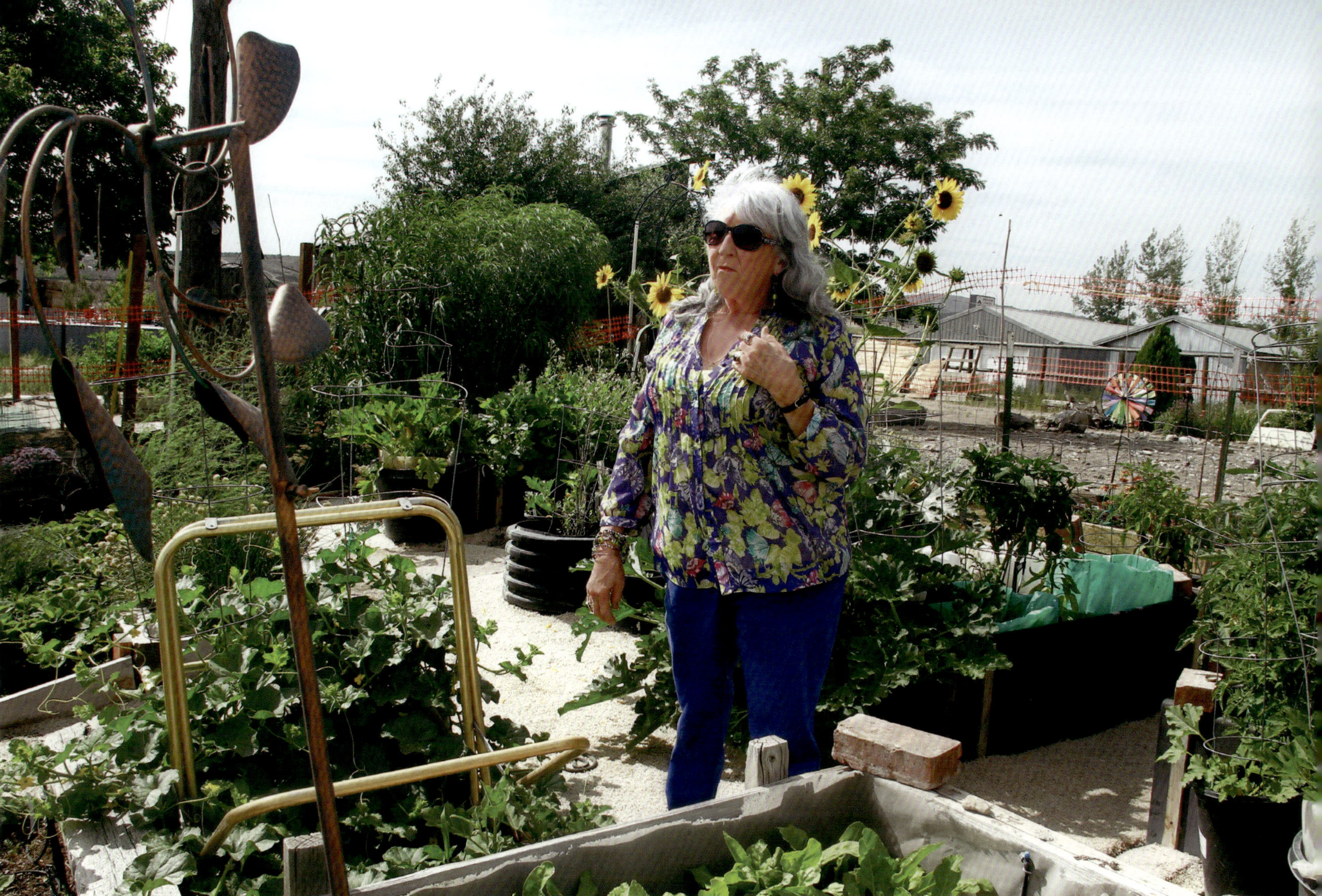

Sarah Sweetwater's sculpture garden.

thoughtful statement appreciated by those who work outside the world of mainstream art, manipulating such media as paper pulp, wood, rusty metal, thread, stone, clay, cloth, glass, and trash-dump throwaways. Many employ techniques familiar to their history as women, like stitching, weaving, designing the interior of a home, making do with less, and so on to bring their visions forward. Increasing numbers of craftspeople create nonfunctional objects that are now classified as art, and increasing numbers of artists express their vision using media formerly relegated to craft. The line has blurred, and few collectors, gallery directors, and others seem to care.

The old art versus craft debate is almost history, and the artists in this book have bridged that gap. They have taken leaps into the unknown, sometimes by choice of media, like cloth, wood, vinyl, paper, string. Other times, they invented techniques such as welding metal to tufa as Kay Minto did, or in Danaë Bennett-Miller's case using the lost wax casting method normally employed for jewelry making to create large public sculpture. In the past, craft was identified by its function and/or material, but whether objects exist as decoration or as symbols, it is the power of their presence that links them to art and obscures their relationship to the tradition of craft. For what art has no function? Power rests in objects that are created for use as well as contemplation. You will find references to Wild Women Artists in various chapters. They are a group of professional artists who network and exhibit their work. The group is discussed in detail in chapter 11.

MAPPING THE STORIES

"One must believe that private dilemmas are, if deeply examined, universal," wrote May Sarton in *Journal of a Solitude* (1973, 60), "and so, if expressed, have a human value beyond the private." An important part of the mapping experience in this book is a brief life story of each artist. As the women spoke of coming to their fullness during extremely trying situations, I came to realize that story keeps art alive, drenches it with power. A great work of art does not just suddenly appear. Rather, it is the result of the artist's story. Her roots and longings, her lifestyle, spirituality, and training all converge into each piece. You appreciate at a deeper level the drama and perfection of the end product when you have an awareness of its beginnings and middles. National Public Radio interviewer Terry Gross says she loves interviewing artists because they are "the people we designate to open up their lives for examination so we can understand better who we are" (Gross 2015, 37).

Each of the thirty-two women discusses the loops in her journey. Each artist is quite different from the others—not only in her artistic practices, but also in the cultural forces

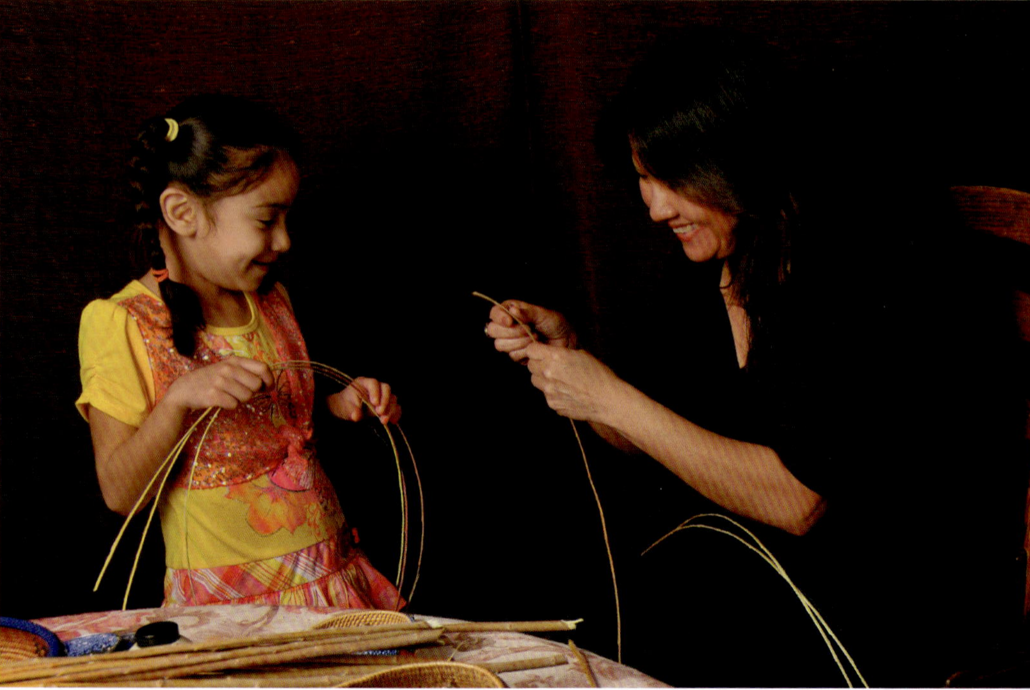

Rebecca Eagle teaches granddaughter, Monica, to work willow.

that stimulate and inspire her; and we become aware of a multiplicity rather than a sense of sameness in the art she produces. Each has stepped away from the typical center of art to take new and unfamiliar roads back to her true beliefs and beginnings.

Some of the artists are daughters of World War II veterans with mixed outcomes from those relationships, from harboring pride in their fathers' accomplishments to bearing the brunt of what is now labeled post-traumatic stress disorder, a condition that might have precipitated joblessness, anger issues, abuse, and/or alcoholism. In these situations, the daughters found release and personal reward in private corners, creating art that soothed their souls. Some either grew up alone or became little mothers themselves by caring for younger siblings when their mothers, sole breadwinners, were forced to work outside the home (child support was optional and child care was not available in those years). Being women, these artists have cared for children, grandchildren, parents, or partners when needed. Most discovered their talents while enrolled in elementary and high school art classes that were then (but not now) part of the curriculum. Art provided an escape to a happier world, where outcomes could be invented and baffled hearts could find a home. Jill Atkins said, "It is a shame that art is now considered so frivolous that we have to cut it."

At least two artists were struck with infantile paralysis as children and several others dealt with breast and other cancers. Three felt unable to care for their children as single mothers back when child care and equal pay were not options, and they sadly relinquished their children to their fathers' care. Almost all experienced other traumatic events at some point in their lives, and from them they developed great wisdom and strength. The women mention mothers, grandmothers, aunts, nurses, and teachers who encouraged them. One artist said nobody did.

Today, many of these artists are bringing wellness to the souls of their communities, working on public art projects, teaching the underserved, organizing tours and events, and resurrecting community pride.

"Women have to do it all," Elaine Parks says. "If you want to make art, that's fine. But you also have to keep the house going." The women in this book buy the groceries and birthday presents, bake the homeroom cookies, pick up the dry cleaning, drive the children to dance class or 4-H or scout meetings, prepare a feed for the round-up crew, and volunteer at schools, libraries, and nonprofit organizations. Multitasking is second nature, and their artmaking eddies around cooking dinner, gathering cattle, teaching school or tai chi, conducting business, and other life endeavors. Some postponed their serious creative work until retirement, while others have postponed or decided against raising families in favor of developing their careers. All perform juggling acts. While this might seem a sad state of affairs, these women made personal life choices, and all of the parts of their lifestyles have contributed to their culture and the unique types of art that you're about to see. Working with myriad materials at hand, they have created authentic works intended to make the world a better place. I've come to think of this book as one avenue of hope. Because artists, in telling their stories and bringing forth newness to the world, do indeed provide hope. And if they can do this, so can others in any way that works for them.

It isn't always easy for people to decide for themselves about "good art" and "bad art," or even just "Is it art?" because the field has become mystified to the point where many don't trust or are even embarrassed by their own responses. Artists themselves are often separated from their audiences and influenced by the values of those who exhibit and/or purchase their work. Have no doubt: the women in this book are their own bosses. Their art does not celebrate meaninglessness; each has ventured outside imposed art contexts and developed an authentic style as distinctive and independent as the place that nurtures them.

Still, they face challenges. Arts advocate Courtney Martin wrote in *American Prospect Magazine* (2011), "So what do female artists need? They need space, literally and metaphorically, money, the capacity to advocate for their own work, and the networks necessary to make artistic effort lead to opportunities."[3] The overwhelming fact remains that a woman's experience in this society—social and biological—is simply not like that of a man's.

To facilitate the mapping process, I presented each artist with ten questions, and their responses became the bones of their essays. Some answered fully, others chose to answer the questions that resonated. The questions were

1. *Where did you grow up and what were your creative beginnings?*
2. *How did you get to your present work?*
3. *Does your heritage play a part?*

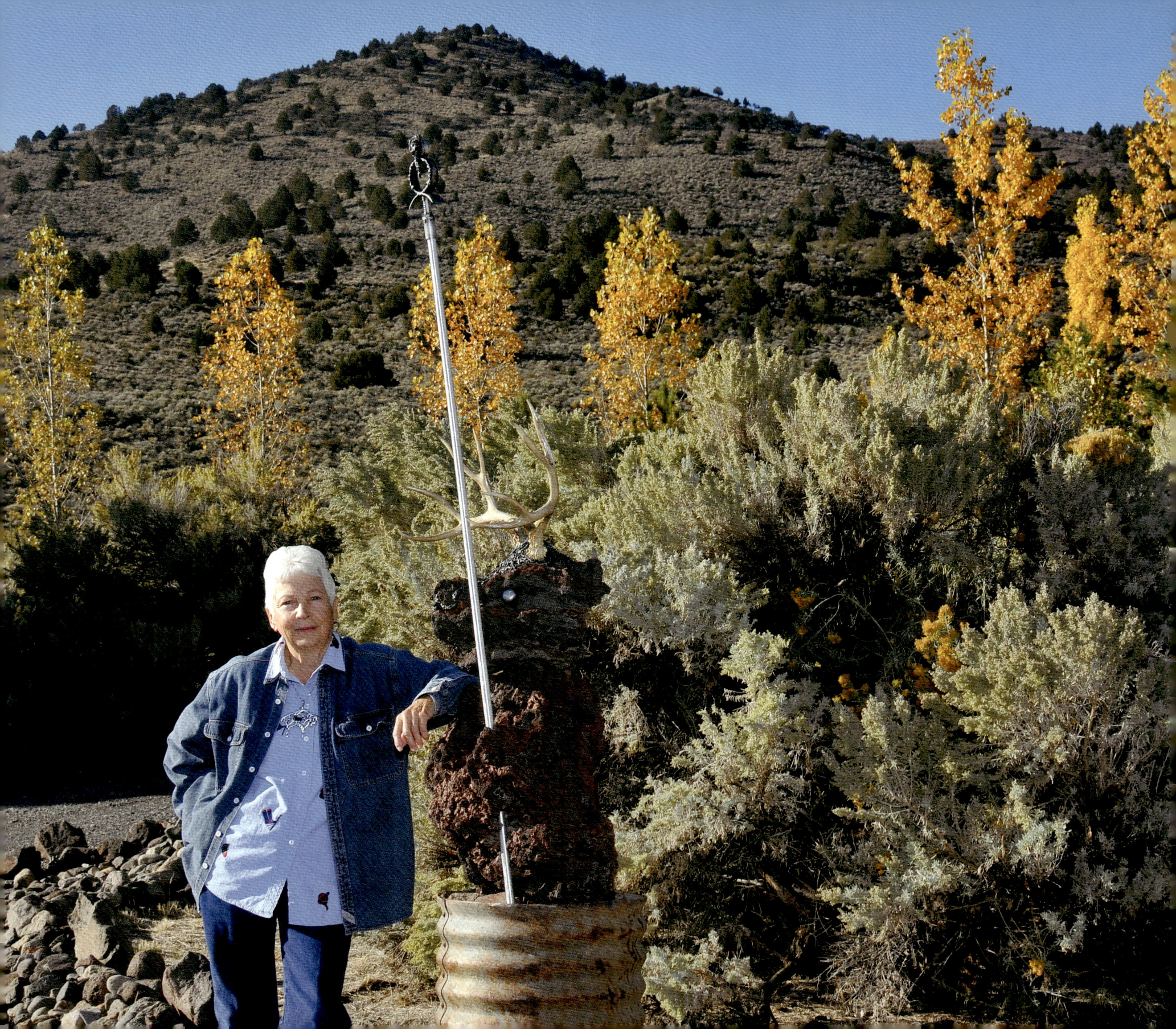

4. *What does it mean to you to live in the Great Basin?*
5. *Who were the role models who encouraged your artistic path?*
6. *What is your process?*
7. *Name important books or readings.*
8. *What motivates you to keep going?*
9. *What transformative experiences have brought you through to where you are today?*
10. *In praise of failure, what made you strong?*

I have grouped the artists in various chapters according to the nature of their work and, inspired by Lucy R. Lippard, PhD, in her book *Mixed Blessings* (1990), have defined each chapter by a gerund, because the gerund (from the Latin "to be carried out") is the grammatical form of process. Finding chapter headings was a challenge, because artists and their masterpieces shift like the terrain under their feet, and creative work requires constant intervention and change. This first chapter, "Mapping," introduces and explains the book's direction. Chapter 2, "Landing," looks at the visual and spiritual influences of Great Basin geography. The land is the one common element that engenders a big dream, a purposeful path, a vision. Succeeding chapter headings—"Firing," "Building," "Advocating," "Spiriting," "Staging," "Cheering," "Honoring," "Exploring," and "Dreaming"—describe the focus of the artists' work.

The women in this book seem both ancient, connected to those cultures that have preceded them, and contemporary, because they have blazed trails to create new art forms that nurture an old, old memory—one without words—that lies deep within all of us.

With a vision, a big dream, a purposeful path, sprinkled with a little humor and a little feistiness, these artists keep their feet on the ground even while their heads are in the clouds as they show us new ways of seeing and envisioning. Their creative rivers flow deep. They and their contemporaries are the standard-bearers for future generations.

Notes

1. The saying is attributed to abstract-expressionist painter Ad Reinhardt.
2. In 2002 Ms. Hodge defined the noble media as bronze, oil, and marble at an art workshop in Tahoe City, California.
3. Martin goes on to say, "No wonder statistics, however shocking, don't seem to jolt art-world powerbrokers into behavior change. No wonder visual culture is still largely created by only one half of the potential artist population."

Kay Minto outside her studio.

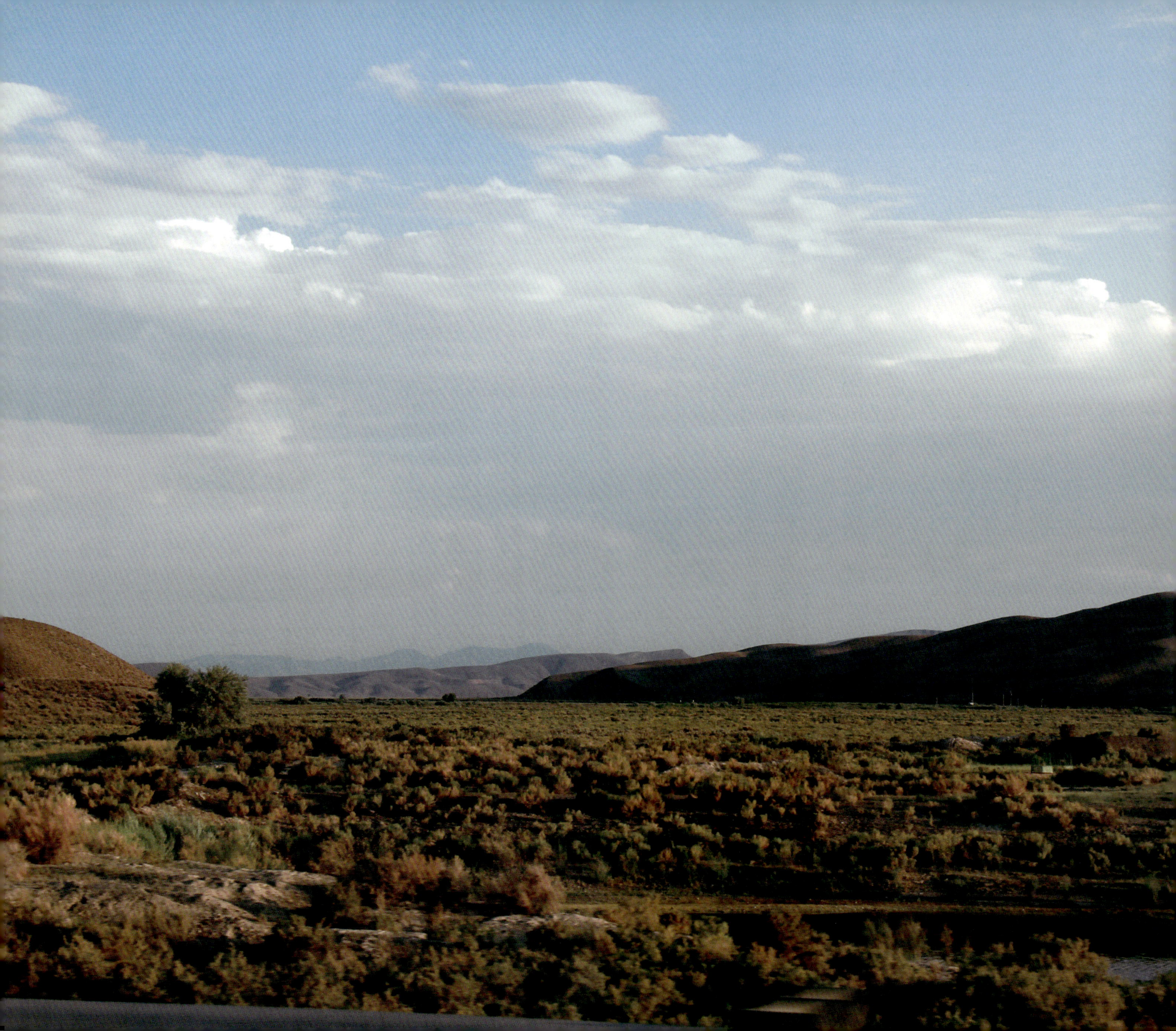

LANDING

Today's Great Basin women artists are true originals, rooted in a land of unique geography, a stew of cultures, and story unlike any other.

People call the Great Basin a lonely place, even a wasteland, maybe because an immensity of time and space hovers over the land, and those unaccustomed to it feel a sense of displacement. Others, like me, see surprising beauty and mystery among the miles of tumbling sage-covered hills—giant fat velveteen bodies at rest, offering miracles and sweet surprises, sheltering fertile valleys—Gardens of Eden that are hidden like secrets in the shadows of the hills. And if you don't think those hills offer miracles and sweet surprises, try meditating in a sweat lodge, or camp in the outback with only a campfire at night, and feel embraced in a great dark and starry silence. Or check out Shoshone spiritual leader Corbin Harney's book, *The Way It Is* (1995, 41, 71). He said Native ancestors healed their sick with sage, a prolific shrub, and "Today we're still doing it." Harney looked on sagebrush as a living being, and interpreted its voice: "I don't care how wet I am; when you ask me to warm your body, I'll burn." He said people also made soup out of the tiny balls on the sagebrush, with jerky or deer meat mixed in. And in Utah author Terry Tempest Williams's essay, "A Sprig of Sage" in David Landis Barnhill's edited work *At Home on the Earth: Becoming Native to Our Place* (1999, 119), she had this to say: "Out of my pouch falls a sprig of sage. I can crush its leaves between my fingers and remember who I am. I belong to the Great Basin."

Bill Fiero, in his *Geology of the Great Basin* (1986), says there is no land in the world that is as amazing as the Great Basin—mountains still rise, shorelines etch the valley slopes. Titanic forces lock in massive conflict. Richard Francaviglia, in his *Believing in Place: A Spiritual Geography of the Great Basin* (2003, 59), credited geologist Kenneth Diffeye with the observation that "the earth is moving. The faults are moving. There are hot springs all over. The world is splitting open and coming apart." The unceasing struggle between fire and water created the grandeur that is the Great Basin. This astounding landscape, where three mighty rivers—Humboldt, Sevier, and Quinn—run inward and disappear, is unique in the world. The quest for water never ends, and the Nevada topography ranges from the North American low point at Badwater Basin to the highest point of the contiguous United States, less than a hundred miles away at the summit of Mount Whitney.

The Great Basin, that perpetually landlocked region that lies between the Sierra Nevada and the Wasatch Range, takes up a good-sized chunk of the entire West, including most of Nevada, half of Utah, and parts of California, Oregon, Idaho, and Wyoming. It spans anywhere from 113,000 (geography) to 200,000 (hydrography) square miles. And since most of the water runs inward, then why shouldn't attitudes do the same? Flowing toward the center, they bubble into a stew of creativity. As author Wallace Stegner wrote, "The Great Basin is a unifying force; wherever you live in it, you flow toward every other part."[1]

Still, there's more than uncommon geography here. Gretel Ehrlich in her book, *The Solace of Open Spaces* (1985),

Beowawe area, south of I-80.

believes that all of us live in a culture that has lost its memory. I'm not sure that statement is true in the Great Basin. Here, stories and memories seem to linger like the mighty bristlecone pine, the oldest known tree anywhere in the world. While the land itself is on a trajectory of movement and change, the myths continue to simmer in the corners of our minds. Utah artist and world traveler Jann Haworth put it succinctly: "There's a different blood here." Haworth might have a point.

My father roamed this country back when stories were passed along about cattle rustling, water witching, and a lost Wells Fargo gold shipment. Once an old cowpoke told of underground water he'd discovered. He'd chased a yearling down a rock-slippery canyon and wound up at the bottom, near a crevasse. There, he heard water gurgling from deep down below. Curious, the cowboy tied a rock to his long rope and lowered it into the fissure. The rope never reached bottom.

Many tales are much older. We try to interpret petroglyphs, etched chronicles in stone—some carved nearly 19,000 years ago; and today's Native people have stories of their own.[2] Take Sand Mountain, near Fallon. There, if you hold yourself still and let a desperate quiet saturate the air, the sand begins to sing. The People say this is the sound of the Great Serpent Kwansee, dispensing guidance and protection. When the sands shift, as they frequently do, Kwansee is shaking the earth, sensing imbalance and disrespect of the land. Many ancient myths float around the Great Basin, and, like Kwansee, they frequently center around geographical landmarks such as Pyramid Lake's Stone Mother, whose tears formed the lake, or Mount Timpanogos, near Provo, an Indian maiden lying down. At Red Rock, north of Reno, the old people said the earth was scarred long ago when giants fought each other over territory. And Shoshone elder Lily Sanchez speaks with reverence of flying wolves and water babies that draw respect at her home reservation of Duckwater.

Harney (1995, 26) said things that come from Mother Earth have life. "The Rocks are the same way. The rocks talk—they eat like we do, they breathe air like we do. They are the same age as whatever was here thousands of years ago. Some of your people are just beginning to realize that the rocks have a life." So even rocks have tales to tell.

Pioneer trails cross the land, and stories of the California, Applegate, and Oregon Trails and the Great Mormon Crossing remain sources of pride, not only to the descendants of those hardy folk, but also to those who still discuss the great migrations of bold-spirited people who came for gold, silver, a fresh start, or God. Basques arrived from the old country to herd sheep and carved their yearnings into the bark of mountain aspen. Their resiliency is legend, and one family, the Laxalts, produced a United States senator and a college professor who founded the University of Nevada Press. The university also formed an international center for Basque studies.[3]

Latinos continue to pour into a land that welcomes them, and both the University of Utah and UNR, support Latino research and study centers. African Americans came later and dug in their heels, determined to create their own space, some by building their own community in Black Springs, Nevada.[4] Chinese laborers traveled ten thousand miles to help build the transcontinental railroad, supply fuel for the mills and mines, and do a little mining of their own before returning home or fanning out across the Great Basin and beyond. Today, the University of Utah's Intermountain Consortium for Asian and Pacific Studies has created an education pipeline across that state.

Wild horses, fodder for heated arguments over their handling, still roam free over sagebrush hills. Buckaroos—cowboys and cowgirls descended from the Spanish vaquero tradition—still ride the range, and on long winter nights they soap their saddles, braid horsehair riatas, and set down poems to present at the National Cowboy Poetry Gathering in Elko, Nevada. Each year a Burning Man city rises in the

Black Rock Desert, where thousands gather to honor art and community and depart a week later, leaving no trace. On family farms and ranches, women then and now work alongside the men. If the men were injured or even if they died, the women carried on. Women continue to carry on. They not only run the ranches, but they've also built the culture—the libraries, museums, and the arts. They've been a hardy group, much like their forebears who tackled the deserts and mountains and channeled the rivers to settle here.

And because the federal government owns so much of the land (nearly half of the eleven Western states and nearly 80 percent in Nevada, according to the Conservation Biology Institute in Corvallis, Oregon), a vast wilderness is available to explore. You can ponder the stories that lurk behind such old stomping grounds as Lonesome Polecat Road, Surprise Valley, Toejam Creek, Pancake Summit, Fandango Pass, Wah Wah Summit, Lost Wallet Rim, and Steptoe Valley. When you walk out across the bare hills in the day or night, away from cell-phone range, you will discover that the light is alive and the moods and colors change every hour. You can rest your eyes on a distant mountain folded into more mountains and contemplate the soul of the earth. You can wonder what surprises, fertile valleys, loom around the next draw. Like the pathfinders of old, you can explore the magic that is the Great Basin.

In a recent lecture tour in Utah, the Guerrilla Girls (www.guerrillagirls.com), a group that advocates for women's equality in the arts, reported that equality for women artists is not happening in New York.[5] They said that the farther away a woman artist goes from New York, the greater her opportunities. And thus emerges the fruitfulness of the Great Basin. Those born here grew up tough and carry the myths of the land, and those who came along later brought a pioneering spirit that lingers in everyone who touches the ground and strikes out into the wild. The women artists in this book have dug deep and pulled out inspired and innovative work—art that doesn't imitate. They have struggled to find their own frontiers and have succeeded. Their creative rivers originate here.

Today's Great Basin women artists live gutsy, independent lives in this land of big skies, wilderness, and open spaces, where they can walk for miles in silence, tread and touch the earth, smell willow and sage and mud, hear wind swish through trees, and, like my father, tell a few stories of their own. Even the city dwellers retain the pioneering spirit of the early settlers, breathe the stories and myths of wild horses, of proud Native, Basque, African, Asian, and Latino culture, of hardy ranch life and cowgirls and cowboys.

Artist Sue Cotter said it all: "The Great Basin is the one region of the United States where I feel at home, where I could merge forever with a rock outcropping, a sagebrush, a creosote bush, or a lone raven on a fence post, and I would be content. The Basin makes you stop, be still, then move slow, explore carefully, sit down in silence, and absorb an indefinable presence."

Yes, Great Basin women artists are true originals.

Notes

1. Wallace Stegner said this while describing his friendship with Walter Clark (Laird 1983, 55). Clark grew up in Reno, Stegner in Salt Lake City. From opposite ends of the Great Basin, they came to share a vision of the West.
2. Great Basin tribes are many: Bannock, Chemehuevi, Kawaiisu, Mono, Paiute, Panamint, Shoshone, Washo, and Ute.
3. The Basque homeland is in the Pyrenees, which straddle France and Spain.
4. In 1952 Helen and Ollie Westbrook bought an acre of sagebrush land and engendered an entire community where African Americans could build, live, and raise their families (Townsell-Parker 2010).
5. From the FAQs at the Guerrilla Girls website: "We're a bunch of anonymous females who take the names of dead women artists as pseudonyms and appear in public wearing gorilla masks. We have produced posters, stickers, books, printed projects, and actions that expose sexism and racism in politics, the art world, film and the culture at large. . . . We wear gorilla masks to focus on the issues rather than our personalities. Dubbing ourselves the conscience of culture, we declare ourselves feminist counterparts to the mostly male tradition of anonymous do-gooders like Robin Hood, Batman, and the Lone Ranger. . . . The mystery surrounding our identities has attracted attention. We could be anyone; we are everywhere."

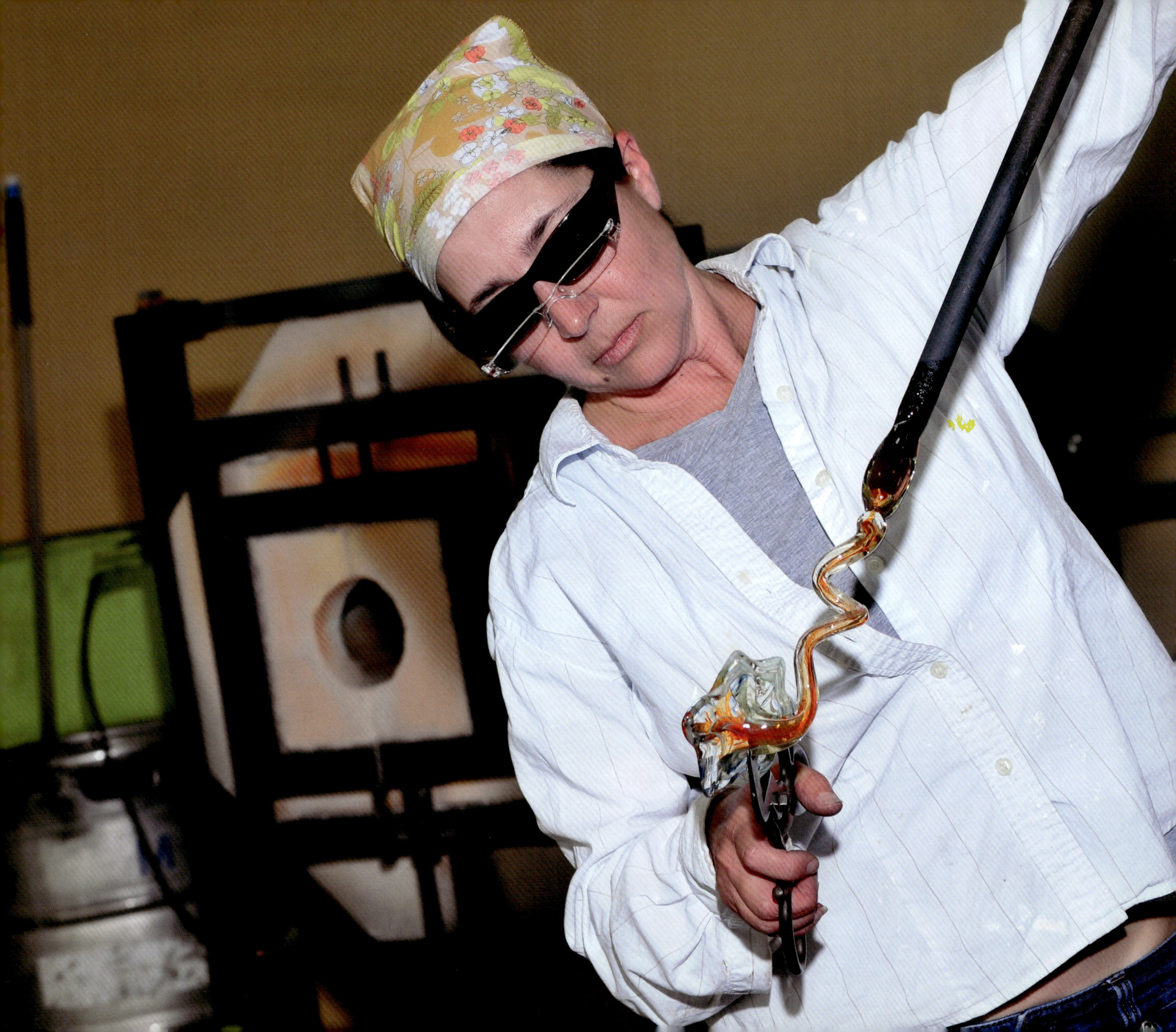

FIRING

We cannot hold it. Mysterious, mesmerizing, and powerful: Why does fire pull us? A campfire provides warmth, a cooking base, and a cozy atmosphere for singing, storytelling, or simply gazing. The flame shapes are fluid, dancing here, leaping there, and creating lives of their own. Fire can melt, and if taken to the extreme, destroy. And yet to look at fire is to be almost drawn into it. In Nevada's Black Rock Desert, fire has become the central force of an annual art event with the torching of a great wooden figure, Burning Man.

The four artists in this chapter rely on fire to develop their art forms. Carola Nan Roach and Kristen Frantzen Orr use metal rods to plunge raw glassy material directly into red-hot flames and, maintaining that high temperature, expertly manipulate the material into one-of-a-kind sculptures. Susan Glaser Church's fire involves the heat and sparks that are by-products of her welding technique. Rebekah Bogard, who is discussed in a later chapter, and Barbara Glynn Prodaniuk finish their ceramic work inside kilns that have been fired at high temperatures for many hours.

CAROLA NAN ROACH • BORN 1964

Carola Nan Roach was set up to fail, but her unstoppable drive to succeed was just too great. Her jet-propelled path to fulfillment has mostly evolved around art-glass sculpture, to be exact. And the buzzword is *alchemy.*

Our interview took place on March 20, 2015. Her brown eyes widen and seem to grow larger as Roach describes her highly perfected technique of blowing hot glass into a copper basket mold, when each element faces the possibility of destruction. "Copper can burn and melt, and at the same time you have to be intuitive of the crazy alchemy of glass," she says, her hands slicing the air as if to punctuate her statement. "And," she adds, "if the glass is too cold, it'll break." This same alchemy is at work when she twists a blob of hot glass around an iron rod, first inside a 2100–2400 degrees furnace, and next in the slightly cooler "glory hole," then shaping it with tools, adding color and more glass, and repeating the process.[1] The sculpture that finally emerges is a result of intuition, well-honed technical knowledge, physical endurance, and luck. Or *alchemy,* as Roach calls it.

The Merriam-Webster dictionary redefines the medieval process of alchemy, identifying it as the scientific "power or process of transforming something common into something special." Dennis Hauck defines the word *alchemy* more loosely, calling it a magical course of personal transformation. And Carola Roach has achieved success in both the scientific and philosophical definitions of the word.

"Nothing ever held me back," confides Roach, who was homeless as a child. During the interview, we sip water and chat across a table set against the wall in one of two large first-floor rooms that make up her Reno gallery. Glass sculptures in a variety of sizes, colors, and genres occupy shelves or soar from pedestals. Here a sword crookedly plunges into a rough-hewn block of glass. Behind it, winged figures in various stages of abstraction seem ready to fly or hover above their shelf, while a table in the next room holds three glass tiers of colorful frosted and decorated glass cupcakes

Carola Nan Roach expertly shapes the molten glass.

that look like they're fresh from the bakery. Another day we'll visit her workspace, Burnt Knuckle Studio, where she shares furnaces and equipment with other glass artists.

Roach's highly regarded work is the result of extended study—bachelor of fine arts from California College of the Arts, master of fine arts from Tulane University, and study at the world-famous Pilchuck Glass School in Washington. Her glass sculpture has juried into numerous solo and group exhibitions in art museums, galleries, and cultural centers from California and Washington to Texas, Louisiana, Alabama, Florida, and Japan. Her public art projects include a collaborative event in downtown Los Angeles and an artist residency in Artpark, New York. Her work has been reviewed and/or appeared on covers of various publications, and for several years she owned Feng Shwa Glass, a gallery and teaching studio. Oh, and did I mention she has been an art instructor? Yes, at Buffalo State College, New York; Pilchuck Glass School, Washington; Tulane University, New Orleans, Louisiana; Art Center College of Design, Pasadena, California; and the Tokyo Glass Art Institute. She was also artist-in-residence in several venues.

All these accolades I've gleaned from Roach's resume; she mentions none of them in our interview, but nods, smiling and moving her hands as she describes her path to the present. That's when I learn that pulling molten glass from a 2700-degree oven is familiar territory. Roach has been jumping into and out of the fire since childhood.

A New Yorker by birth, Roach at age six and her brother, Kevin, at age eight, moved with their parents to New Mexico. Their father, Robert, completed school and Roach fell in love with the high desert. Two years later, in 1972, the family headed for Berkeley, California, where the so-called hippie movement was in full swing; riots and unrest defined the days and her mother, a psychologist, wanted to study the movement. Study she did, divorcing Robert and taking up with a new man whose anger issues forced the Roach children to eventually flee to their father's flat. There, alcoholism consumed Robert's life and that of his ever-present friends. Poverty reigned. Roach and her brother were able to attend Berkwood, an alternative

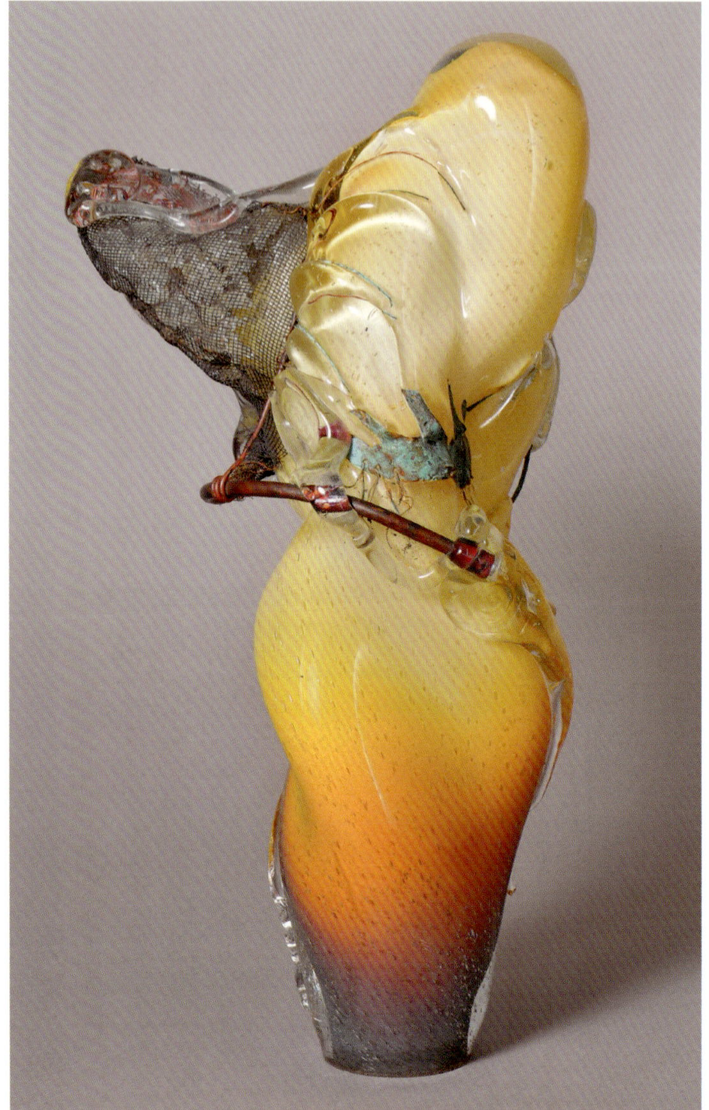

Carola Nan Roach, *Furor Poeticus*. Blown glass and copper; 17 x 8 x 7 in.

school, because their mother worked as the school secretary and their tuition was waived. There, students could choose their own course of study. Roach chose art, and her entire elementary school years were devoted to sculpting and drawing.

"It was great for the development of my art," she says, "but academics were lacking."

When Roach entered junior high school, she could not read. Fortunately, the public alternative school she attended, Odyssey, was small. She says, "I learned to read and everything else for the first time." She learned quickly—so quickly that she graduated from high school in two years. "My brother had done the same thing. He paved the way."

These were the growing-up years. Maybe her shyness came because of her poverty (they were living on welfare). She was also dishwashing at a restaurant and had little time for a gaggle of friends. Maybe it was her home situation, where Robert and his buddies were having brawls, and she didn't feel safe. But at age fourteen, Roach moved out. "I had an opportunity to take care of a big old house in Berkeley," she recalls. "It was empty and scary, and my dad only gave me half of the welfare check." A friend stayed for a while. They threw their sleeping bags on the floor, and even though school was farther away, she was safe.

"I share this because not having a stable family has affected me. Now I own two big homes and a ten-acre property. It [early life] made me more driven, perhaps."

Soon, Roach was able to move with her brother into a flat with several apartments, which she rented out. At age fifteen she was managing the whole operation while still in high school. Evenings found her at the library, researching scholarship possibilities, for she was determined to go to college and study art. I ask what kept her from getting involved in the drug scene. "I was focused on the art. It kept me away from that. My good friend Kristin's mother, Melody, was always there for me." She paused and those brown eyes seemed to gaze inward, "If kids have just one adult—if they know somebody cares—I always knew Melody cared."

Roach graduated from high school at sixteen and received a full ride scholarship to the California College of Arts and Crafts (now the California College of the Arts) in nearby Oakland. "I would walk by the glass area, and in the hallway was a big glass case holding the work of all these living artists. It was right next door to the hot shop where they did the glass. Amazing!" There were classes in painting, sculpture, and drawing, but from then on, Roach's focus was glass. Extremely shy and younger than everyone else, Roach found support from an unexpected corner, glass instructor Marvin Lipofsky.[2] Known at school as an authoritarian, he must have seen potential in Roach, because he gave her his full attention, and Roach blossomed, creating glass forms and inventing new ones.

She also connected with famed glass sculptor Therman Statom, a visiting instructor. The two became fast friends. Statom became a mentor, and it was through his generosity that she learned about the Tulane glass program. She recalls, "Therman introduced and recommended me to Gene Koss, head of the glass department at Tulane. I became the first woman to be accepted to the glass graduate program. Not something I was trying to do, didn't even know it at the time, and after me there were many more women accepted." She also worked as Statom's teaching assistant at Pilchuck.

Roach graduated from college, and, because of more diligent research, was able to get a scholarship and an assistantship at Tulane University. But first, our jet-propelled artist had another idea—to travel around the world. Since her dishwasher days at age fourteen, Roach worked odd jobs, from apartment management to making sandwiches at delicatessens. She sold her artworks to an increasingly appreciative group of admirers. And she saved her money and built a nest egg, a habit that remains with her to this day. "By the time I was nineteen, I had $10,000 saved." Her contemporaries were not feeling the same fire she was.

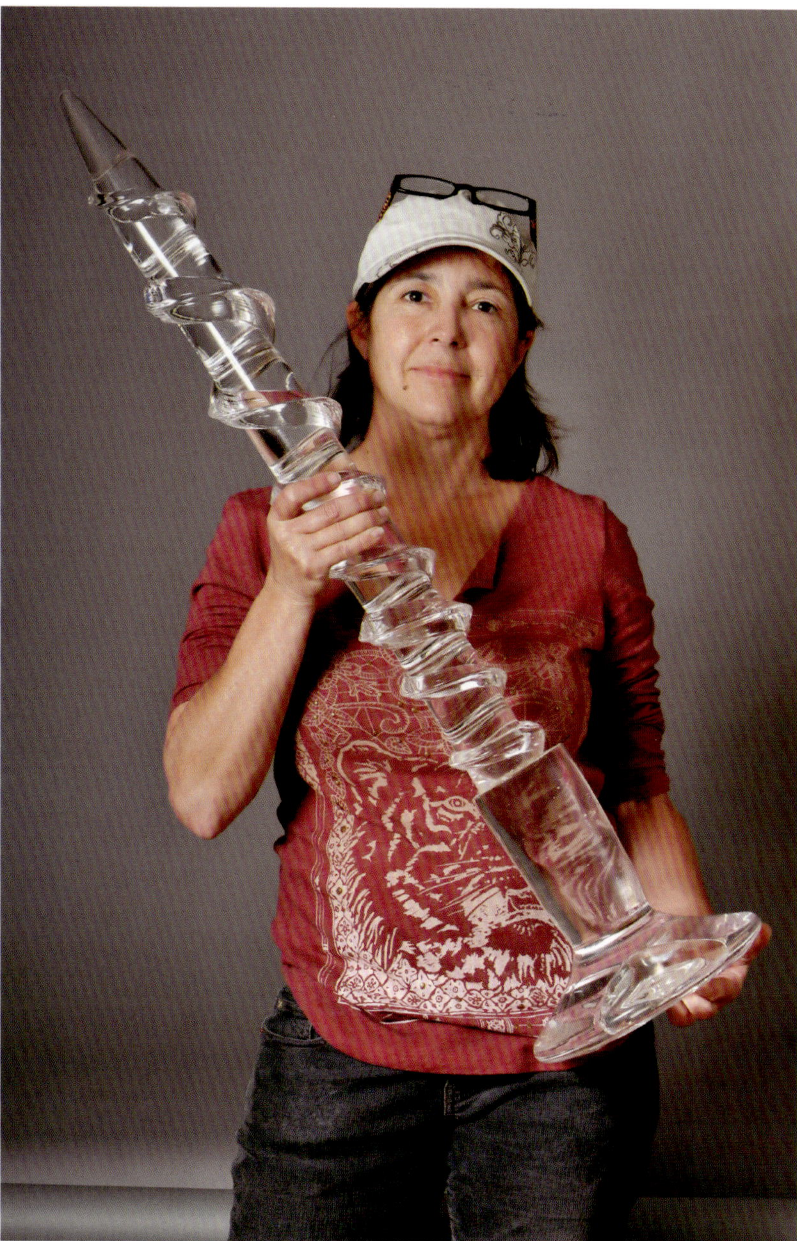

Carola Nan Roach holds *The Big Screw,* one of a series responding to those who do not honor, or who "screw over," others and the earth.

"They were not doing so well," she remembered. "I knew, for the sake of self-preservation, it was time to go." Typical of Roach's style, she threw herself into her travels.

She wanted to see the old masters she'd studied in school. "In Europe I went to churches and museums and saw amazing murals." And in Southeast Asia she saw a different kind of art, integrated into rituals of celebration and prayer. "It was much more a part of everyday life." She learned the language easily in Indonesia, and in Thailand she entered a Buddhist retreat, meditating ten hours each day. "I always throw myself into things." Yes, we knew that.

Back in the United States, Roach entered the master of fine arts program at Tulane and plowed into other explorations, arranging exhibitions and setting up gallery representation. She'd always remembered the New York relatives they'd left so many years earlier, so she returned to her roots and reconnected with her aunts and grandmother.

A teaching career followed, and as Roach recalls her teaching days, she shakes her head, releasing wisps of chestnut hair from its ponytail, "I realized about then that I'd finally overcome my shyness. I was confident. It happened when I wasn't looking." And then she adds a comment about another positive force in her life—her father. "In spite of everything, he encouraged me in his way."

Roach's process is part intuitive when she draws the molten glass in three dimensions. She says "An idea evolves, and the work becomes the result of the inspiration. Other times, it is through work that the inspiration comes. And once you know the glass, you get a feeling of what's going to happen." She adds that attaining that knowledge of what the molten glass can do takes years. Many of her pieces grow from personal symbology. The glass houses are obvious, but only Roach can create a crooked arrow to symbolize something that has gone wrong. "Wings keep showing up too," she says. "There's a sense of guardian angels." And from the beginning, when she was coloring pictures in elementary school until now, as she creates work for exhibition, she tells me, "Art has been a way to access something I couldn't get to emotionally or intellectually." It is this intuitive knowledge, combined with an irrepressible will to throw herself into the mission at hand, that infuses her work with the strength of the ages.

She writes, "The sculpting of molten glass is hard, hot, dirty, demanding, and quite magical. There is a certain alchemy involved when working with hot glass. The final form is smooth, calm, classical—the female figures, their insides a cacophony of movement and color, frozen in that one moment in time."

Several years ago, she traveled to Reno to visit her brother, Kevin, and his family, and instantly the Great Basin triggered memories of that New Mexico high desert of her childhood. She adds, "It's the light of the Great Basin that carries into my art. That is one of the reasons I moved here—big sky, wide-open space, and the light! Love it!"

KRISTEN FRANTZEN ORR • BORN 1951

We can trace the ancient art of glass beadmaking back more than three thousand years. Glass beads have been used for adornment, trade, currency, and religious ritual in cultures the world over, yet until recently the art of making these beads has been shrouded in secrecy. Kristen Frantzen Orr was on the cutting edge of the development of flameworked glass beads in the United States, and this quiet, introspective woman had no idea that one day her one-of-a-kind sculptural beads would lead to her designation as one of the "Top 40 International Beads/Beadmakers."[3]

Orr is not one to brag about the dedication and experimentation that eventually brought the mantle of fame she now wears with a great deal of modesty. Yet her exhibition record is long, and includes museums and galleries around this country and worldwide. Her work is in public and private collections internationally, including the permanent collections of Corning Museum of Glass, New York; Kobe Lampwork Glass Museum, Japan; and the Sweeney Collection Museum, New Mexico. Her pieces appear on the covers of three books and in many other books and publications.[4] With a rigorous teaching schedule that takes her east, west, and overseas, it's difficult to see how she manages to continue creating the major works of art that have brought her such renown. But she manages it all. Coincidence? Not quite.

As we headed to her basement in Spring Creek, Nevada, on September 28, 2013, I had to pause and pet my official greeters—two very curious Pembroke Welsh Corgis. That led my eyes to a fascinating assortment of antique doorknobs in all shapes and colors displayed in a basket, part of a front room art collection; others acted as kitchen cabinet pulls. I couldn't help but notice the array of houseplants that draped around windows and over bookshelves, a vibrant welcome to nature and life. We bade the Corgis goodbye, and I followed her downstairs to a different world from the one we'd just left.

Orr's studio takes up most of her home's basement. She has two torches set up for flameworking, each with its own ventilation system that exhausts through an outside window. An annealing kiln sits near each torch, and so does a fire extinguisher (a safety measure that Orr has never needed to put into service). An open window across the room provides fresh air, even in cool weather. Against one wall, a pellet stove keeps her warm in winter. Behind us are shelf upon shelf of glass rods about a pencil's thickness in diameter, and mysterious beadmaking materials, as well as tools and equipment she's accumulated over the past twenty years. Her entries in the book *1000 Beads* (Logan 2014) included such media as glass, a raven-shaped bead, handmade crocheted copper wire beads, shredded currency, and pebbles.

Orr is demonstrating her flamework technique, a type of glasswork where a torch is used to melt glass. This process of making beads by winding molten glass around a mandrel is sometimes called lampworking, because early

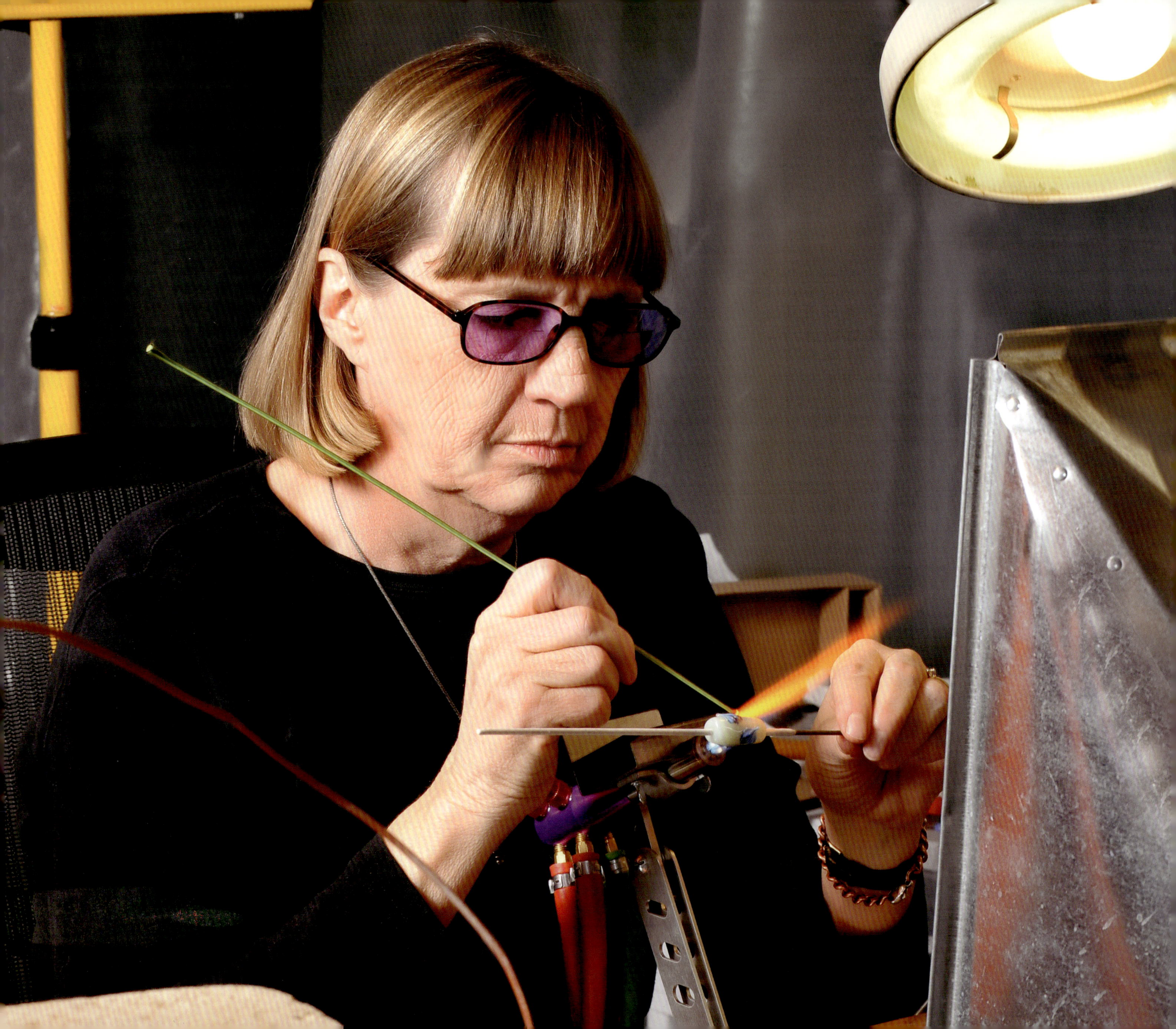

Venetian glass workers used oil lamps as their heat source to melt glass.[5] Today, Orr uses a glass worker's torch that combines a mixture of propane (fuel) and oxygen (accelerant) to achieve perfect control.

She explains that making a bead is a bit of a dance, because she needs to keep the molten glass in motion. Timing and temperature control are key. If a bead gets too cool it will crack; if it's too hot the glass will smear or drip.

Once the glass is in a molten state, she shapes it with various tools and her own agile hand movements. Then she adds colorful images—flowers, mostly, in perfect symmetry, using both hands to form and add more color, build imagery, and create depth and layers. With her brown, sun-streaked hair falling forward, a contrast to her turquoise T-shirt, Orr bends over the flame, rotating and shaping the bead. The scene is surreal, as if she's casting a magic spell on the work. And perhaps she is.

Orr is painting with molten glass instead of a brush, using calligraphic-like marks with a minimum number of strokes to convey gesture and movement, thus creating remarkable detail on a very small surface. An hour later, she will have produced a bead unlike any other, one that students pay hundreds of dollars to learn to make and collectors will purchase. She isn't finished yet, because the piece must be annealed in a kiln to prevent cracking.[6]

Before beads entered her life, Orr was a calligrapher, and before that, a watercolorist, but glass seems to have captivated her for good. "When I first started making beads, I was so enthralled." She smiles. "My husband would come into the studio hours later and say, 'Were we going to have dinner tonight?'" The process, Orr says, is captivating. "All the color and the fire—I feel like a moth drawn to the flame. It's like sitting front of a campfire and you can stare into it forever, watching the colors change."

"I'm best known for my floral beads," she tells me, and I think of the whirls of wildflowers that beckoned when I walked along her country path earlier. "I'm most at home in nature," she continues. "I grew up hiking the Rubies and I still get out as often as I can."[7] Orr's love of the natural world is reflected in her work, and she's recently begun

Kristen Frantzen Orr demonstrating the flame-work technique.

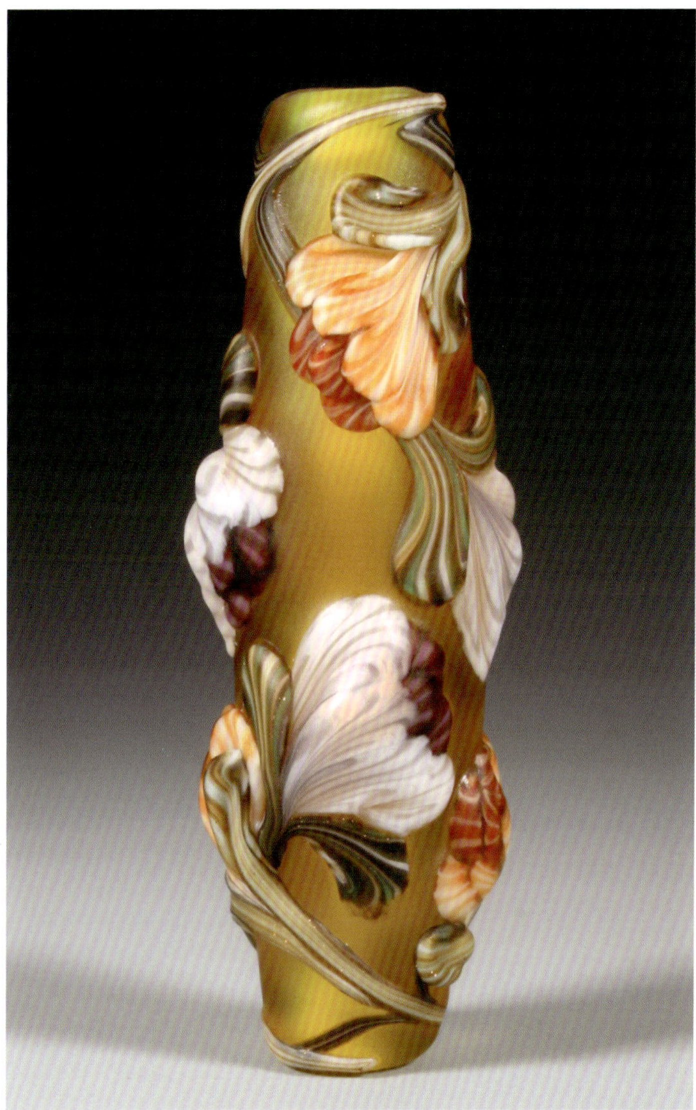

Kristen Frantzen Orr, *Autumn Honey.* Glass bead; flame-worked sodalime, chemically etched; 5 x 1.7 x 1.7 cm. Reproduced by permission from David Orr Photography.

creating glass ravens and bird people, inspired by birds making nests in the trees scattered near her home.

Spring Creek is a half hour's drive from Elko, Orr's hometown, where her father owned the newspaper and her mother did secretarial work. Art was offered in junior high and high school, and Orr enrolled in every art class available. She wanted to pursue an art career, but "I was advised not to attempt something that doesn't generate money. It wasn't practical. I was told I could be a schoolteacher, nurse, or secretary, and I was pretty compliant. But eventually I did become an artist and a teacher."

She set off to UNR, where she earned a degree in journalism. After graduating, she worked for newspapers in both Nevada and Idaho and married Russ, whom she'd met her senior year. Russ worked with the Forest Service in Mountain Home, Idaho. About the time that she realized she hated advertising sales and the competition involved, she became pregnant. David was born in 1975 and Geoffrey in 1978; it was a good time to be a stay-at-home mom and pursue her art, and she began drawing and painting. A move to Caliente, Nevada, introduced her to the group Creative Artists of Lincoln County. She became president of the group and also immersed herself in watercolor, painting mainly Nevada scenes.

When the family moved next to Mesa, Arizona, she said, "I lost the Great Basin landscape. I was kind of in culture shock." They initially lived in a small travel trailer, and when they finally bought a house in Mesa, "I was in this big space with two young children." She began taking art classes—first pottery, then calligraphy (which she ended up teaching for eleven years), and then jewelry. The family became aficionados of Pembroke Welsh Corgi dogs, and she started making dog art to pay for their trips to dog shows. Her search for ways to incorporate color with metals in jewelry led her to the first-ever glass bead exhibit in America in Prescott, Arizona, in 1992. A few interested people decided they were going to figure out how glass beads were made,

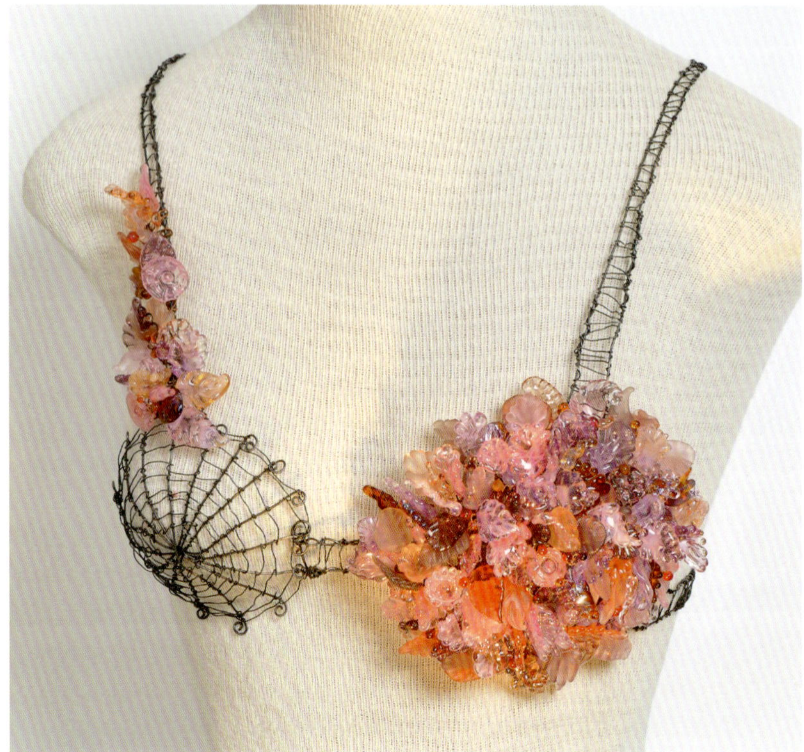

Kristen Frantzen Orr, *Strength and Beauty.* Hand-woven black annealed steel wire with hundreds of handmade flame-worked glass leaves, berries, and flowers constructed into the bra structure; life size on antique dressmaker's bust form; 21 x 14 (w) x 7 (d) in. Breast Cancer series.

and they mounted the Prescott show; at the same time, they formed the Society of Glass Beadmakers (now the International Society of Glass Beadmakers) Orr has been a member since 1993 and was one of the first regional directors of the group.

"It was fascinating," she says. "There were a handful of us in the Phoenix area; we needed more information and started bringing instructors in. Of course, they were all experimenting, too. A lot of what I do now I developed on my own, including techniques for layering and mixing colors and creating textures and patterns to suggest growing plant life. When I started, there weren't many of us and I had to figure out new techniques for myself." She invented new methods and skills out of necessity. To Orr, glass had parallels with watercolor. "You could make new colors and create depth by layering transparent colors of glass." When she began teaching some of these techniques, her career took off; she was invited to teach around the United States and then in Japan and Germany. She says, "The most fun part of the whole thing is traveling."

"I'm better known in Japan or New York or Texas than I am here in Nevada," she says, and smiles at the memory of her first teaching trip to Japan. She'd never been out of the United States and was amazed at the very different culture, where litter did not exist and personal safety was not an issue, not even when people called *packers* would push fifty additional bodies into a train before the door closed. "There I was, towering over everyone," the five-foot, nine-inch Orr laughs. She stayed in a traditional home, sleeping on the floor and bathing by hierarchy. She was the honored guest. "The Japanese people respect and honor artistic endeavors so much more than we do in this country," she tells me.

Once Orr began teaching, her reputation grew, and before long she was in demand. "It wasn't a business plan for me, it was something that just happened." She doesn't mention that the "something that just happened" came about because of the paths that she and a few others took in their desire to experiment and develop methods to produce innovative beads. "I discovered I could make something similar to brush strokes by encasing opaque glass with dark transparent colors."

In 2002 she and Russ had reached their limits of city life, traffic accidents, and air pollution, and got word their aging mothers needed tending back in Nevada. Russ had by this time retired from the Forest Service and their sons had grown and gone. It was time to return home, to the place she thought she'd left forever when she went to college.

"Sometimes you have to leave a place to appreciate it. The clean air, blue skies, the wide-open landscape. And the quality of light."

As for marketing, Orr's unassuming nature steps in and prohibits her from fast-talking salesmanship. She is in the enviable position of being so well known that people and galleries come to her. Her work is currently in several glass galleries, and she'd much rather pay somebody else to sell her work. "It's not my thing," she says, and she means it. She also participates in juried shows and conferences and does two shows each year with the Wild Women Artists. All this is in addition to a rigorous teaching schedule. And, oh, yes, creating distinctive sculptural art, one bead at a time. In her *Strength and Beauty* sculpture, for example, she made more than one hundred glass flowers and leaves on wire and then wove them into a life-sized bra.

I ask what motivates her to continue, and she replies, "I don't feel good when I'm not 'making.' I get depressed." She is still trying new ideas. "There are tons of things with glass and beads left to explore."

Light is ever present in her work. "Light fascinates me. The nature of glass provides a means for capturing light and reflecting it." When she's working at the torch, she becomes centered and her mind "switches over to a quiet place where I can express feelings that are too deep for words." She believes that beads are personal and intimate, both for Orr as an artist, and for the person who wears them.

"And," she adds, "I'm enchanted by the magic of the flame."

■ SUSAN GLASER CHURCH • BORN 1952

It is July 21, 2013. We leave Mountain City highway north of Elko, Nevada, and follow the winding Keddy Ranch Road around sagebrush hills that roll to infinity. I aim the car's cold air blower at my hot face and lean forward to unstick my shirt from the seat back. Behind us, clouds of road dust puff skyward from my tires. Our destination is the northern ranch that lies at the north fork of the Humboldt River, at the foot of Lost Wallet Rim.[8] The Glaser family ranches

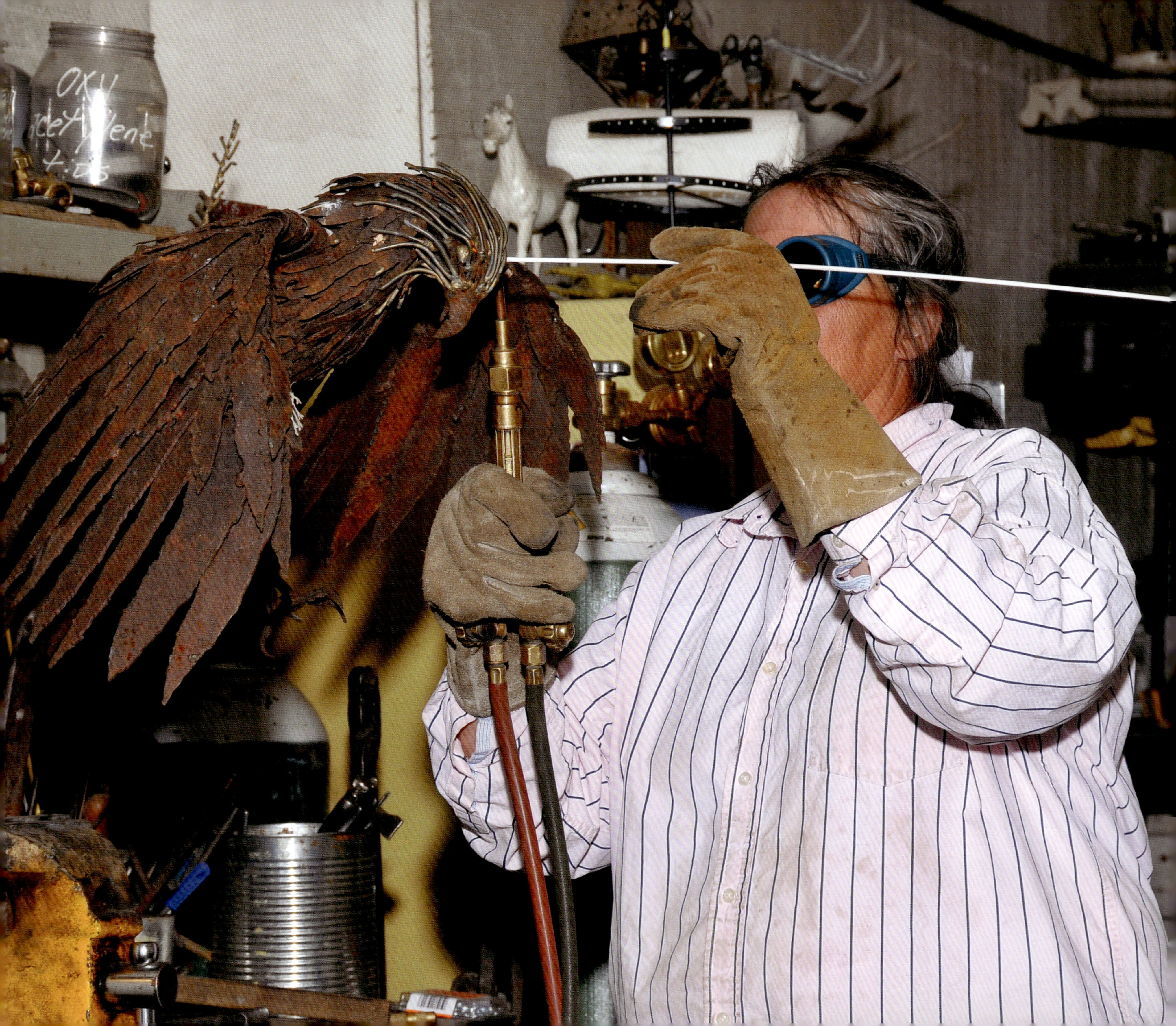
OXY

cover many miles (Halleck, the home ranch, is sixty miles away), and metalworker Susan Glaser Church and her husband, Peter Church, live and work on this one. We hurtle up, down, and around, opening and closing gates, stretching our eyes to find that elusive trail's end. I later learn that Church trucked her sons over this road daily to meet the school bus, and then returned to pick them up in the afternoon. Winters were a special challenge, when she bucked snow, mud, ice, or all three.

We round a curve and there, blazing into view, is the panoramic Keddy ranch. There are grassy fields where horses and cattle munch, barns, outbuildings, and ranch equipment. And finally, nestled under black willow trees, the freshly painted white sprawling family ranchhouse comes in view with its screened front porch stretching end to end. An early day cabin over the hill in back of the house was built in the 1890s. This remote piece of land, with its natural springs and lush grass, has been inhabited by white people for more than a hundred years, and, according to visiting archeologists, by Native hunters and trappers at least seven thousand years before that. "How they survived, I don't know," Church explains as she greets us at the gate and answers our unspoken questions about the ranch's beginnings. The contrast between the stark, treeless drive across the desert and this lush oasis seems to have struck us dumb. All we can do is stare.

"My great grandfather Mathias came through in 1852, freighting cargo to California," Church fills in the silence while we try to acclimate to our movie-Western surroundings, including Church herself. With her ruddy, cheerful face, dark, silver-streaked mane that strains desperately to escape its tie, blue-striped blouse over Wranglers, sturdy stance and easy manner of talking, she seems to have grown like a tree right out of the earth. She ignores my rude stare and continues, "Mathias noticed the river at Halleck and thought it would be good ranchland. In 1869 the railroad came through and he settled that land, and that was the start." She cocks an eyebrow. "But my great-grandmother was right in there, too. She saw that the Keddy here was another greenbelt. It was scrip land, and she found the owner, a Civil War veteran, willing to sell it.[9] She was pretty savvy. Even in drought conditions, we can grow hay here."

We have arrived at haying time. The rest of the family—Peter, brothers, nieces, friends, cousins—had finished lunch, dozed under the black willows for a while, and returned to the upper pastures to bale, stack, and truck the alfalfa they'd earlier cut and left to dry. The job takes several days and, although she'd rather be haying, Church spends her time in the kitchen, because work produces big appetites. Today, though, she takes a break to talk with us. Her long-time friend, Mary, is here from San Francisco and helps Church move her heavy metal sculptures so we can photograph them.

This artist definitely doesn't hold back when it comes to creating. Her pieces range in height from ten inches to ten feet, and her public sculpture can take over the side of a building. She once helped son Andrew make a suit of armor, and today I see a life-size bull, welded from scrap metal, standing in the pasture, surveying the view. Her larger architectural installations can be found in Elko at the Elko County Library and the Great Basin College, as well as in San Francisco. She once mounted one-person and group shows in San Francisco and Park City, Utah, but these days she's pared down to the biennial Tuscarora Days and the two annual Wild Women shows, one in Reno and the other in Elko.

Across the great front yard, a multitude of large sculptures keep company with trees and rosebushes. A skinny-legged metal figure of a woman struts across the grass, her arms thrown outward as if to say, "See? This is all mine!," and just feet away a five-foot rusty metal circle curves as if it's undulating to a symphony. Near a short tree, a quintet of old railroad spikes rise skyward, one upon the other in a delicate left-right balance. The sculptures, all

Susan Glaser Church welding in the ranch machine shop.

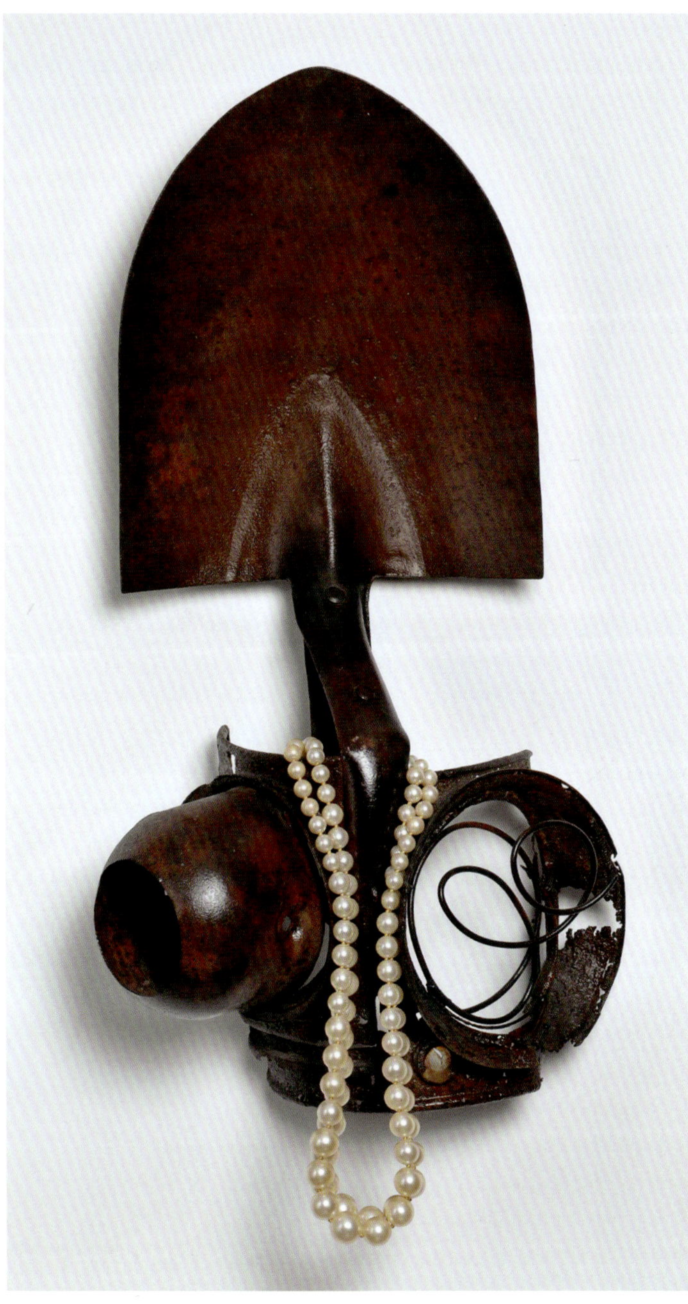

Susan Glaser Church, *Mastectomy*. Welded found objects; 2 x 1 ft. Breast Cancer series.

flawlessly executed, radiate a kind of whimsy that brings to mind the sculpture of Alexander Calder.[10] The previous weekend, Church had trucked them to Tuscarora to participate in that town's biennial Open Studios Weekend, also advertised as Tuscarora Days. She was happy to sell some work there, not only for the revenue, but because the return trip was lighter.

Her work can be realistic, like a bull in the field, suit of armor, quail, and cattails she loves to make, or the candelabra repurposed from scrap metal (one is an old Model T tire pump, while others are made from bed frames). Metal buckets are stressed or shot, turned upside down, and rigged into lamps. She once built a life-size ostrich and called it "Head in the Sand." another time she made "Sink or Swim," a large, complicated piece involving a woman calmly floating in neon waves. Sometimes, though, her imagination takes her to the abstract, where one piece of scrap metal will induce her to build on it until she has created an undulating, non-representational sculpture.

Church's approach to sculpture reflects a Buddhist-like philosophy that sees oneness between life and art and based on the belief that all things are of equal value. This idea has motivated her to transform treasured junk—old materials and objects—in ways that evoke an emotional or psychological response. Her intent can be to give a worn implement renewed presence as sculpture, or to enjoy a bird constructing a nest in her public installation.

We head across the porch where an elderly man snoozes—the father of one of the helpers enjoying the country quiet—and, inside the house, we sit where all the important discussions take place, around the checkered oilcloth kitchen table. The lunch dishes have been washed and stacked, and on the stove a pot simmers away, sending a tantalizing herbal fragrance right under my nose. The kitchen feels like the ranch's command post. From here we can see through to the pasture and around another door to

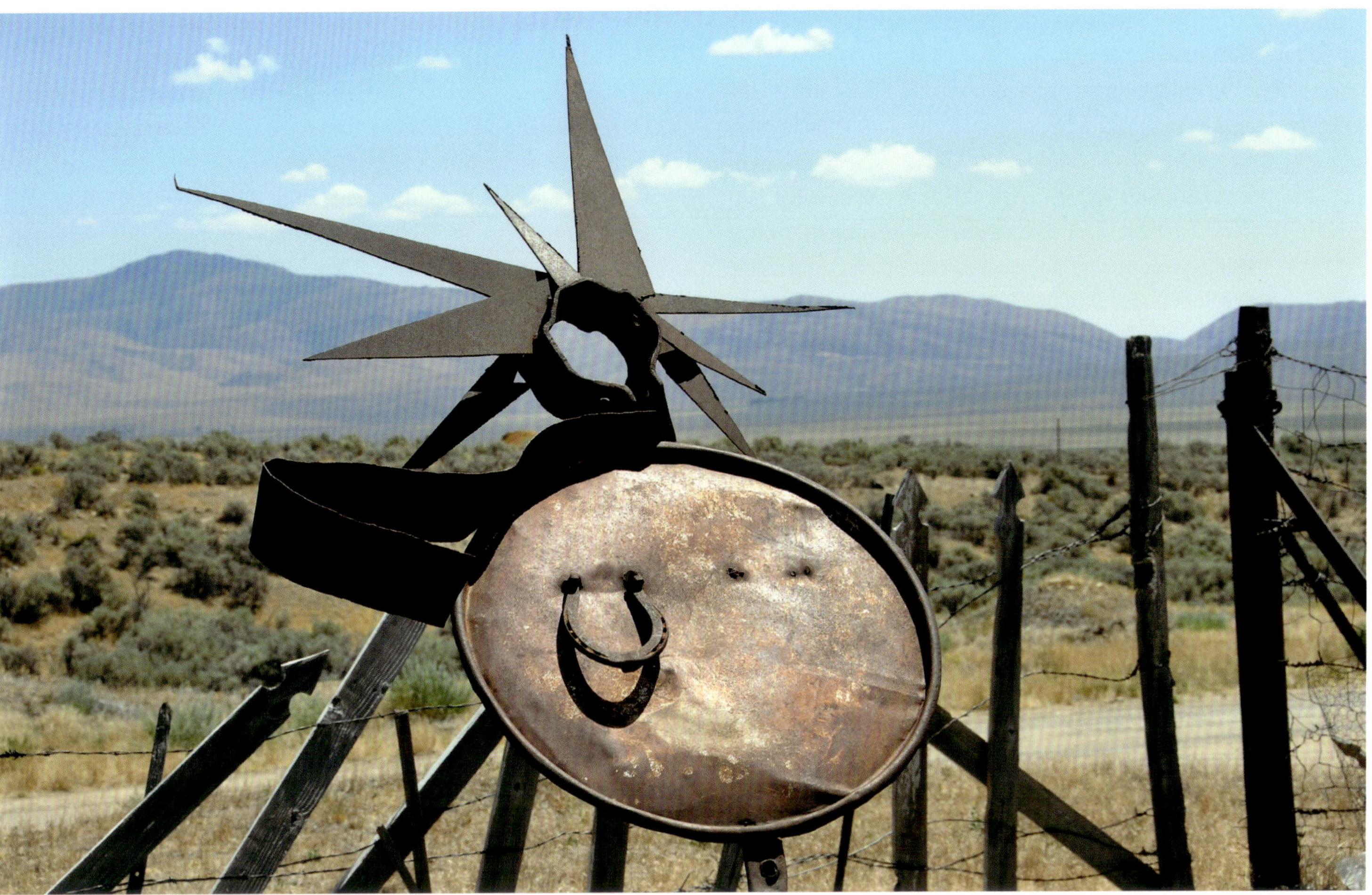

Susan Glaser Church, *Radiant.* Welded found objects; 5 x 3 ft.

the living room, where musical instruments—fiddle, mandolin, guitar—lean against the furniture.

Church follows my glance. “Right now the house is spilling over with people. We live all year isolated, except for haying time. The septic tanks fill up and the beds are overflowing. When family comes, we get to visit in between repairs, and at night after dinner we sit around and sing.”

As if on cue, we hear Peter’s old Chevy pickup roll in. A piece of broken haying equipment needs repair, quickly. Church hurries outside to the shop, dons her welding mask, padded apron, and gloves, and fires up the torch. The sparks fly as she welds the broken pieces together while the rest of us stand around wishing we could help.[11]

That job finished, we return to the kitchen and Church’s story. While she grew up, her dad, Arthur Glaser, was always in the ranch shop repairing something. He was a crafty person, she says, always working on some project. He learned blacksmith techniques from Pete Antone, a German blacksmith traveling through the country. "I still have his anvil. He got me to helping him. I ran a bellows once to make some big lamps my mom saw in some fancy store. They're four feet tall, all forged. I got hooked on that."[12]

The four Glaser children grew up in a house where, with 4-H and other projects, the dining table was never clear. One high school art assignment would plant the seed of her eventual career: students were required to make something from found objects. Her dad said, "Let's go make something," and out to the junk pile they went. On a ranch as old as this one, there is always plenty of *junk*—material left over from obsolete cars, ranch gear, appliances, and so on, and everything is saved for possible use when a newer car or piece of equipment needs a working part.

"Dad pulled out some old-time rake teeth and we made a tripod. Then he showed me how to cut out a hand and an apple. In the junkyard we found an old C-drill that kind of looked like a snake; we just put a tongue in it and a rattle on the end. The hand reached for the apple and the snake is coiled around that. Dad was fun to work with. He said, 'Let's wrap the whole thing with barbed wire and we'll call it 'Forbidden Fruit.' In class, the teacher immediately wanted to buy it and I sold it for $25. What a thrill! I thought 'This is what I want to do: make artwork.'"

Her siblings grew up to have professional careers. One brother is a geologist, the other a physicist, and her sister is artistic director of the Western Folklife Center in Elko. One cousin is a veterinarian living on the home ranch, and another is a dentist in Elko. "They all come out on weekends and give the cowboys a break from feeding cattle. Everyone's still involved at one level or another."[13]

She lifts her chin, and says, "I was the black sheep of the family." As the oldest sibling, she tried college at the University of Wyoming, but dropped out. "In those days, they didn't counsel. I didn't know there were careers in design. I would have loved to go into three-dimensional design." While she was back home, the Elko Library put out a bid for a big sculpture in front of their building, and, never one to sit around, she decided to apply, offering a design of the Ruby Mountains. At age eighteen, she was awarded the contract and, she says, "It was way over my head." She learned, though, and twenty friends helped her mount a thirty-foot sculpture on a new wall. There were several structural issues to solve, and the sculpture stands there today, changing as winter snow blows against it and where, in spring, birds build their nests.

Church eventually enrolled in the Academy of Art University in San Francisco, where she had a welding studio and even worked with neon. She had moved with all her equipment (she mutters, "What silly person would move with their tanks and welder?") and in the larger studio space, experimented with such oversized pieces as *Sink or Swim,* a huge technical challenge, and *Head in the Sand,* mentioned above. "But I didn't have any scrap metal, like at the ranch. Here the stuff is historical and I can pick through a junkyard. There, I had to use new metal."

She joined up with other metalworkers through the California Blacksmith Association and mounted shows both at the Academy and various venues. She met and married Peter, a well-known chef. Two children followed. "Andrew was born within a month of the '89 San Francisco earthquake. We were living in a fourth-floor apartment. It was a crazy time." Soon the little family moved across the bay to Berkeley, where James was born during the Oakland fires. She laughs. "Everyone told us, 'Don't have any more kids.'"

About then, Church began to think of home. She wanted her boys to know her parents and ranch life. The family had been returning for a month every summer to help out, and Peter was willing to give up his job. "They never had good luck keeping people in this part of the ranch. Nobody lasted more than a couple of years. You're on your own doing everything. But that was the job that was open and we said we'd take it." She shakes her head. "If we'd known then what we know now. . . . I knew about haying and branding, but Peter would say, 'How do you chain up a tractor?' and I didn't know. When we got in a jam, Mom and Dad would come, but they were busy with their ranch. But neighbors helped—warning us to have fuel delivered before October or the trucks won't be able to get in, or [asking,] 'Have you chopped your wood for winter?' That winter we had some angels looking over us. But we succeeded, and it's beautiful. We've now been here twenty years. I admire my husband for teaching himself and hanging in there." She smiled, "He's still hanging in there." She remembers one occasion when the situation looked glum, and she reminded Peter, "It could be worse. We could be stalled in traffic in San Francisco."

When the boys reached high school age, they wanted to participate in various activities, so they moved to town, first staying with her mother and sister, and later with her brother and his wife until graduation. "I always say, here it takes a county to raise a child." James and Andrew, now college graduates, return to the ranch frequently. "Now it's summertime and everyone comes and pitches in. It's neat to see them taking on projects that I wouldn't want to do."

After being influenced by the process- and content-based ideas of conceptual artists in the Bay Area, the return to her rural roots revived her interest in giving a voice to objects, materials, and environments that are so often neglected, unfamiliar, or taken for granted. Church resumed her sculpture shortly after moving back to the Keddy and found unlimited inspiration from the natural environment as well as a treasure trove of rusty materials just waiting for her welding torch and imagination. She and artist friend Sidne Teske mounted a show at Elko's Western Folklife Center, and Teske invited her to join the Wild Women Artist group out of Reno.

Things nearly ground to a stop when Church was diagnosed with breast cancer and spent months in treatment, surgery, and thankfully, an eventual recovery in Salt Lake City, Utah. Since that terrifying year when her world shattered, she has resumed her work and has used the breast cancer theme to develop a series. "I saw an old coyote trap and thought that was what a mammogram feels like." She has built on that theme, and her breast cancer pieces are among the most powerful and also the most acquired of her recent work. "I was able to work through some of the myriad of things that happened during that scary time and put those thoughts into artwork. It burned off some anxiety. It was making the best of what happened to me."

I ask Church what's next, and she places a finger to her cheek, then says, "I want to do things here—a nice new front gate for the yard, for instance. I don't want to sell it all. I'm getting very attached to some of it, and if my pieces don't sell, I say, 'fine.'"

Still, she plans ahead. The following is an excerpt from her "Musings from the Ranch," an essay introducing her work and challenges as she prepares for an upcoming show:

> This is the time of year our cattle are coming home from the summer range and are being weaned, sorted, shipped and settled in for the winter. Trying to do artwork in the midst of all this activity is often a challenge, but this year was even more so thanks to one pesky bull that kept breaking through the fence and into my scrap metal pile. I now know the true meaning of a "bull in a china shop" after witnessing what a bull can do while grazing amongst my rusted treasures. I was furious when he disrupted my rows and bins and left barrels of future artwork overturned. Yet, in picking up the mess the bull made I found the perfect pieces for a special sculpture that I am working on for our "Wild Women Go Pink" show. Be sure to come to the Summit Mall and see what the bull and I created![14]

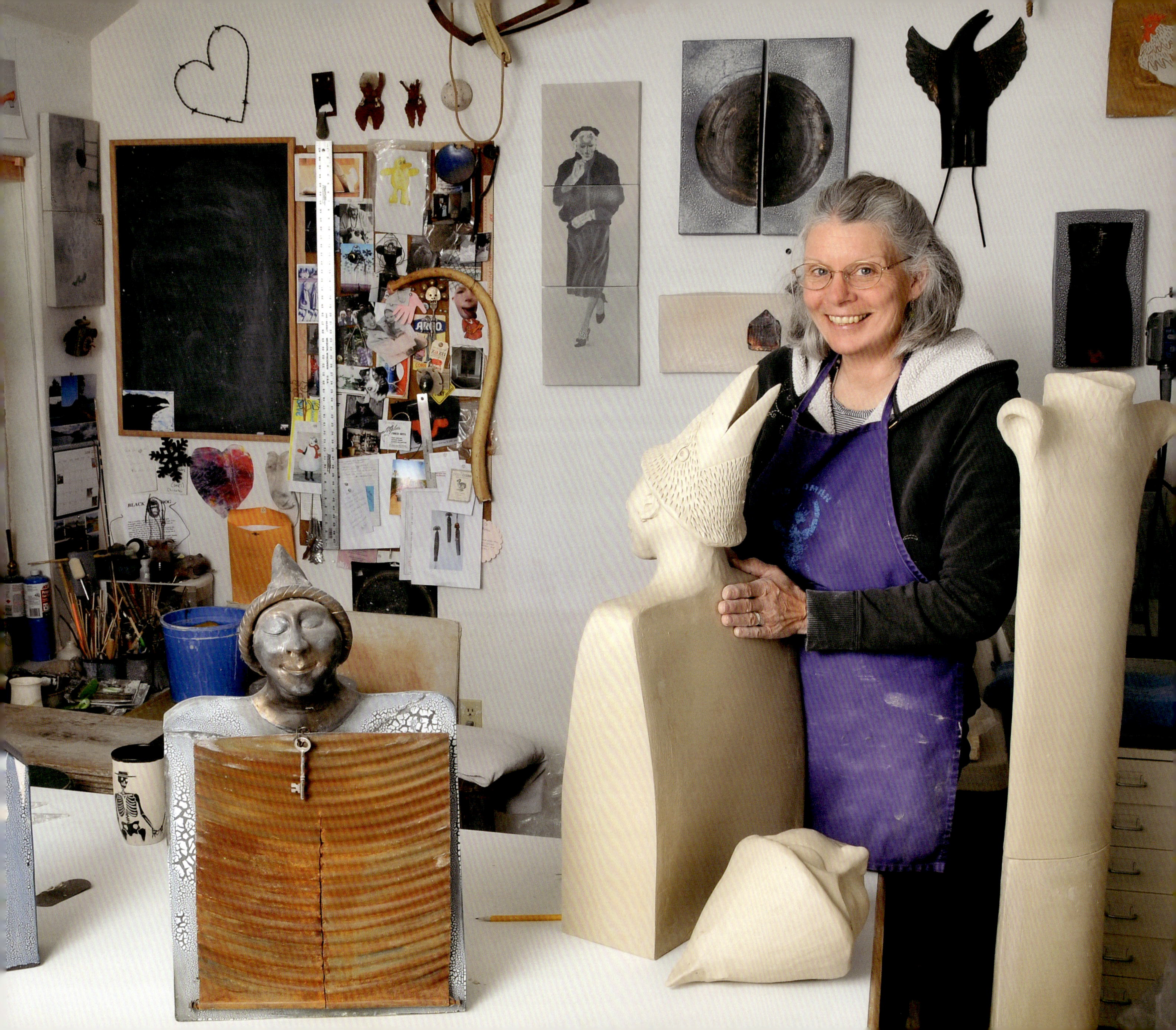

BARBARA GLYNN PRODANIUK • BORN 1954

Barbara Prodaniuk pushes a lump of clay around a slab board, and the action seems symbolic. "I push myself to see how far I can take the work," the California artist says as her hands explore the soft mass in front of her. "That's what's so fun about this job."

Prodaniuk's job is also her bliss, and she tells me, "I'm really fortunate that I get to do what I love." On the day of our interview, June 23, 2013, we step into a studio bursting with tools, equipment, plastic-covered works in progress, and completed pieces. The sculpted ceramic cups, once her bread-and-butter work, have given way to narrative sculpture that gives off a variety of moods, from whimsical to spiritual. *Roller Derby Chicks,* two bird-like creatures riding roller skates, stand beside *Antelope Woman,* a serene three-foot-high figure with a crackly body and antlers rising from her head. Prodaniuk follows my gaze and smiles as she rubs a wrist across her forehead; wisps of gray-streaked hair escape the rubber band to frame a ruddy face pierced with eyes flecked with light. She's preparing for her biggest show of the year: the prestigious Palo Alto Clay and Glass Association show, the largest of its kind in California. She's hoping to have two or three kiln loads out and ready to go. "I'll fill the van up to the roof," she tells me, adding that sales of her sculptural work are climbing rapidly. "People use art like that one"—she points to *Antelope Woman*—"just as much as they use a coffee cup." Her remark brought to mind a Victor Hugo quote: "The beautiful is as useful as the useful," he once said, then added, "maybe more."[15]

Prodaniuk's ceramic work has exhibited in numerous one-woman and group venues in Nevada and California. She is represented at many galleries and art centers in the United States from California to New Mexico, Arizona to Florida, Massachusetts to Kentucky, and beyond. She has juried into the prestigious American Craft Council shows in several cities, including Baltimore, Saint Paul, and San Francisco, and her sculpture has appeared in countless national and regional publications. This kind of commitment takes dedication and work, and, because a show is imminent, Prodaniuk is on the move.

Barbara Glynn Prodaniuk sculpts a bird reliquary before firing.

Her muscular hands, covered with white dust, push, mold, knead, and poke the white clay, a high contrast to her powdery purple apron. Glasses perch on the end of her nose as she speaks, describing the bird-like figure slowly taking shape, and discussing a career that has spanned more than thirty years.

Born in Hackensack, New Jersey, the fourth of five children, Prodaniuk attended grade school in Connecticut, and the magic was about to begin. She saw her first potter during an elementary school field trip to Old Sturbridge Village in Massachusetts and was mesmerized at the sight of his hands, filled with wet slip, forming a container as his potter's wheel turned.[16] She overcame her shyness and asked the man if she could try it, and he retorted, "No, I'm sorry I can't." He was kind. Later, she left her group and sneaked back to the potter's shed, again pleading with him. Again, the man refused. But the memory of hands creating something from a lump seemed magical and stayed with her.

When the Glynn family moved to Las Vegas, Nevada, following her father's (John) work at the Nevada Test Site, she enrolled in a general art class at Clark High School and was finally able to throw a pot. Her mom, Elizabeth, worked for the district attorney, but, Prodaniuk says, "She was always a mother first." John was a veteran of World War II and a Marine sergeant in the Pacific theater. She remembers, "What really colored our lives was his [John] recovery from an accident that caused a traumatic brain injury. He had broken his neck, fractured his skull, jaw, and ribs. It was considered a miracle in our family that he lived, and made a full recovery. But that process took a long time and a lot of effort from both my mother and father. He had to re-learn everything, including who all his family members were. My parents taught me tenacity, that sometimes life gives you challenges, and you have to find your way through them."

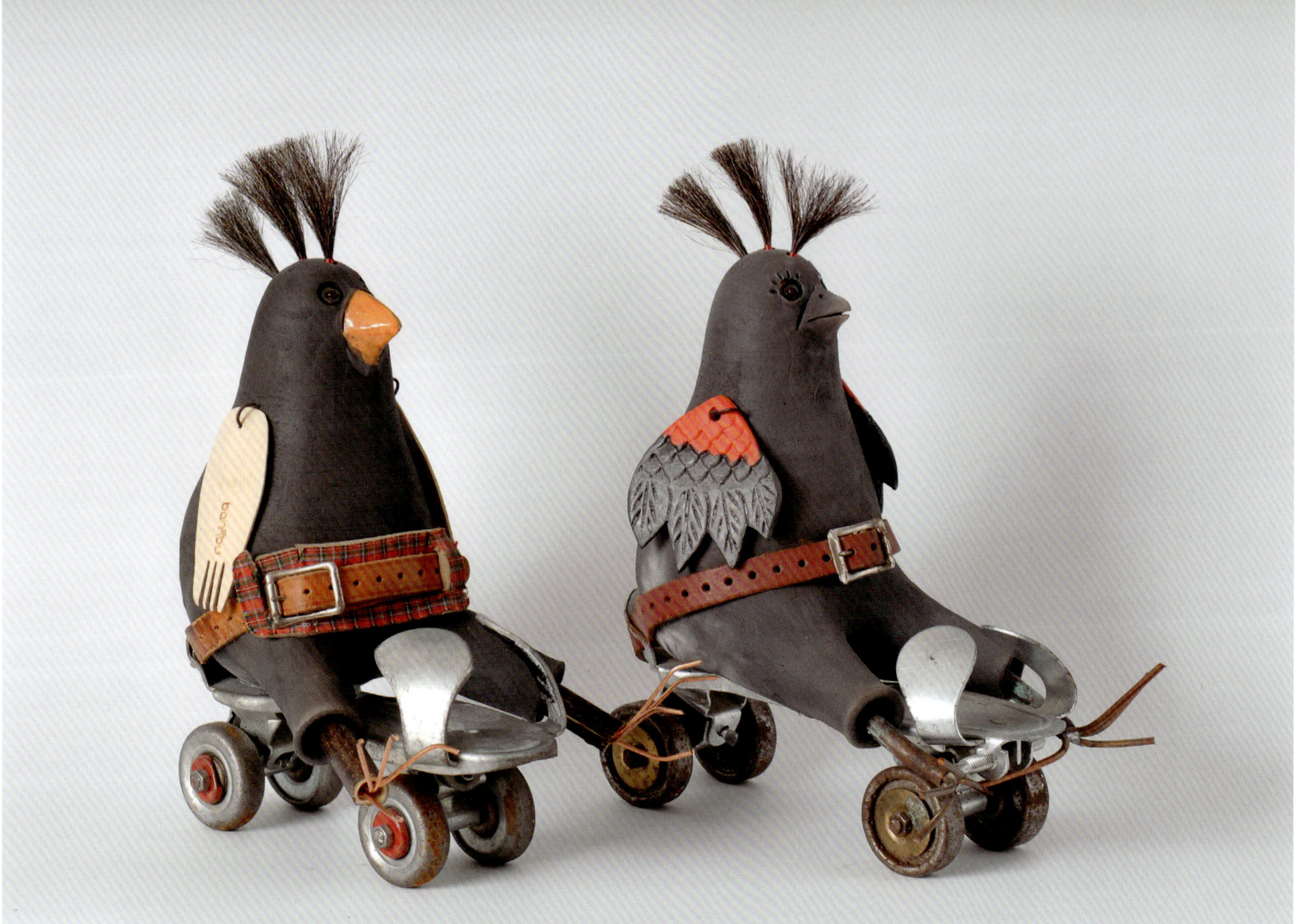

Barbara Glynn Prodaniuk, *Roller Derby Chicks.* White stoneware; raku fired, black bamboo, metal, vintage roller skates; 12 x 12 x 6 in.

John drove his family out into the desert, where they hiked and picnicked and watched the stars explode in the big night sky. Those happy times discovering nature's offerings, and a father's love, play into Prodaniuk's relationship with the out-of-doors to this day.

Her dialogue with clay began in earnest at Moorpark College in Southern California, where she was named ceramic lab assistant, and there she found her mentor, Kirk Aiken. She received her associate of art degree, and Aiken helped her land an apprenticeship with master potter John Schulps as she finished her bachelor of fine arts at California State University, Northridge. While a student there, she met fellow sculpture student Orest Prodaniuk. She graduated and, determined to make her living with her ceramics, rented space from fellow potter Frank Masserrella. Next, she headed east and established her first studio among the tall timbers at Donner Lake. In 1986 she and Orest married, and three years later they designed and built their home, complete with studio, in a forested area near Truckee, California, where the Sierra Nevada range meets the Great Basin. Here, the couple raised daughter Alex and son Nick. Prodaniuk built a large kiln in back of her studio, which has a separate entrance. Whether she does raku, sawdust, pit fire, or high-fired work, all her necessary equipment is right at hand.

"Every time I open the kiln, there's something that doesn't work. You can use it if you can get over your expectations," she says, adding that she learns more from her mistakes than her successes. "Letting go of things is hard, but you have to let go in order to reach for what is possible. Remember the story of the three bowls? The empty one is to be treasured because you can fill it with possibilities."[17]

During summer, buyers visit the studio while Prodaniuk offers a snack from the adjacent kitchen and describes current work displayed on shelves and pedestals in a corner exhibit area. Visitors can also look around her studio and delight in the myriad of tools, materials, and inspirations that go into creating a single sculpture. One shelf is piled high with jars of various colors of slip (a liquid clay base), and on the floor stand buckets of glaze and rolls of tar-paper for making patterns. Across the room, drying racks hold slabs in various stages of completion, and a rolling rack is loaded with unfinished pieces (I notice some deer head people taking shape). A huge slab roller holds more work in progress, and I realize this upcoming show is a big one. A large planning calendar hangs on one wall, and over her desk a tall bulletin board is plastered with clippings, images, and photos, the most prominent being those of her mother and grandmother.

She smiles at the 1913 *Good Housekeeping* magazine cover with the lovely young brunette Helen Kelly (her grandmother) on front, a gloved hand holding a wrench as she kneels before a tire. Helen will be the subject of a future piece; her father's mother, Agnes Glynn, has already been

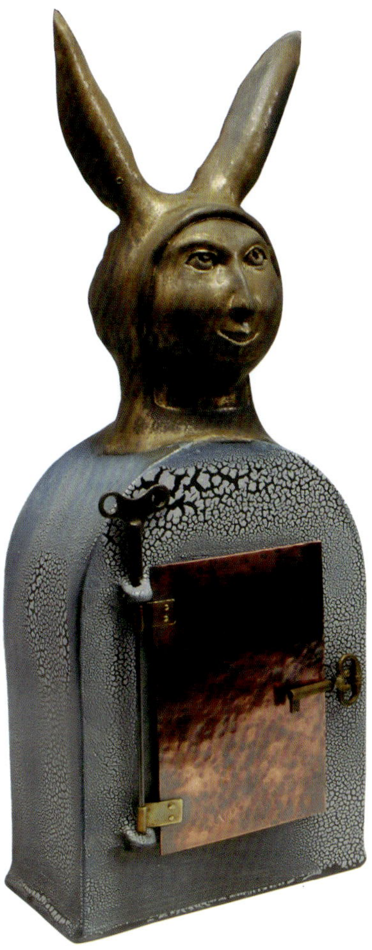

Barbara Glynn Prodaniuk, *Rabbit Reliquary.* White stoneware fired to cone 10; hammered copper, vintage clock key, hand formed hinges; 18 x 9½ x 5 in. Reproduced by permission from Barbara Glynn Prodaniuk.

immortalized in clay. Many of Prodaniuk's family members created with their hands: a brother is a wood turner, her great-grandfather was a blacksmith, and a grandfather whittled pocket-sized animals for the grandchildren.

Prodaniuk identifies small artifacts that might one day go into some of her pieces (*Roller Derby Chicks* was inspired by a pair of old roller skates she found). Shelves spill with weaving bobbins, small shed deer antlers, old toys, an antique rolling pin, shoelaces, champagne corks, wishbones, kelp, and things that make texture, like mesh bags. She laughs. "I have a tendency to be a packrat."

When her professional life began, Prodaniuk became a ceramics instructor at Sierra Nevada College in Incline Village, Nevada. But her struggles to combine teaching and motherhood came to a head during an overnight student field trip to Pyramid Lake, Nevada. With Alex and Nick toddling along, the group set up camp near the Stone Mother.[18] The students finished their dung-fire assignment, and Prodaniuk instructed them in the pit fire process, ordering a slow, gentle fire. It was getting late and Nick, who was less than two, badly needed a diaper change and bedtime preparation. She went to her car to settle him in, and returned to discover her students had used every stitch of the wood to create a blazing bonfire. "This is not what you do for a successful pit fire." She smiled at the memory, but it wasn't funny at the time.

"It wasn't working. You have to choose between being a teacher and a potter and a mother all at the same time," she tells me. "So I chose mother and potter." Her hands pause on the figure she is building, and her eyes lose focus. "I could only work fifteen minutes at a time back then. The kids would bring things to me." She smiles. "Nick's plastic frog ended up on a pot. They grew up around me, changing so much." Alex is now a college art graduate working in San Francisco, and Nick is a college junior. "Motherhood is a big transformer," she says.

She lifts a flat bamboo stick to the top of her clay figure, and begins to shape it; I watch as the blob slowly becomes the head of a crow. I ask her about the crackly body on the *Antelope Woman* and learn it's a technique she developed through trial and error. She calls it *mud crack glaze* and says the tufa formations and dry riverbeds around Pyramid Lake inspired it. Much of her inspiration comes in flashes when she's out in nature, and most mornings will find her taking long walks through the meadows, watching for wrens, rabbits, ravens, quail, and deer, thinking about the trees, seeing the ways smooth stones rest up against one another. Andy Goldsworthy and his work in nature is a huge inspiration, and William Morris's glass pieces tell life stories and urge her to do the same.

"In the spring I did a show in Minnesota and drove across the entire Great Basin," she tells me. "I have truly learned what my father was talking about, loving this land. The sky is so big. You become part of the landscape, much more so than if there was more plant life. The textures are amazing."

For twenty years Prodaniuk was part of a group of professional Great Basin artists who call themselves the Wild Women. Their networking helped shape Prodaniuk's work and ambitions. "This group really gave me a wonderful place to grow and develop as an artist. It was a major point in my life. Having a group of artists to encourage you, to bounce ideas off of, to spark ideas when you're in a slump, and to validate your path, is extremely valuable."

For now, the crow figure has taken shape beneath Prodaniuk's hands. She has created a large hollow at the front of its body, shrine-like, and she explains the cavity can hold whatever special object the owner wishes. "It's a collaboration between artist and owner." The crow smiles slightly, seeming to take pride in its accessory, a small rusty washboard that Prodaniuk gleaned from a junk pile in Tuscarora.

In 2015 the artist engaged in reexamining her situation, or, as she puts it, "taking the Goldilocks approach to finding my place." Two years earlier, both her mother and brother-in-law passed away, and Prodaniuk did what many artists do—she expressed her grief in her artistic creations. She worked around the Mexican Day of the Dead theme, and suddenly skeleton faces and bodies became cups accented with crows. As she worked, she began to realize how short life really is, and felt she needed to "get on with stuff" and leave some of the comfort behind. She took a temporary break from the Wild Women group and is thinking ahead. "I'm in a transformative state," she says. "I'm fifty-nine. The kids are grown and gone, and I'm looking at the next phase in life—what I want to do, where I want to go. My husband's job [as a contractor] is so physical, he deserves a shot. I know I can't do shows forever. Maybe I need to get myself established with more galleries. I might change my website and build it so that it functions as a store. Who knows? She opens those eyes flecked with light and grins. "I'm always looking for the next lily pad."

Notes

1. A glory hole is a small furnace for keeping glass malleable. The glass artist reheats/keeps the glass hot as she works it at 1,800 degrees.
2. Lipofsky, a central figure in the American Studio Glass Movement, founded the glass program at the University of California and later, at the California College of Arts and Crafts (now the California College of the Arts).
3. In addition to this designation, Frantzen Orr was listed in the top five artists who received the highest score from jurors in *Glass Line Magazine*'s list in the June/July 2012 issue to commemorate the twenty-fifth anniversary of *Glass Line* and the twentieth anniversary of the International Society of Glass Beadmakers.
4. Her pieces appear on the covers of *Masters Glass Beads* (Lark Books 2008), *Inspiration in Glass* (Ostwald 2015), and *Beads of Glass* (Jenkins 2003). Her pieces have also appeared in countless other books and publications.
5. The mandrel is a steel wire that has been dipped in a special clay slip called *bead release.* The bead release allows the finished annealed bead to be removed from the mandrel, leaving the bead hole.
6. Annealing involves heating a piece until its temperature is uniform throughout, then slowly cooling it.
7. The most prominent range in Elko County, Nevada, the Ruby Mountains run south-southwest for eighty miles. They were named after the garnets found by early explorers. Their canyons, valleys, and steeply carved granite mountains can be seen from Lamoille Canyon Road, a National Forest Scenic Byway.
8. The headwaters of the north fork of the Humboldt River begin here.
9. Land scrip and land warrants were certificates from the land office that granted people private ownership of certain portions of public lands. The greatest volume of scrip was given to war veterans. For more information, see the Gale Encyclopedia of U.S. History at www.gale.com.
10. Calder, an American sculptor (1898–1976), is famous for originating kinetic *mobiles* and also his stationary sculptures, which were called *stabiles.* He also produced wire figures.
11. Arc welding uses an electrical arc to melt the work pieces along with the filler material, and that is what joins the pieces. The process takes steady hands and an eye for detail.
12. A smith using hammer and anvil once performed one of the oldest known metalworking processes, forging. Although the industrialization of forging has changed the process, artists and others still use a forge (hearth) to heat metal to a temperature where it becomes easier to shape. With tongs, the metal is moved back and forth from hearth to anvil while the smith works it with a hammer. To finish, the work piece is transported to the slack tub to rapidly cool the work.
13. The Glaser family stories can be heard on video at Elko's Western Folklife Center and on National Public Radio's "This American Life." See Western Folklife Center, 2008 "City Boy in the Country," 2007 "The Facts of Wife," and 2006 "Winter Feeding Workout."
14. No longer found available online. In 2014 this was at www.wildwomenartists.com.
15. Victor Hugo (1802–85) was a well-known French poet and author. His best-known works are the novels *Les Misérables* and *Notre-Dame de Paris* (*The Hunchback of Notre Dame*).
16. Old Sturbridge Village is a living museum that re-creates life in rural New England during the 1790s through 1830s. It is the largest living museum in New England.
17. In Sue Bender's *Everyday Sacred* (1996), there are three bowls: the first is upside down so nothing can go into it; the second is right side up but cracked and debris filled, polluting anything placed in it; the third bowl is clean and ready to receive and hold whatever is poured into it.
18. The Stone Mother is a tufa formation at the lake, on the Pyramid Lake Paiute Indian Reservation. She has engendered creation stories, and the area around her is sacred.

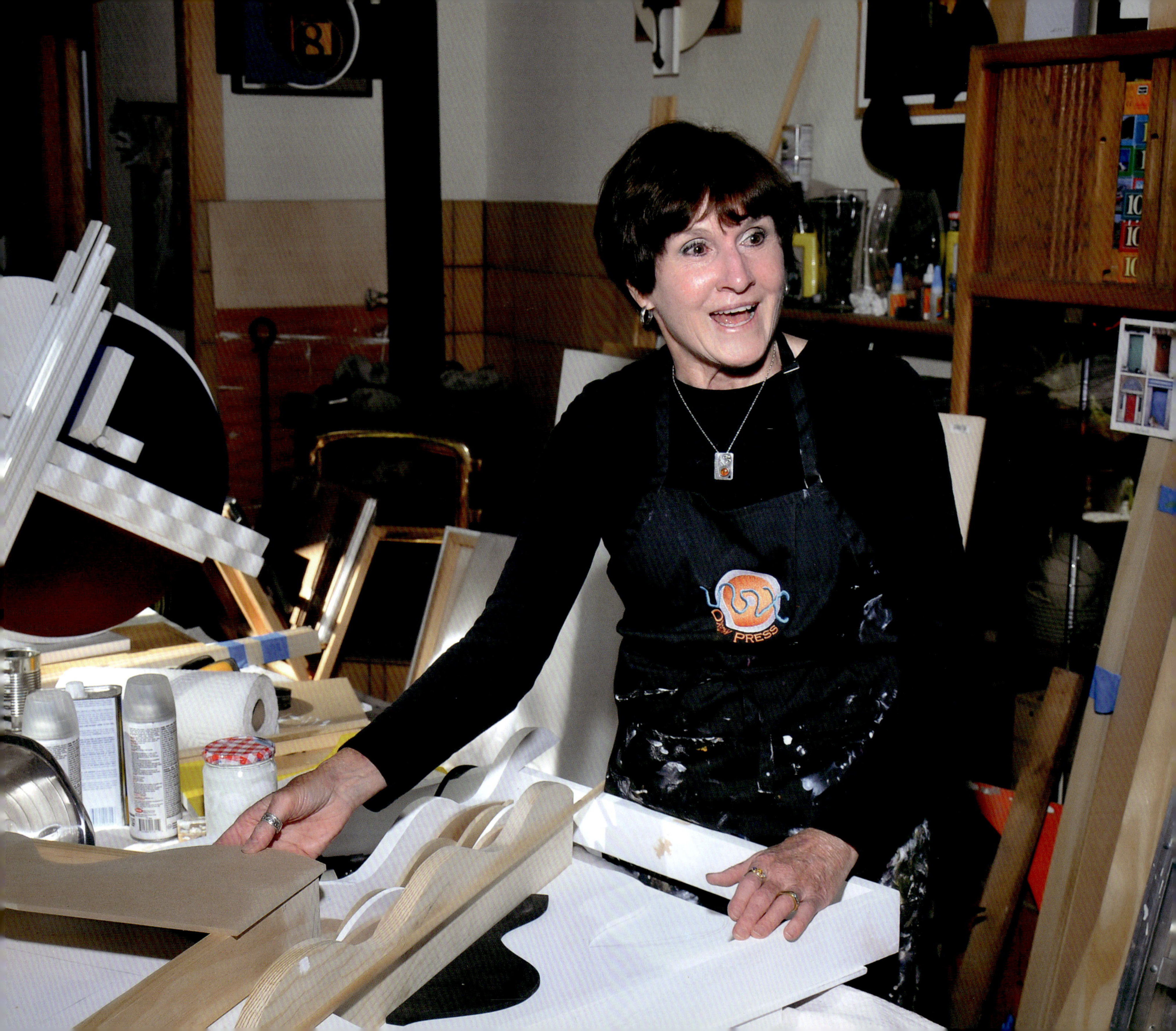
PRESS

BUILDING

To build or construct something normally requires a planned process of ordering and uniting homogeneous pieces of material to produce a uniform structure in conformance with a specific set of plans. This definition could apply to an office building, a computer, or a bicycle.

But a constructed piece of sculpture is radically different. Artists use a variety of materials, from hard to soft and in various sizes to create one-of-a-kind pieces that have taken shape and clarity in the maker's imagination. Generic patterns are not considered.

While Elaine Jason, Danaë Bennett-Miller, Gretchen Ericson, and Mimi Patrick are far apart in media, process, and their finished pieces, they have all envisioned their three-dimensional works of art first and then developed construction techniques that would bring their imaginative concepts to reality.

ELAINE JASON • BORN 1942

If you were to ask most artists how long it takes to complete one piece, they would probably reply, "All my life." Elaine Jason is no exception.

The first time I saw one of her structures, layered in a sort of deliberate way with pieces of wood and neon, I wanted to know more about the work and the artist. And as she describes the layers of her eventful, at times chaotic, life, I appreciate the power that is embedded in every piece she creates. "These . . . aren't intended to be mere abstract forms," she explains, her silver-hoop earrings dangling against dark shoulder-length hair, "but a way that I relate to life and space."

Elaine Jason assembling wood forms after cutting them.

On August 25, 2013, I stand before her work, *Never/Always,* and am reminded that art and life cannot be separated. We build an understanding of the world by reflecting on our own experiences, and Jason's early tumultuous years of witnessing and participating in move and change paved the direction of her work. Today, her structures of wood scraps and life passages blend with a kind of harmony into something new, like jazzy music, art forms the world has never seen.

Well, the world is seeing it now. Jason's sculpture has exhibited in solo and group exhibitions, at colleges, universities, art centers, and galleries around the country. Her work can be found in such corporate collections as Lockheed Martin, Philips Interactive Media, and Kaiser Permanente. Her many grants and awards include funding from The Andy Warhol Foundation for the Visual Arts and a recent Pollock-Krasner Foundation, Inc., individual artist grant for $15,000. This artist is definitely no amateur.

Life wasn't always so easy. Today, she says her work is all about balance, fun, and composition, but, growing up in post–World War II Los Angeles, change was the only thing she could count on. Her family moved from town to town, and she moved from school to school. The family battled its own private war with her father's alcoholism, violence, and unemployment. She remembers, "I knew how to hide." Jason was enrolled in kindergarten at the early age of four, and probably the best thing to come out of a challenging, disruptive childhood was art.

When she was seven, she discovered infinity on the back of a box of corn flakes. "On the box was a picture of a

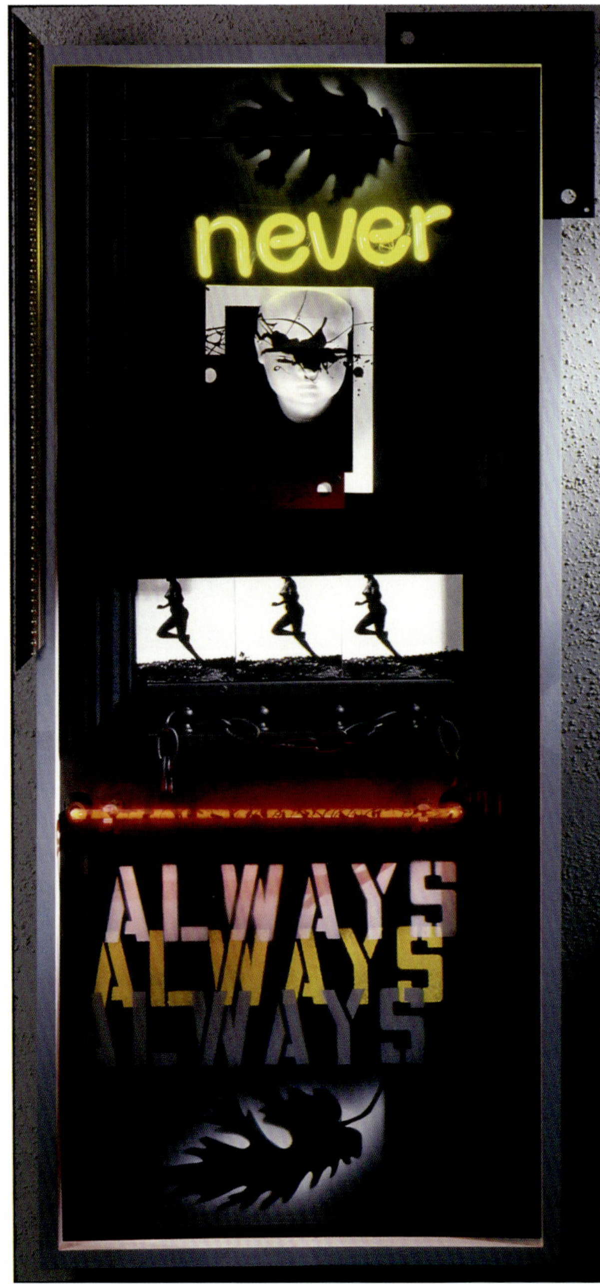

Elaine Jason, *Never Always.* Mixed media of found objects, neon, spray paint, acrylics on board; 53 x 28 x 7 in.

boy and a girl looking at a box of corn flakes with a picture of a boy and a girl looking at a box of corn flakes, and on and on. That same day I discovered my ability to draw. In my seven-year-old mind, I thought if I could copy the picture, and draw it smaller and smaller, that I could figure out how it worked, or find the end, or see if the end existed. I found how easy it was to copy pictures and objects and almost anything I wanted." She crosses her arms and I hear a catch in her voice, "For years to come, my drawings became a sanctuary from the terror of my childhood." At school, she received an A in art, and from that time forward she thought of herself as an artist and continued to create wherever she went.

When Jason was eight, her parents divorced; her mother raised the family as a single mom, and Elaine became a latchkey kid. During their many moves, she witnessed the growth of an entire city, which, she says, evolved into cities within a city. Farmlands were destroyed to make room for subdivisions and freeways. Building was everywhere, and the sky turned from blue to brown almost overnight. She says, "It was the beginning of my love/hate relationship with architecture."

Like the box of corn flakes, she was fascinated with the patterns made by mile after mile of homes under construction, the skeletal frameworks forming vanishing points against the horizon. Under a microscope at a school science class, she marveled at the cellular forms of a plant or a butterfly's wing. Her sculpture today reflects those early influences.

After high school, Jason studied at Chouinard Art Institute (now the California Institute of the Arts), and after college she was determined to make a living with her art. She married, moved to San Francisco, and began producing small, affordable pieces that she sold as a street artist. She created larger works and found galleries to carry them. Her income and stature as an artist grew. A daughter was born, then a second, and later a third. Jason was able to do what most artists only dream of—she purchased a home in Sebastopol with her art income.

But all was not well at home. Just at the blossoming of her career, she was forced to give it all up when she made the decision to escape an abusive husband and take her daughters to Nevada to obtain a divorce. That year was traumatic, no doubt tumultuous. Yet she soldiered on. She eventually remarried, and in 1983 Jason was fortunate to move into a studio home in Sparks, Nevada, with beautiful views of downtown and what she describes as "the bold relief" of the Sierra Nevada. "This area will always remain a sanctuary for me," she says. "A place to be free and safe and a place to create art." The influence on her artwork was profound. She could visually link all those experiences of constant change with a contemplative spiritual space. She began to construct and to arrange diverse materials into works of art, and they came outside the frame and off the wall. This new direction grew. Colors became brilliant and sculptural elements evolved.

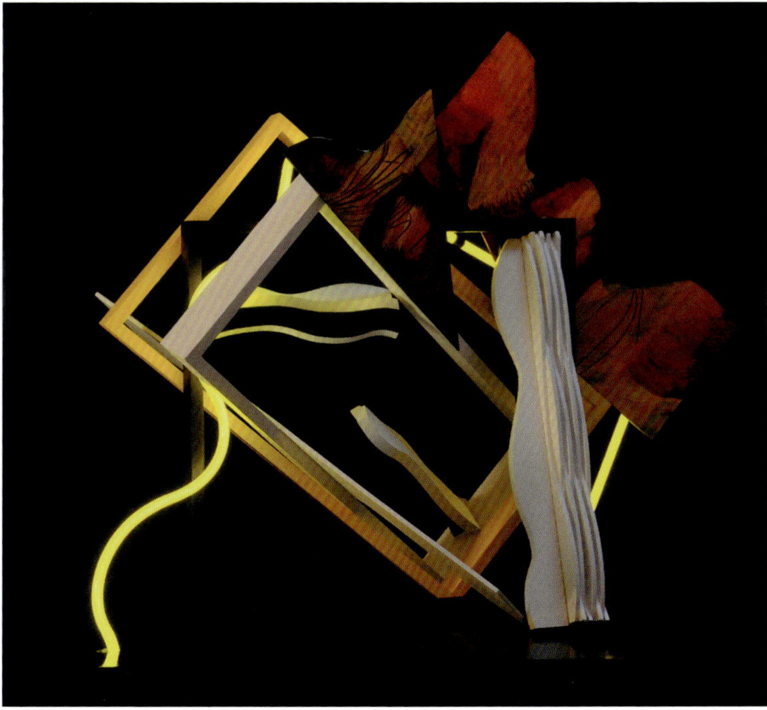

Elaine Jason, *Night Flight*. Painted wood; acrylic colors, neon; 46 x 47 x 37 in.

"When I got my first band saw I was in heaven," she says. And once again she went to work.

In this unfamiliar Reno/Sparks community, Jason began promoting her work. She attended openings and met supportive artists, beginning with the recently deceased artist Nancy Peppin. She met the late Chelsea Miller Goin, an art curator. "Chelsea came to my Sparks studio, saw my large body of work, and invited me to have a one-woman show at the Nevada Museum of Art." Gallery owner Peter Stremmel suggested she contact the newly opened Deluxe Gallery, and she arranged a show there and began to sell her new work. UNR professor emeritus and artist James McCormick was an early mentor and remains so to this day. Ever ambitious, Jason put a portfolio together and approached the Lake Gallery in Tahoe City, California, with a persistence that finally paid off. Other galleries from Mexico to Arizona, Chicago to Florida, and back to Nevada, followed, and the irrepressible Jason was on her way to establishing herself as an artist.

She found neon builders and picked their brains. Ken Hines taught her wiring, and she began incorporating neon tubes into her work in the mid 1980s. A whole new epoch in her career began, and by 1990 she was showing at the Museum of Neon Art in Los Angeles, landing a solo show there in 1995. Many people see the Louise Nevelson's influence in Jason's work.[1] Jason mentions the sculptors Marisol and Louise Bourgeois, who "worked and exhibited until she was ninety-nine," and Dorothea Tanning. "My role models," she says, "are women artists who have continued to make art until they died."[2]

And Jason is doing just that, in spite of personal challenges. One day, at the peak of her career, she returned home from an out-of-town show to find an empty house and a note on the kitchen table—her husband had walked away from the marriage. Unsettled times followed, but there was always her art, the one constant that brought rewards and satisfaction. By this time, her daughters had launched their own professional careers, and Jason obtained a job in Tahoe City, California, until she once again found her footing. One casualty was her Nevada home of twenty-five years, but move and change is a constant in Jason's life, and is even a kick-start for her work, which is evolving even now.

Health has challenged her also. She's a breast cancer survivor, and has had other health challenges. But they haven't stopped her from skiing, and she's learned to move forward despite physical handicaps. "I make my work lighter," she tells me, "and I ask for help."

Help might come from husband Ron, whom she married several years ago in a ceremony at the top of nearby Snowmass Mountain. "Then we all skied down." She smiles at the memory. "Life hasn't been boring," she says, then cocks her head. "But sometimes boring would be nice."

Somehow I doubt Jason will ever be bored. At our interview, she waves an arm over what was once a pool table, now covered with white cloths and a strong base for building her constructions. Her studio is crowded with hand and power tools, woods and found objects, paints, sketches, transformers, and electrical wiring, finished sculptures and works in progress. She rarely begins with a drawing. Instead, she approaches her work like a puzzle that she solves as she goes along, shaping wood and fiber board on a band saw, and sanding the sections. Next she'll add primer. At some point, after assembling "founds" and leftovers, she'll arrange and rearrange them with neon until the finished composition emerges. But she's not finished yet, not at all! Next she will create a sketch of the work before taking it completely apart. After that she'll paint each element and, finally, will rebuild the piece according to her drawing.

She will refine the composition several times before she's satisfied. The many shapes and sizes, cut to embody a vision that only she can see, come together slowly, deliberately, until a perfectly balanced whole has been created. It seems she is attempting to impose order on the chaos of an ever-accumulating pile of memories and wood scraps, harmonizing disparities. The overlapping shapes and layered planes of her life and art create glimpses into partially obscured interiors, much like the interiors of memory.

What motivates her to keep going? I want to know.

"I cannot imagine myself not making art. All of my life I've been creating in one form or another. Art is my identity. Being an artist is who I am. Without making art I would surely vanish." She gazes around her studio, from the massive tools to boxes of wood strips; from finished pieces gleaming in the sun on walls and pedestals, to works in progress on her table, before turning to me. "This is my addiction. I'm always still working for the perfect piece," she says. "I plan on doing this until I drop."

■ DANAË BENNETT-MILLER • BORN 1959

Every time art renews itself, something entirely fresh happens: something is born that has never been seen before. Danaë Bennett-Miller folds individual slabs of wax into sculpture that, when completed, will play the heaviness of bronze against the lightness of air. The finished piece becomes a poetic balance of what you see and what you think you see. She has tapped into a well of innovation to fill her sculptures—all of them animals of one kind or another—with movement and life and even a kind of poignant frailty that suggests a determination to carry on in the face of our own impermanence.

There was a time when Bennett-Miller met her own impermanence, and, lying in her hospital bed physically and mentally consumed, she had no idea that one day she'd produce larger-than-life public sculpture, achieve representation in prestigious galleries, be reviewed in national publications, and create innovative work for private

After the poured hot wax has cooled on the work table, Danaë Bennett-Miller shapes and texturizes it to form a part of a bird form, then pulls it up.

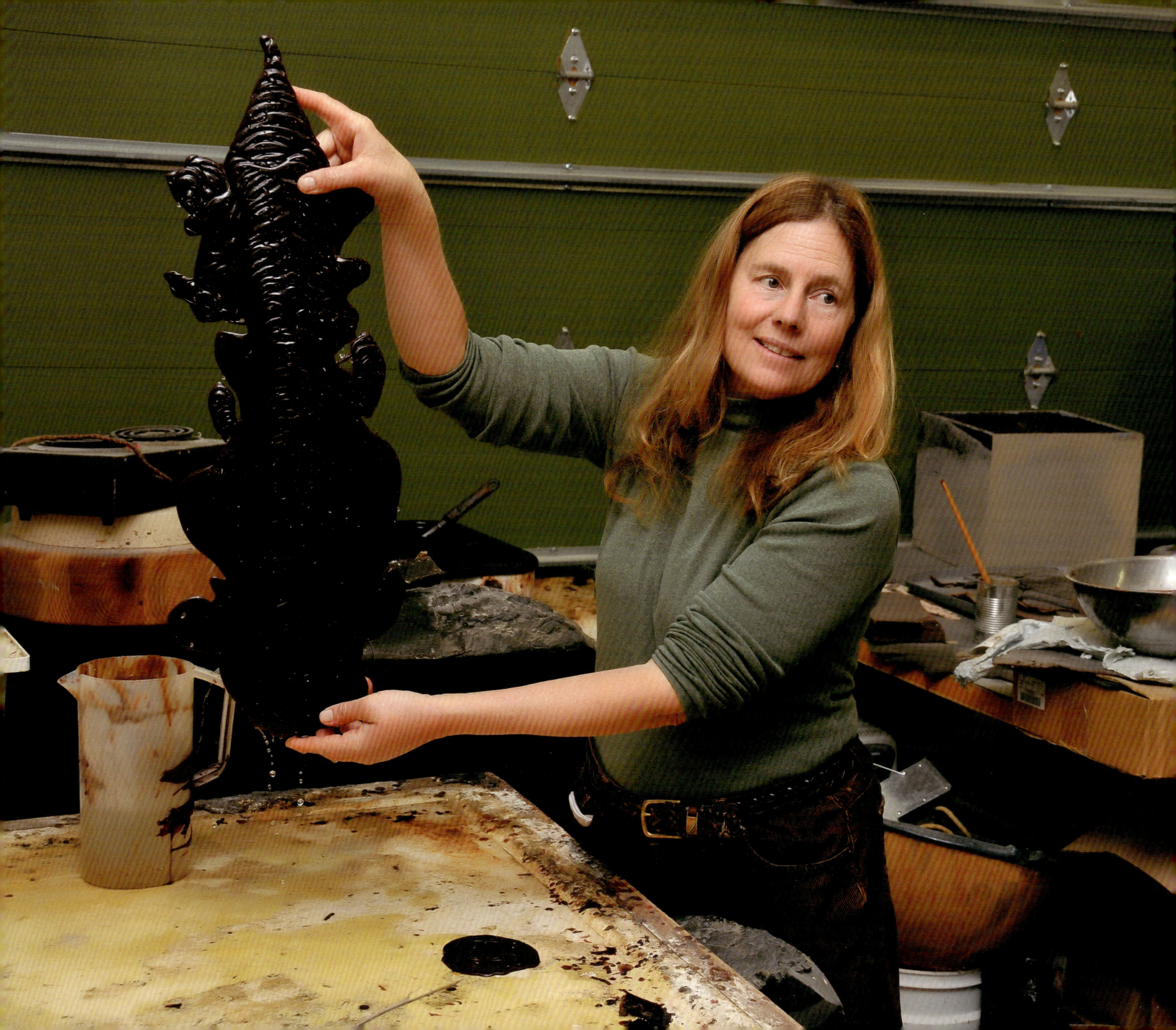

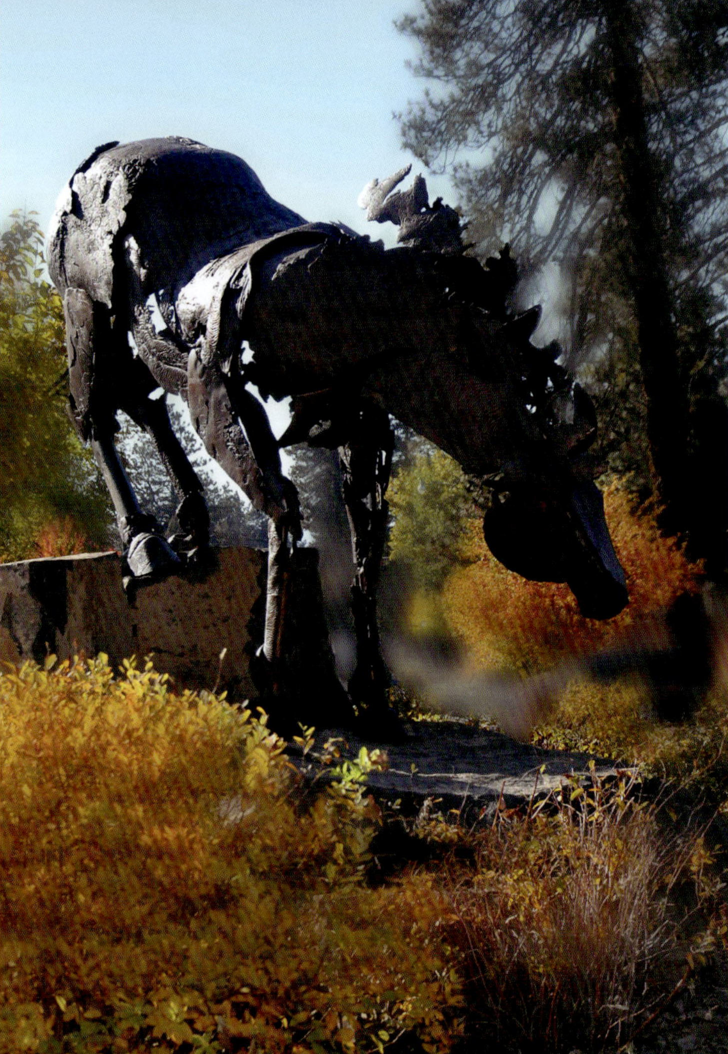

Danaë Bennett-Miller, *Bueno: Homage to the Great Basin Buckaroo*. Wax forming, cast bronze; 12 x 11 x 4 ft.

collections. The frequently mentioned Chinese symbol for crisis that can also mean opportunity comes to mind, for as this artist clawed her way back to the state of possibility, the puzzles of her life began to fit together.

Bennett-Miller has a deep familiarity with animals, ranging from buffalo to jackrabbits to cranes, horses, deer, elk, ravens, and more. "The animal shapes just come to me," she says, her dark eyes piercing the air. "I need to be around them. I'm more interested in the energy of the animal and how the material can express that energy." She pushes a hunk of blonde hair behind her shoulder. "Pouring the wax does that for me. You're given a gift of making this pretty piece, and I want to work with that."

Bennett-Miller's unique sculptures are the results of a finely tuned process that her extensive background in the arts helped her nurture and perfect. Her family encouraged her to pursue her twin passions of art and wildlife. "I never really cared for dolls," she says. Born in Greenwich, Connecticut, to a Greek mother, Mary Louise, and an industrial designer father, Louis William, she grew up traveling to cities where her father's work beckoned. He always had a basement workshop where his daughter loved to create. "He had milling machines and lots and lots of tools. He would hand us materials, like wire and wood, and we'd make things." At the age of eight, she started riding horses and drawing them, and her parents encouraged her—most of the time. Her mom wasn't real happy when her daughter pushed her fingers around warm candle wax or the hardened cooking grease left in the gravy pan. But those experiments were precursors to the wax she works with today.

In high school, which offered a wide array of art classes, she made the decision to become an artist, and after graduation Bennett-Miller attended the University of New Hampshire where art was her focus. "They had a really great animal science department with a horse program, too. And when I was able to, I sneaked in horsemanship." While she was at university someone gave her a hunk of wax to experiment with, and "I built up muscle memory and brain memory. Now, when creating a piece, I have more success because of all those early failures." In 1981 she received her bachelor of fine arts in sculpture and joined the University of New Hampshire's staff in the sculpture department. She maintained the school's foundry, furthering her knowledge of casting processes, an experience that would help her immensely years later.

In 1982 she decided to explore her mother's heritage and immersed herself in a cultural program at the Athens Center for Research and Hellenic Studies in Greece, and the following year she enrolled in a sculptural course in Crete through Manhattan College. Finally, she returned to the northeastern United States and pondered her future. Would she teach? Somehow support herself making art? Find work in an art-related field?

She learned of an upcoming shamanic workshop near Boston and decided to sign up. The experience gave her breathtaking access to another realm and opened her mind and heart to interconnectedness and her own inner sources of power. She discovered that her power animal was the elk, and right then Bennett-Miller decided to move west, where these animals primarily live, and to pursue further art studies at the University of Washington in Seattle.[3]

Often her professors expressed dismay that she continued creating the animals that had been with her since childhood but she persevered, and in 1986 received her master of fine arts degree.

Bennett-Miller wanted to teach, but where? She'd traveled all her life and it was time to settle down. She found a job at a photo lab in Palo Alto, California, created art in her spare time, and began to work with horses at a local stable, riding hunters and jumpers. There, she met the man who would become her husband, but in an unfortunate twist of fate, the idyllic life of making art and riding horses she'd planned was not to be—not yet, anyway. Her husband became increasingly controlling. He was especially adamant that she was not to "waste her time" making art. But the worst was yet to come: she had a severe horseback riding accident. Surgery was required, and as she lay alone in the hospital, morose, in pain, and unfulfilled, she realized this was not the life she wanted. She filed for, and was granted, a divorce.

A friend from the horse world invited Miller to head north to Sisters, Oregon, for a visit, and she jumped at the opportunity, once more becoming involved with the horses she loved. One June night just before the annual Sisters Rodeo began—they called it "Locals Night"—she met Ron Miller, a rancher from the vaquero tradition who lived in nearby Tumalo. They talked into the night about horsemanship and art and everything in between. In 1994 they were married at Lake Tahoe, Nevada. Bennett-Miller moved to Tumalo, "and I've been here ever since." They built their house, a mini ranch, of foam block and stucco with enormous vertical skinned pine logs inside.

At our interview on October 7, 2013, I see that antlers and a steer skull are stacked by the fireplace, below an immense wall hanging of ancient steer petroglyphs similar to the Paleolithic cave paintings in Lascaux, France. Original art hangs or sits in every available spot. Outside, horses prance around their corrals and a sheepdog works to keep the turkeys and geese in their yard. Bennett-Miller helps son Logan with the two hundred chickens that he raises and shows in the region. The home place, a cattle ranch, is east of here and Ron works there. When the artist isn't in her studio or at a show, she works alongside him, moving cattle and branding calves close to the wildlife that inspires her sculpture. "We'll see antelope, elk, rattlesnakes," she says. Rabbits and deer are there to be enjoyed and studied. "It's important to capture the essence and spirit of the animal."

She continues, "I rope, I brand. Oregon women are independent and hardworking. They will jump into every aspect of what has to be done. We work hard and if everything fell apart—well, my husband is inspiring because we can do anything."

And all the while Bennett-Miller has made her art—first from a trailer while they built their home. Next, she worked on the kitchen table, then in the chicken coop, and now in a corner of a spacious outbuilding that also stores poultry supplies. "A studio is next," she says with a laugh.

Her public sculptures are very different from traditional bronze sculptures, because they are created in sections

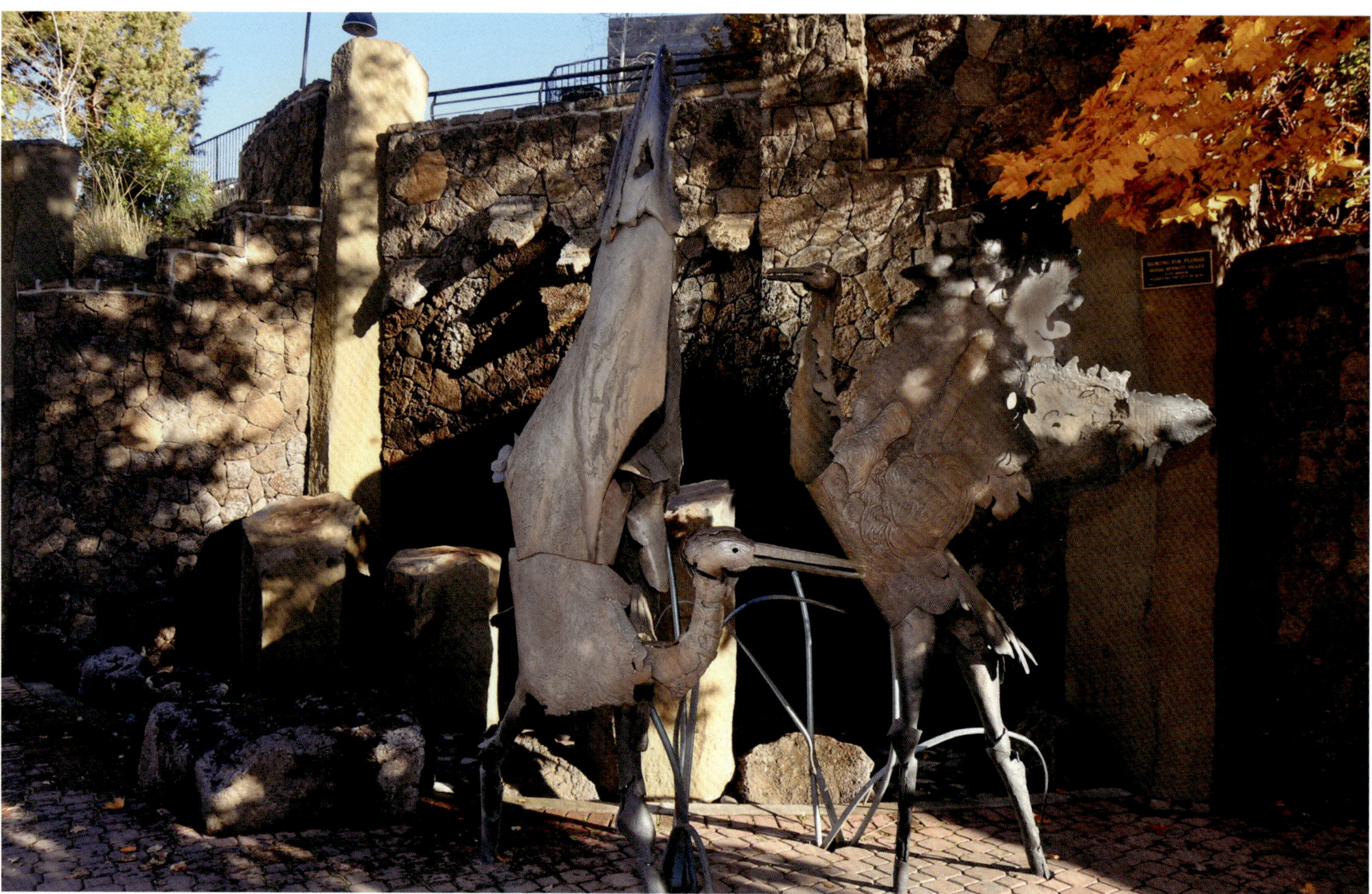

Danaë Bennett-Miller, *Dancing for Flossie.* Wax forming, cast bronze; 11 x 10 x 8 ft.

with space between the various parts. It is this aspect that gives her work the "poignant frailty" I mentioned earlier. "The negative space is as important as the positive space. I've always been attracted to the light and airy feeling, as opposed to most bronzes, which are dense."

The life-and-a-half size bronze *Bueno, Homage to the Buckaroo* that graces a roundabout in downtown Bend is one of her proudest achievements. Inspired by a horse her family owned, she says, "He had a huge body and a huge heart. He was a very kind horse and taught a lot of people how to ride." Bennett-Miller used Bueno's actual back and hindquarters to make a plaster mold. "He stood there while the plaster set and got hot. He could feel it tightening up, but he didn't move. So when this old horse died, my son was so sweet because he said, 'Old Bueno is still there; his back is in the sculpture." Bennett-Miller's mother cried for joy when she first saw it, and she credits her parents for their support. "They allowed me to be who I am, and they never put art down as a possibility, even though they didn't know how to help me obtain my success with it." (Her parents, now in their eighties, live nearby.)

Other public sculptures include *Dancing for Flossie,* giant cranes amid cattails and fountains in downtown Bend; and *She Loved all the Birds, Especially Cranes and Herons,* a ten-foot-tall great blue heron in Sisters. In addition, in the Deschutes County Health Services lobby is a life-size piece incorporating neon to display two elk. Of course, her power animals would be exhibited in a place where they can pay tribute to the underserved.

I watch Bennett-Miller demonstrate her technique while Susan Mantle photographs the process. A few chickens squawk and crow from their cages behind me; they are bathed and ready to go to a poultry show this very afternoon.

First, the artist pours water over a plaster surface that sits atop a sturdy stand. (Water keeps the hot wax from sticking to the plaster.) Next, she dips an old dented saucepan into hot wax melting nearby in an electric roasting pan. Finding the exact temperature and mix of waxes has taken years of trial and error. She pours this molten wax from the saucepan in an uneven but controlled puddle along the plaster slab. At this point, she might or might not have an idea in mind. If she's planning a specific animal, she pours to follow a previously drawn sketch. As the wax cools, Miller gently pulls it from the plaster and begins to form it. She remarks that the demonstration piece in her hands resembles a wing, and if I stretch my imagination, I can see it does.

She will continue in this manner, shaping each piece into an animal part—a head, beak, torso, hoof, leg, and so on. She says, "At work, you tune everything else out. And if you're not in a good frame of mind, nothing will work." Her affection for wax isn't just technical. "It has a life of its own. When you work with something over the years you become familiar with it. I have this bond with the material, and it gives me everything."

While the wax is still warm, she'll take an X-ACTO knife and cut away parts she doesn't need. Sometimes she'll incise into it, creating texture.

She took time to build a relationship with the foundry, and must transport the completed wax model to Joseph, Oregon, several hours away. She needs to be present for the entire casting process, working with the men who build it, one section at a time, translating the shapes into bronze.

She also uses the lost wax process for casting glass, which she then incorporates into the bronze. Bennett-Miller says that combining glass and bronze adds another level of lightness. She pours liquid glass directly into the mold, in yet another leap into innovation.

Bennett-Miller also creates smaller work for private collections, but none of it is an easy task when you're working with bronze, a material known for its solid presence. Because she works with wax, her original piece is destroyed in the casting process; unlike traditional bronze sculpture that begins with plaster, she is unable to cast in editions. "About 95 percent of my work is one of a kind," she says. And she likes it that way. "To me, there's a freshness in a piece of work that's the only one."

Her hope is to eventually invite people to come and learn to make art, remembering the professors who derided her for making mere "uninteresting" animal objects. It was difficult to get through those unfavorable critiques, but she was determined to follow her own path. "There are many levels of art in the world. I may never be a New York artist." Many artists have particular career goals, like being in museums, and that isn't necessarily her direction. She would like everybody to explore the field of art, and she wants to help them in their efforts. "Anybody can make [art]. It makes us feel whole. If you feel empty, it's because you're not making something."

Bennett-Miller will never have that problem, because she is involved in many artistic endeavors and most of them involve an innovative style that incorporates heaviness and light, negative and positive, frailty and strength. By choosing a small part of what went before, and by isolating a kernel of it, she has foregrounded a seed that seems to be growing into the next big thing.

GRETCHEN ERICSON • BORN 1965

What English literature and the Fibonacci number sequence have in common with Gretchen Ericson's knotted sculpture is a question I have to ask as I interview the Reno artist over tea at Aroma Café, a Russian restaurant, on February 16, 2014. The artist demonstrates her technique as we talk, manipulating thread into a macramé knot around a core of thread and pushing it firmly against a hand-carved mold, another knot added to row upon row of hundreds of identical overhand knots. It will take her thirty minutes to knot one round, and this piece, an oblong, pod-like shape about two-thirds finished, has consumed hundreds of hours. "I don't know many people who are crazy enough to do this kind of work," she says, laughing. "But," she adds, "it's very meditative, and in this hectic world we live in, I can feel at peace as I work, lost deep in a place of rest and renewal."

Knot enthusiasts say that civilization is held together by knots. Our shoes are tied by knots, the materials in our clothing are themselves glorified knots, fibers twisted together. Doctors suture wounds and tie knots, cables supporting suspension bridges use principles of knotting in ropes of galvanized steel wire.

Knots predate the axe and the wheel, and some scientists say that the first knotters were animals, gorillas who tied simple knots as they interlaced branches to build nests. In this digital age, knots remain indispensable. On the deck of NASA's Mars rover, Curiosity, cables are tied down with a variation on the reef knot, used by mariners hundreds of years ago to trim their sails. Knots are used by practically every person on the planet every day. And the most recent application has entered the field of art. In *The Ashley Book of Knots* (1944), Clifford Ashley wrote, "The simple act of tying a knot is an adventure in unlimited space."

Ericson, with her knotted sculpture, has joined a handful of others around the country to put a new spin on an ancient tradition. With variations of simple half-hitching of nylon cord around a linen thread cord, over a mold she has carved into a sculptural form, she creates a structure that grows as she works, until the final knot completes the piece. Little specialized equipment is needed, which allows for latitude in design and concept. "There is no end to the possibilities," she says. She considers knotting to be a skin over the form she has designed. "You can cover it, stitch on it, paint, layer, and do anything you want with it." Because of the length of time required to create each piece, Ericson's exhibits are limited. She was part of a Los Angeles Knotters Collective show at the Nevada Museum of Art, has shown with the Great Basin Basketmakers, and exhibits annually with the Wild Women at various venues.

Her English literature background fostered a love of story, and some of her *baskets,* as she calls the sculptures, tell stories. In *Ni' Hodisxos,* tiny architectural figures are placed inside three coiled baskets, her representation of part of the Navajo creation myth. "It's a fascinating story—they explained what we're doing here and how we got here." Ericson coiled the baskets, covered them with a mixture she concocted, and "that became the canvas to tell my story around."

I notice that the artist refers to her work as baskets, when I want to call them fiber sculptures. She explains, "Baskets are traditional holders of things; taken to another place, I see baskets as narrative. If I use a skin over a form or cover an actual basket, I have allowed a story to be built, that story being either a dream, a representation of nature, or just a thought."

Born in Reno, the daughter of a teacher mother and a father who is a partner in a civil engineering firm, to whom she remains very close, Ericson remembers a solitary childhood. "They sent the children out all day long. I was all

Gretchen Ericson knotting over a mold.

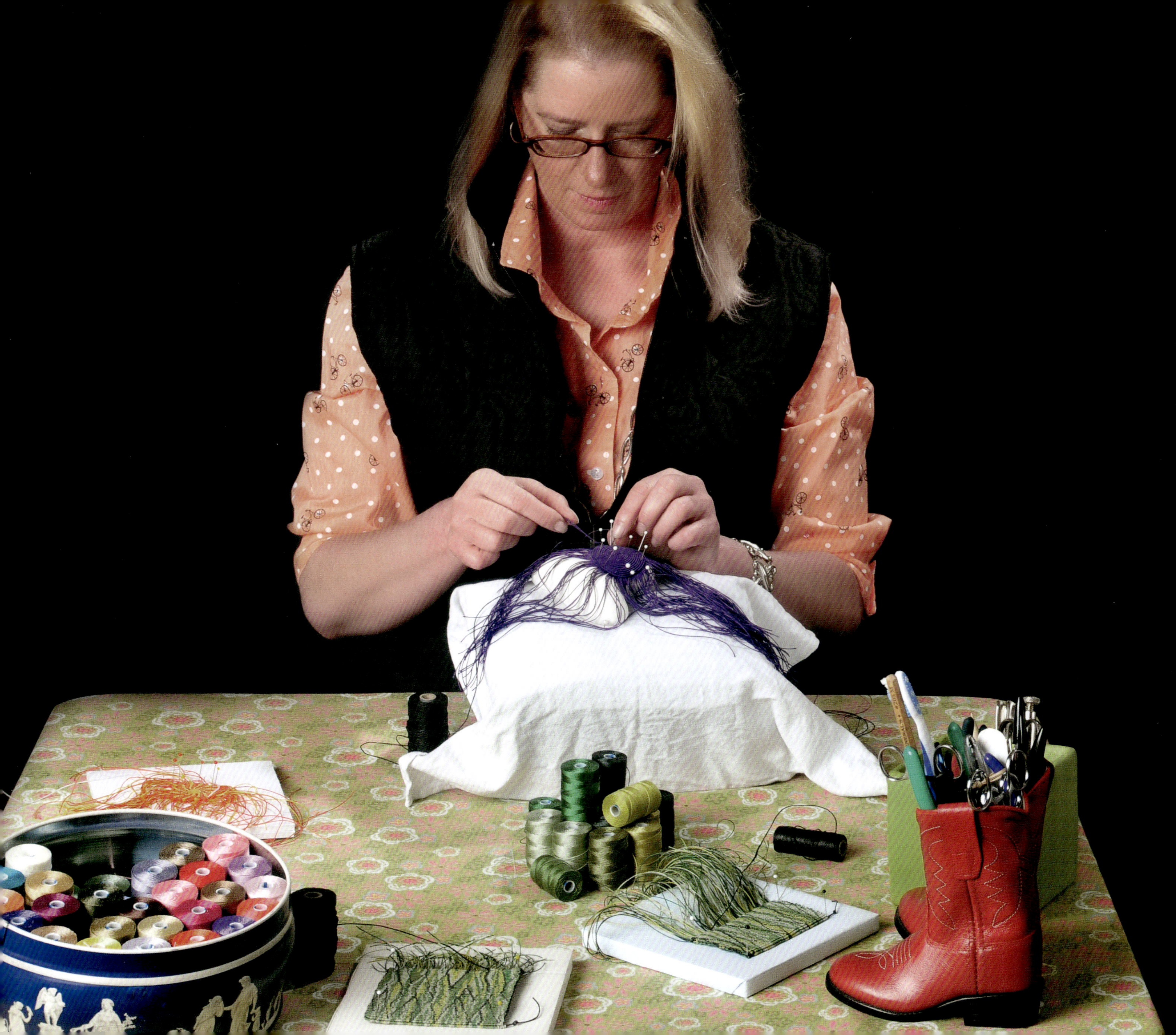

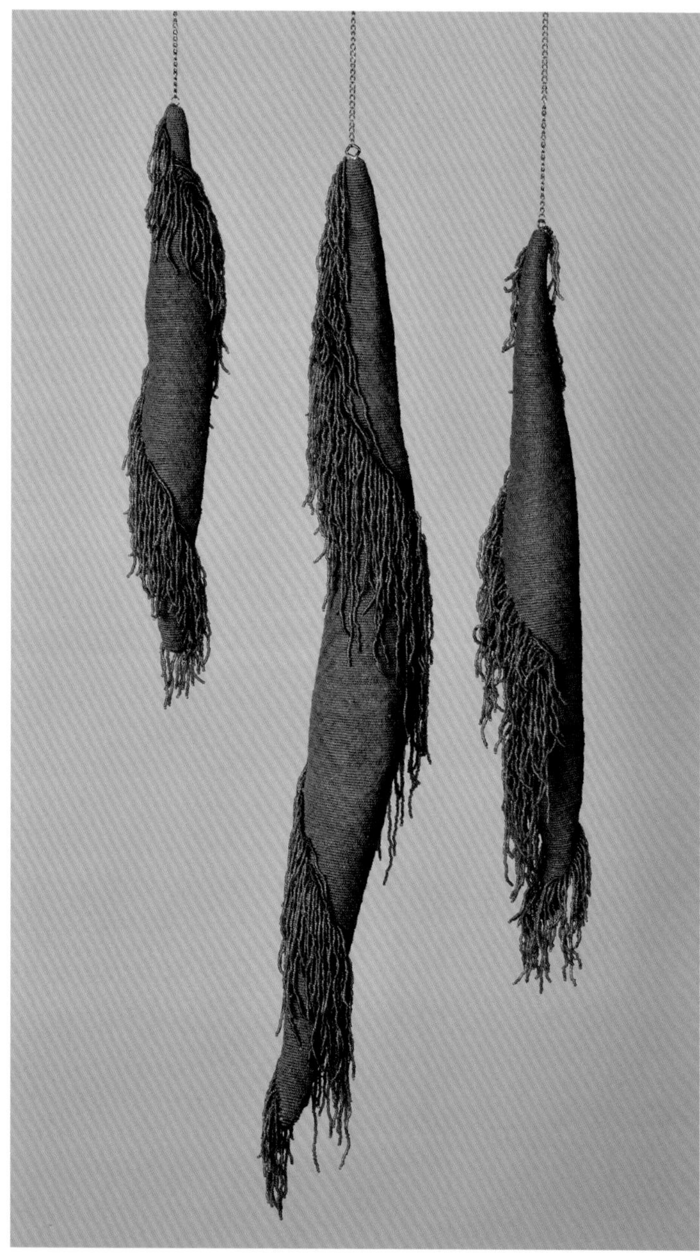

Gretchen Ericson, *Pods*. Mixed media of knotted waxed linen over a wire armature; variable dimensions from 25 to 14 in.

by myself in the field every day making little things out of sticks and grasses. I was a shy little girl. I had no clue I was making sculptures." Her aunt taught Ericson and her sister how to crochet, but it didn't click. "The joke in the family was 'Where's Gretchen? I don't know, she was down by the river playing with sticks!' I wanted to sit at my little spot at the river gathering little piles of sticks, hanging out by myself making things." She joined the Campfire Girls (now Camp Fire) and soon learned how to make a pine-needle basket. She also remembers her mother doing needlepoint and taking it on family outings, and that idea taught her about moving around with her art, an activity she does during this interview.

Art was an elective at Reno High School and she always signed up, although sculpting was of a practical nature like making ceramic bowls or cups. She had a drive to make things, and when she enrolled at San Francisco State University she taught herself how to do folk art pieces in papier mâché and then sold them. She was determined to graduate in four years so she could move on and find employment, and she succeeded.

After some retail jobs, she went to work in 1990 for a medical software company in Burlingame, and that's where she fell in love with computers and software. "Computer technology was so new. The Internet wasn't there yet. Being involved with computers was so much like being an artist," she says, "and it still is. I could take words and make something. It's technical but it's very creative, too." She fell in love with it and stayed within the computer industry.

She moved to San Clemente to work for a software company, a company that employs her in Reno today, and from her home computer she does all the testing, documentation, and new product design. "It's very creative and fun. Most people wouldn't think a visual artist would find that interesting, but it is, and it's creative." Then she adds, "It's also intense and technical." Creative. Fun. Intense.

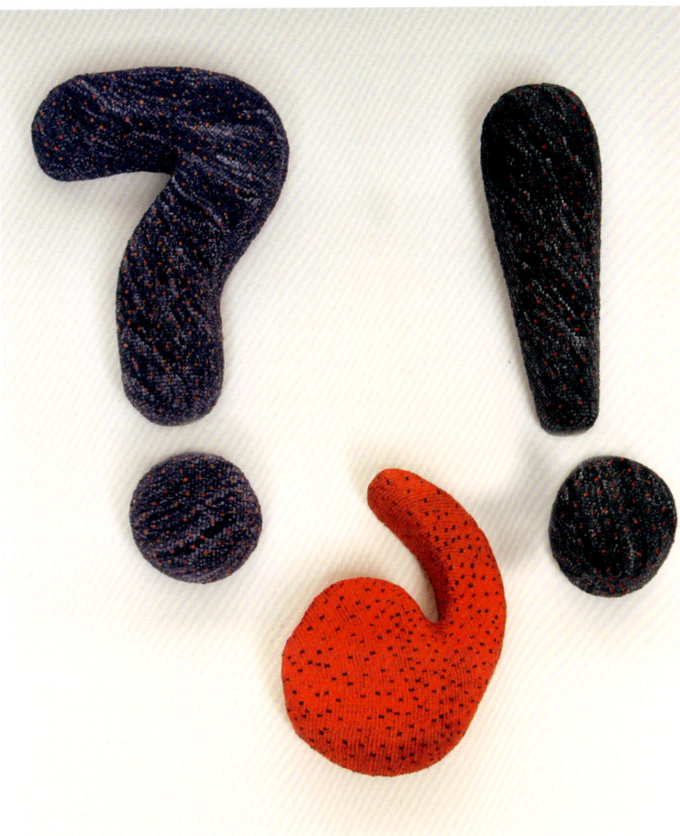

Gretchen Ericson, Punctuation Series. Mixed media of hand-painted waxed linen thread knotted over carved foam forms; 12 x 16 x 2 in.

Technical. Those are words that could easily describe her present artistic work.

Ericson, like many other artists, exhibits the characteristics of an introvert, as described in author Susan Cain's *Quiet: The Power of Introverts in a World That Can't Stop Talking* (2013). While extroverts are rewarded in our society for their outgoing natures, introverts work quietly, behind the scenes. Cain reports that solitude is an important key to creativity and cites experts who say that only when one is in deep silent concentration can she go directly to the most challenging part of the work. Introverts, says Cain, spend time inside the intellectually fertile environment of their own heads, and this is where discovery often begins. She cites examples of introverts: Bill Gates, Rosa Parks, Albert Einstein, and Eleanor Roosevelt, among others.

Back in 1998 when Ericson was living in Orange County, California, her life was a little too solitary. She was lonely. She'd felt disconnected from her artist friends in the Bay Area, and for the first time in her life, she was on her own. One day she wandered through a craft show in Irvine. "I turned a corner and saw a woman sitting there with the most incredible pine-needle baskets I ever saw in my life!" The woman was the well-known basket artist Nadine Spier. Ericson not only became acquainted with her, but she also enrolled in Spier's classes. "I learned the basics. You have to learn techniques, and she taught me about being open and sculptural. I used long needles from the Mexican weeping pine, and I could get my coils so long and delicate." It took her back to her childhood and the Campfire Girls, but these baskets were entirely new. "It opened up a whole new world to contemporary basketry. "You didn't have to use a pattern and you could open up and try new directions—much like programming in computers." She added, "You try it and see what happens."

Ericson eventually made her way back to Reno, and when Los Angeles artist Rosalie Friis-Ross was invited to teach a Great Basin Basketmakers conference workshop in knotting, Ericson signed up, and she was hooked. "I couldn't push the limits any longer with pine needles. Knotting was [so innovative]—you can do anything: cover any form and even create your own forms. I can express anything I want—a thought, a dream, part of a conversation. It has become my great love. I'm obsessed with experimenting."

She also uses technology to design her fiber sculpture, and that's where the Fibonacci sequence comes in. "The Fibonacci sequence is basically what a coil is. You can get a very nicely proportioned spiral, and if I'm doing a series, I use the sequence to make sure each piece stays aesthetically proportioned." To explain in a nutshell, the first two numbers in the Fibonacci sequence are 0 and 1, and each subsequent number is the sum of the previous two. (0 + 1 = 1, 1 + 1 = 2, 1 + 2 = 3, 2 + 3 = 5, and so on.) Ericson says she sees it as "a numerical chain letter." Sometimes she uses a reverse Fibonacci sequence to determine where exactly to begin.

She's obsessed with experimenting, never knowing whether the trial pieces will fly or fail. "After all," she says, "half of success is failure." The experiments always teach her something. "Who knew that marine toilet paper is far superior as a paper base than printed newspaper? Or that the cotton cord found in the hardware store is much prettier and easier to use than expensive cotton cord from the fabric store?"

In addition to Friis-Ross and Spier, Ericson looks to the greats—nationally known knotting artist Jane Sauer, and the notes, vessels, and drawings of another national artist, Lissa Hunter. Native American literature has moved her into dreams and ideas, and it helps to be "so close to the Washo and Paiute people," who live and work in the western part of Nevada.

"It would be easy to say I live here in the Great Basin because my whole family lives here, or that it's familiar because I grew up here, but that does not begin to cover this place I call home. There's a lot of life downtown, and in a half hour I can be in the desert, so quiet and fragile. Or I can be in the mountains among the pines. All these different worlds I can be in within minutes." She continues, "The diverse opposite environments directly feed into my desire to create in opposites, using traditional basketry techniques with unexpected materials. And also," she continues, "my work represents my overall sense of place here in the Great Basin. It reminds me that the solid, almost impenetrable permanence is actually very fleeting and fragile."

MIMI PATRICK • BORN 1941

On March 25, 2014, we travel along Highway 50 east of Carson City, Nevada, and just beyond the small community of Mound House we turn onto 341, a narrow, winding road where deserted miners' cabins and fairly recent buildings rise from sagebrush fields and old mine tailings tumble from the hillsides. Virginia City was focus of a spectacular silver discovery—the Comstock Lode—in the late 1850s, and today is listed on the National Register of Historic Places. But we're headed to nearby Gold Hill, site of early day (and very recent) mining as well, and to Mimi Patrick's studio.

Eighteen years earlier, Patrick bought this place, a former schoolhouse along the tourist road to Virginia City, to live, create, and sell her art. Her rustic sign crowds a huge lilac bush and reads, "Argenta Earth and Fire, Pottery and Stoneware." The door opens to her gallery, where various artworks grip pedestals and walls. Patrick has made a name for herself with pottery—first utilitarian ware, then sculptural works that she sometimes incised and carved, sometimes sculpted into figures or abstract forms. In recent years she has transitioned from clay to wood.

I stand before a box-shaped sculpture on one wall. Toward the base of this box, small legs zigzag outward on each side, their wood shoes pointed to the sky in a zany kind of dance. Higher up, jointed arms twice the size of the legs protrude with their own rhythm. Two wood doors open at center front to reveal an ocean-like interior, with shells resting on stands in various heights against a background of painted blue and white bulbous shapes that are flush to the back and gesture toward a center ocean of ultramarine.

This isn't a typical human form I'm looking at, because there's no head. In its place, a small figure made of various found objects stares wide-eyed, waving its wing-shaped hands in glee. Or is it distress?

As I gaze at this form, more questions push into my brain. Those couldn't be penises in the background? Does that seashell have an eye? And does its little mouth grimace,

Mimi Patrick assembles a wood figure.

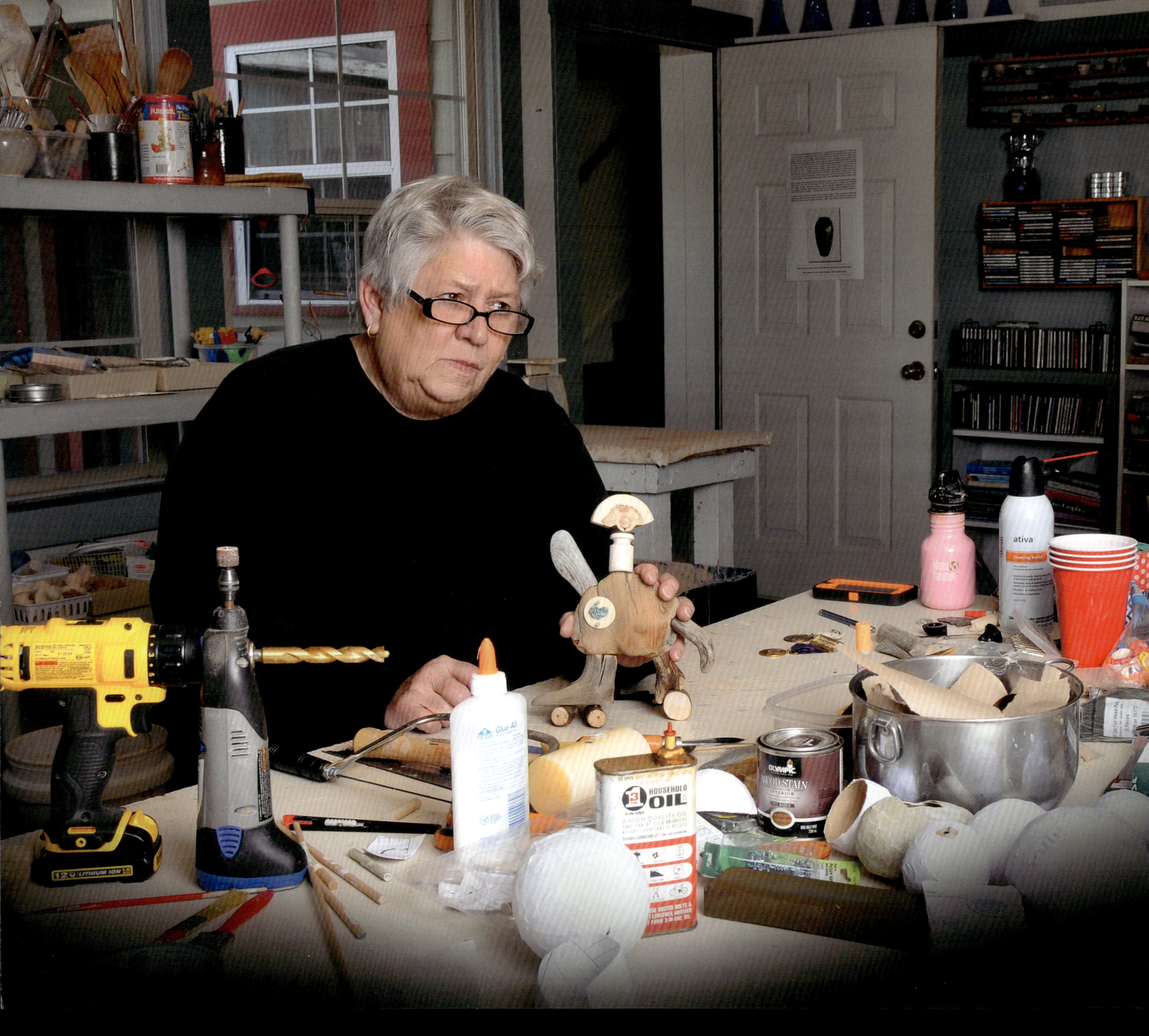
Glue-All
HOUSEHOLD OIL
OLYMPIC
WOOD STAIN
ativa
12V LITHIUM ION

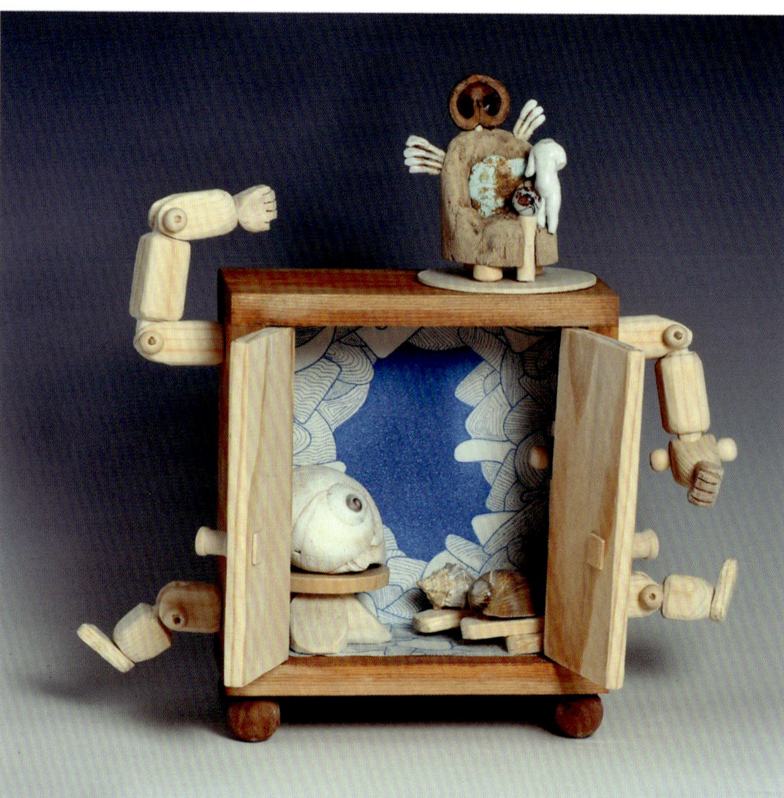

Mimi Patrick, *Untitled.* Mixed media of wood, shells, turquoise, deer teeth, found object; 12 in. high.

or does it smile? I back up and study the entire piece. Is it dancing or is it, like Humpty Dumpty, trying to catch itself from falling? Or maybe both?

This foot-high box sculpture, representing Patrick's newer work, might be communicating on behalf of the artist herself, for she tells me, "I moved to Gold Hill eighteen years ago, and reinvented myself. Now I need to do it again."

Indeed, this artist is in the process of making new decisions on all fronts—how to put clay on the back burner after forty-three years, how to adapt to changing directions in creating her wood sculptures, and mostly, how to sell her home and studio and move back to Reno, a community she happily vacated eighteen years earlier.

In the adjoining studio I pull out my recording i-Phone, photographer Mantle arranges her equipment, and Patrick sits at her worktable and picks up a wood figure in progress. A silky down of silvery white hair hugs her face in a thick cap, and her hand clutching the sculpture is wide and muscular, fingers stubby, nails cut short. She picks up a file and begins to work on the figure, which, like the box, gives off a feeling of what French artist Jean Dubuffet called *art brut* (raw art). He said those works were created from solitude with pure and authentic creative impulses, where worries of competition and acclaim aren't present. *Art brut,* Dubuffet said, is immune to the influences of culture.

Patrick talks into my recorder, and while she explains the work of assemblage artist Joseph Cornell that "hid in the back of my mind all these years," I find myself blown away by her huge studio. The work table is scattered with glue bottles, a tin bowl of paper strips, a set of drill bits, various pieces of wood—new wood, driftwood gathered elsewhere, old weathered wood found on walks through the hills. ("Three things I really like," she says. "Glue, sharp things, and dirt.") Outside in back of the property, an eighteen-cubic-foot gas kiln rises from the ground; inside, floor-to-ceiling shelves spill over with tools—dremels, drill bits, power sanders, and more. Pottery equipment remains—a pug mill for reprocessing clay, slab roller, wedging board, and a wheel and stool. Elsewhere shelves hold work in process, more hand and power tools, glazes, work from a previous printmaking class, a CD player, and hundreds of little numbered pots containing test glazes. I ask what the closed doors on some of the shelves would reveal and she replies, "magical things" found during scavenging trips through the Comstock hills—old gears, Nevada turquoise, rusty metal, pieces and parts of dolls, marbles, and more.[4] Fish posters decorate a wall—Patrick is an avid fisherwoman, as her sculpture sometimes indicates—and I see a quote attributed to Robert Caples: "We're shaped by the things we shape—it's as simple as that."

Mimi Patrick is indeed shaped by her work and life. Born at Washoe Hospital (now Renown) when it was just one building, Catherine Grace Patrick is a fourth-generation Nevadan. *Grace* is a family name—her mother was Grace, her grandmother, Grace Gracey. Three generations of Graceys are buried in Virginia City. Her Manx great-great grandfather arrived in 1860 from the Isle of Man; her grandfather was a brakeman on the Virginia & Truckee Railroad and moved to Reno with his job. While Patrick's mother and sister, Nancy Gracey, painted beautiful landscapes and still lifes, Patrick says, "I was the kid who was making houses out of large boxes and rummaging around in ditches and little creeks, putting together scenes with sticks, grasses, rocks, and mud. Reno was so rural in the forties and fifties. I once built a raft and was going to float down the Truckee River, but they caught me." Both Grace and Nancy sewed, but "I was hopeless at it and still am." She smiles a grin rather like the one on the seashell. "I was a rebel, but really more of a tomboy."

A Reno High School drawing class under John Iacavelli caused plenty of frustration—more two-dimensional art that did not compute. Mimi's father, Edward John, a telephone company executive, died suddenly in 1959, and her mother returned to the workforce. Patrick obtained a degree in French from UNR, married, and moved with her husband to San Francisco while he finished law school, and then to Germany as her husband fulfilled his military obligation. Daughter Kristen was born in 1967 and son Stephen in 1969. Back home in Reno, Patrick tried her hand at various three-dimensional artforms like macramé and stained glass, but nothing seemed to grab her. Then she enrolled in an adult education pottery class at Wooster High School, with Genelle Rae instructing, "and," she says, "I knew instantly that was it."

In 1972 Patrick enrolled in art classes at UNR, and eventually taught pottery at Truckee Meadows Community College and the YWCA. She remodeled a greenhouse into a studio, bought her first kiln, and, with a friend, gathered other local potters together and formed the Nevada Clay Arts Guild. The group applied for grants and invited nationally known potters to present seminars and demonstrations. They organized group shows. Over the years

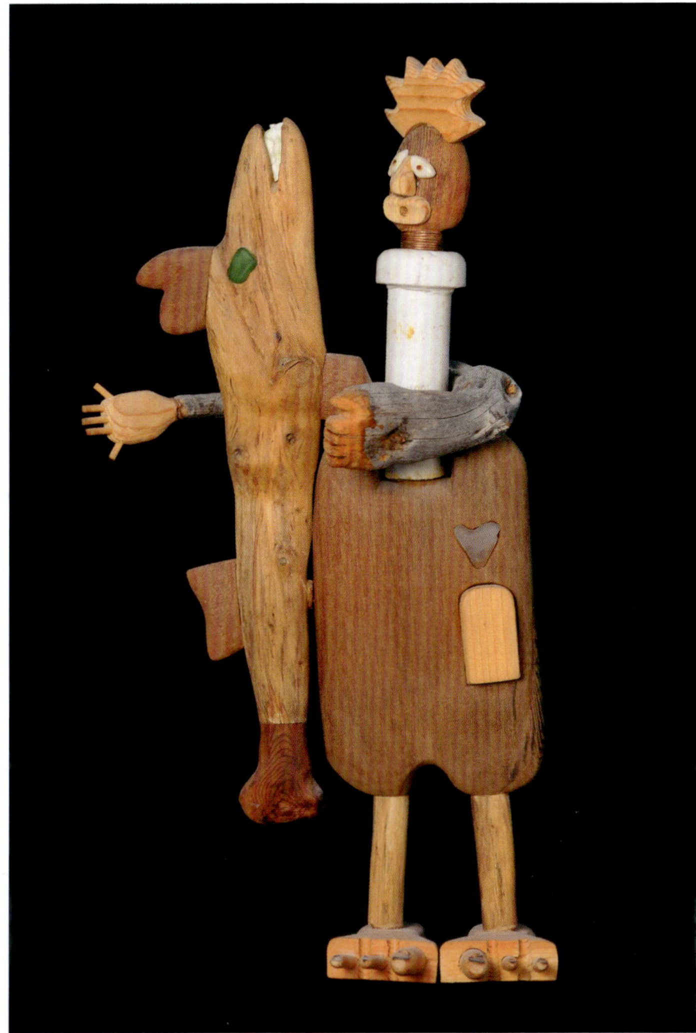

Mimi Patrick, *Untitled*. Mixed media of wood, bone, beach glass, porcelain insulator; 14 in. high.

Patrick exhibited and sold her work all over the Great Basin of Nevada and California. She participated in several Wild Women shows and exhibited with Artouring at the Nevada Museum of Art, John Ben Snow Foundation and Memorial Trust, River Gallery, and Metro Gallery (Baltimore, Maryland), and the Artists Co-op Gallery Reno, to name a few.

And then she hit a roadblock—divorce. Just three credits short of receiving an art degree, and with two small children to support, Patrick went to work for Nevada Bell. And all the while she made time to keep her hands working the clay. But, she says, "After seventeen years of torture at Nevada Bell, I got out on early retirement. And I've never been sorry."

Then one day, shortly after her children had left home to seek their own fortunes, a serendipitous event happened. Patrick, eating her taco lunch at work, dropped it on the floor. She stooped to pick it up, and there she spotted a newspaper folded open to real estate ads. One of those ads "popped out at me. It said, 'Gold Hill Large Workshop.' I took Friday off and came to look at it." The place, a former school built in the 1940s, was perfect, with living quarters upstairs and even a separate cottage for potter friends or maybe rental income. "A good friend had just passed away and I thought, 'If this is what you want to do, you'd better do it!'"

Patrick sold her Reno house in six days, moved to Gold Hill, and became a full-time clay and wood artist. As with the Clay Arts Guild in Reno, Patrick once again created community, helping to build and to operate the St. Mary's Art and Retreat Center in Virginia City; she was also one of the hundreds of teachers who presented classes and lectures at the now flourishing Center. She worked with the old Fourth Ward School and the Virginia City Convention and Tourism Association. Today, the St. Mary's Art and Retreat Center is thriving.

Recently, some physical challenges have arisen, and Patrick is contemplating a move back to Reno, where medical facilities are available. The nearby Comstock Mine threatens to close down the road that brings tourists to her studio on their way to Virginia City; if that were to happen, sales would abruptly end. Then there are the new and exciting explorations in wood that have torn her away from her beloved clay while at the same time inspiring a myriad of new possibilities. After working in clay for forty-three years, her hands are painful, but that little setback won't stop her.

"I'm going to keep on working," she declares. "I have to, because [otherwise] I'd be locked up somewhere. This is a compulsion for me. I can't stop. When I grew up, there were only limited acceptable life choices for girls ranging from wife/mother, nurse, clerical secretary, to teachers. I do not denigrate those choices, but I did not fit into them very well. When I discovered clay at thirty, it was a turning point for me. I have worked at many things, but art was the only thing I wanted to make my life." Then Patrick rephrases an earlier statement, "I've got to reinvent myself again. And I think I'm on the road."

I think she is, too.

Notes

1. Late American sculptor Nevelson was known for her monumental, monochromatic wall pieces made of wood, and her outdoor sculptures.
2. Maria Sol Escobar, who adopted Marisol as her name, was born in Paris of Venezuelan parents. Escobar forged her own path in sculpture, fusing Pop Art imagery and folk art. Louise Bourgeois's sculpture was manifested strongly in feminist-inspired art and in installation art, through a variety of media. Dorothy Tanning gained fame as a painter, sculptor, and writer and she worked until she died at age 101 years.
3. People who present shamanic workshops say that long before the rise of our current societies, indigenous ancestors discovered methods for seeing the capabilities of the human body-mind-spirit complex. A workshop may offer what they call shamanic journeys to establish connections with spirit helpers and teachers, ancestral spirits, and possibly descendants to help solve problems or foster healing.
4. The Comstock Lode (named for Henry Comstock), near Virginia City, was the first major discovery of silver ore in the United States and sparked the silver rush. The entire area is now referred to as "the Comstock."

ADVOCATING

Advocacy is a process in which groups or individuals use different types of methods to advance their ideas, drawing attention to a variety of beliefs or decisions.

Artist and art critic Suzi Gablik's book *Has Modernism Failed?* (1984) won readers with its passionate description of contemporary art that seemed to be without purpose. She spoke of loss of vitality in the art scene and said we need relatedness and rootedness.

Next, in *The Reenchantment of Art* (1992), Gablik proposed the idea that we embark on "interaction and connection," in which the artist attempts to restore lost harmony between humanity and earth. She feels that artists need to find new traditions or to recover old ones, embracing a revitalized sense of community, among other issues.

Several artists advocate for a more humane embrace of people and affairs of the world, and this chapter will focus on four of them. Jann Haworth, Sarah Sweetwater, Jean LaMarr, and Joan Giannecchini have strong views but have followed far different paths to bring attention to them. They have indeed changed the world through their art and their advocacy.

JANN HAWORTH • BORN 1942

If you feel breathless after a conversation with artist Jann Haworth, it wouldn't be a surprise. She wasn't dubbed "the most important artist living in Utah today" for nodding her head in silent agreement.[1]

Since Haworth left for college, and probably long before that, she has always plunged in to life. "We are among the first women to have stepped onto the stage in any numbers. Historically we have barely spoken."

She writes, "I am interested in what happens to the viewer in that I want them to be engaged whether or not they are art aficionados or 'the wo/man in the street.' I want the art to be democratic, and I want to break new ground, invent new form, discover if I can do what I think I can't do." And the rewards have been many: Solo shows in Utah, London, Amsterdam, Milan, New York City, and Paris; group shows in the latter locations as well as Edinburgh, Minneapolis, Cincinnati, Dallas, Wyoming, and Idaho." Her awards include the Grammy in 1968; her public collections include the Hirshhorn Museum and Sculpture Garden in Washington, DC, Tate Britain, and more.[2]

There have been fellowships, public art projects, designs for television and theater, and founding or cofounding schools. Currently, she is the creative director of the Leonardo Museum in Salt Lake City. The museum is reconfiguring the usual expectations of a science facility by combining the creative arts and technology with its mission.[3] Haworth further elaborates, "My part of the Leonardo is to find ways that offer original hands-on experiences that stir curiosity of young people and adults; experiences that use old technologies in new ways, that unlock the science in art and the art in science. We need to have centers that get people away from passive experiences." She recalls driving around the city one snowy December and noticing there were no snowmen. "Our hands aren't wet and our feet aren't cold with making a snowman anymore. Our children and

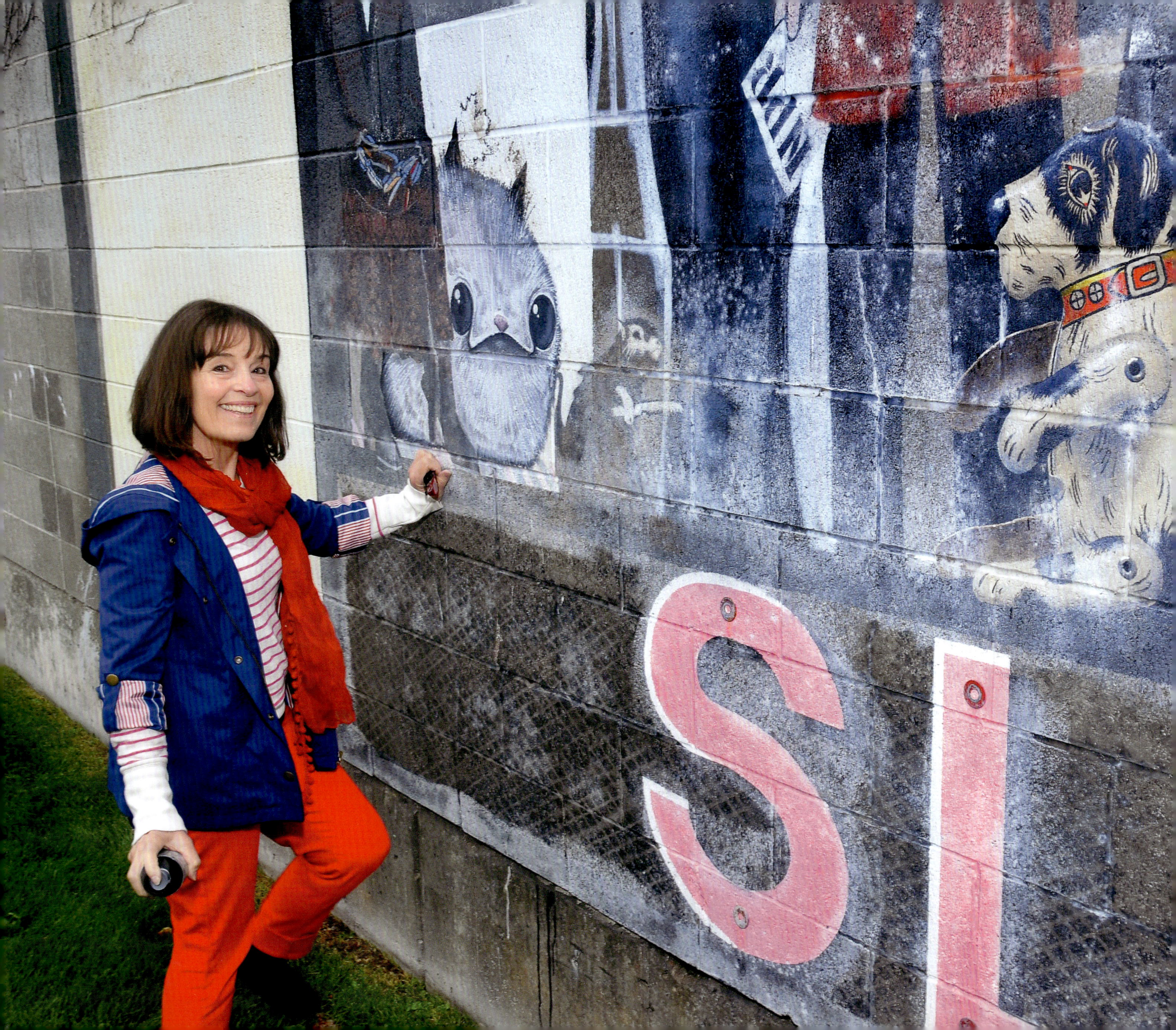
SI

grandchildren are safe inside in front of a screen shooting things. We use exercise machines instead of walking. We should be worried."

It's all I can do to break into her fascinating ideas on new teaching approaches, but this interview on September 26, 2013, is supposed to be about the artist herself, and right across the street, painted in vivid color on a cinder-block wall, is a mural for which she has gained recognition all over the state and beyond: *SLC Pepper,* a life-sized civic wall mural that Haworth calls a "riff" on the Beatles' Sgt. Pepper's Lonely Hearts Club Band cover. In 1967 she and her then-husband, Peter Blake, cocreated the Sgt. Pepper cover that won them the Grammy for Best Original Album Cover.

"The original cover, famous though it is, is an icon ready for the iconoclast," Haworth said, "and I like the idea of creating one of the several rip-offs of the original." She adds that the Salt Lake City team "turned the original inside out . . . with ethnic and gender balancing, and evaluating each face to appear on the mural as catalysts for change in social and artistic pursuits." The viewer might spot Martin Luther King Jr., Edward Abbey, the Peace Pilgrim, Jean-Michel Basquiat, Diane Rehm, Eve Ensler, the Guerilla Girls, Mother Teresa, Cesar Chavez, Alice in Wonderland, the Dalai Lama, and more than ninety others in the life-sized crowd.[4] Stage III of the mural would be to create a grassed ramp up to the front row of the crowd with the idea that the public could then pose in the front row and become part of the crowd for a photo moment, creating a sculpture in the process.

Susan Mantle and I recently viewed Haworth's work in a four-woman exhibition called "Work to Do" at Brigham Young University (BYU) Museum of Art in Provo, Utah. Her stuffed and embellished *Charm Bracelets* span one wall, one bracelet above the other, each in public collections in Utah. Against another wall hangs *Pom Pom Girl,* a leaping cheerleader frozen in a mid-air jump, and between these pieces is a family diorama. Across the room in a Plexiglas case is the seated *Old Lady* that appeared on the cover of the original *Sgt. Pepper's Lonely Hearts Club Band.* Within the diorama, titled *The Set,* a latex version of the original Old Lady illustrated the intricate detail of these pieces. All are created from various fabrics stuffed with batting, thread, and buttons supported by wooden armatures. BYU Museum of Art curator Jeff Lambson said Haworth "purposely created them from materials and domestic associations . . . to question preconceived notions about women in art, and more broadly, women's roles in society." He added, "Her work is poignant and telling, sly and humorous. It pokes fun at art history and questions high and low art subject matter and materials, with all the strength of Pop Art's trademark tongue in cheek irony."

Fabric isn't her only medium, though; a visit to her website unveils corsets and Minnie Mouse allusions in vinyl. Corsets freely mix fashion, theater, music, film, and animation. Each one is both a figure and a piece of lingerie made of vinyl, fabric, and found objects. Explaining her work, the rosy-cheeked artist speaks as if she's about to smile. For her, "It is the idea that drives the piece, and the choice of materials needs to support the intention and mood of the idea. Form Follows Idea. That is very, very important to me."

Haworth was born and raised in Hollywood, California. Her mother, Miriam, was a distinguished ceramicist, printmaker, and painter. She also taught her daughter how to sew. "I was eight when I made my first petticoat and from that point on I made dolls, their clothing, and almost everything I wore." Her father, Ted, was an Oscar-winning production designer whose many film credits included the cult classic *Invasion of the Body Snatchers.* "I followed him on the sets and ran around the back lots." Another of her father's films, *Jeremiah Johnson,* introduced him to Sundance, Utah, and he eventually retired there. This cinematic background influences her past and present work. "In the sixties what later became known as *installations* were, in my visual language, *sets*, and I peopled them with replicant stand-ins."

Jann Haworth finishing a collaborative mural, *SLC Pepper.* A grassed ramp will be installed so that the public can pose and become part of the moment, creating a sculpture in the process.

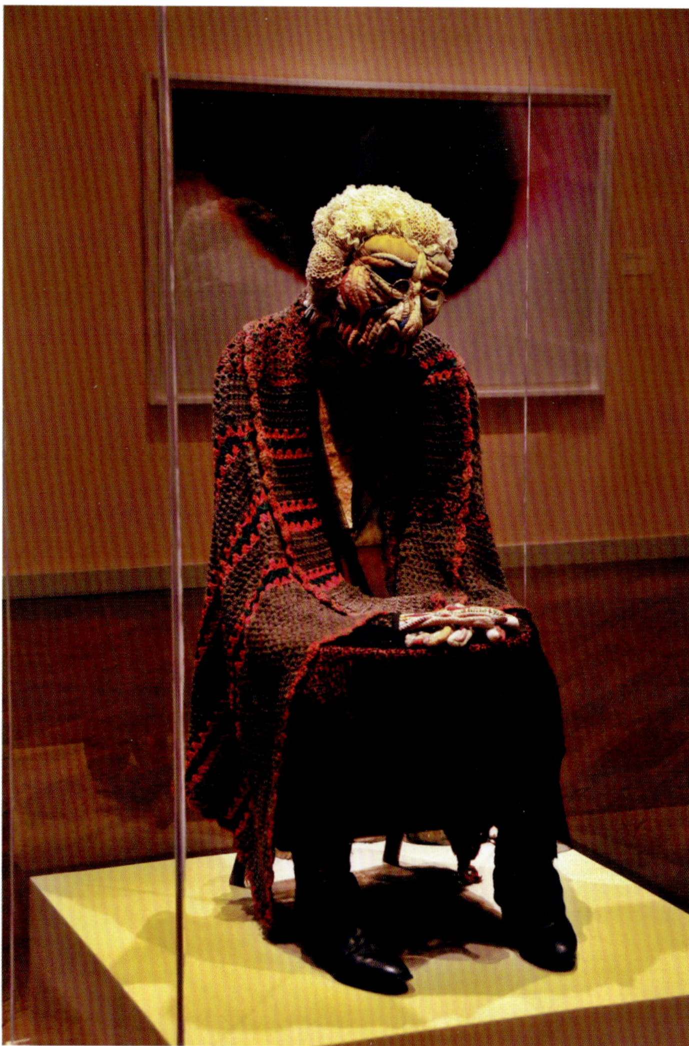

Jann Haworth, *Old Lady I*. Mixed media of fabrics, wooden chair, and stuffing; life-size figure.

The concept of the stand-in, the fake, the dummy, the latex model as surrogates for the real, came from being on the sound stage, on "location, in the prop room and the casting studio with my dad."

After two years at University of California, Los Angeles, Haworth moved to London, England, in 1961, where she studied art history at The Courtauld Institute of Art, and fine art at the Slade School of Fine Art. She reveled in being a vocal woman artist in a conservative, male-dominated institution like the Slade. "It was something to push against," she says. "The assumption was that, as one tutor put it, the girls were there to keep the boys happy. He prefaced that by saying it wasn't necessary for teachers to look at the portfolios of the female students. . . . They just needed to look at their photos."

It was head-on competition with the male students. "I was annoyed enough, and American enough, to take that on. I was determined to better them, and that's one of the reasons for the partly sarcastic choice of cloth, latex, and sequins as media. It was a female language to which the male students didn't have access." She began experimenting with soft sculptures and progressed to life-sized figures, such as the original *Old Lady* that eventually took her place on the Beatles' album cover of *Sgt. Pepper's Lonely Hearts Club Band.*

Haworth is recognized as part of the London's Swinging Sixties that gave birth to the British Pop Art movement. Her work uses American images—a surfer, a pom-pom girl, doughnuts, Mae West, Minnie Mouse, cowboys, and Shirley Temple. Her daughters Liberty (1968) and Daisy (1974) were born. She continued exhibiting and founded and ran the Lookingglass Elementary School, an arts-and-crafts primary and middle school near Bath.

In 1979 Haworth and Peter Blake parted. In 1981 she bought a small farm and a house south of Bath with writer Richard Severy. His daughters together with hers rather suddenly made a family of seven. The five girls, and later their own son, became the inspiration for eight published children's novels, and three books on making art. Severy wrote and Haworth illustrated. In the next twenty years fine art took second place to her commitment to the farm, a new baby, plotting and illustrating children's books, and raising farm animals and kids.

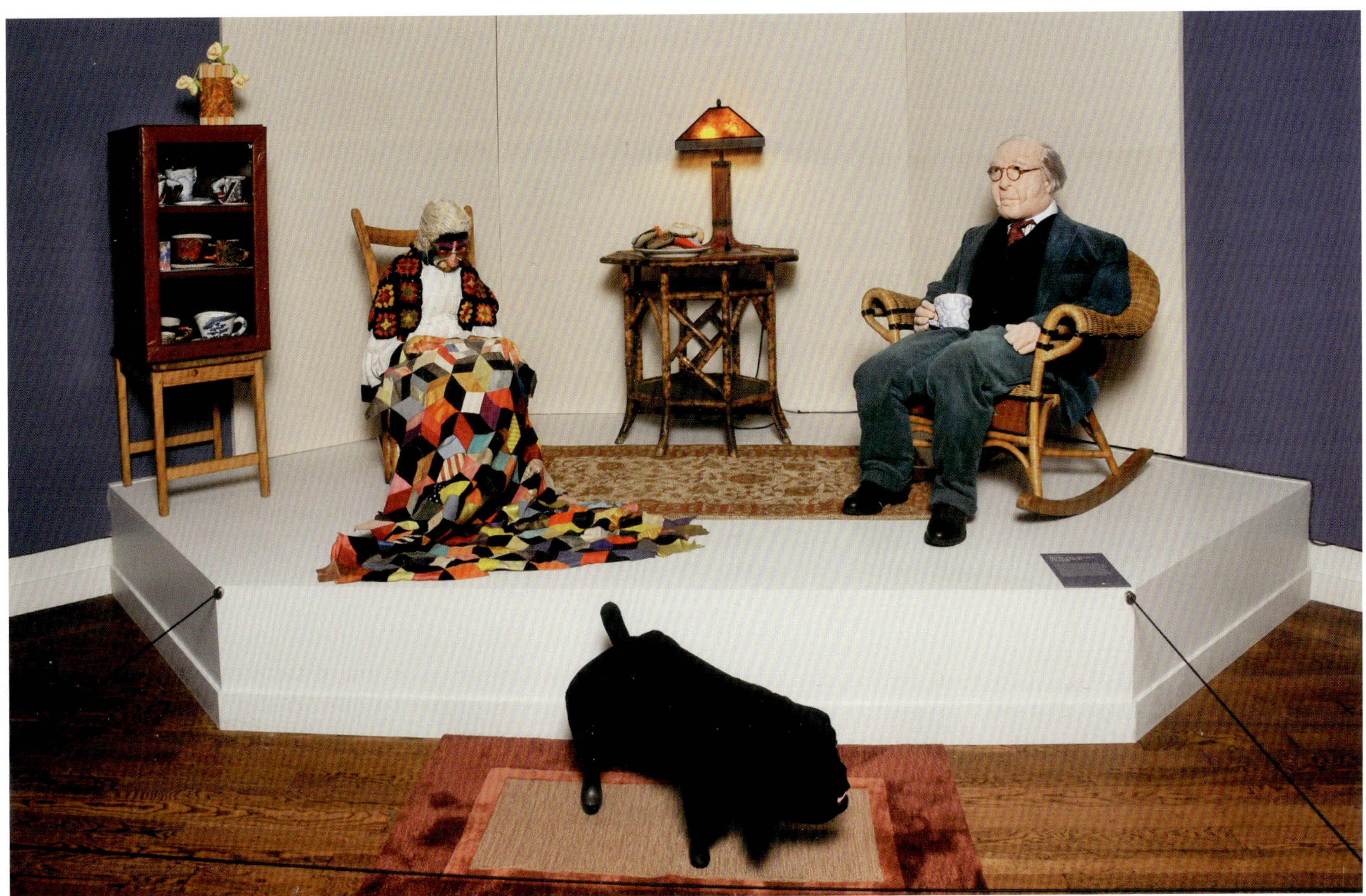

Jann Haworth, *The Set, 1962*. Mixed of media miscellaneous furniture, cloth, Kapok; life-size figures and dog.

In the 1990s she mounted two more solo shows at Gimpel Fils, a London gallery specializing in contemporary art, and then it was time for a change. In 1997 she was awarded a Churchill Fellowship to study American textiles. The trip became a major turning point. Instead of returning to the United Kingdom, she took up an offer from Sundance Mountain Resort to create an art facility. She created the Art Shack Studios, the Sundance Recycle Hot Glass Studio, and was cofounder of the Sundance Mountain School—one of the first six charter schools in Utah. "As an American returning to the U.S. after more than thirty years, I felt more European than Californian, but the contrast was exhilarating. The 'best kept secret'—Utah—was so exquisitely beautiful, welcoming, dreamlike that every day was like being reborn. I had lived for many years in the 'country' in the UK, but the great wildernesses of Utah were shocking in their wild intensity."

Many things grew out of the time teaching and working in the Art Shack. Haworth got to know people in and out of state. Her daughters joined her in Sundance, and her son grew up and graduated from the University of Utah with a film degree.

Then the fates twisted. Severy died of cancer after a six-year battle. Haworth's mother died five months before him. The story of loss, the sorrow, crushing debt, the imminent danger of losing one's home, all come at the same time when cancer strikes and is fought. "Because of amazing people in this place, I had help that was close to magic. There is more to this story than words can begin to tell," she says.

A new life begins. Children grow up, and new ideas and work sift into reality. The Leonardo offers great opportunity for an idea person. Haworth's brain still ticks with possibilities yet to come, ideas about the entire field of art. She writes,

> The role of the gallery is changing—the art fair is strengthening—the dealer's role and relation to the artist is different. An artist presence in the world is largely communicated digitally. Sales arise often online—reputations are built in the secondary market.
>
> I have lived close to three myths: Hollywood, Swinging London, and now The West. Some myths are fading. The Hollywood myth of gods and goddesses—retouched and filmed through gauze—now goes under the plastic surgeon's knife. The myth of London, the Beatles, and the great teenage scream of idolization that celebrated them have [*sic*] grown old."

"Those myths are dying," she says, and then she reminds me of the myths of the West—the wild horses and the Native Americans are alive, and the rodeo cowboy is still riding. "There is a living myth here."

Haworth now divides her time between Sundance and Salt Lake City, and the ideas continue to roll. She's formulating plans to do a mural project of women who are catalysts for change. She plans on inviting women from various communities to participate and add to the piece, which will roll up and travel. ("Like Guernica," she says.[5]) She credits her energy with living in Utah. "Dry air helps you to think clearly and inventing things is part of the resourcefulness of the West. And when you're surrounded by desert, it loosens your mind."

With Haworth, we're pretty sure there is more on the horizon. We just don't know what she and Utah might conjure up.

SARAH SWEETWATER • 1940–2015

Sarah Sweetwater died before she could see to fruition the publication of this book. What follows is the result of the interview that took place on July 23, 2013.

When art introduces potent, empathetic, and powerful material to the uninitiated, our understanding of the world is forever changed, according to noted artist and activist Favianna Rodriguez. And nowhere has her view been more aptly illustrated than in Elko, Nevada, where artist Sarah Sweetwater has planted seeds of cultural activism that have been felt around her town, state, country, and world.

She has defied the odds. Back in Texas, bedridden in the room she shared with parents and her other two siblings, she couldn't possibly foresee a future of attending college, carving sculpture with the quarry marble of Michelangelo, bringing art to a community, producing multicultural festivals, seeding the beginnings of what would become the National Cowboy Poetry Gathering, or touring the world. (She has traveled to fifty-plus countries escorting more than three thousand people.) Sweetwater has accomplished all those things and more.

"I was told I would never walk again or have children," Sweetwater tells me today as I gaze in wonder at her

Sarah Sweetwater shaping marble, sparks flying.

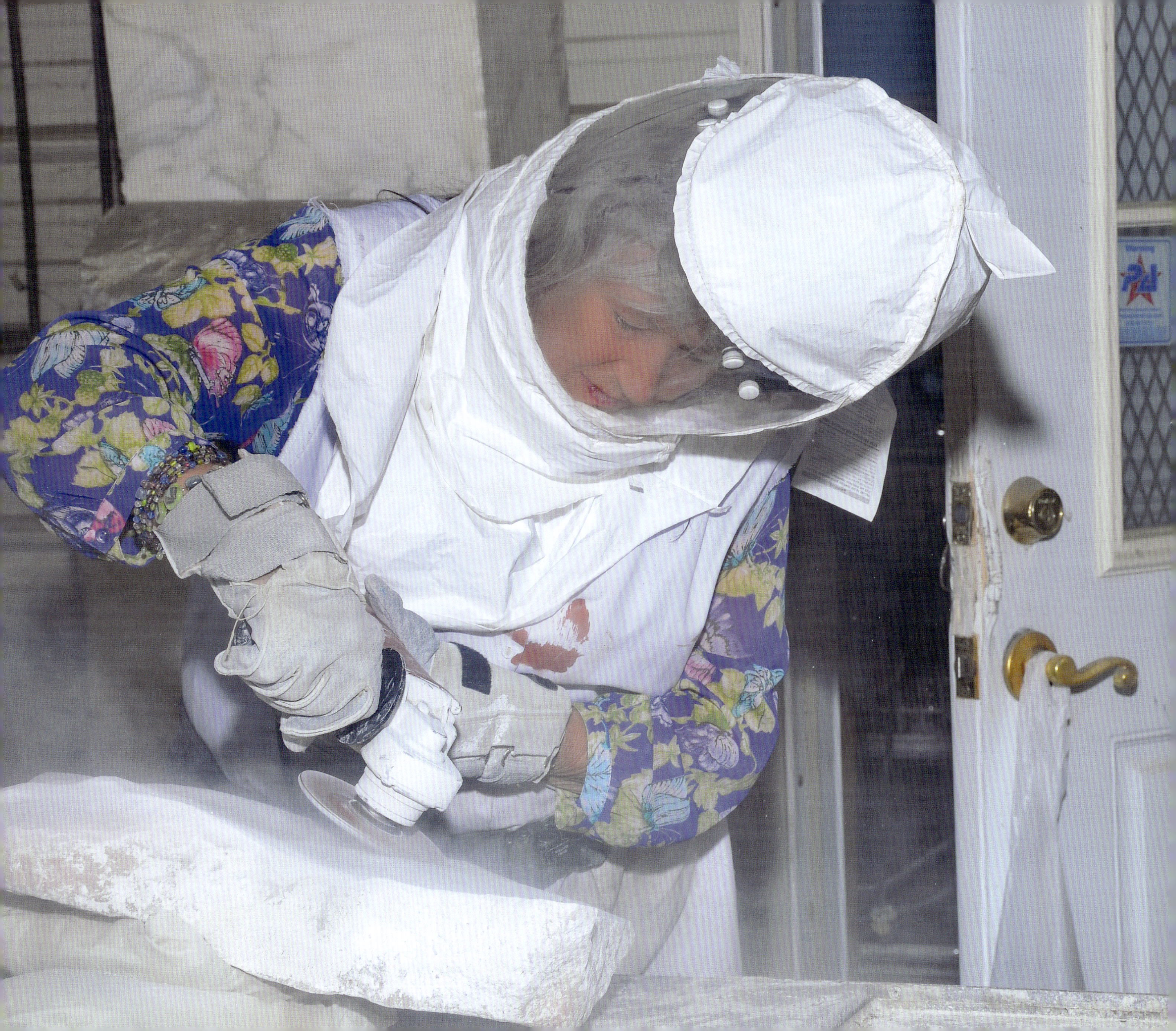

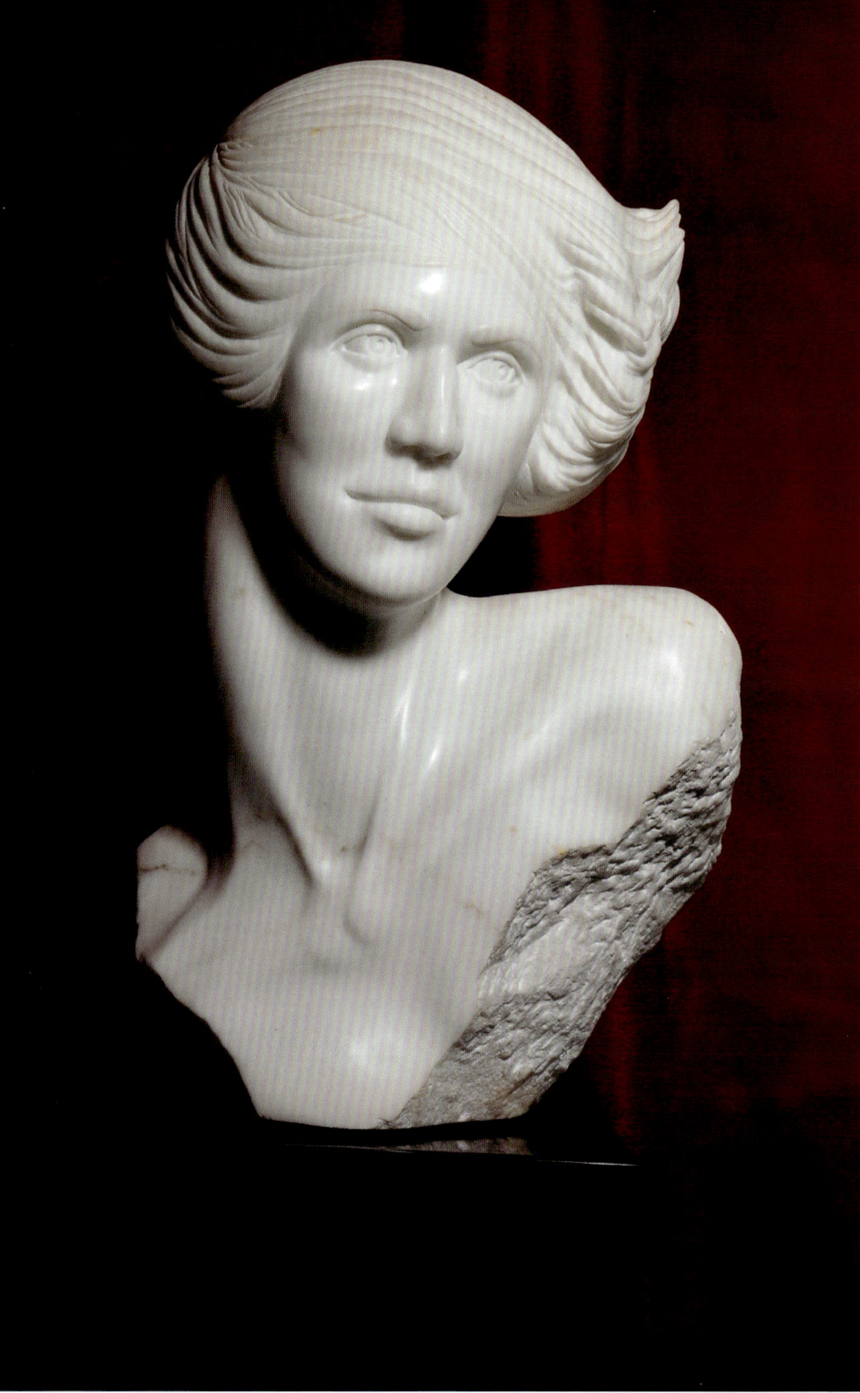

Sarah Sweetwater, *Maya*. White Italian Carrara marble on black marble base; 30 x 14 x 10 in.

museum of a home. "And I just said, 'Sit back and watch me.'" She smiles at the memory and runs a hand down the silken, white-marble neck of her favorite classical sculpture, *Maya,* the first marble piece she made and the one she won't sell at any price.[6] *Maya*'s neck is elongated and, contrary to the submissively posed female sculptures of Europe, Sweetwater decided to create a different woman, one with her head held high. "She became Maya, a strong woman who's willing to stick her neck out."

Sweetwater's home bubbles over with three stories (she designed and helped build the top two) full of art in all varieties and sizes. We walk through rooms of paintings, folk art, sculpture, and ordinary items like toilet tissue holders from various countries that, arranged floor to ceiling on a bathroom wall, are a fascinating study in color, design, and the definition of art.

The two of us settle at a table that has been arranged for company (she has frequent visitors), with colorful straw placemats, interesting napkins cleverly folded, several unusual salt-and-pepper shakers, and a centerpiece of homegrown flowers and local weeds. She begins her story, and I soon realize that this woman has been sticking her neck out most of her life. It's no wonder she keeps *Maya* around for reminders.

She was born Sarah Whisenant to a conservative, blue-collar family, where the front bedroom was rented out, and Sarah, her parents, and two older siblings slept in the second. Hard work ruled their days. The few pictures tacked to the living room wall came free with the Cloverine Salve her mother purchased from a traveling salesman.

One day, the little girl returned home from first grade with a headache and stiff neck. By week's end she could no longer walk. The verdict was polio, and she ended up at Parkland Hospital in Dallas, sharing a ward with fourteen other girls.[7] Over the next eight years, Sweetwater underwent thirteen experimental surgeries, and while hospitalized at the Texas Scottish Rite Hospital for Children in

Dallas, her parents were permitted visitation only between two and four on Sundays.[8] "Times were hard and my parents couldn't always come to see me during those two- to three-week hospital stays." But the lonely child had two major awakenings that were to set the direction of her life. First, her kind and generous hospital caregivers represented previously unheard-of cultures to the white Protestant girl: the nurses, orderlies, and bedmates were a mix of African American, Latino, Asian, Native American, and Catholic. An African American nurse twisted her hair into rag curls, and the Mexican orderly would bounce a quarter on her fresh-made sheets. The nuns came and smiled as they delivered chocolates and oranges in their long black habits with the crisp white headgear. This was pure theater to the little girl from the Texas outback. "At home, people discriminated against these people. But I learned to love them in the hospital."

Her second awakening was artistic, for on Tuesdays and Thursdays the patients were treated to occupational therapy. "I learned to weave at age six from a blind woman," she says. "I made decoupage from used greeting cards, and created all kinds of items from donated recycled materials. I learned to express myself with my hands." It distracted her from the pain and homesickness and took her to another realm. Surgery meant being bedfast at the hospital, and later needing a cast leg for at least three months at home in the days before television, cell phones, and electronic games. "I made my first dress at age nine when my mother moved the sewing machine to my bedside and fixed it so I could run the leg lever with my good leg." Writing, sewing, drawing, and other handiwork kept her busy, and Sweetwater writes poetry to this day. As we talk, she frequently expresses herself in a kind of story language. "The diverse patterns in the fabric of my life have been woven with Polio, and through Rotary's programs I am adding new richness to the patterns," she writes in an e-mail, eloquently describing her current teaching trips to various lands through her Rotary Club of Elko.

She married range conservationist Leland Campsey, and with first-born daughter, Keri, commuted 174 miles round-trip daily to West Texas State University (now West Texas A&M University), obtaining a bachelor of arts degree in art education—the only one in her family with a college degree. After Alice, the second of three children, was born, Sweetwater began teaching, a career that was to become a lifelong passion. In 1967 Leland took a range management job in Elko, and she fell in love with the town; soon a third daughter, Melissa, completed the family. Sweetwater began teaching art at the Elko Community College (renamed Northern Nevada Community College, and then Great Basin College), introducing such traditional arts as weaving, carving, painting, drawing, and fiber arts. "Teaching college was my way to birth other peoples' creativity. I was a midwife, in a way, and I loved it."

She also expanded her own work from her home studio ("My kids never knew what was going to be on the stove—a pot of dye, melting wax, or chili"), drawing, painting, and developing explorations in sculpture.

In 1974 she mounted her first one-woman show at Elko's Northeastern Nevada Museum; it would be the first of nearly one hundred exhibitions in museums, galleries, and public spaces around the West.

The title of that first show, "Stripped Bare," proved to be prophetic, for Sweetwater began to strip her own layers down to the core, and there she discovered the drumbeat of her own heart. She and husband Leland obtained an amicable divorce. That summer she took a workshop at the Tuscarora pottery school; she said the experience of living away was "like panning for gold." She took her hometown of Sweetwater as her last name and then reconnected with the behaviors she'd learned so long ago in the children's hospital: "Once again, like back then, I wanted to look at life through another window. . . . Just like Leonardo was Leonardo da Vinci [meaning Leonardo of Vinci], I became Sarah of Sweetwater." And the window she looked through in the ranching hub of Elko County, Nevada, opened up to reveal cowboys. Lots of cowboys.

"When I started working with cowboys and their poems, others didn't especially appreciate them. But I'd already learned to recognize in people something deeper than skin color or status. I've been fortunate because I want to know their hearts." She took her big tape recorder and went out to the bars and ranches. "I had a drive to collect this culture that people didn't think was worth listening to. They were the preservers of incredible art forms—poems, leather tooling, songs, rawhide braiding." They called her the "schoolmarm" and eventually became comfortable around her. At the old Tuscarora Bar, the first time someone shared a personal creation with her, a cowboy named Blackie brought out a tattered piece of notebook paper from his back pocket and read her one of his poems. Then poems by Curly Fletcher, a famous old-time poet, were recited. Joe McKnight was the first who demonstrated the braiding of horsehair ropes.

"I was able to weave all this together—poetry, the songs they sang, crafts." In 1975 she combined the traditions of these cowboy artists, such as saddle making, leather tooling, and storytelling, along with the Tuscarora potters, Native American artisans, and local quilters. She found Basque sheepherders to provide wool for weaving and spinning, and a local German woman to warp looms, while a ranch wife carded wool and others demonstrated dulcimer and banjo making. These people came together at Northern Nevada Community College (now Great Basin College) creating the Pioneer Arts and Crafts Folklife Festival, which was possible by grants Sweetwater applied for. Later, more traditions—Mexican, Chinese, Mormon, Polish, East Indian singing and foods—were added to the mix. Festival organizers established a popular folksinging group and even published their own songbooks.

"Remember," she says, "our small rural community is a hard-working, isolated town—Salt Lake City is 240 miles away and Reno is 289 miles. The college opened new opportunities to people from all backgrounds and supported the festival wholeheartedly."

Representatives from the National Council for the Traditional Arts and the the American Folklife Center visited the festival on several occasions. Sweetwater applied for more grants and secured donations, and the festival, which expanded each year, became the grassroots movement for Elko's National Cowboy Poetry Gathering, where today thousands of people converge every winter from around the world to enjoy and capture the spirit of the West. Thanks to Sweetwater's efforts, the Elko gathering reinvigorated a tradition that is now being duplicated in other Western communities.

Meanwhile, her employer, Northern Nevada Community College (now Great Basin College), needed its art instructor to obtain a master's degree. So in 1976 off she went, daughters in tow, to the University of Utah in Salt Lake City, where she worked two jobs and received her master's degree in education, art, and human relations. Professors Mamiko Suzuki and M. C. Richards influenced her thinking. "M. C. Richards made us shut our mouths and make art. You can't find your inner self unless you shut up to students."[9]

She also met a man named Hal Cannon. A member of a string band, Hal offered to bring the group to Elko, and Sweetwater applied for the grant to pay them. They stayed at Sweetwater's house and she took Hal to meet the cowboys; he became extremely interested in the festival. So interested, in fact, that he accepted a part-time position on Sweetwater's grants for the next two years. In 1981 she obtained a National Endowment for the Humanities fellowship and went to the Berkeley Folklore Program at the University of California, where she worked on her Nevada Buckaroo project.[10] "I was able to collect and put everything on tape and photograph and draw the cowboys." The images of cowboys she'd interviewed appeared in her one-woman

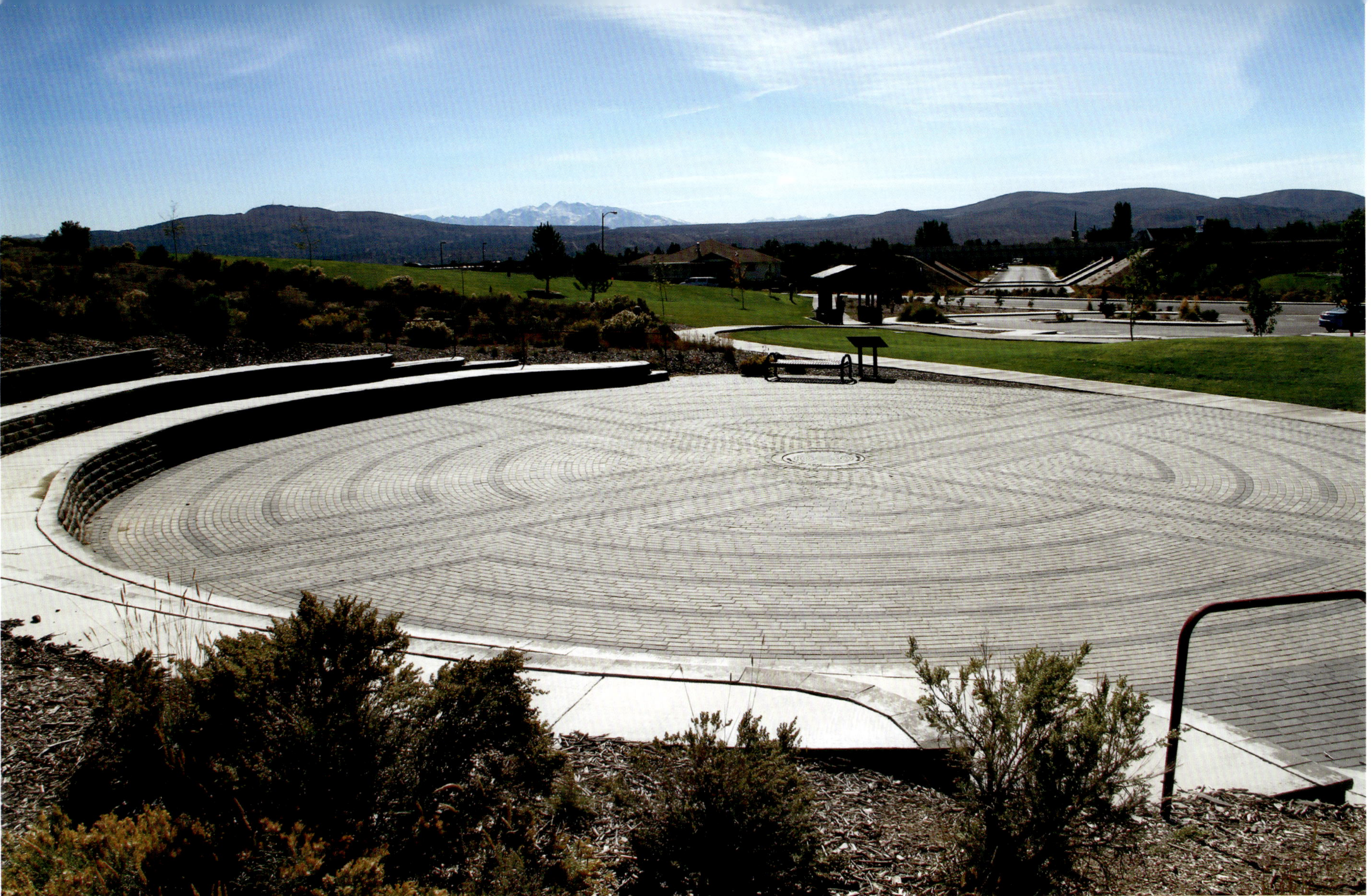

Sarah Sweetwater, *Labyrinth*. Located in Elko, Nevada, Peace Park with amphitheater; 67 ft. in diameter.

show in Elko in 1984. Cannon saw an opportunity to develop this project into something of his own.

There was no room for Sweetwater. "What happens to me happens to a lot of women who birth something," she says. "I was so incredibly naïve." Cannon is now thought of as the originator of the National Cowboy Poetry Gathering. "But it was my child," she says. "It was rustled from my herd in 1980 and another brand put on it in 1985."

Undaunted, Sweetwater got to work. She built a second story to her house, then a third, and began collecting art that would fill every nook and cranny. She carved wood—a spinning wheel, a dulcimer with a woman's head as the tuning head, other pieces. She was named chair of the Department of Art at Northern Nevada Community College (now Great Basin College). And she found her true voice in stone, which was to stay with her always. She took a sabbatical to Italy to study with renowned sculptor Pasquale Martini and returned with eight tons of marble. Another summer found her in New Mexico, learning how to use pneumatic tools from Navajo artist Doug Hyde. "Much of my work is about digging up women's history." She nods towards *Maya.* "Whether it's the fragmented lives of women I have carved in marble or the bronze work, I find my art reflects my own growth as a traditional stay-at-home mother into the world of a single parent raising three daughters."

She won numerous awards, including the National Institute for Staff and Organizational Development (NISOD) award for Excellence in Education; Outstanding Woman of Northeastern Nevada, and the State of Nevada Governor's Arts Award for Excellence in Folk and Traditional Arts. Her art projects skyrocketed; she's exhibited extensively, created and installed several public commissions, and was one of four finalists in the national competition to create and install Northern Paiute teacher and activist Sarah Winnemucca in the national rotunda in Washington, DC. Meanwhile, this teacher/artist delivered lectures and workshops around the West, developed school curriculum guides on various cultures, and conducted educational travel. The global educational tours, developed through Great Basin College to study various cultures of the world through art, ended, but Sweetwater has continued the tours as a personal vision. She also traveled on behalf of Rotary International's National Immunization Days in support of polio vaccines. In Benin and Ghana, both countries in West Africa, she delivered soccer balls and school supplies from her Rotary Club of Elko and taught the children to draw cowboys, passing out twelve dozen bandannas so the children could have a bit of the cowboy West. She repeated the venture twice in India, teaching more hand skills. "In 1947 I learned to weave," she says. "And in 2013 I taught polio survivors to weave."

Sweetwater also participated in the development of the City of Elko's Peace Park and, with volunteer help, constructed a large public labyrinth; she created another large labyrinth in Ely, Nevada, in that city's sculpture park.

Retired? Not by a long shot. Sweetwater's studio, now a few blocks from her home, is full of projects completed or in progress. Across the road, on Sweetwater Street, she's hard at work developing sculpture in her large organic garden. Since it is located on Sweetwater Street between Silver Street and River Street, she lovingly calls it Sweetwater at Silver River. Busloads of people now come to see her art-filled home, which she has transformed into a museum (she calls it the Sweetwater Museum of Art and Kuriosities). The museum is a small private museum, open by appointment only. "We also have 501(c)(3) [status] and will be offering small workshops in the creative process, guiding art tours of the museum, and offering house concerts." She still writes poetry and sculpts, and recently started the Paula Bear Wright Storytime program in Elko County schools. Two books and more travel are in the works.

Has it been easy? Not always. Because of polio, one leg is one inch shorter than the other, and she wears two different shoe sizes; walking is difficult, but she continues her travels. She's had numerous surgeries, but, as she reminds me, every major breakthrough is often preceded by adversity that makes us wiser and more understanding of other people's misfortunes.

"I've learned mostly from women," Sweetwater says. "Not because men are bad, but because through women we finally begin to recognize ourselves. I remember a quote: 'Your only job is to remember who you really are.'" She touches the marble *Maya* once again. "I'm grateful for everybody who's taken me by the hand and pulled me through the next knothole."

In later correspondence with Sweetwater, she wrote:

> One other thread that is running through my life from hospital stays with black nurses and other cultures is my passion for equality. Currently, I am working on a sculpture of Rosa Parks. Partly that is out of my passion for public art that will create attention for women who have made a difference in the lives of their people. And partly from those not-to-be-forgotten times I had with my nurses of color in Dallas. Sarah Winnemucca, Rosa Parks. . . . These sculptures show women in that moment in between . . . that moment when [they] decide to step off the river rocks of their native peoples and onto the sawn-off timber of the white man's world. . . . That moment when Rosa decides that in order for her to stand up for her people she has to sit down. I recognize that my sculptures of these women capture that moment of decision. Do I stay in the comfort of my world or do I step out into the unknown and show courage for the change that is necessary[?] When you look at the Rosa Parks sculpture you are not sure if the gesture is to rise up or to sit down. . . . That moment like the space between notes that makes the music. With Sarah Winnemucca, you see her caught in that space between.
>
> The activist artist Favianna Rodriguez said, "Art is also about us shaping our human experience, but through beauty, form, reflection, and critical analysis." This is why I believe in the power of art to shape thoughts and change hearts.

JEAN LAMARR • BORN 1945

California artist Jean LaMarr addresses discrimination by combining heart, head, and hands to produce a range of art infused with power and history, sprinkled with a little satire. Invigorated by a deep Native pride, the Northern Paiute–Pit River artist learned early how to reach the widest audience with her messages of change.

"A teacher once told me that one painting would be in one home or one museum, but a print or video or mural will reach everyone. One painting might be worth a million dollars, but prints will reach millions of people." And LaMarr went to work. Her fine prints, sculpture, murals, dioramas, interactive installation, and videos have set forth from her studio on the Susanville, California Indian Rancheria to exhibit in public arenas and some of the most significant museums across the United States. Questioning American Indian stereotypes, such as Longfellow's Minnehaha and Knott's Berry Farm Indian Maiden, LaMarr's message has reached thousands of Native and non-Native viewers. In so doing, this artist not only counteracts centuries of anti-Indian repression, but has also helped to reclaim the power and authority of indigenous art in the Great Basin and beyond.

Today, October 15, 2014, as she moves around her studio, pulling out box assemblages and organizing an installation to be photographed, her curly black hair flying, she shows no signs of slowing down. "I just enjoy it," she says. "It takes me away from my stress and troubles. It's my avenue of rejection of the idea of the vanished American Indian. People think we're all dead, but we're not."

LaMarr likes a sense of community. She founded the Native American Graphic Workshop, a teaching space and fine print studio, and recently hosted well-known Great Basin Native artists Jack Malotte, Melissa Melero, and Ben Aleck, where new ideas and techniques were shared. She worked with Malotte to create a community mural, "Our Ancestors, Our Future," on Susanville's Lassen Street; together they painted prominent early Native people from the area, a result of her research. In a public park in Berkeley, California, she created a four-wall mural, *The Ohlone Journey,* that narrates the history of the Ohlone people. In both murals, LaMarr countered popular narratives of native disappearance from these regions, thus

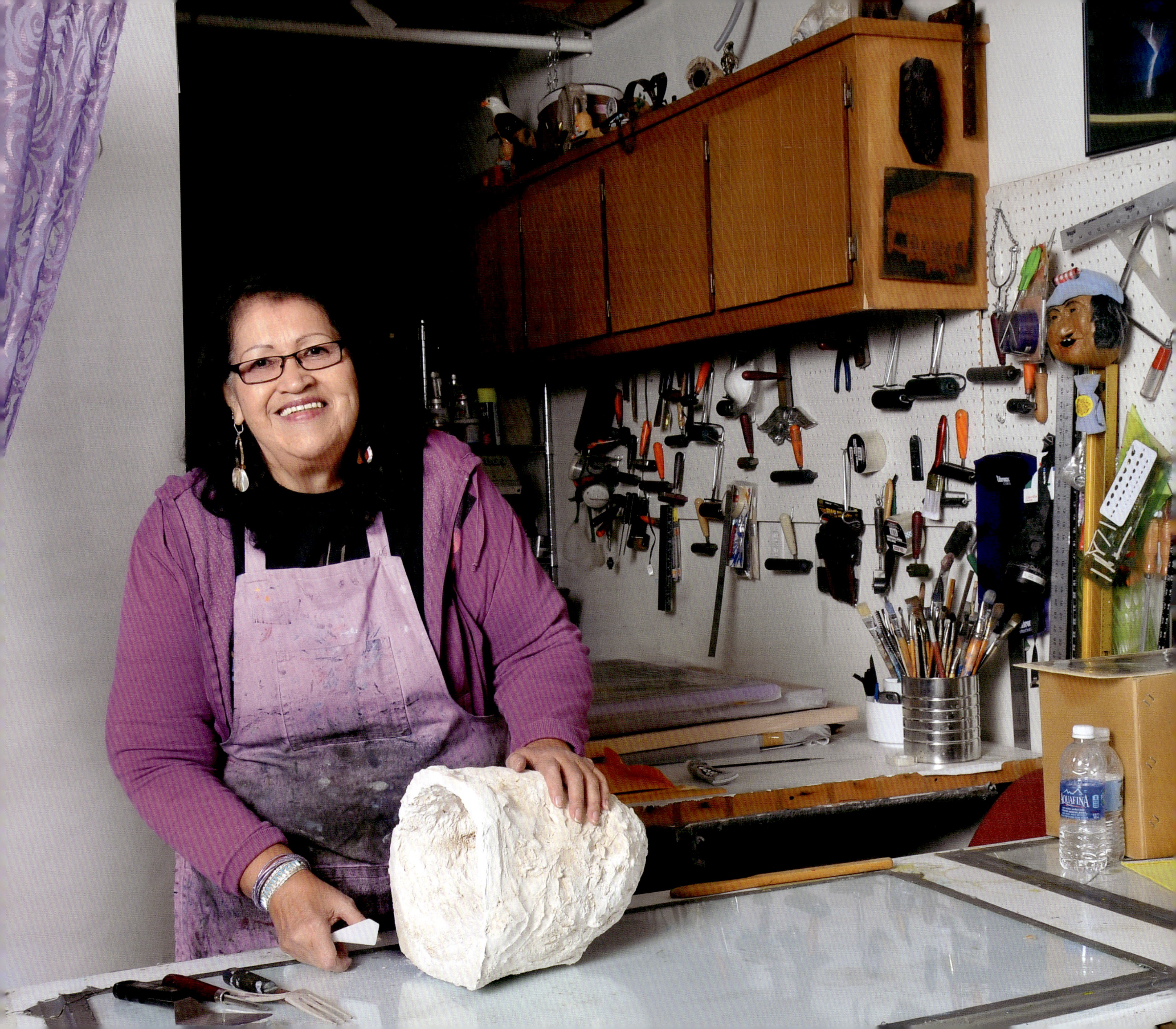
AQUAFINA

reclaiming the significance of indigenous people past and present.

Her satirical, interactive installation at the Heard Museum in Phoenix, Arizona, was titled *Princess Pale Moon.* (One could almost hear the song "Indian Love Call" wooing through the perfect trees and across the shimmering blue lake.) The beautiful princess, who had a removable head, is postured in her native garb among a clichéd forest setting beneath a round silvery moon. Viewers could don one of several stereotypical headpieces (feather headband, a black wig with braids, child's war bonnet, and so on) hanging at the side. The wigged viewer can then pose in the princess's open headspace, to be photographed as part of the idyllic scene, and gain insight into what a contemporary Native person must feel to be the subject of such stereotyped labeling. *Princess Pale Moon* has since returned to LaMarr's studio and is not for sale. "I want to see it in a special place," she says.

LaMarr is confident, though. Her work has shown in such special places as museums, contemporary art institutions, and cultural centers around the United States and abroad. With arresting titles like *Watchful Eyes, Bridging Two Worlds,* and *500 Years of Resistance through Women's Eyes,* her art has exhibited in solo and group shows from South and Central America to Washington, DC; from New York to New Zealand; and from California to Germany, with dozens of stops along the way. She and her work have been featured in exhibition catalogs, magazines, and books such as Lucy Lippard's *Mixed Blessings* (1990) and Peter Selz's *The Art of Engagement (2006),* both of which are comprehensive surveys of artists' roles in politics and culture. LaMarr has directed murals and poster and portfolio projects, and been an artist-in-residence through the California Arts Council. She has also been a teacher, not only in her own Native American Graphic Workshop but also at the Institute of American Indian Arts in Santa Fe, San Francisco State University, Wellington Polytechnic Institute (renamed the Wellington Technical College) in New Zealand, California

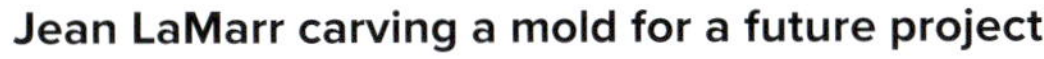

Jean LaMarr carving a mold for a future project

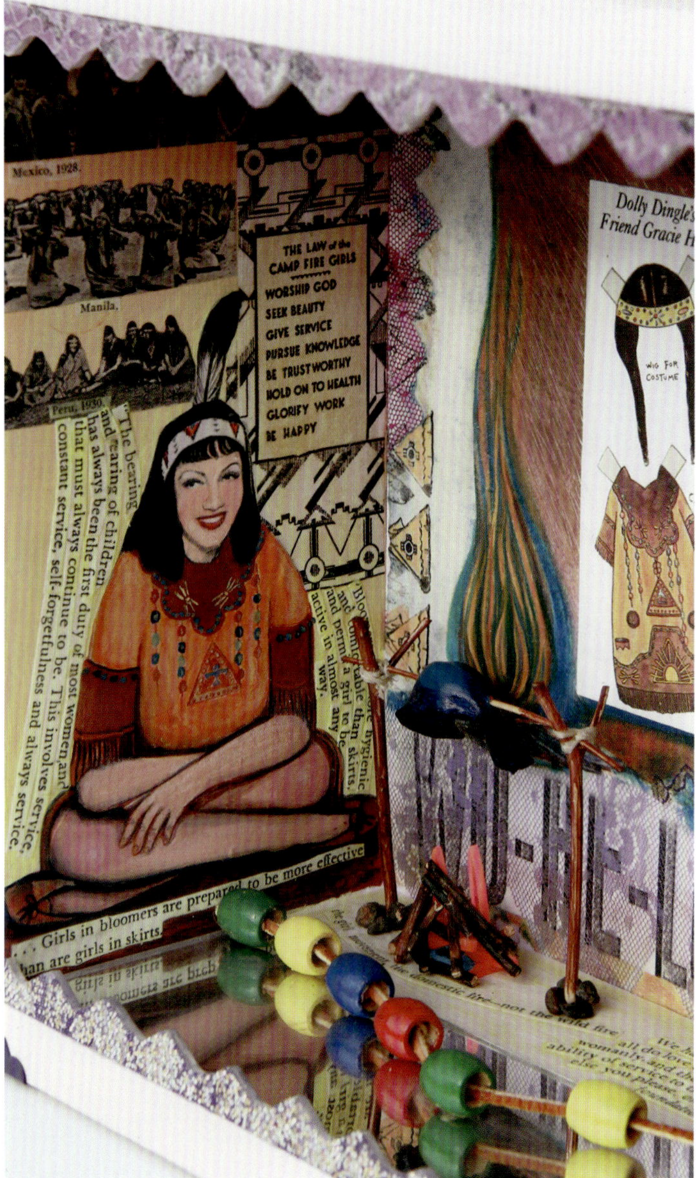

Jean LaMarr, *Dolly Dingle's Friend.* Mixed-media box assemblage; 12 x 12 x 2 in.

Correctional Center in Susanville, and many other institutions. When this artist says she wants to see her diorama in a "special place," she has plenty of options.

Her story of a poor Native girl who grew up on a hillside outside the little town of Susanville to become a renowned artist is remarkable. Born in Susanville, LaMarr's grandmother's friend, Mrs. Astor, presented her with a name—Pahima Gutne—meaning Purple Flower Girl. "All the girls were named after flowers," she says, and I notice at our interview that LaMarr is dressed head to toe in purple. Her vivid purple sweater is emblazoned with a dreamcatcher motif.

The young LaMarr and some of her sisters (she was one of six) went to the forest every day and collected rocks, sticks, and feathers to create little houses. She remembers coloring in the book her mother, Esther, a native of Wadsworth, Nevada, gave her and braiding rugs from cast-off men's neckties with her grandmother. But mostly, art supplies were considered frivolous, and her father, Leonard, discouraged artmaking. However, she says, "My uncle was a fantastic artist. He would draw cartoons about coyote and there, all of a sudden, it would appear on the paper. We couldn't wait until Saturday night when he came over."

She was a shy child in kindergarten. "I was one of the last ones to get up to the easel. I finally got up there and painted something so beautiful. But a boy got angry. He got black paint and ruined it." LaMarr felt the brunt of jealousy and racism all through her school years, but "I just let it roll off my back." Growing up, her family didn't have much food, but she says, "Through it all I kept making art."

In fourth grade she created her first mural: "Sir Frances Drake Christianizing the Indians." ("The teacher had me do it since I was Indian.") The mural experience would always stay with her.

Most Native children dropped out of school after eighth grade, but LaMarr continued at her father's insistence. Despite receiving some top grades in high school art, the girl felt her teacher's hatred. "If I disagreed with his politics, he gave me an F." She added, "I did all the work—screen printed, designed. He put his name on it. As and Fs, that's all I got." As in kindergarten, she not only ignored his criticism, but she also developed a stubborn pride in being Indian that began to grow. Around this time, she was invited to create a poster for a Maidu Bear Dance ceremony. When the posters began disappearing because community members were collecting them, she realized that through this visual art she was "bringing information to people, beckoning them into our world, and trying to make them understand it."

But her father was adamant that she choose a career in banking, the Forest Service, or the Bureau of Land Management. "He wouldn't allow me to do artwork at home. I'd have to hide or do it after he went to bed." Later, when professionals began to recognize her abilities, "he changed his tune."

The Indian Relocation Act of 1956 encouraged Native Americans to acquire vocational skills and assimilate into the general population. It paid moving expenses and provided some training and other benefits. LaMarr signed up, was accepted, and attended a technical institute in San Jose. The instructor advised her to consider college, and she enrolled first at San Jose State University and later at the University of California at Berkeley. Her sister was living there at the time, and LaMarr entered a new phase—citizen activism. "It was the time of occupying Alcatraz, and we supported that. We were making signs and demonstrating."[11]

She joined a group of Chicano artists who were creating murals and posters to protest discrimination, and again LaMarr experienced the amazing power of art to serve revolutionary ends and bring communities together. She created the Ohlone Indian mural at this time, and learned screen-printing, sculpture, papermaking, and video. She also became interested in the Chicano shrine-like boxes and later would develop a Native Pride series inside similar assemblage box forms.

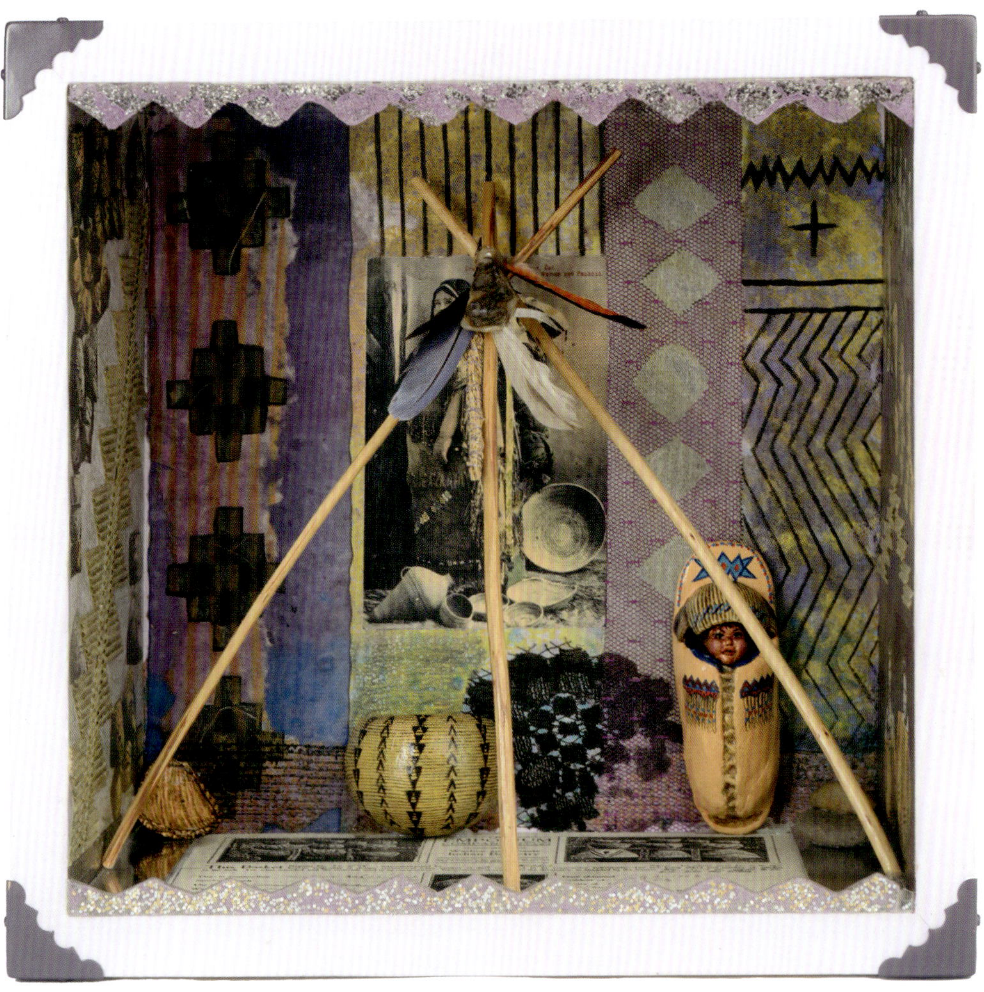

Jean LaMarr, *Washo Indian Woman and Papoose.* Mixed-media box assemblage; 12 x 12 x 2 in. Reproduced by permission from the Nevada Museum of Art, Carson City.

While attending the University of California, Berkeley, LaMarr taught classes at the College of Marin and San Francisco State University. She met and married designer and teacher Spencer Shaw, but kept her name, and her son, Rory, was born the following year. Marriage and motherhood did not stop the drive to create. She participated in all the Chicano shows and was invited to exhibit at prestigious institutions. Soon she was being discussed in publications and her reputation grew. She exhibited at the Museum of Modern Art in New York City.

LaMarr received some encouragement along the way. One day she was walking around the museum grounds of the Kansas City Art Institute and a stranger introduced himself; she learned he was well-known artist Warrington Colescott. "I was blown away!" Another supporter was multimedia artist Paolo Carosne. Anthropologist Susan Lobo, PhD, helped her learn oral history techniques to research Native history and culture, and LaMarr's interviews unearthed much of the history of Great Basin Paiute people and how they came to Susanville. "I wanted their stories—hand games, bear dance, old time songs. She [Lobo] helped me learn how to interview." Many of LaMarr's activities and art reflect those historic personal interviews.

Her Susanville physician, Dr. June Glenn-Lawson, was a mentor. "Dr. June," as LaMarr affectionately calls her, "said, 'You gotta be out there. You have to let women know that you're doing this—not for yourself, but for other people who wish they could.' We Native Americans aren't supposed to brag about ourselves, so Dr. June's advice put it in a different perspective."

LaMarr's box assemblage *Minniehaha Lives: Boxes, Postcards, Indian Women* (referring to Longfellow's romanticized fantasy of Native women) shows six postcards examining representations of Native American women. Native women were assigned the role of princess or squaw. Other boxes look at the contemporary and commercial views of the Indian maiden, fair-skinned sexual animals through cartoon imagery, or a white girl appropriating an Indian religious ceremony in paper doll clothes.

Of special interest to LaMarr is her box assemblage *Washo Indian Woman and Papoose.* The piece is about Nevada's most famous Indian basket artist, Dat-So-La-Lee, but LaMarr has given the weaver anonymity to illustrate the plight of the many excellent basket weavers whose names are lost to history.[12] Nevada Museum of Art senior curator Ann M. Wolfe, in *Tahoe: A Visual History* (2015, 450–51), said LaMarr felt that Dat-So-La-Lee's reputation was built largely by businessman Abe Cohn and his wife Amy Cohn. The Cohns were the exclusive dealers for Dat-So-La-Lee baskets, and Amy invented elaborate stories and titles for them.

"The Cohns basically owned her," LaMarr said. Her box sculpture tells this story and includes a reproduction "Certificate of Authenticity" like those that Amy Cohn regularly made for Dat-So-La-Lee's baskets. Lamarr used the certificate and Cohn's assigned the title (*We Inherit the Right to be Free Like the Birds*) in her assemblage. "At least the Cohns gave her a name so that she has some legacy," LaMarr added. Often, nameless Native weavers were photographed alongside their baskets. "By doing this, the baskets became more 'authentic' and 'exotic,'" LaMarr explains in *Tahoe: A Visual History,* "thereby increasing their value even more" (2015, 451). A postcard depicting an anonymous Washoe woman and her child stands at the center of LaMarr's box sculpture in homage to the many unnamed weavers who produced baskets for personal use and non-Washoe consumers.

Today, LaMarr is back at the Susanville Indian Rancheria, mentoring and receiving help from local youth, who follow her every word. She is founding member of the newly formed Great Basin Native Artists collective, the first of its kind in the Great Basin. She still teaches, mentors, exhibits, and creates art, because, as she said earlier, "I enjoy it. It's my avenue of rejection of the idea of the vanished American Indian." And referring to a famous California ski resort, she winks and adds, "And pretty quick I'm going to deal with Squaw Valley. I just hate that word!"

Jean LaMarr isn't finished yet, not by a long shot.

JOAN GIANNECCHINI • BORN 1943

When conceptual artist Joan Giannecchini was young, her mother called her crazy, not realizing that her daughter's creative mind was steaming along on the twin engines of intellect and curiosity. (And what engines! Horsepower through the roof!) Giannecchini (pronounced John-a-keeny) had the kind of lust for life that transforms us or runs over us or both, and in her attempt to overcome a feeling of shame that accompanied the childhood label *crazy*, she powered through life with compassion and insight, eventually bringing art—sculpture, watercolor photography, installations, and performances—to the masses. Through her art she generates aha! moments—an awareness of people and issues previously unnoticed—for viewers to take with them.

The Tuscarora, Nevada, artist's work has appeared in galleries and museums throughout the United States and Africa. In Soho (New York), she cofounded the Dentures Art Club, dedicated to bringing artists and nonartists together to stage performances and happenings on socially relevant themes. (Rock groups had just begun taking unconventional names such as the Talking Heads, and Giannecchini's group chose a similarly witty tag, Dentures, as a reminder not to take things too seriously.) She performed in New York City venues including the New York Feminist Art Institute and the Soho Repertory Theater. Her collaborative piece on role and romance in 1950s America, "Charms" (using Barbie and Ken dolls as props), was staged at the Franklin Furnace and several dinner theater venues in New York City.

Her public installations include work in Central Park and the New York City subways, where she and husband Stan drew attention to the dangers of New York City's streets by installing life-size stick figures in tableaus of violence (and were arrested for their effort). Giannecchini has written and published on environmental matters. Her presentation "Ecotourism: New Partners, New Relationships" at the 1992 IUCN (International Union for Conservation of Nature) conference in Caracas, Venezuela, was published in 1993, and is often quoted.

Giannecchini received grants from the New York State's Blue Mountain Center to initiate various public projects.

Joan Giannecchini in her studio.

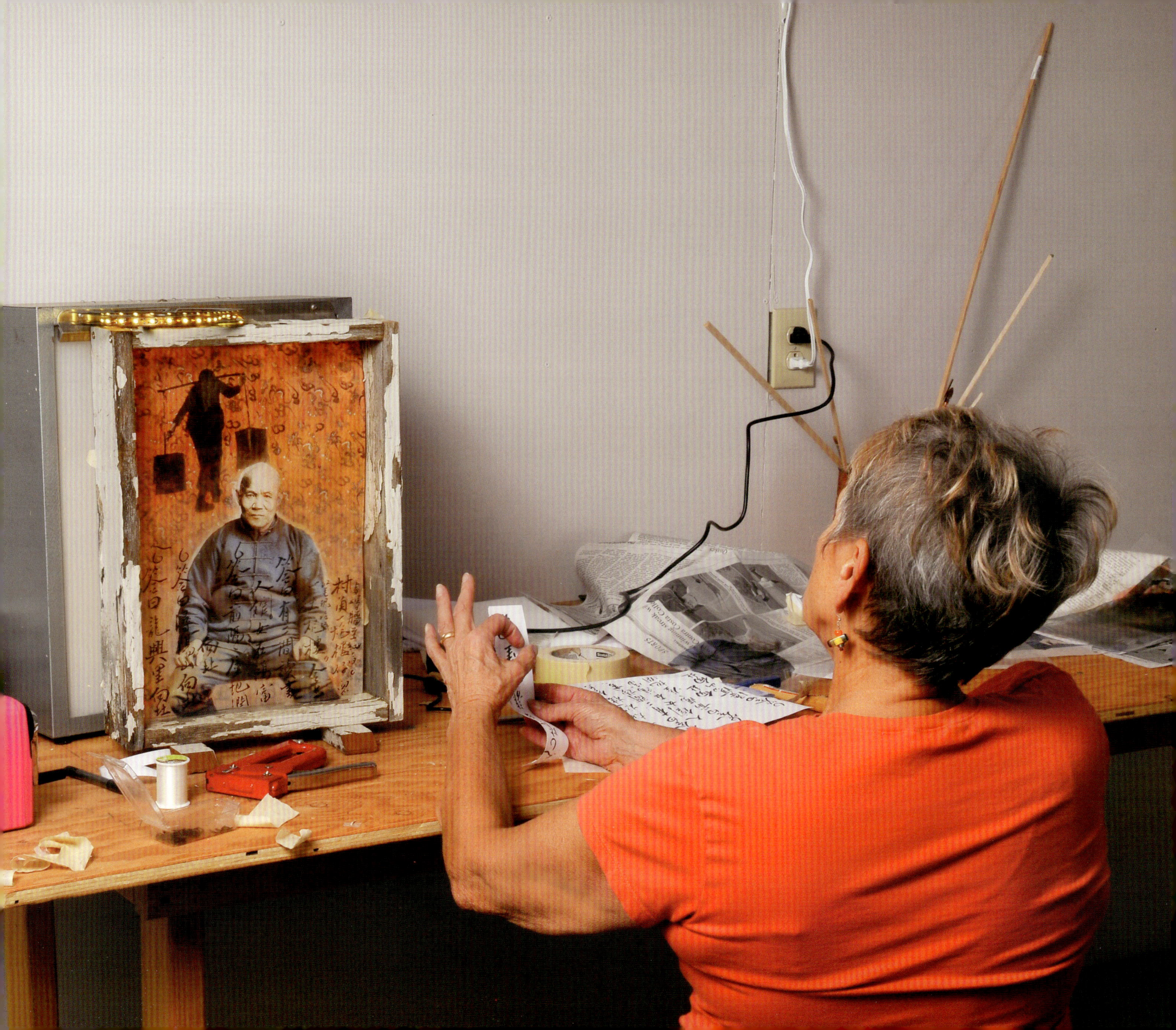

Her Dentures Art Group received a $10,000 grant from a loosely formed group of small businesses who called themselves "Small Business for Nuclear Disarmament" to join others in producing a participatory art extravaganza, "Say Goodbye to Nuclear Weapons," at an antinuclear rally in Central Park. Upon the countdown, thousands of balloons with an image of a mushroom cloud were released by the audience to blanket the sky as a visual symbol of the overwhelming danger involved with nuclear proliferation. "Everybody started crying," she says.

The second time we met, on October 20, 2014, Giannecchini and I are in Reno following up on the initial interview at her Tuscarora studio. This time she described the long, complicated process involved in creating her recent layered three-dimensional series, the Celestials series, about the presence of Chinese people in the Old West. Her intention was to honor those early pioneers and to highlight their disappearance from our national memory. I'm curious about Giannecchini's past installations and performances and seek to understand the common thread that stitches together her diverse forms of art. As she replies, her appearance seems to sync with what I know about her energetic lifestyle. Her short ashy hair spikes here and there, so the wisps and waves oblige and create their own lively shape. Her dangly earrings move as her mouth opens in a big smile and erases her mood that minutes before dimmed her eyes. She explains her approach.

"I want to draw attention to people and situations that maybe have been overlooked or degraded. I will get the idea first and then I figure out how to communicate it." The idea, once solidified in her mind, will manifest in one of a variety of art forms. The Celestials series came to life when she learned that four thousand Chinese people once inhabited the 1872 mining town of Tuscarora, and yet they are now forgotten. "Even their bones were sent back to China." After extensive research, Giannecchini decided to resurrect an imagined past that would suggest the

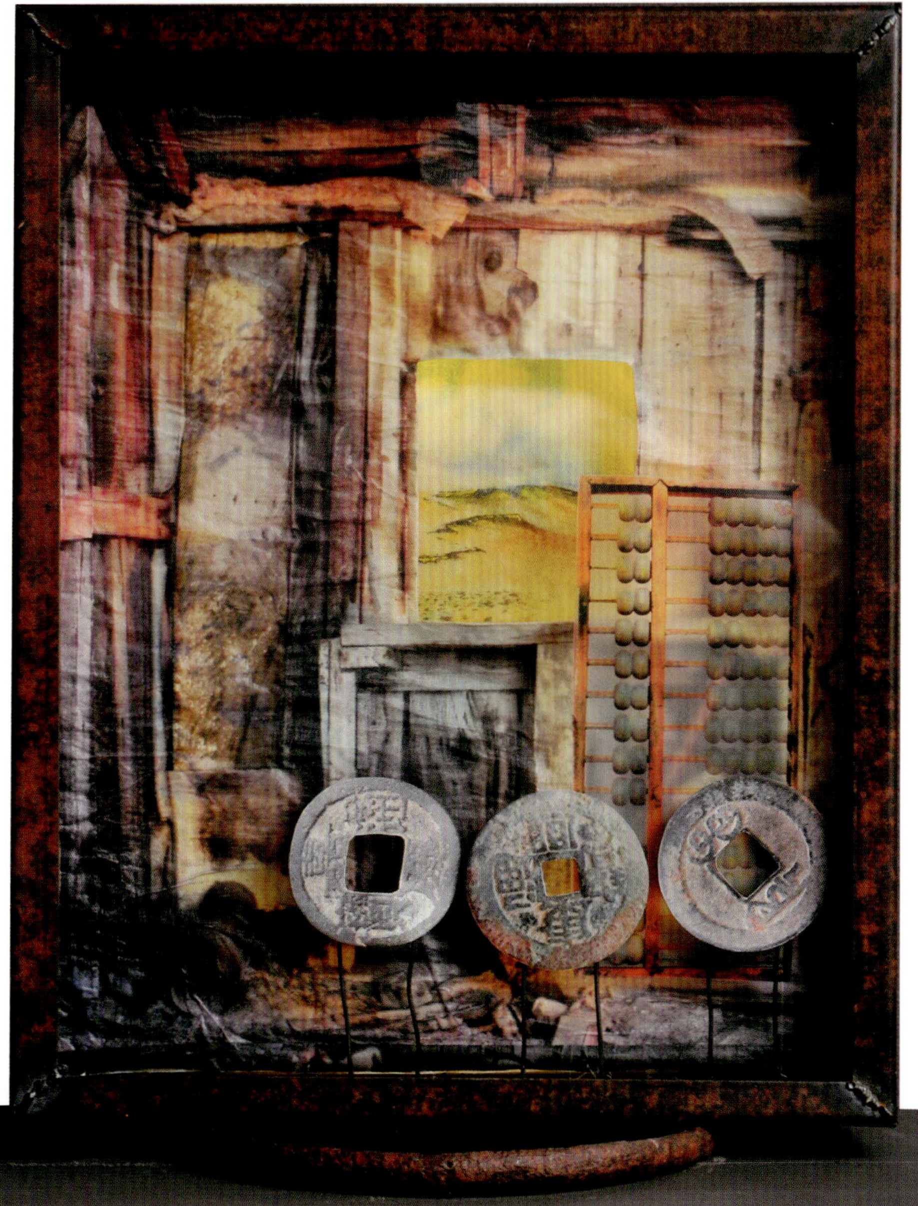

Joan Giannecchini, *Square Holed Elder Brother.* Mixed media; 18 x 14 x 3 in.

hardships, loneliness, uncertainty, and immense bravery of these early immigrants. She located and digitized archival photos from railroad and mining camps to create computer-manipulated mockups. Then she carefully printed the images onto a variety of mediums including vellum, silk, and acetate. She layered several of these semitransparent images so they appeared ghost-like inside large frames that were three to four inches deep that she had constructed of wood and metal found among the weeds and bones of Tuscarora. "I had to learn how to weld first!" She painted the images in muted tones, added rusty objects, and unearthed wood, old mining fragments, and LED lights that shot up from below to cast ethereal shadows on each piece. This project of twenty works was seven years in the making.

Giannecchini's work has blasted into the world as a result of her own poignant growing-up experience. Born in San Francisco, she moved at age six farther north to the home of her mother's people. Her father, a Navy veteran of World War II, was, she says, "high strung." Her father was half Mexican, her mother Italian, and when they moved to a small town, the parents were self-conscious about their ethnicity. Looking back on those unhappy years, Giannecchini believes she might have been suffering under more than the strain of simply growing up. She had a difficult time concentrating both at home and in school. Art was wonderful, but she couldn't focus. Unable to follow sentences or even instructions, she began to wonder if her parents were right in labeling her crazy. This characterization brought forth all the pent-up frustrations of a small, intelligent girl who could still out-think and out-talk her teachers and parents. Angry most of the time, she acted out with words and actions, and her wild side got wilder.

Upon hearing Giannecchini's story, I was reminded of John Merrick's plea in the true-life movie, *The Elephant Man*. Merrick was cornered, and in desperation turned to plead to an angry crowd: "I am a human being! I am a human being!" Giannecchini did not yet believe she was a full human being. Encouraged by her brother, Don Snyder, she entered college but promptly flunked out. Shortly thereafter, she married and gave birth to a child, but when the baby was two years old she realized she was not emotionally prepared for motherhood. Knowing the girl's father would be the better parent, Giannecchini left her daughter with him in the most wrenching decision of her life. Today, she is proud of the effort made by both mother and daughter to form a close and lasting bond. "My daughter is a lovely, successful person—the proof of the pudding."

Meanwhile, the artist, who did not yet know she would become one, went to Europe; that trip turned out to be the great beginning of exploring her own capabilities. She hitchhiked for a year, and then returned to settle in Los Angeles to become a hippie. She dabbled in art classes and discovered she loved art, especially clay. "I got immersed in this creative community. I was growing up, finally, and for the first time I felt I was home." The man she lived with at the time was a filmmaker, and in 1973 he enlisted Giannecchini to travel north with him to Oakland to film the mayoral campaign of Bobby Seale, cofounder of the Black Panther Party and recently released prisoner. There was a violent eruption at an Ike and Tina Turner benefit concert for Seale, and in the fallout a dispute began between the filmmakers and the Panthers regarding possession of the film. Giannecchini didn't like the threats, but she did like the East Bay, and decided to move there to join an art collective in Oakland, where friends studied papermaking, glass, weaving, and pottery.

When she experimented with clay, but wanted to explore it more fully, she consulted with the internationally famous sculptor Stephen De Staebler. He had recently received his master of fine arts from the University of California, Berkeley, and elevated ceramic's categorization from craft to fine art. De Staebler's advice would set the trajectory for her life: "Don't go to college yet. First you must explore everything you can through your work."

Giannecchini moved to New York where rent in downtown Manhattan was still cheap and work and artmaking were plentiful. Seventeen years later, she obtained a bachelor of arts degree in Art from SUNY (State University of New York) Empire State College and a dual master's degree in art and science from New York University. Because her focus was eco-tourism, she needed to take additional classes at both Fordham University and Georgetown University in order to complete the degree she had envisioned. She wanted a focus on education about environmentally sustainable tourism, but also needed hard science to fulfill requirements, and the field was too new to find those classes in one place. She met and eventually married playwright Stan Kaplan, and the two of them collaborated on several performance projects. Another time, they designed a life-size Monopoly game in Central Park addressing city management issues, inviting passersby to be human players.

She says, "I found this man and he taught me how to love." The woman once considered crazy and unteachable had hit her stride and become a respected, innovative force in the art world.

Giannecchini and Kaplan moved to Zimbabwe, where Stan volunteered for a job working with poor people. Giannecchini fell in love with the raw, earthy environment of Africa, and it was difficult for her to return to the United States. When a friend invited her to visit Tuscarora, she found a peace and openness akin to that in Zimbabwe. "The interface between the land and the animals was more immediate than any place I'd visited." But Stan, a native New Yorker, had to be convinced. It took a plaque over the cash register at Tom's Taylor Canyon tavern north of Elko to change his mind. Beneath two smoking guns, the words read, "We Don't Call 911," and Stan said, "This is the place for us!" The couple eventually purchased a singlewide trailer, the one that was featured in the movie *The Long, Long Trailer* starring Lucille Ball and Desi Arnaz. They added a huge family room, built a separate studio, and settled in to

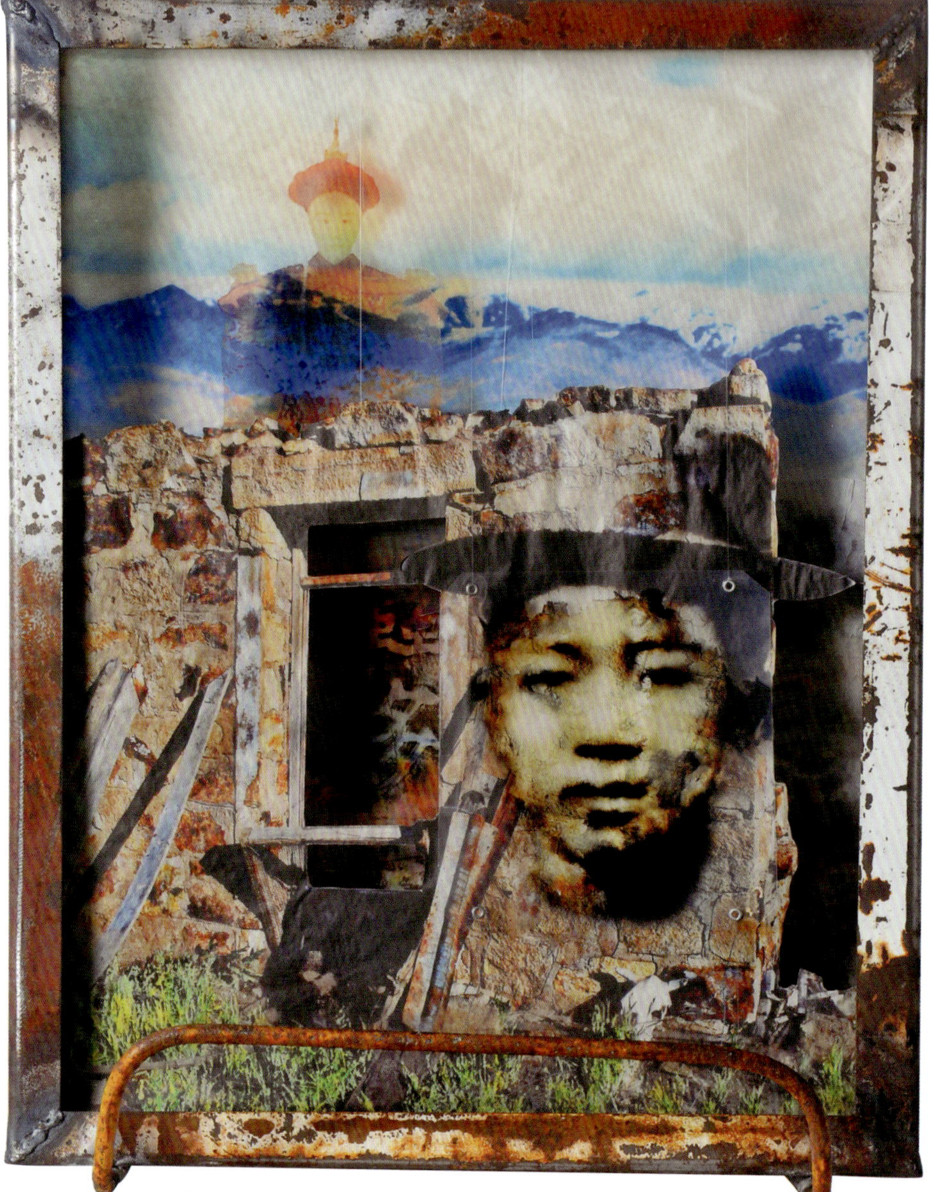

Joan Giannecchini, *China Man*. Mixed media; 16 x 20 x 3.5 in.

write and make art. They currently split their time between Reno and their Northern California farmhouse. It is when they leave Reno and drive east across the Great Basin that they become still. "Then the visions and ideas that drive my work take hold, inspired by all the beautiful shades of beige that pass along the highway, the empty expanse that rests my mind and feeds my creativity."

Giannecchini also conducts workshops in nonviolent communications each month at the Susanville, California, high-security prison with the Alternatives to Violence Project, established by the Quakers. "As long as those prisoners are going to be alive, they have a right to a fulfilling life just as much as we do!"

She has advice to those who are considering a career in arts: "Experience things and don't close the door behind you. Collect them; they're little gems. You can look back on them later and see they've helped you. And if you don't think you're ready, then get a job and move along. Take that shotgun down and shoot it out there, and wherever those little lobs go, head that way!"

That's what she did. And at the risk of sounding boastful, Giannecchini says she's proud of making a difference. "People talk about fine art, and about crafts, but creativity is the functional word here. The creative impulse has to do with having another dimension. I can speak, act, support. When I make art, I just extend those efforts."

Notes

1. The statement is attributed to Jill Dawsey, former curator of the Utah Museum of Fine Arts.
2. Other collections are in the Museum Ludwig, Cologne; Arts Council England; Museu Coleção Berardo, Lisbon; São Paulo Museum of Modern Art; Utah Museum of Fine Arts; and Utah Arts Council.
3. The museum's goal is to model a creative cross-disciplinary thinking in art, science, and technology. She sees her role in the museum as part of a team that is pushing the definitions of what a museum is. And that combining these seemingly disparate topics not only resonates with her approach to fine art, but also offers a new creative scope wherein form has to be found in wider range of subjects than she has used in her solo work.
4. The mural location was donated by a local restaurateur, scaffold by the father of one of the artists, and creative support from Spy Hop staff, KPCW Radio, Youth City, and the local, national, and international artists who cut stencils and sprayed the portraits.
5. *Guernica* is Pablo Picasso's famous antiwar masterpiece that was rolled up and returned to Spain only after democracy was established.
6. This goddess symbolizes spring—new life, rebirth, love. She is also known as "the maker" and "the grandmother of magic." She has her own star in the Pleiades cluster. She is connected to the Hindus and to the great civilizations of the Mayan people of Central America.
7. Often called infantile paralysis, poliomyelitis is an acute viral, infectious disease. It was one of the most dreaded childhood diseases of the twentieth century. Polio epidemics have crippled thousands of people, mostly young children. A network of Shriners Hospitals for Children cared for children with polio and other conditions, regardless of their ability to pay. Polio vaccines, developed in the 1950s, have dramatically reduced the global number of polio cases per year.
8. Sweetwater credits those surgeries for her healing and ability to walk today.
9. The late poet M. C. Richards was a writer and potter who created art of many genres that wove together all her concerns.
10. In 1981 she obtained a National Endowment for the Humanities fellowship and traveled to the Berkeley Folklore Program at the University of California to study the Nevada Buckaroo Project on file there. From this information, she located and interviewed some northern Nevada cowboys, whom she recorded and photographed. Their images appeared in a one-woman show in Elko in 1984. (This author also saw Sweetwater's show. It was one of the first exhibitions in the newly formed Sierra Arts Center in Reno.) Cannon saw an opportunity to develop her work on the Nevada Buckaroo Project into something of his own.
11. In 1969 a group of Native people who called themselves "Indians of All Tribes" occupied Alcatraz Island, a former federal penitentiary off the coast of San Francisco, in order to bring Indian rights issues to the attention of the federal government.
12. Dat-So-La-Lee (née Dabuda), a member of the Washo people (ca 1829–1925), was a renowned basket weaver and one of the most famous native artists of the twentieth century.

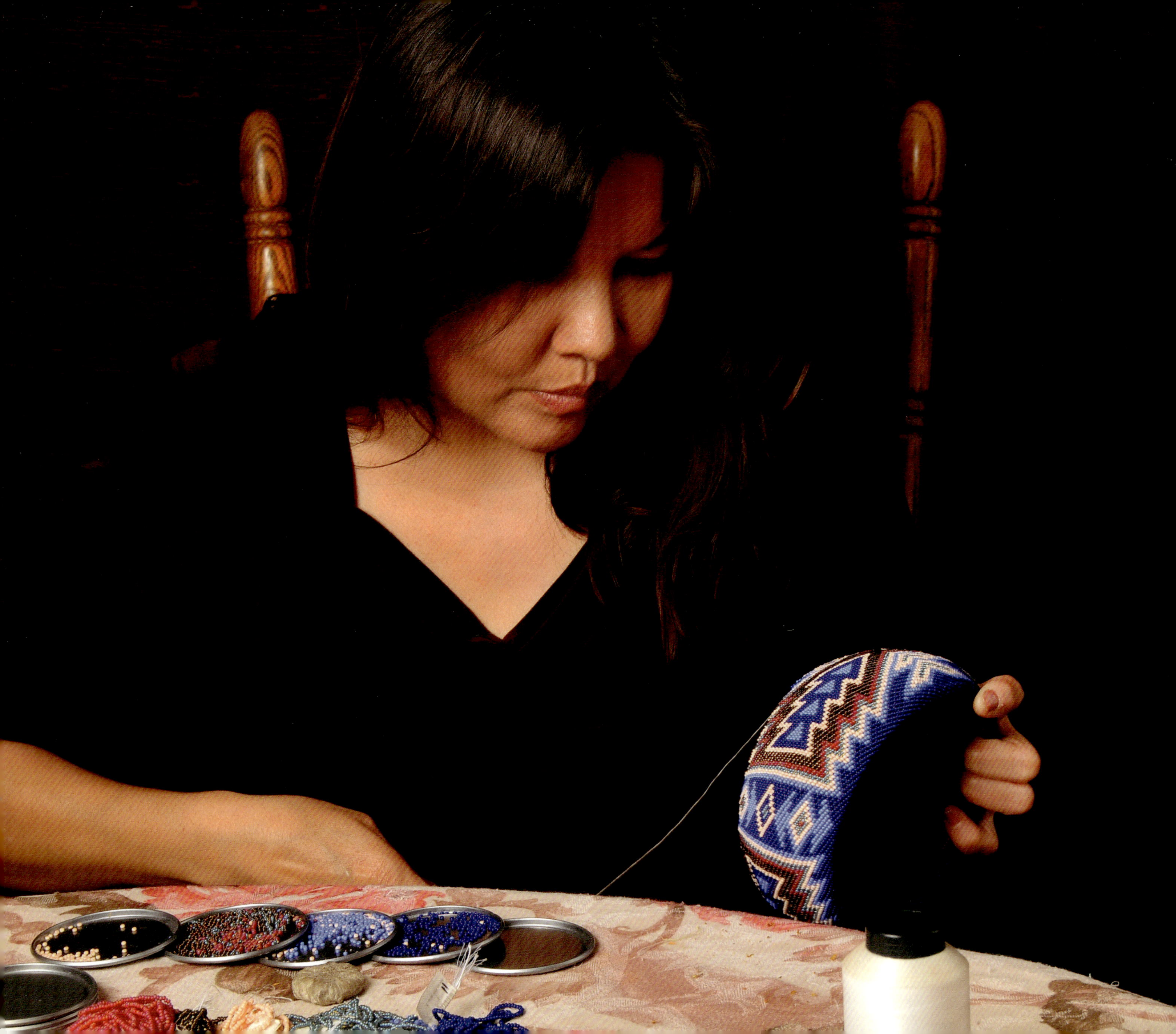

SPIRITING

Metis medicine woman Evelyn Eaton said, "Artists are the Shamans of the World" (1982, 97).

Cathy A. Malchiodi, a leading expert in the expressive arts, says that, historically and cross-culturally, artists have been core leaders of their communities and often assumed the role of shaman. They haven't been seen as individuals in pursuit of personal expression but instead were acknowledged as the creative source of insight and wisdom for the collective group. Today, the use of art as a spiritual and transformative practice is experiencing a revival.

Rebecca Eagle, Tia L. Flores, Kay Minto, Patricia Wescott, and Kathleen Curtis place spirituality in the center of the art they create. They believe that, by making art a spiritual practice, they are cultivating a relationship to the mystery and are helping us to learn, as they have, to surrender to a process greater than ourselves. By making art a spiritual practice, these artists take time to relate with the sacred, and to remind others of the possibilities along this path.

REBECCA EAGLE • BORN 1964

March 29, 2013, was a cloudless March afternoon, one of those days that feel like a preamble to summer, at the time of our interview. Rebecca Eagle lowers her needle and willow basket to the round kitchen table and gazes out the window of her immaculate home on Nevada's Pyramid Lake Paiute Tribe's Reservation, where sage-covered hills glitter with ochre, sienna, red, and gold colors in the late-afternoon sun. A small cradlebasket adorns the living room wall, along with other objects and family photos.[1]

Rebecca Eagle beading a basket.

With her smooth, nimble fingers, slim build, and shiny black hair tumbling over her shoulders, she does not look old enough to be a grandmother, but she is. Standing nearby, her six-year-old granddaughter, Monica, wearing a sparkly pink outfit, smiles and ducks her head.

The handmade basket in Eagle's hand will eventually be wrapped with an image that right now is taking form in her mind. Beads, separated into various colors, fill the orange juice can lids arranged on the cloth-covered table before her, and she will snag each bead with her threaded needle to begin creating a net of elaborate imagery. Her imagery has made her the most distinctive Native American–beaded basket artist in the Great Basin, and perhaps in the entire country.

Eagle does not follow a pattern. She has gone beyond her fine geometric designs to imagine and to create scenes of the American West—Yosemite, the Grand Canyon, the Ironhorse Railroad, the lakes (Pyramid and Tahoe), and such Native themes as the basket dance, the Stone Mother, and more.[2] Incredibly, she visualizes the completed image in color before she begins. There are no sketches, no graph paper, and no notes. She figures everything, down to the final count of beads in up to fifty colors, mathematically in her head. She begins at the top and, one bead at a time, she dips her needle and begins the row-by-row process of creating an image—a process that will take four months to a year to complete.

Her *Tahoe* basket (publicized as *Lake Tahoe*) begins with the name. *Tahoe* is the English translation of the Washo people's name for the lake, Da-ow. Eagle worked a bead-netted stitch over a Washo coiled gap-stitch willow basket, with western California redbud and bracken fern root as the design. Beaded symbols include dragonflies and butterflies as signs of change in life's constant process. She thus creates her own storyline: Tahoe in the beginning of change. Using a kaleidoscope of forty-two colors in size 10 beads, this piece took more than 567 hours to complete.

"Rebecca is an innovator in beaded portrait baskets," anthropologist Catherine S. Fowler, PhD, explains.[3] "She is an artist, especially in the kind of story she puts on the baskets." Fowler went on to say that beadwork portraiture has been done at the Fort Hall Indian Reservation in Idaho, where Rebecca once lived, and this could have been her inspiration. "But Rebecca has gone way beyond that," Fowler said in an April 2013 telephone conversation with the author. "She is an artist with beads. She pioneered a new concept."

I study this unassuming woman whose eyes complement a dress of the same dark earth color. How did Eagle achieve what nobody else has? Amazingly, her journey began with tragedy—the worst, she says, of her entire life. She puts the basket down and lowers her eyes. Her voice shakes as she tells the story, the one that began at Fort Hall, the home of her Shoshone-Bannock father, Harvey Eagle, where the family resided. She was just nine when her mother, Jeanette Mitchel Eagle, passed away in 1974. Eagle, who had been born in Reno, was sent back to live with her cousin, Norm DeLorme, his wife Bernie, and their children at the Reno-Sparks Indian Colony. Her grief abated only when her cousins and grandmother, who lived across the street, began to talk about willow and how it could be transformed into a basket. Grandma Adele Muzina Sampson showed her how to gather straight and strong willow sticks by scoping surrounding areas in the Truckee Meadows. Then she showed her how to split each willow into three strands to make strings for weaving. In Northern Paiute culture novices learn by observation, so Eagle watched her grandmother and learned the intricate preparation process of willow work.[4] She learned to make baskets from Bernie and beadwork from Norman. She remembers watching her mother when she made beadwork, which inspired her to devote her energy to making baskets and brought her ever closer to her.

"Growing up, my mom Jenny and grandma Adele took my hands and showed me more than just working them to do chores," Eagle explains in her soft voice. "They gifted me the tools and dedication to make baskets and beadwork art. . . . I knew as a young girl I wanted to be just like them. I knew my heart was in the right place, creating." In 1988, when Eagle was twenty-four years old, her grandmother Adele passed away.

Eagle wandered the next years, searching for a place to belong. She first tried several Indian Schools. At Phoenix Indian High School she did pastel and charcoal drawing of faces of old people. Teachers insisted that students focus on Native American styles and themes, and Eagle developed a pride in her own Paiute-Shoshone heritage that remains with her today. She met well-known Southwestern artists, and at the University of Phoenix felt privileged to collaborate with them. She was thrilled when her teacher bought all of her artwork. Finally, Eagle returned to Reno and enrolled at Wooster High School, where she was placed in an advanced art class and relished every bit of it. Here, with the help of Bernie DeLorme, she participated in her very first art show. Norm and Bernie took her to Bridgeport, California, to see various beaded baskets and a butterfly pattern, but try as she might to understand the pattern technique, it escaped her.

Eagle gave birth to two daughters, Yvonne and Miranda, and moved to Denver, where son Jason was born. She enrolled and graduated from Floral Design School of Denver, accredited by the Accrediting Council for Independent Colleges and Schools, and there she developed a sense of artistic freedom. Then, always close to her dad,

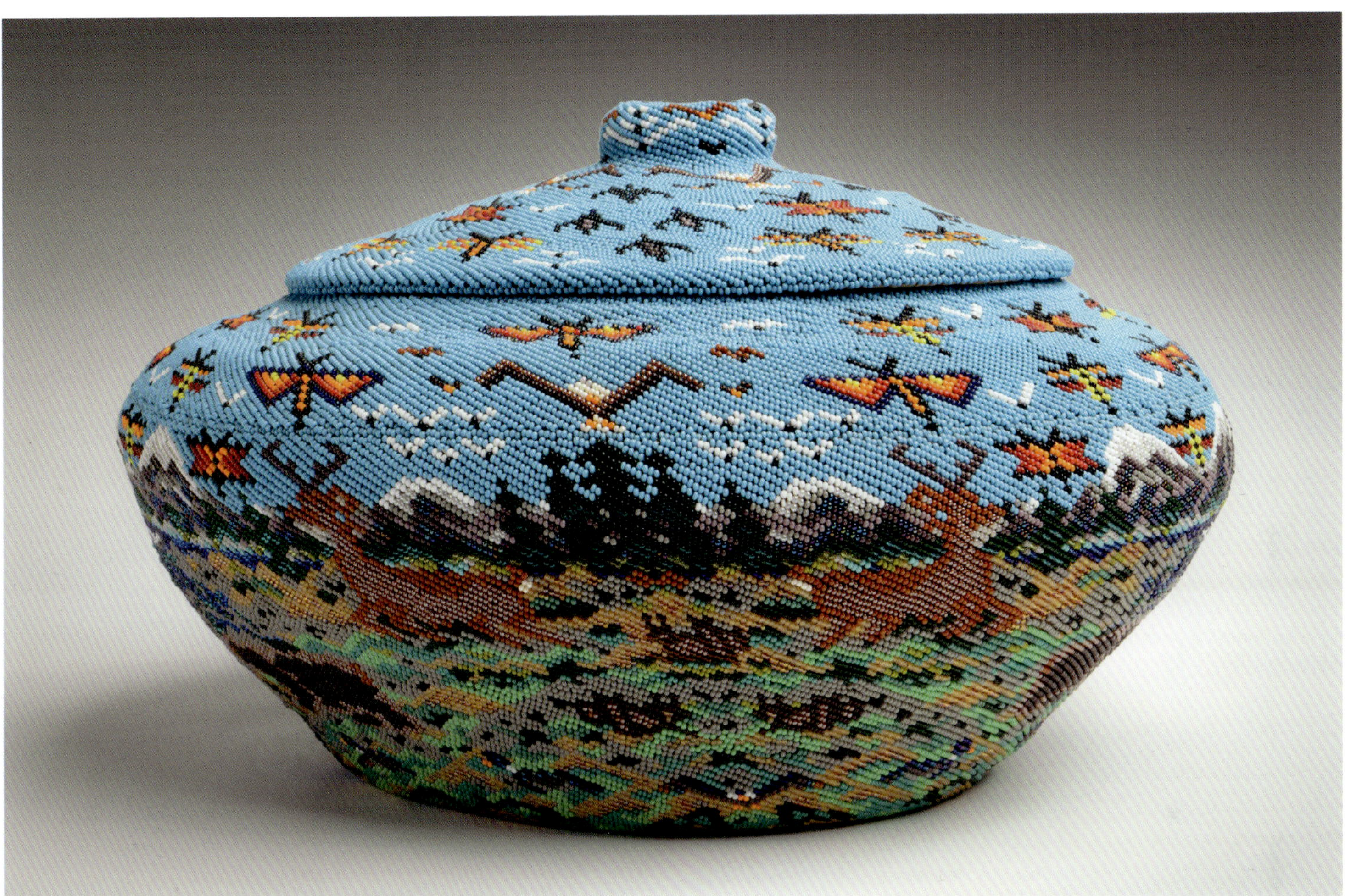

Rebecca Eagle, *Lake Tahoe*. Pictorial beaded degikup; 9 x 14 in. (diameter). Collection of Jackie (Mrs. Gene) Autry, reproduced by permission from the Nevada Museum of Art, Reno.

she moved back to Fort Hall in 1987 where she had spent so many happy childhood years. She was always enrolled and a member of the Pyramid Lake Paiute Tribe's Reservation. She moved into her present home in 1990.[5] She found a good willow patch, where the willows grew straight and strong, and began making baskets in earnest, often adding beads and remembering the beadwork techniques learned years earlier from Norm and Bernie.

Collectors sought out Rebecca Eagle baskets and the earrings she made. She began to win competition ribbons for her perfectly executed miniatures and small baskets. Her baskets have exhibited in museums, including the Clark County Heritage Museum in Henderson, Nevada, the Nevada Museum of Art, and the Nevada Historical Society in Reno. She was part of a group show, "The Art, Culture, and History of the Northern Great Basin . . . ," organized by

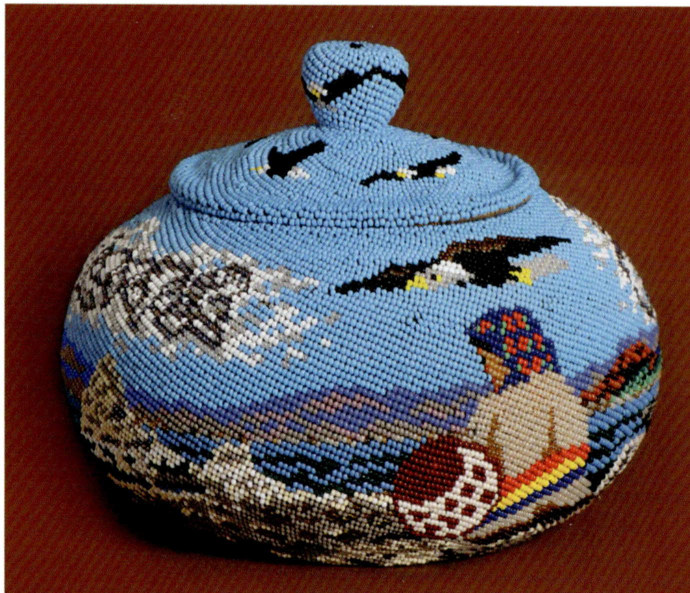

Rebecca Eagle, *Lake Tahoe/Pyramid Lake*. Decorative gift basket; 6⅛ x 7¹⁄₁₆ in. (d). Photograph by Susan Mantle, reproduced by permission from the Nevada State Museum, Carson City.

the I. P. Stanback Museum and Planetarium in Orangeburg, South Carolina; the show traveled from Washington, DC, to several destinations before returning to Nevada. Eagle has presented, exhibited, and sold her work at shows, galleries, conferences, and symposiums around the country as well as up and down the Great Basin, and her first-place awards and ribbons are too numerous to mention. The UNR, department of anthropology, and the Nevada State Museum in Carson City, has each acquired one of Rebecca Eagle's portrait baskets for their permanent collections. *Lake Pyramid,* which resides at UNR, entails a pictorial beadwork over a Washo gap-stitch coiled basket and is woven with willow and sunburnt willow. There are twenty-two seed beads (size 10) of various colors, and it took Eagle more than four hundred hours to complete. Eagle's basket storyline is, "Pelicans dance romancing the desert lake breeze, winged relatives of air follow."

"I'm grateful to come from a family of great teachers," she says, "and in return give thanks to the Creator, Heavenly Father, and Mother Earth."

Eugene Hattori, curator of anthropology at the Nevada State Museum, described Eagle's Tahoe-Pyramid basket that resides in the museum collection. "Rebecca said the Lake Tahoe side represents her Washoe heritage and was inspired by an Edward Curtis photograph of Dat-So-La-Lee." He pointed to Washoe basket images in the clouds, and then indicated the figure, which held a blanket and wore a silk scarf. "The red, yellow, and blue band is on a trade blanket. The silk scarf with red beaded roses is like the one her grandmother wore."

Hattori went on to describe the Pyramid Lake side of the basket, where "the Stone Mother [is] anthromorphised as Rebecca's grandmother, and the basket replicates one in the museum collection." An eagle flies over the Stone Mother, and beaded clouds contain images of the five chiefs of Pyramid Lake. The pictorial beadwork of *Lake Tahoe/ Pyramid* is designed over a coiled Western Shoshone basket with a lid. As in her *Lake Tahoe* and *Lake Pyramid* baskets, Eagle's technique entails a netted bead stitch overlay, favoring the two-bead hand-stitch method with thirty-five seed beads (size 10) of various colors. This basket's storyline is, "The Mother of stone sits with her basket receiving blessings from the clear blue waters, eagles circle above sacred skies, gifts from the Creator; we are thankful."

Eagle was featured on public television, along with Norm and Bernie and other weavers, in two programs: "The Way of the Willow" and "Exploring Nevada." Afterward, she was invited to participate with the Nevada delegation at the fortieth annual Smithsonian Folklife Festival in Washington, DC. In 1998 she was awarded the Governor's Arts Award for Excellence in Folk and Traditional Arts.

And so we see that the greatest tragedy of Rebecca Eagle's life—the death of her mother—became a transformative experience.

But it's difficult to make a living as an artist. Ask any artist. Eagle worked at the Amazon warehouse, florist shops, and various other venues, and her basket and beadwork lagged.

Then came another breakthrough—her mentorship by art dealer and collector Gene Quintana, of Gene Quintana Fine Arts in Carmichael, California. Mr. Quintana offered to pay Eagle to stay home and create baskets, and she accepted. The two began to collaborate on ideas for beaded imagery, and Eagle was off and running. In the next fifteen or so years, she created thirty-three baskets for his collection, some covered with scenic images of the American West and Southwest. Unfortunately, with the two exceptions mentioned above, these incredible baskets no longer reside in the Great Basin. In spite of this, it must be recognized that Mr. Quintana's patronage fostered an excellence and a creativity that is unrivaled anywhere in the country. Eagle received the gift of time and space to do what only she could do.

During our interview, she pulls down her photo book and slowly turns pages in which each one illustrates a basket more spectacular than the previous one. Eagles soar, bears, deer, bighorn sheep, and butterflies circle the baskets. On the image of the Tahoe basket, she points to a crescent moon, its tips pointing upward. "See, that's a lucky moon," she smiles. "That's when you gamble."

A train circles one spectacular basket; one side depicts colorful Arizona mesas near Phoenix, and on the other, the California–Nevada Sierra. Looking from artist to image, I am struck by the dichotomy of this unassuming woman and the drama and blazing color of the baskets she has created.

Although she is an expert weaver of willow baskets, Eagle also beads over baskets made by other weavers, a custom that was developed not by her, she said, but by Native people who created for the tourist industry more than a half century ago.

"They beaded over other people's baskets back then," she explains. "Some women didn't know how to make baskets and they traded so they could bead." She went on to elaborate: "And I don't bead over just any basket." She usually sews on Washo, Shoshone, and Paiute baskets, but would be reluctant to bead over a Navajo basket, because of ancient taboos. She said Quintana would supply the baskets for her, and he knew which ones were acceptable.

Quintana sold most of the Rebecca Eagle baskets in his collection to Mrs. Jackie Autry and assumes they will eventually go into the Autry Museum of the American West in Los Angeles, California.

Is Eagle finished? I don't think so. At the completion of the interview, she is leaving for an extended stay at Fort Hall to tend to her ill father. Family is everything to this woman, who now is saying goodbye as daughter Yvonne leaves for work, and whose dark eyes rest lovingly on Monica, who had listened quietly through our entire interview. "The best parts of my life are my children and grandchildren," she says, ever modest about her incredible accomplishments.

"Long after we are dead and gone," Mr. Quintana said, "her baskets will endure. Rebecca is the new Dat-So-La-Lee of the beaders."

Accolades like this do not change Eagle's path or the way in which she views her world. While her work is unparalleled in this country, she remains the same woman she always was, devoted to her family and heritage. "Respect the great earth, honor the teachings, and cherish the moments in time," she writes in her personal statement (undated). "This vision is life handed down from one generation to the next."

TIA L. FLORES • BORN 1960

Author Cathy A. Malchiodi, in her book *The Soul's Palette* (2002, 210), asks the reader to imagine casting a pebble into a quiet lake and noticing the circles ripple outward in

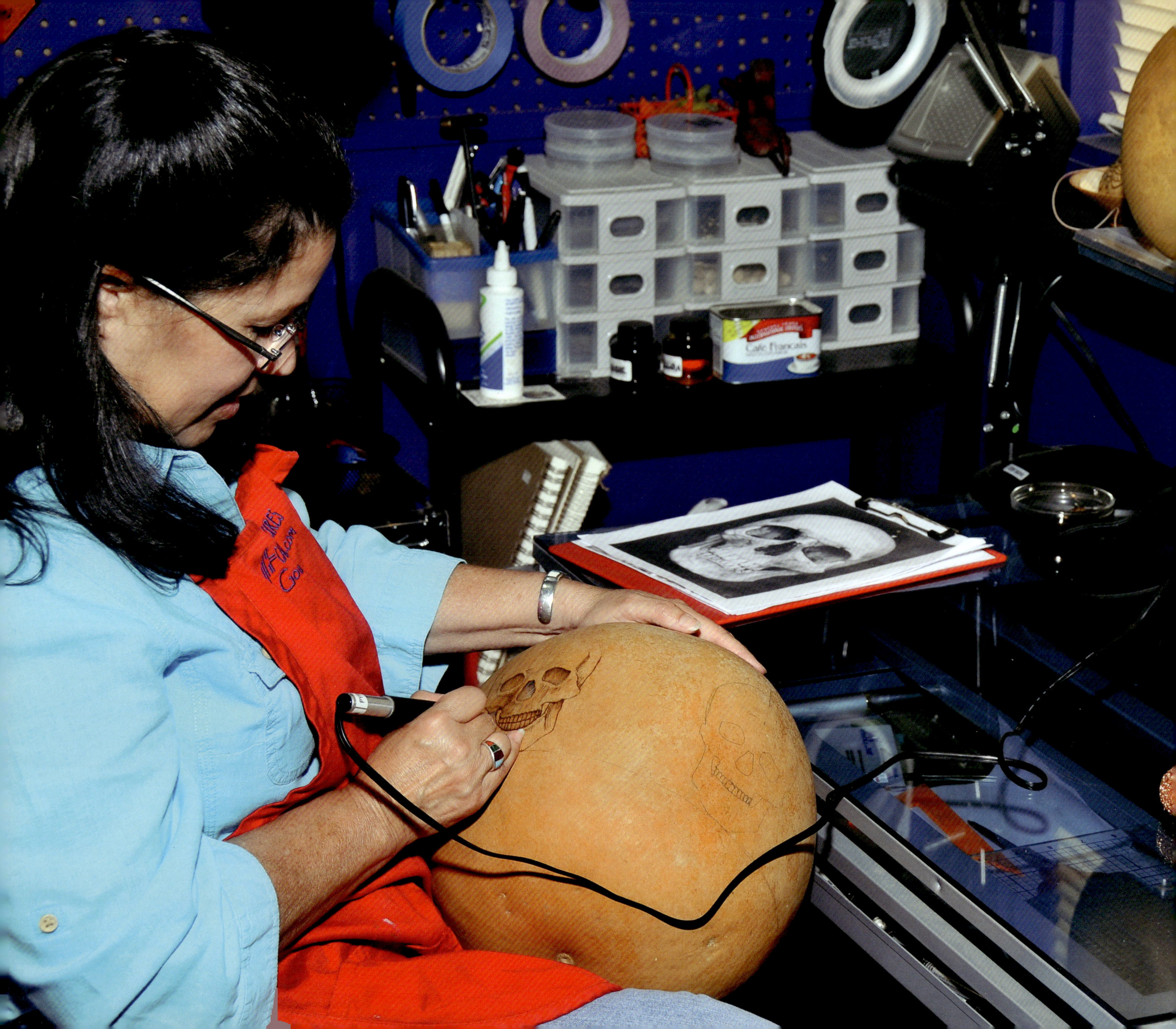
Cafe Francais

the water. "When we let our images reach beyond self-expression to symbolic intentions, we create art that cares not only for ourselves but also for the souls of others, even those we do not or may never know."

Although the two have never met, Malchiodi's words eloquently describe the life and creations of gourd artist Tia L. Flores. Flores creates with artistic wisdom acquired over years of exploration. From her studio in south Washoe County, Nevada, she makes visible the mythology of people and animals of the world. Like ripples in water, she scatters her unique brand of spiritual knowing to the larger community in her exhibits and teachings, and in the calendars, cards, and poetry she fashions.

It wasn't always this way, of course. On August 8, 2013, I gaze around her compact studio as she draws an image on a gourd and tells her story. Power equipment covers walls and a shelf at one end, while raw gourds in various sizes and configurations rest along an upper ledge. Sculpting tools, paints, and dyes are within reach, and works in progress line other shelves. One area holds smaller, inspirational pieces; nearby we see marketing brochures, cards, calendars, and folders she designed. Flores's worktable overlooks the natural vegetation on her land, and as she talks she pulls back a strand of shiny black hair and shoots occasional glances at a nearby wall area filled with images of the animals and women who inspire her.

A fourth-generation Nevadan, Tia was born Tammie Louise Flores in Las Vegas to her seventeen-year-old mother, Eva Lynne Robinson. She was, Tia says, "very fiery, and so much fun," a lover of animals, and also artistic despite hours spent away at work. One day Lynne found an infant gray tree squirrel on the side of a dirt road. "She named him Alvin, and they adored each other." Eva built Alvin a home in a large cage, and he lived in the middle of their living room.

Their small neighborhood on the north edge of town ("back when there were more animals than people") nestled just below the Red Rock Mountains. When she was four her parents divorced and her father left while Lynne found work. Flores and her two younger brothers spent summers exploring the desert, building elaborate forts and collecting various reptiles to study. She says, "It was the prehistoric-looking horned lizard that brought joy to our adventurous young hearts."

Flores started school and was intrigued by the shapes of the letters of the alphabet. "Today when I'm feeling stressed, I will use words—maybe write letters, maybe create patterns and shapes from the letters." Art was part of the curriculum, and Flores won first place in a Valentine art contest in first grade (she made a Valentine mailbox shaped like a slot machine). From that time forward, the girl wanted to be an artist. At age eight she checked out a book from the school library, E. L. Konigsburg's *From the Mixed-up Files of Mrs. Basil E. Frankweiler* (1967), about a runaway girl who discovered New York City's Metropolitan Museum of Art. "It introduced me to Michelangelo." Today, a copy of that book is part of her collection. She had some enthusiastic art teachers and compares her early experiences to today's school art offerings. "As a native of this great state, it saddens me that the arts have been defunded and removed from our schools, especially at the elementary level in Washoe County [Reno/Sparks]. I cannot even imagine what my life would have been like without an art education. Not only was creating art my passion, but it was my safe passage to a world I could escape to when life was unbearable." When she was twelve, she wrote a poem:

at times when i'm feeling down
And there's no one around
i escape to a far away world
Which I create.
With just a pencil, brush or pen
My world begins.
Through a time of its own

Tia L. Flores burns images into a gourd.

Where I'm never alone
To a place full of beauty and pleasure
For this is my world. My treasure.

Then everything changed again. Her mother entered her third marriage and worked swing shift.[6] Child care was nonexistent in the late 1960s and early 1970s, and Flores took on the role of mother, caring for her brothers—cooking dinner, cleaning, and engaging in most other caregiving activities. During that difficult time, she says, "Art became a necessity."

She still remembers high school art teacher Mr. Walter Jacobsen, who introduced new media and concepts. "Many of the things I learned from him I try to pass on to my own students:

Honor and be grateful for your talents.
Learn from others but use your own voice.
Challenge yourself and share your process with others.
Treat your art with care and respect.
Presentation is 90 per cent.
Enjoy the process.

She took part, along with eight other students, in creating the first high school citywide mural project in Las Vegas, at the Dula Recreation Center. (Theirs was one of four murals.) She learned printmaking and was planning to be an artist. She received an internship to illustrate products for brochures but her family discouraged that pursuit. Next, her teachers found a college art scholarship, but her mother dissuaded her from applying. Even today, parents, fearing financial roadblocks, rarely encourage children to follow a career in art.

Flores went to work at an automotive retail store and soon was promoted to assistant manager, where she created the store's advertising posters. She believes this early experience of combining art and words contributed to her current profession as communication and marketing manager at Reno's Coral Academy of Science.[7]

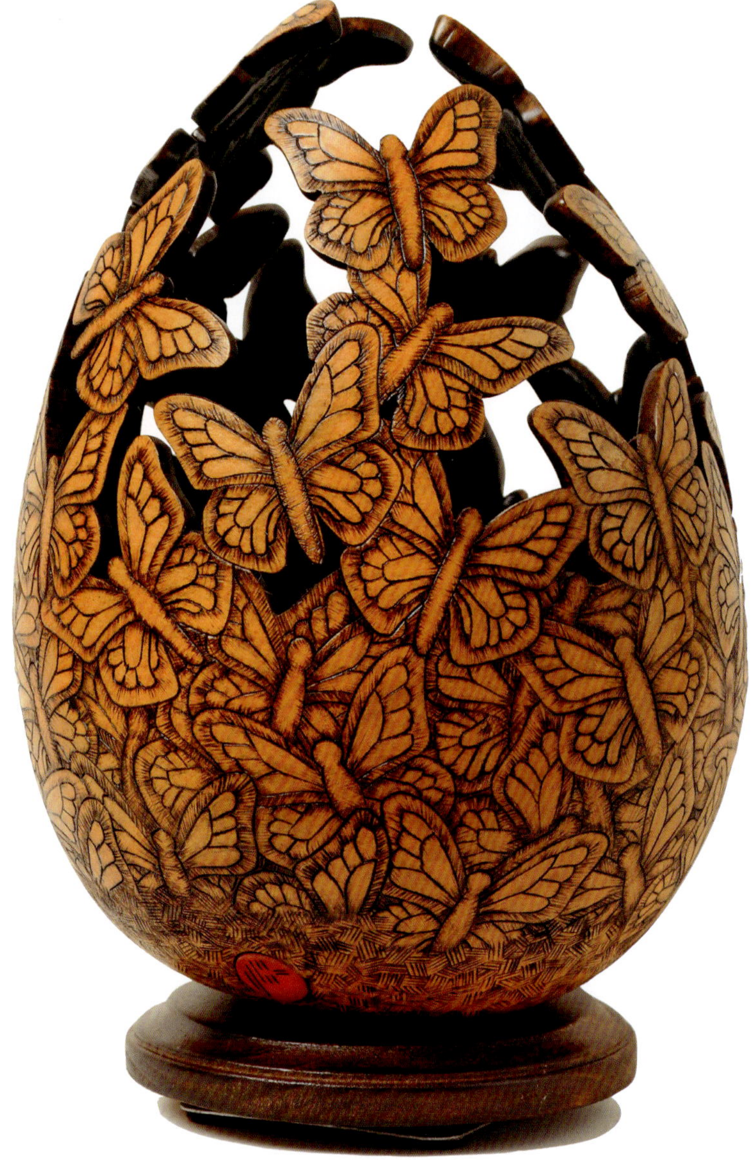

Tia L. Flores, *Papalotl, Monarch Butterfly Gourd.* Monarch Butterfly Gourd; carving (mini jigsaw) and pyrography (woodburning) on hard-shell gourd; 11 x 7 in.

In 1979 she moved to Reno to enroll in architecture classes at UNR. She worked part time at a bank, and then, to get the health and other benefits the bank offered, Flores went full time. Her banking career began.

"I loved my job," she tells me. "I could design forms so their banking systems would work better." She was promoted and began to design training materials, then created workshops and presented them state wide. "It was my creative outlet." She was on her way to a life career.

But after twelve years in the banking industry, a traumatic event launched its attack and changed her future forever: her bank merged with a larger one and management eliminated her position. They offered her a job in San Francisco, but she declined. This great shock and loss was a low point in her life, a gut-punch to the pride she took in her work as well to as any professional future hopes, and she reeled, a stone that ricocheted to the bottom of the lake.

The only good news in this upheaval was a strong severance package; she now had resources and time to seek a new path. At first she returned to architecture, this time at Truckee Meadows Community College. In another stroke of bad luck, her inspirational teacher, Tim Chapman, passed away suddenly, and when there was nobody to teach the program it collapsed.

Some people, when met with great misfortune, begin to examine themselves more deeply. As Flores put it, "When things turn away, you search for who you are." The questions "Who am I? What am I doing here? Where am I going?" are asked during vision quests in some Native cultures, and appeared as far back as the ancient Greeks in the adage "know thyself" (inscribed in stone at the Temple of Apollo at Delphi).[8] Flores tackled questions she hadn't confronted before, and wrestled with them to pull out some kind of meaning and purpose.

She reconnected with aunts and uncles on her father's side. "After all, their Native American belief system is in my blood." She participated in a Native sweat lodge. She learned about her paternal grandmother, Anastacia, and felt drawn to the rich cultures of the Aztec and Navajo people of her heritage. She also remembered the ways in which her maternal grandmother, Louise, influenced her love of the vast beauty of the Nevada desert.

When the book *Medicine Cards* (Sams, Carson, and Weneke 1988) came into her hands, she explored the concept of animal medicine. The cards and book comprise a system of divination that its authors hope will bring forth the reader's intuition. They wrote, "When you draw on the power of an animal, you are asking to be drawn into complete harmony with the strength of that creature's essence" (13). Flores learned of various symbolisms of animals like wild horses, birds, and reptiles such as the horned toad ("representing youth and innocence, as well as dreams and imagination"), and the rattlesnake (*tecuancoatl* in Aztec).

She continues, "You could pull a card and it would tell you something you needed to know. I fell in love with them, studied them, and did spreads with friends who did totems." One of the book's authors, David Carson (a Choctaw) wanted to meet her, and on the one-year anniversary of Lynne's death, Carson did a reading. He told Flores that her mother was the owner of Spider Medicine, which symbolizes storytelling. After that, her deep yearning was to create art that could tell the stories she realized had been in her heart all along.

At the same time, she began an artistic exploration, first with beadwork and then with leather. In 1994 she enrolled in a gourd class at the Nevada Museum of Art, taught by well-known Reno gourd artist Cheryln Bennett. "I knew as soon as I touched a gourd that it was my connector." She began working with gourds on her own, experimenting with their possibilities to narrate stories, developing new techniques such as pyrography, carving, resist, dyeing, and burnishing.[9] She used a drill and sculpting tools to make certain marks and a saw to sculpt the gourd into designed shapes.

Nephews Brandon and Tyler, who spent their summer

months with Flores, referred to their aunt as Tia, and the name stuck.[10] Her self-reinvention seemed complete.

Flores takes pleasure in holding the gourd while she works on it. "There's no paintbrush between me and the gourd. It's very comforting, and almost as soon as I cradle it, there's a sense of calmness that comes over me. I think this is the way it's supposed to be. I think of them like pregnant women. They have a seed in them and if I planted and watched, it would produce."

As the old saying goes, the rest is history. "Once I found my medium, it was natural to keep searching for influences from my heritage. And I really connected. I could interpret my love of nature, of animals, of the stories of strong women. Everything had a meaning and therefore value." Using the native term for gourd, calabaza, Flores has interpreted the graceful rattlesnake, eagle, butterfly, quail, and hummingbird, as well as women in ceremony, flowers, and many more objects that are abundant with spiritual meaning.

Flores conveys stories and personal beliefs in her gourd sculptures. Butterflies, for example, "completely transform their shape to become beautiful. The Aztecs believed that the monarch butterflies carried the souls of their warriors to the spirit world." One day, driving to an exhibition, she turned on National Public Radio news only to hear of the tragic killings in Afghanistan of nine American soldiers. "I couldn't get it out of my mind," she says. "I thought it ironic that I was participating in an art show on this beautiful summer day while these families were being notified of their loss, bearing the burden of unbearable grief." She hugs her arms close to her body and says, "I'm not an outspoken antiwar advocate. I don't participate in rallies or write protest letters. I am an artist. My art is my voice." Flores went home and began working on a calabaza sculpture dedicated to the loved ones of the nine soldiers. She called it *Imagine Peace*. The bottom half of the artwork is inscribed with thousands of Chinese peace signs. "Every time I burned one in, I was putting peace out into the world." *Imagine Peace* is reproduced in her 2009 calendar.

Flores's work is in high demand, and she participates in exhibits locally and regionally, including the Nevada state legislature. She has been featured in *Pyrography Magazine*, on HGTV *That's Clever!* and on YouTube. She participates annually in Reno Open Studios, a self-guided studio tour. But these days she has cast her stones into deeper waters. She has joined Reno's Coral Academy of Science: in addition to being its communications and marketing manager, she's also its high school art teacher, including graphic, digital, and studio art. She has taught at VSA Nevada (now named Arts for All Nevada) for many years, and this work is a calling for her.[11] No matter how busy, Thursday evenings will find her teaching a class there.

"I'm creative every single day," she says. She has become interested in the connection between art and mathematics: she presented a sold-out workshop called ArtSciMath at the National Art Education Association conference in San Diego, California. She recently met with Nevada U.S. senator Harry Reid when a Coral Academy of Science High School student was presented with the Congressional Award silver medal.

What does it mean to live in the Great Basin? "Well, Nevada is not a wasteland," she says. "One of the oldest living things is in our state—the bristlecone pine. It's not flowery, but it has strength, endurance, and purpose." She talks about the abundance of wide-open spaces. "How can you be in a place where you can't see?"

Tia Flores continues down her path, casting stones upon lakes and sending ripples far and wide. She wrote the following for a special art piece created in honor and memory of her mother and grandmothers:

Stand barefoot upon the brown belly of our Earth Mother
and feel our presence.
All those who came before you and those who have yet
to come.

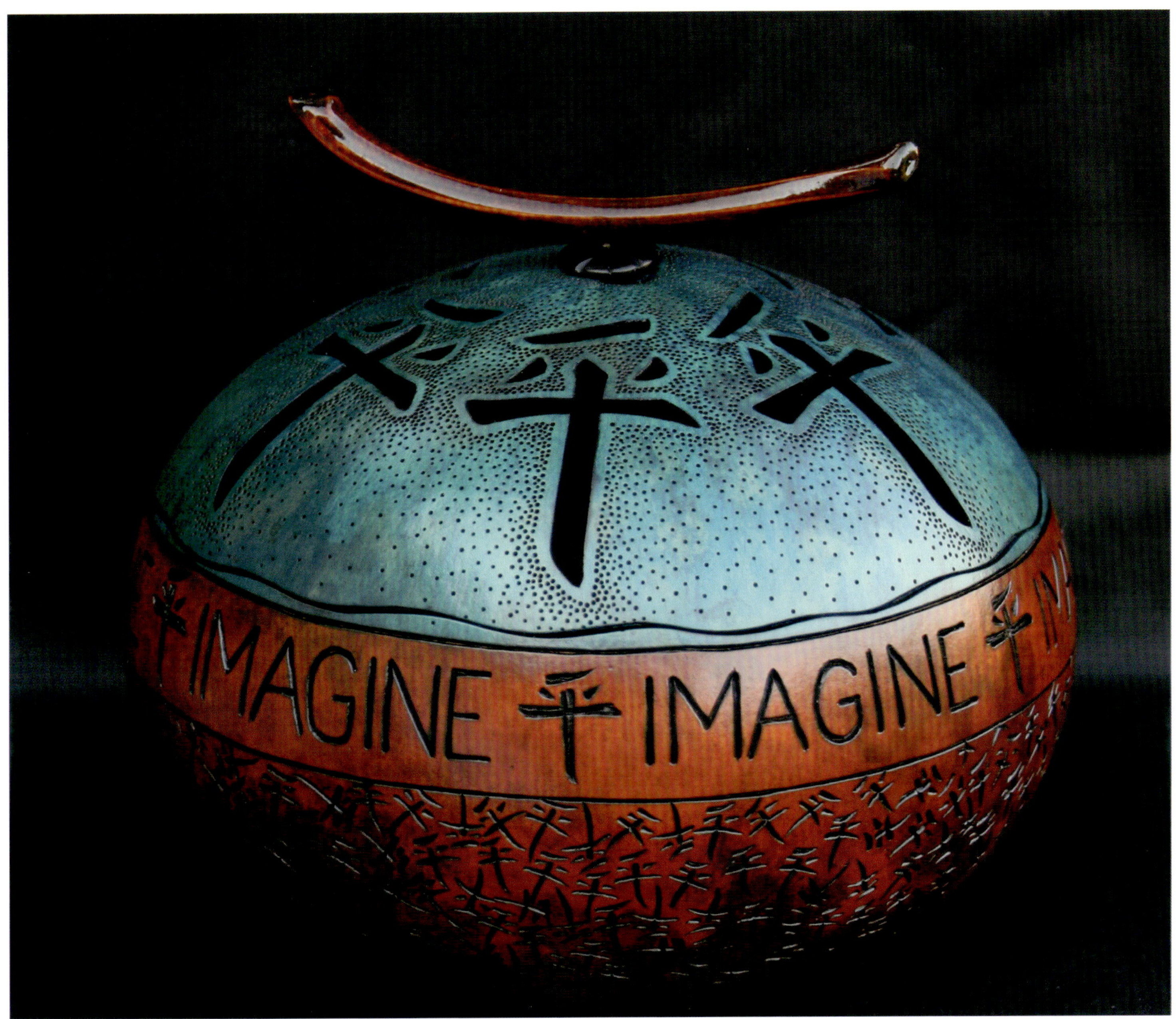

Tia L. Flores, *Imagine Peace.* Gourd; carving and pyrography on hard-shell gourd with leather dye; 7½ x 8 in.

We are the past, present and future.
Together, we stand barefoot upon the brown belly
of our beloved Earth Mother
and we are one.

KAY MINTO • BORN 1941

As I stand beside Kay Minto at the top edge of her Lava Rock Ranch on October 17, 2013, and gaze down over the antler tips of her sculpture, *Greeter*, to the little winding road we'd recently climbed, then to the whole of Surprise Valley below, I have to catch my breath. The lakes, the lush green pastures where deer and cattle graze, the smattering of ranches outlined with cottonwoods, and the pine-, fir-, juniper-, and sage-dotted hills seem almost unreal under a cloud-puffed blue sky; the quiet is broken only by the sounds of a hoot-owl or meadowlark. Recently, this ranch, with its sculpture park and a home and studio that Minto built herself, was chosen to be part of National Geographic's Geotourism project, a venture that honors local sites with cultural or historic value.

I have a difficult time understanding how the artist is able to create at all when she's confronted daily with the panorama below. But create she does, and not just your normal sculpture, oh, no. After years of experimenting, Minto has become the first artist in the country to develop a technique for welding metal directly onto lava rock. Folks in nearby Eagleville, California (population 59), Modoc, and Lassen Counties affectionately call her "the rock welder." And whether she realizes it or not, Minto has much in common with the lava that she welds to create one-of-a-kind sculptures that have been variously described as abstract-realistic, poetic, witty, and thought-provoking.

The rocks were formed from erupting volcanoes. They can handle the expansion and contraction of the intense heat from gas tungsten arc welding (GTAW, or TIG welding, as Minto calls it) that the artist employs as she builds luminous glowing puddles of aluminum that will adhere to the stone, bringing to fruition one of a multitude of sculptures she has created.[12] Like the lava, Minto has been through her share of natural upheavals, too, but walking through the fire has led to a life she wouldn't change for anything and to an art career that is as unique as her sculpture.

Greeter is one example, and the first piece we see after we turn off of State Route 447 at the parked water truck, as directed, and head up a gravel road. Soon the antlered lava rock figure, its metal eyes gleaming in the afternoon sun, its staff held high in welcome, swings into view, and we know we've arrived at Minto's home and studio nestled right up against the Warner Mountains and the western edge of the Great Basin. The artist, with her thick white hair, rosy cheeks, and Levi's jacket, is out the door and smiling as I pull up, and soon we are in deep discussion over her style of walking in the world.

She sometimes steps back to become a "distant observer, getting outside myself and looking at the situation from different angles," she says, adding that this technique fosters original thinking. "Thus, I discover there are all these different ways to make sculpture. Just as there are all these different ways to live."

Minto definitely speaks from experience. Little did she know back in Oklahoma City, Oklahoma, the place of her birth, that she'd face personal and physical losses that many will never know. Back then she just knew she wanted to be an artist. At the age of eight, she earned money by selling drawings to neighbors for twenty-five cents. Her dad, James, kept a little black book, and Waggoner (her name then) deposited her money with him, and "I babysat for money and learned budgeting that way."

At a Del City High School presentation, where she gave a talk, a wealthy local businessman approached her. He offered her a full college scholarship on the condition that she major in business and then commit to work in his development business for four years. It was tempting, for Minto needed to pay for her own college education. But after much

Kay Minto welds metal to lava.

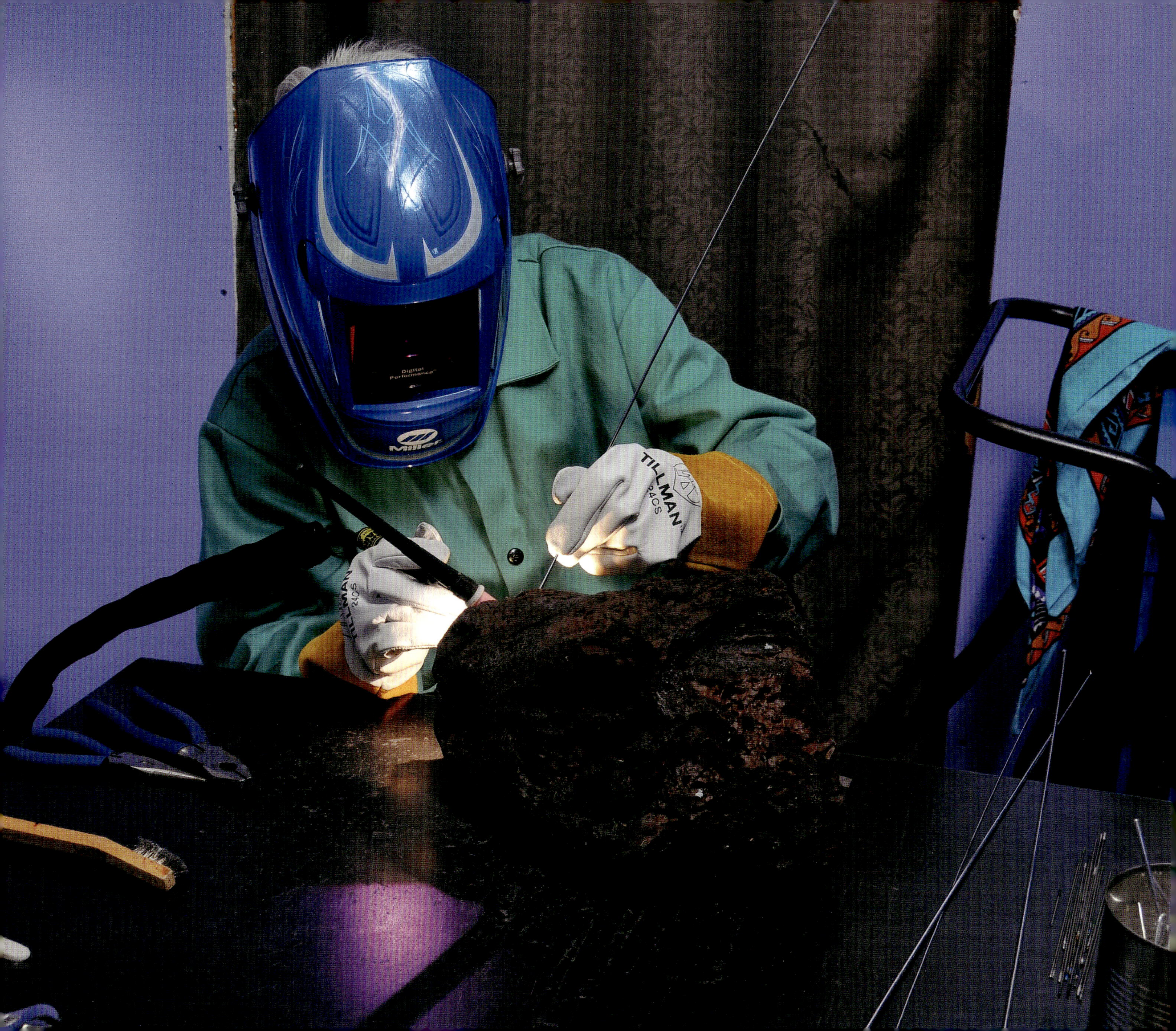
Miller
TILLMAN
24CS

deliberation, she declined. The reason? She wanted to be an artist.

Her art teacher, Monte Hoke, inspired her to go to college and major in art, and she received the Lew Wentz Art Service scholarship, enrolled at the University of Oklahoma in Norman, and received a classical art education.[13] She also worked at the Fred Jones Jr. Museum of Art at the University of Oklahoma as part of the scholarship requirements, and it was here that her future began when a David Smith exhibition came to the museum, and she became enthralled.

The idea of metal sculpture interested her to the point that she enrolled as the only woman in a basic course in oxy-acetylene welding in the industrial arts department. Then she took her newfound skill back to the art department, entered an art show, and won a purchase award.[14] That same year, she was nominated as one out of ten outstanding students of the year.

Things got even better when she next met the man who was to become her husband, Wally Minto, son of a California rancher. They packed all their belongings in back of Wally's hay truck and moved to the Minto ranch in Eagleville, which has been in the family since 1865. Minto jumped into ranch life as if she were born to it. Wally's widowed mother, Edyth, "Mom Minto" to Minto, ran the ranch and was her role model, teaching her about living and working on a remote cattle ranch—including how to kill and dress out a deer, which the family needed for food. "I was scared spitless of her. She had the voice of God," Minto says, smiling, and the two became fast friends. She has now lived in Surprise Valley for more than fifty years. "I became comfortable in the high-sage country and the wilderness canyons, growing deep roots and embracing the silence and solitude."

The couple raised two boys, Tyler and Trent, and ranched. Art took a back seat for fifteen years while Minto helped her husband found and develop a program he named "Alpha Awareness." A natural speaker, Wally began traveling to teach his theories. Minto drew the Warner Mountains and then used hand tools to try out stone carving. "Great art," she says, "has something embedded in it by the energy of the artist." Minto imagined energy going through all her art and felt a connection, even a communication with the rocks. "Those stones gave me the courage to do what I do now."

She wanted to integrate stones with metal and decided to learn TIG welding, "the brain surgery of welding," at Lassen Community College in Susanville, California, under the direction of John Mulcahy. It wasn't easy for her to return to school in midlife to an all-male environment. "To take molten metal and draw with it was incredible." She smiles at the memory. "I wondered how lava rocks would accept GTAW. It had never been done. I had learned that the hard stones like marble and granite don't react well to the expansion and contraction with the heat; they flake. But lava rocks have already been fired by Mother Nature. And lava is more porous, so it handles expansion and contraction well."

She pursued it, and in no time welding on lava became Minto's signature style. Through trial and error, she learned to weld the rocks using a slightly cold temperature. She became an expert at drilling holes, pinning, and pegging things in place, learning how to deal with structural issues. "Unfortunately, all of my beautiful, structurally correct welds are buried underneath texture. I had to learn to develop this texturing process, and I had to break the rules to get what I wanted. The process is a constant one of looking and listening to what the materials are saying." Each piece has its own story, and Minto has created a portfolio to reveal her motivations. "Art is a language. It's not decoration. It communicates something."

Just as lava is a by-product of a violent, explosive, and heat-intensive reaction, many of Minto's most famous sculptures are the result of a trying personal journey. In 1992 her thirty-year marriage was reaching an end, and

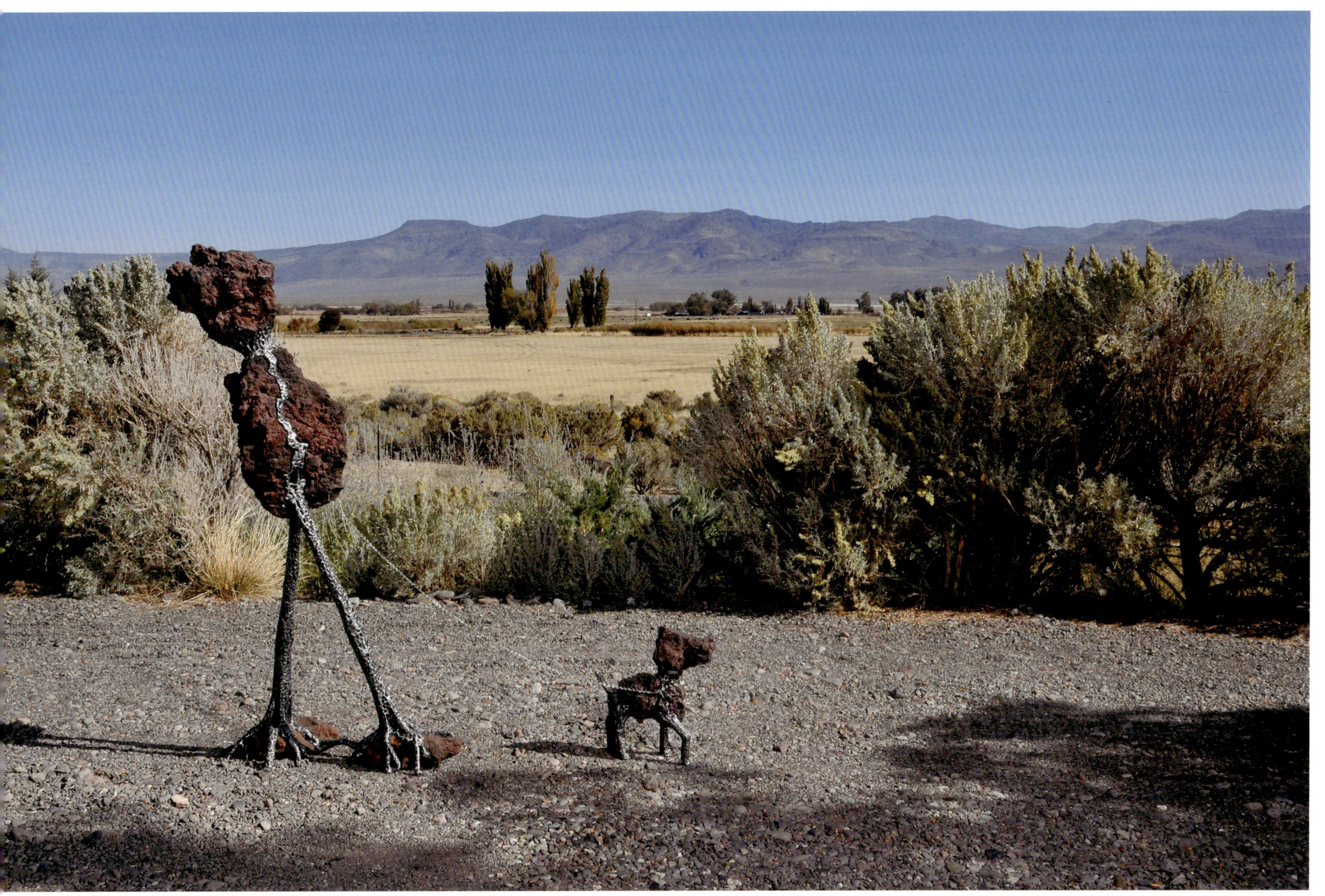

Kay Minto, *Walking the Dog.* Mixed media of lava rock and aluminum; 5 ft. 4 in. x 5 ft. 8 in. x 14 in.

Minto was diagnosed with breast cancer, a result, she says, of "the cumulative effect of years of stress and internalizing my pain." She opted out of chemotherapy and radiation after her modified radical mastectomy, and as she lay alone in her hospital bed following the surgery, she dreamed of the Nike of Samothrace, the winged goddess of victory that was carved circa 200 BC. She awakened and knew she must do her own version of the goddess, as well as choose a more holistic healing approach, drawing on some of the knowledge she'd gained from years of Alpha Awareness study. A week after surgery, she went back to the weld shop to begin her emotional and physical healing process with the help of lava and GTAW. She also began learning tai chi and investigated other alternative healing strategies.

From Minto's pain came the sculpture *Nike of Mastectomy*, a curved rock with her heart to the sky and her wings outstretched as if in flight. After months of work and adding molten metal drop by drop under a cloud of blue-gray smoke, Minto completed the sculpture. With completion came a sort of closure to a difficult life chapter. Together, Minto and Nike leapt into the void, no longer bound by earth's constraints. They were women who flew.

"Finishing the *Nike* for me was a sense of graduation. Thoreau admonished, 'We must walk consciously only part way toward our goal, and then leap in the dark to our success.' I truly feel that my life began again with that sculpture. March 8 is my second birthday—and it's been over twenty years that I have been cancer-free."

Nike of Mastectomy debuted in the rotunda of the United States House of Representatives in Washington, DC. It has traveled the world and served as a source of inspiration and healing to countless people affected by breast cancer. It was part of two traveling exhibits, "Healing Legacies" and "Art.Rage.Us," and exhibited at Tulane University, the Glenbow Museum in Alberta, British Columbia; San Francisco; Youngstown, Ohio; Los Angeles; Saint Louis; and Hong Kong, to name a few. Other

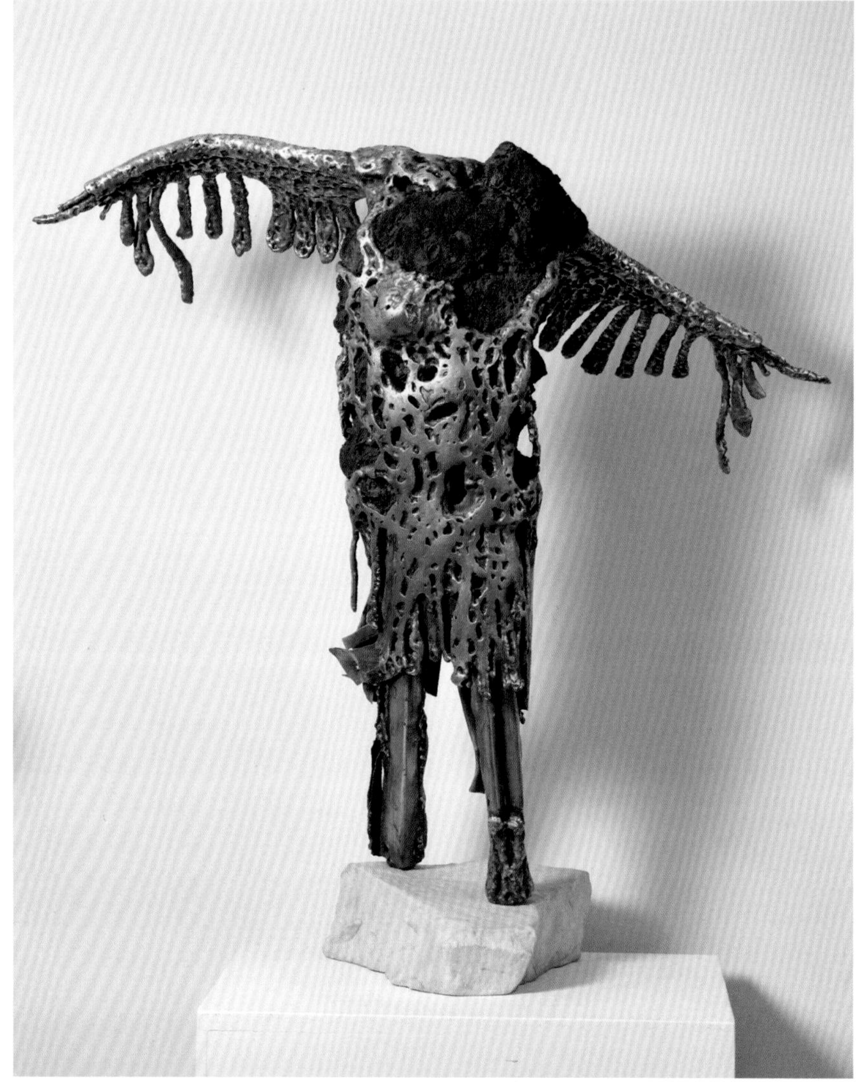

Kay Minto, *Nike of Mastectomy.* Mixed media of lava rock, aluminum; 29½ x 29 x 14 in.

exhibitions were in Reno, Nevada; Redding, California; and various cities in Oklahoma. Her work has been published in several magazines, and she has won outstanding awards and purchase awards in various venues. Recently, she was one of three national winners, Miller Welding Heroes, in a welding contest sponsored by Miller Electric Manufacturing Company.

"I've been told I should live in a place that appreciates sculpture—Seattle, New York City, some large area," she says. But she is rooted here.

As we stroll along the sculpture garden path Minto fashioned among thick stands of sagebrush and juniper, she points out various pieces—some patterned after prehistoric birds and animals—and chats about her life in Surprise Valley. Schoolchildren like to peek around turns in the path and discover a sculpture that Minto has "blended with the land." She describes clearing sagebrush and hauling rock with her hands as she prepared to build her home and studio, with help from her son, Tyler. "We don't get to hunt every year—it's a lottery drawing now, four to five years, if you're lucky." Ever resourceful, she shoots a deer to fill her freezer for the winter, saying she hunts intuitively, and "I only take the deer that offers himself."

She learned following cancer surgery that tai chi practice can boost one's immune system. Presently, she teaches it in the neighboring towns of Cedarville and Alturas, and doesn't let a morning go by without going through her own tai chi practice, which heightens her awareness of energy. Julia Cameron's *The Artist's Way* (1992) has been an important book, and her library is filled with books on healing energy, including Brian Greene's *The Elegant Universe* (2003). Louise Hay's *Heal Your Body* (1982) has been with her for many years, and she reminds herself to nurture herself first before tending to others.

Minto believes that energy is the new science, and that everything is interconnected. "In carving, welding, performing tai chi, or pruning sagebrush, there is an intangible world at play." Much of her thinking comes from readings and personal experience, and the rest from the nature of her valley. She says, finally, "As the sun rises over the Nevada range and lights up the golden aspen on the California mountains behind me, I catch a glimpse of snow on the Oregon crest. And so my morning ritual of tai chi gently ends with a profound appreciation of the beauty and energy of this place."

PATRICIA WESCOTT • BORN 1947

Patricia Wescott holds a deep-rooted doctrine in her heart: "If you believe that something can happen, it does," she says. "You need to be in tune, listening to the wind, or wherever the inspiration and message come from. If you ask for it, it's there." And this spiritual trust has guided her art journey from the time she was four years old.

When she and her husband, Don, retired several years ago, they decided to return to the Great Basin, the land of her ancestors. The couple searched the rugged outback for many months, orbiting the shadow town of Wabuska, Nevada, in ever-growing circles.[15] One autumn day the two rolled down a sagebrush-lined road north of Wellington, and as Wescott squinted skyward to the west, she spotted a group of red-tailed hawks circling a piece of land.

"That's it," she pointed to the grassy earth beneath the circling raptors on the day of our interview, May 24, 2013. "There is our place." It felt like she was coming home.

And it was. Wescott designed a house with many windows, and then sited it so they could see the eight mountain ranges skirting the valley.[16] Their home of many rooms was erected, and while Don pursued his interests in geology, Wescott began to create artworks that she'd held inside all her working years: a *Bamboo Prayer Spirit* that came to her in a dream, a healing talisman for returning warriors from Iraq and Afghanistan, and outside, swaying in the ever-present wind, the larger-than-life *Wabuska Woman.* For media, she uses resources gathered from the land—metal from old junk heaps, feathers, stones, pods, bones, or sinuous sticks burnt from a long-ago fire that must be patiently massaged to their former beauty. "The rusty metal and burnt sticks all have a purpose, just like humans all have a purpose. You can feel it in those sticks."

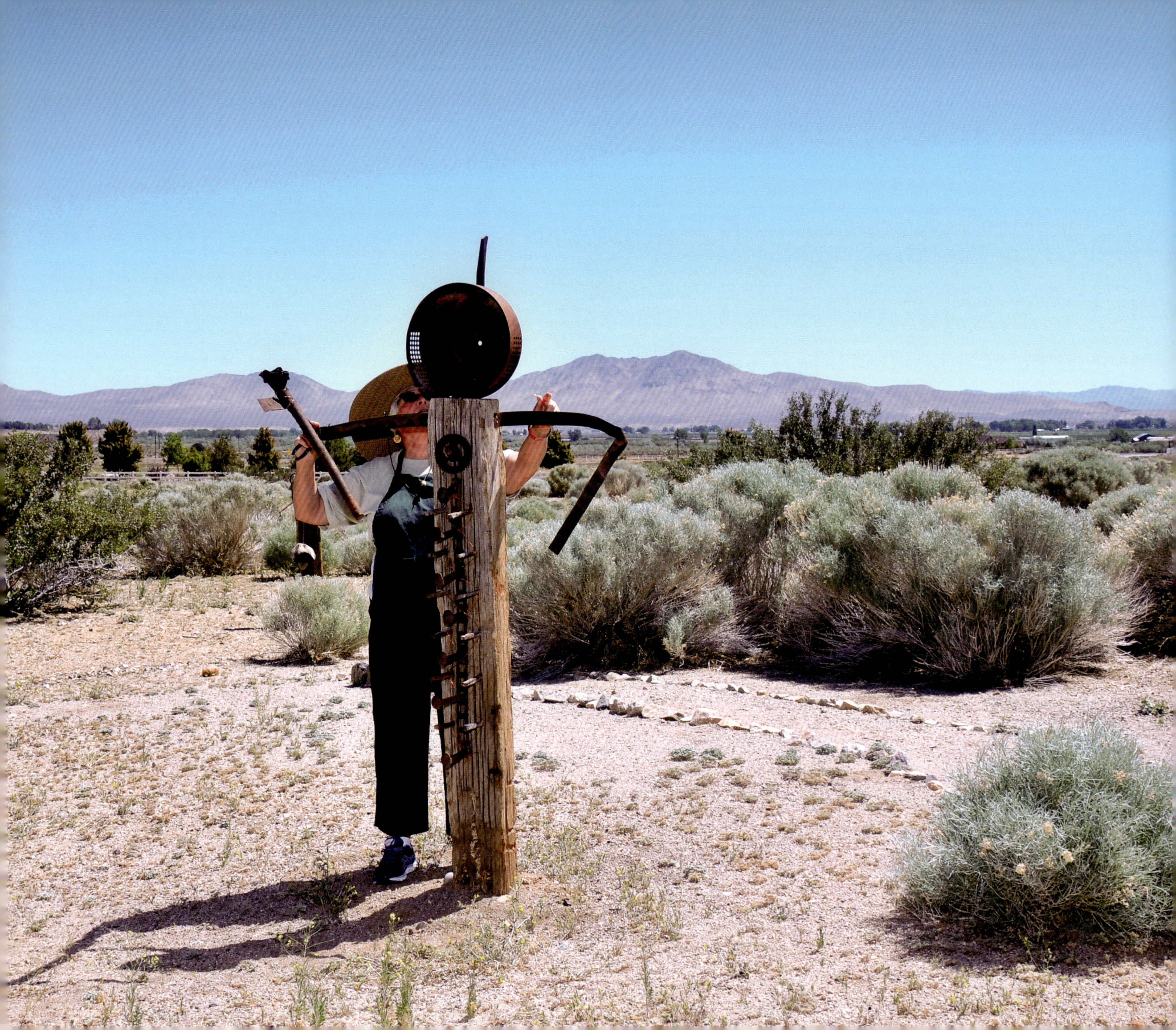

She adds, "I want to cohabit with the environment. We kept all the stone, sage, and ephedra, as you see." She waves her arm around the outdoors and speaks of being in touch with the elements. "I can sit out there on a rock for hours and not see anyone or anything. Every sense is alive. The smell of sage after a rain is special, and there's a unique fragrance of willow, mud, water, and wind that's indescribable. They could make a perfume out of that. I can even smell the snow coming." She thinks for a minute. "I feel the Native people are walking with me. I've been here in this place before."

Wescott's gift of envisioning might have been seeded in her childhood—a childhood in Big Pine, California, where, from the time she could walk, she spent her waking hours out of doors with her family, finding images in clouds, rocks, and trees, and fishing and camping near water and native vegetation. Sadly, her mother was addicted to prescription drugs, so as a child she spent a great deal of time with her Swiss grandmother, Emilie, and German grandfather, Paul Nikolaus, who had moved there from Wabuska. Emilie taught Wescott to knit and crochet when she was four, and the feel of the soft fuzzy fabric over her hands has carried directly into the art she creates today. Many of her current pieces are integrated with handspun yarns, and soft texture is a defining element. "My grandmother was one of the most influential people in my life," Wescott declares, her brown eyes shining.

Although she drew and sketched at every opportunity, enrolling in high school art was not an option, as her parents considered art supplies to be "frivolities." She yearned to be the first in her family to attend college, even though her father announced in no uncertain terms he was not paying for it. So she began to visualize and prepare. Wescott worked three jobs in high school, kept a straight A average, became a cheerleader, and was involved in school government. "I stayed out of trouble. I always had a plan because it was up to me. I stayed focused on my goals." She was chosen to attend Girls State and received the American Legion award.[17] "It was awesome to meet girls like me who had visions and future plans. I realized I wasn't crazy." During that time she was also caring for her mother, cooking, and keeping house, while, she says, "Dad was a martyr." Her father rarely spoke except in negatives, and living in that situation felt oppressive and hopeless, as if there were no tomorrows. Wescott wanted out.

She tried Whittier College in Whittier, California, where professors encouraged her to attend California State University, Fresno. Wescott enrolled, and her mentor-teachers purchased her books for the entire four years of her attendance. Scholarships, loans, her supportive teachers, various jobs, and her seasoned practice of envisioning the dream sailed her through to graduation with a double major in art and education. While creating art in college was not the focus for prospective teachers, learning about it was, and Wescott's fascination with art burned brightly.

At age twenty-four she met Don, a twenty-six-year-old veteran of both the Korean and Vietnam Wars, on a blind date. "I wasn't going to settle for just anyone," she says. "I had a list of what I needed in a husband." The two clicked right away and recently celebrated their forty-second wedding anniversary. Both agree they are blessed. Neither one really wanted children. "If it doesn't fulfill you to have a child, then you shouldn't," Wescott declares.

Today, the Wescotts's children are the wild animals in the great outdoors near home, while inside the artist creates small characters—personas that are quiet presences in various rooms of their home. *Cat Woman* honors her cat spirit. *Moonwalker* carries all her wares on her back, including sticks for her fire. "She's a nomad traveling the desert." Wescott describes *Bamboo Prayer Spirit*, a figurative sculpture of gourds, fabric, and more, holding a bamboo prayer stick. "She was a vision," Wescott explains. "I saw her on the side of a hill praying in a bamboo forest." Later, Wescott watched a TV special about the gorges in China, and says, "I

Patricia Wescott working on *Wabuska Woman*. She has constructed similar figures to be placed in each of the four directions surrounding their home.

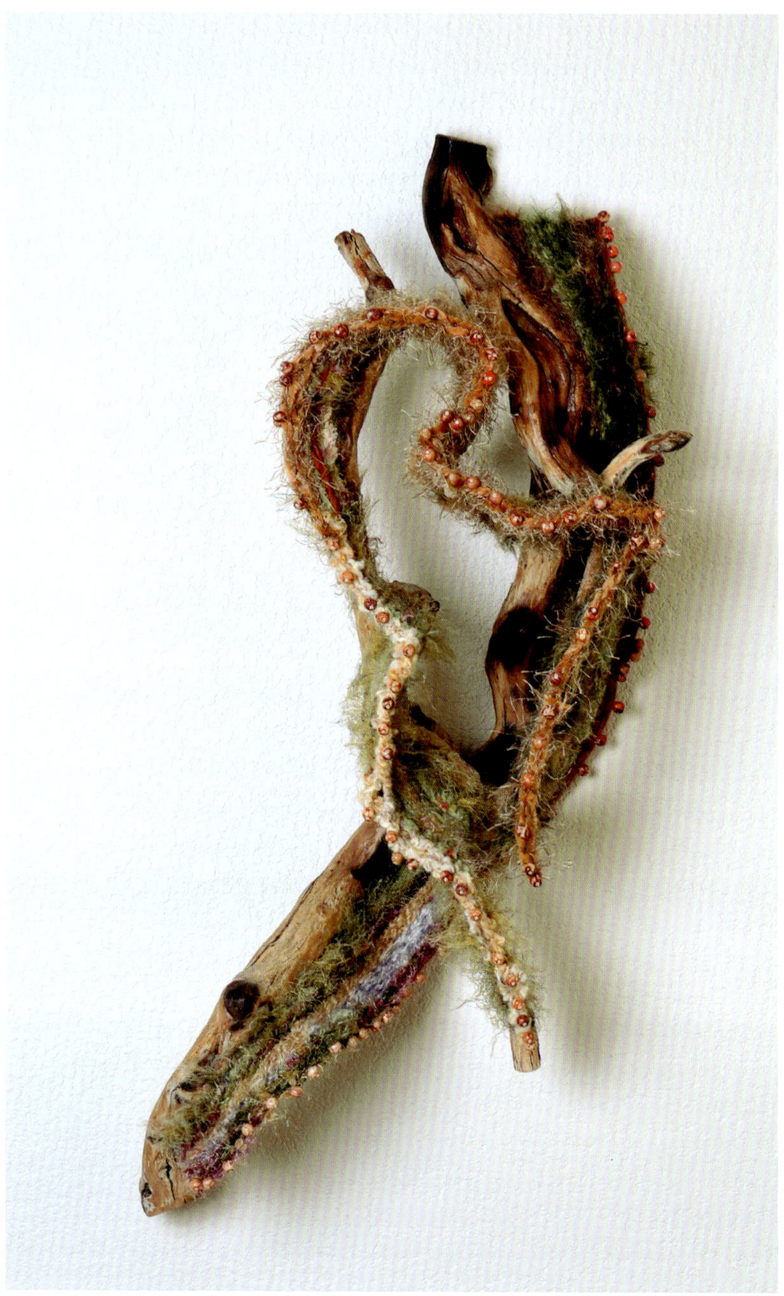

Patricia Wescott, *Out of the Dark, Into the Light.* Mixed media of burned root, bamboo skewers, yarns, beads; 14 x 31 in.

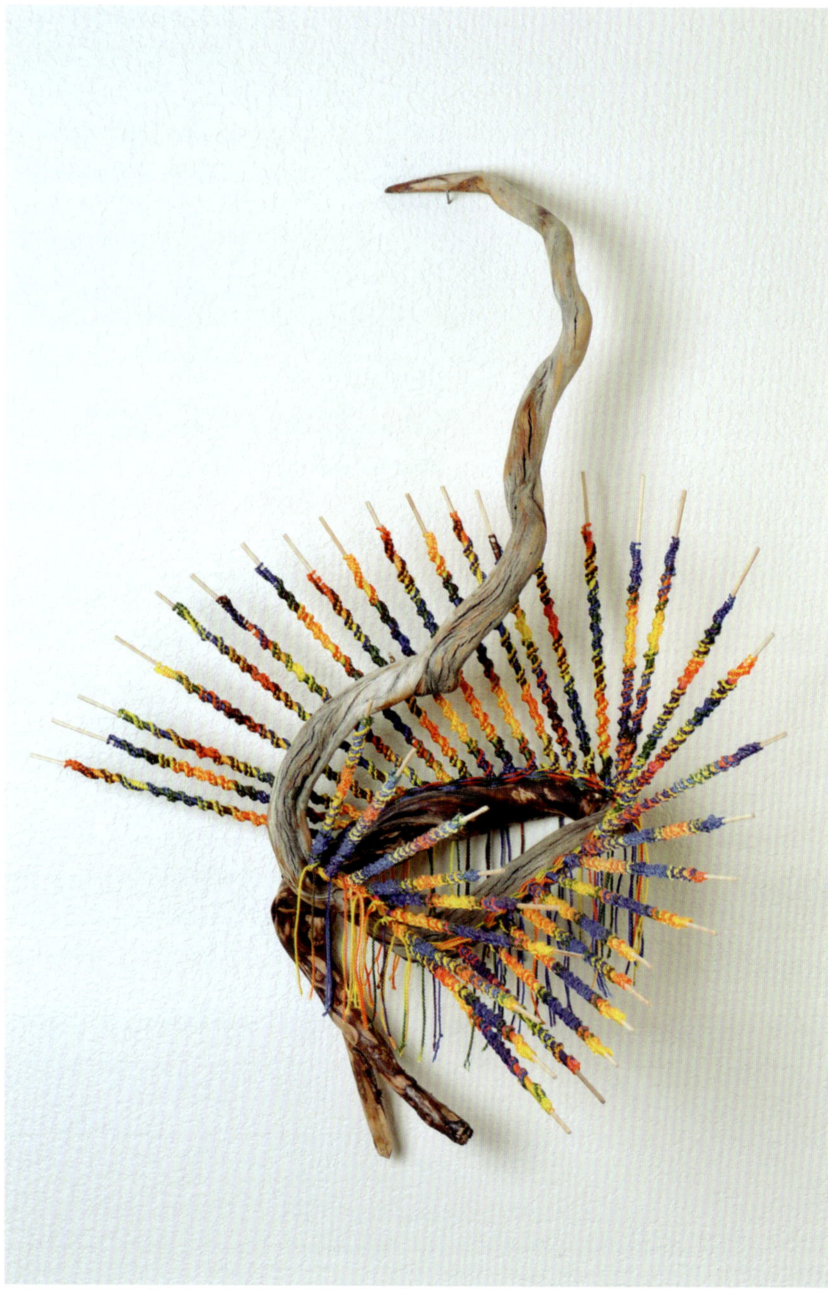

Patricia Wescott, *Dragon Spine.* Mixed media of root, bamboo skewers, string; 22 X 28 in.

realized it was a real prayer, her praying for her land not to go into the water." She sobered. "I got goose bumps when I realized that."

The warrior talisman of gnarled wood and various fibers alludes to those who return from war and need to heal. She pointed to the stick. "This piece of wood was burned; it took me a week to clean it up. I wanted to restore it to its natural beauty. Some parts are burned beyond repair. When you come out (from war), you are burned—but inside you are beautiful."

Wescott is currently developing a piece to be called *Try and Catch the Wind*, and she will dye dryer sheets to resemble prayer flags and weave them on individual sticks. She is a devout recycler. "I can't throw things away," she tells me.

We step out the back door, past the prayer walk that the couple is building to circle their property, and view the imposing *Wabuska Woman* swaying in the afternoon breeze. In Wabuska, Wescott found some old metal package strapping, and her husband discovered an old railroad tie that might have been driven over by her grandfather a century earlier. Wescott pounded spikes into the sculpture and attached the strapping. The figure's head is an old cover from an engine with rusty gears she found on an abandoned ranch.[18] Standing tall among the sage, grasses, and bitterbrush, *Wabuska Woman* (*White Grass Woman* to the Washo people) seemed to be a sentinel of her place, a sort of Statue of Liberty for the Great Basin.

Wescott eventually became a school art director for the Monson-Sultana Elementary School in Tulare County, California, while working for the Tulare County Office of Education. During her working years in special education, she taught art projects to students with both physical and mental disabilities in five schools, from preschool through eighth grade. She would travel to each school, her Honda van stuffed with all the materials needed for the day. The experience not only engendered a very clear sense that staying in one's authenticity was the real stitching in the fabric of life, but also encouraged her to experiment with a wide variety of media. To this day, everything is possible when Wescott builds a sculpture.

As she neared retirement, she asked herself, "What's next?" Wescott joined the Fresno FiberArts Guild and enrolled in workshops given by professional, enthusiastic teachers. "They were great and powerful people," she said. "Interest groups expanded concepts into any media and mixed them with contemporary ideas." She took gourd and basket classes at the Discovery Center (now Garden of the Sun Demonstration Garden) in Fresno, and there she met Carol Rookstool, dean of curriculum for the Fashion Institute of Design & Merchandising in California. Rookstool was first a role model, then a friend and mentor, and the two remain close to this day. That experience at the Discovery Garden set her on the path of her own discovery, a path she still travels, finding inspiration everywhere she looks.

"I joined the Great Basin Basketmakers in Reno and entered a show before we ever moved. I met Cheryln [Bennett], who got us into the [Artists Co-op Gallery Reno] Co-op and the [Nevada] Rock Art Foundation.[19] Now Don and I volunteer every week." She adds, shaking her head in amazement, "I was handed all these blessings on a platter."

Wescott has her own unique approach to creating a sculpture, and during this time she stays completely away from social media. "They really interfere with my process," she tells me. And her workplace must be clean and free of clutter.

First, Wescott is in what she calls the *smoldering* stage, creating and dreaming. Here, she needs to be "tuned in and have my receivers wide open and be willing to experiment with new media or combinations." Sometimes this period is overwhelmingly abundant. Next comes *doodling,* where her multiple ideas are set to paper. She doodles in the car and during meetings on scraps of paper and in her many journals that burst with ideas. Interestingly, she envisions her pieces completed in all dimensions before she even begins. Next, at the *gathering* stage, she brings together all the parts that will make up the finished piece. This stage could last an hour, a day, weeks, even years. Then comes *the hunt,* where she searches for parts that make the piece come alive. And finally she reaches *the zone,* the actual creation process, where she blocks out the outside world. "I don't eat or pay attention to time, sound, anything. It's not necessarily healthy, but that's what I do."

Sculpture in all shapes and colors grow from her hands, and Wescott is frequently invited to participate in art sale shows. But she disdains resumes, most shows, sales to collectors, and the like, echoing sentiments of the late American sculptor Elizabeth Catlett. This African American sculptor and graphic artist wrote, "I do know that I followed an alternate path as an artist. I was not interested in making money and becoming famous. . . . When I physically transform a raw material into an aesthetic expression of the life of my people, I feel complete as a human being."[20] She is what UNR art professor Rebekah Bogard would call "a rugged Nevadan." Wescott creates sculpture that comes from her own depths, regardless of trends, acceptable media, or salability. "I don't care whether or not I'm accepted into the art world," she says, leaning against *Wabuska Woman*'s warm wooden torso. "I don't need that validation to continue or not continue. I'm just comfortable in my own skin."

"My head is full all the time. A rock, stick, ball of yarn, string at Lowe's Hardware, or an item from a cooking store can get me going. And the Internet is my oyster," she says. "Life!"

As photographer Susan Mantle and I point the blue Camry toward Reno and our busy lives, I reach the hilltop, brake, and turn to view the Wescott home settled so comfortably into its desert environs. I look upward and see two red-tailed hawks circling.

KATHLEEN CURTIS • BORN 1941

Author Dawna Markova (2011) believes we've been trained to think of ourselves as perpetual motion machines, like stair climbers in a gym. And how, Markova wonders, can we be in conversation with what is hidden inside so we can slow down and explore those things that make us more alive?

Earth-sculptor Kathleen Curtis discovered how to have that inner conversation. But when she first embarked on the path of a spiritual artist, she wasn't having any kind of conversation at all, at least not to her way of thinking. She was simply moving in bumps and false starts toward a finish line she could not yet see. Back when she dropped out of high school art class, she had no idea she'd one day be a professional artist, building mythical beasts and goddesses inspired by dreams and ceremonies, using mud, of all things, as her medium of choice. Curtis's work has appeared in museums and public spaces as well as national publications, and has been represented in galleries across the country. She coauthored a book about Native American basketmakers of the Great Basin and has been in demand to offer museum workshops and private mentoring.[21] These days she creates artwork in her studio/barn and gardens with the same red earth she has used in her sculpture for many years.

On the warm day of our interview, on June 24, 2013, she strides down the lane to meet us, her gray hair swinging in rhythm with dangly quail earrings, and her smile radiates the wisdom of a woman who knows who she is. Curtis is the only artist in this book who does not live and work in the Great Basin, but that region is, she says, her inspiration. She mentions trips to Pyramid Lake and participating in ceremonies there, being blasted by wind and sand, wading in the water and watching the pelicans soar, "all of it becoming part of me." She recalls listening to Native people's stories and collecting earth, sticks, bones, and rusty objects along the way. "I can almost smell the warm earth and the sage, see the rabbit brush blooming in the fall." Especially in Nevada, she says, the earth is in evidence, without

Kathleen Curtis sifting earth, the first step in creating a sculpture.

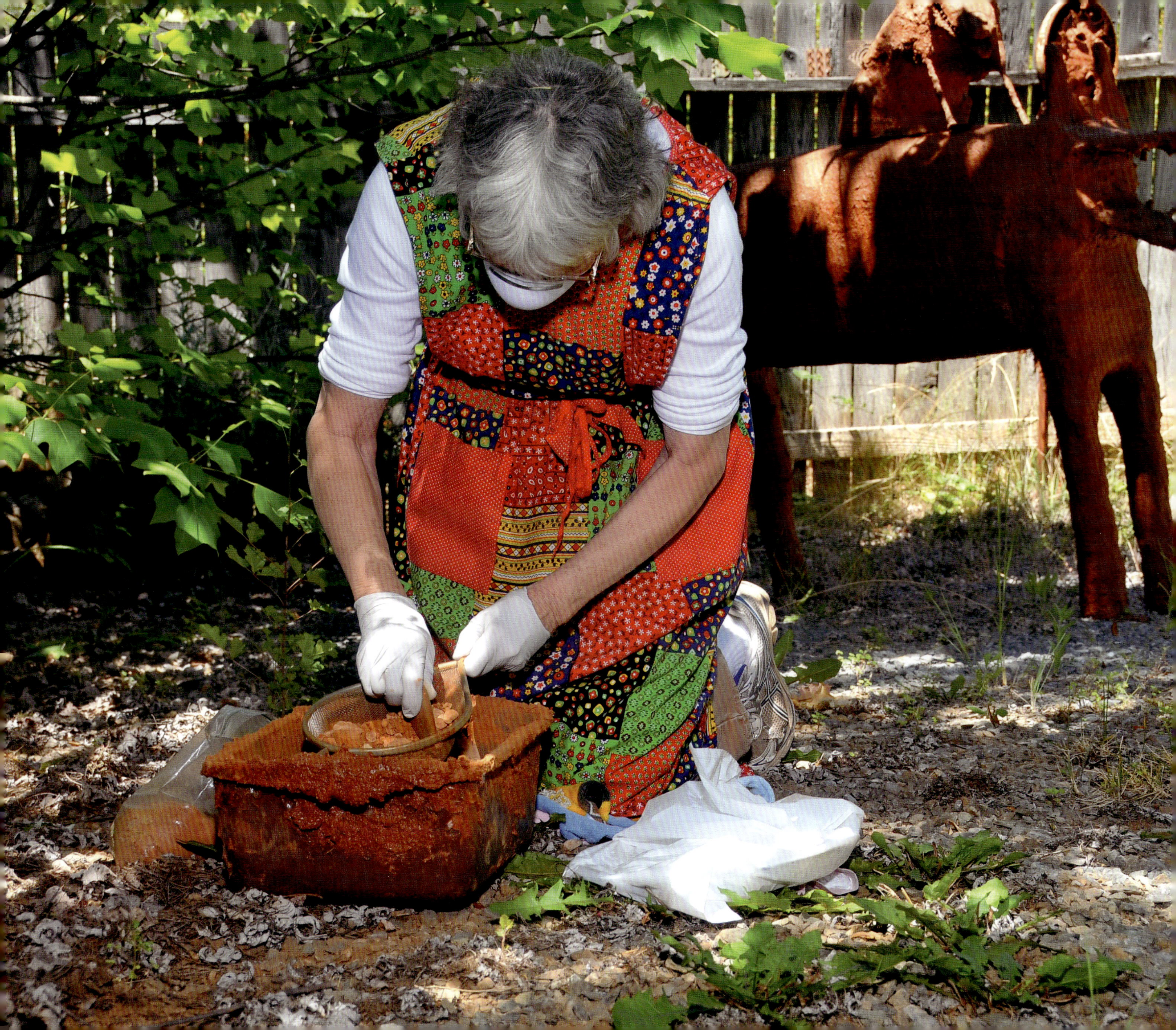

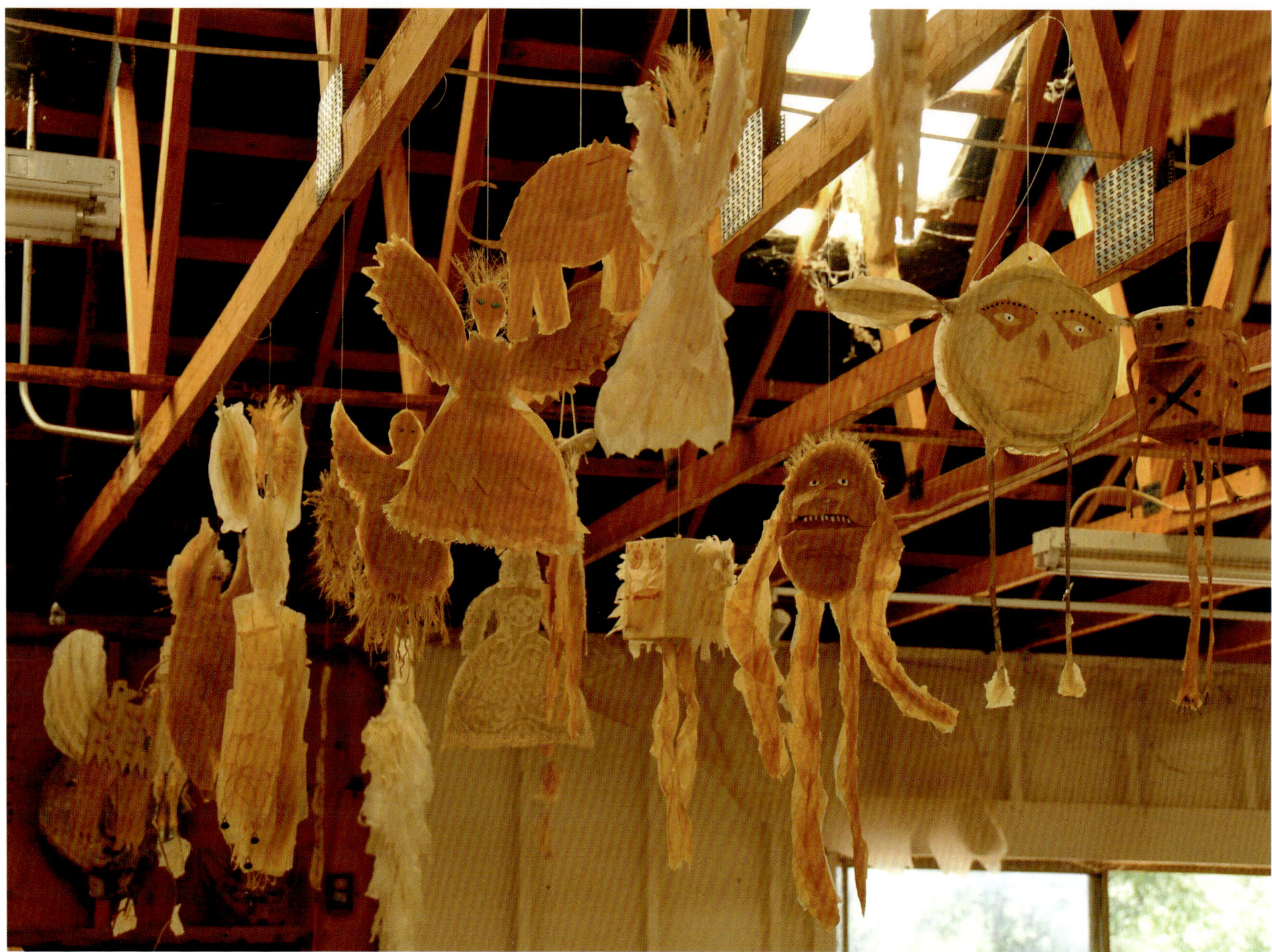

Kathleen Curtis. Dancing figures swaying from Curtis's studio heights.

distraction of multitudes of trees. "The texture, the shapes of the hills—it's in me."

Curtis introduces us to *Ranger Bob,* her larger-than-life earth sculpture standing at the fence to welcome visitors, and we head to her barn/studio. I walk through the outsized door into her studio and am greeted by a happy crowd of human- and animal-like objects fluttering from strings attached to ceiling rafters. Some of the translucent figures have raffia hair, their faces smiling or worried or bemused like Charlie Brown in a Peanuts comic strip. Long paperish legs and arms swing in the cooling breeze that wafts between the two open barn doors. For centuries, dolls like these have emanated to humans a sort of holiness, and these fragile dancing ceiling figures seem to be our welcoming committee.[22] Curtis made them from used-tea bags and coffee filters, treated to a state of near-transparency. But there is so much more than paper in these presences that swing joyfully from the heights.

A shelf along an entire wall holds small, labeled jars of earth that friends have brought from their travels. Curtis will use this earth to make her small healing earth goddesses, portable sculptures that she gives to people who need healing of one kind or another. Traveling friends carry her healing women to countries around the world, including Turkey, countries in Europe including Ireland, Machu Picchu in Peru, Australia, and to Nevada's Black Rock Desert and Hawaii in the United States, and to other locations. "It's my way of healing the earth," she says simply. The rest of the studio is filled with rusty relics from a ghost town, sage, stones, bones, stacks of handmade paper, fibers, and the skull of a wild mustang. An altar holds prayer sticks, feathers, messages, candles, icons, and more. In a large corner gallery completed sculptures adorn walls and pedestals. Nearby, her idea table holds work in progress, and she mentions some that will become prayer sticks that are meant to be touched, shaken, and prayed over. When a person she knows or reads about seems to need a prayer, she will create a prayerful blessing on a treated coffee filter, embed it with feathers and crystal dust, and place it with others inside what she calls a *prayer basket.*

We pull up chairs to talk, and Curtis notices me watching a spider crossing the floor. "They are welcome here," she says, and then begins her story.

Born in Portland, Oregon, Curtis remembers only one thing: rain. Soon afterward, the United States was embroiled in World War II, and her father, Tony Moore (a dentist), was assigned to March Air Force Base (now March Air Reserve Base) in Southern California. The family moved to nearby Riverside, where she grew up. As an only child, she always drew pictures, and her parents encouraged her. Her dad, who enrolled in a painting night class, took one of his daughter's drawings to show, and the instructor said, "This is the best picture in the class!" That comment encouraged Curtis, and not only did she continue to draw, but she also began designing doll clothes; it was the beginning of her love of three-dimensional work. In the unfortunate high school art experience, the teacher had insisted on a focus on perfect perspective and color charts; it was enough deterrent for her to skip art until enrolling at the University of California, Berkeley. There, with continued support from her father, she majored in the subject.

"Everything was very free at Cal," she says. "You could do anything!" Teachers Glen Wessels and Karl Kasten were very encouraging, and Curtis painted to her heart's content. She fell in love and married graduate school student Dick Curtis, who was home from the Marines, and she obtained a teaching credential ("That's what women did those days!"). She taught school during the day and painted at night, adding collage and assemblage to her work. The couple moved to Donner Lake, California, where her husband established a dental practice and Curtis began teaching through California's Artists in Schools program. There, she developed various techniques that would serve her later; feltmaking, weaving, papermaking, and coiled basketry were her favorites.

Her basket works grew. They stopped being utilitarian and became large, sinuous sculptures that eventually wound up in galleries and national publications.

Three events happened to rearrange her artistic path. First, Curtis met Tahoe City, California, spiritual artist Jonda Friel and others, and they formed an informal group that began holding ceremonies. She remembers the first. "We made a structure out of living willows by tying them together." The friends sat under the structure and brainstormed the powerful yearnings of one another, and then they translated those meanings into sketched symbolic images. Around a central altar, created with special talismans each had contributed, and under the fragrant willow dome, the women spoke of their dreams and yearnings. Then they returned home to build on the symbols and discussions that arose in the circle.

It was the first of many ceremonies to take place in secluded nature sites between Lake Tahoe, California; and Pyramid Lake, Nevada. The women would begin with passing smoke over one another, or smudging, with handmade fragrant sage bundles. Sometimes they designed colorful symbols on the ground—crushed blue corn, dried yellow sunflower petals, red ochre from the earth. There might be song, drumming, or dance. Developing ideas that people can work magic by creating a vision and then directing energy toward it inspired Curtis and her friends to conduct fire ceremonies, where they symbolically burned old outmoded traditions and discussed fresh beginnings to freely bring the work of their souls into the world.

The second event that impacted Curtis's life was more concrete: The Walt Disney Company planned to clear old growth timber at nearby Independence Lake, one of the most pristine alpine lakes west of the Rockies, and develop a mighty ski resort and recreation area. For the first time in her life, Curtis fought back. She joined other environmentalists and worked to halt the development, and the group was victorious.[23] She'd become aware of the importance of protecting the land and its animal inhabitants from more unwanted growth and attended meetings and wrote letters for other proposed projects. Curtis applied for and received a seat on the Nevada County planning commission, and there she was often the lone dissenting vote. But by now the activism had settled in her bones. She joined others at isolated Rock Creek, Nevada, where Shoshone medicine man Corbin Harney, in his work to prevent the area's development, described the talking waters and heart-healing pond and spoke of other ways in which this ancient gathering place was sacred. She participated in a memorable sweat lodge there, sitting with others inside a covered mound of willow hoops and perspiring floods of impurities in the steam generated from fiery-hot rocks. Later, during a Citizen Alert trip across Nevada, Curtis sat one night with a group around a bonfire at the Duckwater (Nevada) Reservation, to hear Shoshone elder Lily Sanchez tell traditional stories about flying wolves and water babies. Back home at Donner Lake, she initiated an Earth Day project where children made tiles, prayer flags, and other objects along a fence to bring attention to the value of the environment.

Curtis continued creating her sculptural forms, and now they were becoming ceremonial, touched with symbols and shaped for ritual activity. She began to daub them here and there with the earth she'd been championing for so many years. Meanwhile, hostilities at the planning commission were escalating; the anger generated was not conducive to her art or health. "I figured," she says, "if other people wouldn't step up, maybe it wasn't worth the grief." She abandoned her environmental clashes, and interestingly, when she left, "Other people did step up and formed a conservancy."

She took time out to collaborate on a book about Native basket weavers, and she says it was one of her most important accomplishments. Her favorite artist of all time is Betye Saar. Other inspirations came from Lucy Lippard's writings and from reading about the lives and determination of artists Georgia O'Keeffe and Louise Nevelson.[24] She was moved at the way the late San Francisco Bay artist Susan Seddon Boulet created paintings of women who morphed into animals—deer, mountain lions, wolves.

Threading throughout her book, *The Spiral Dance (1979)*, was a question that author Starhawk suggested we ask ourselves: "What is sacred to me, and where are my life energies going?" It was Curtis's time to express her vision of a holy

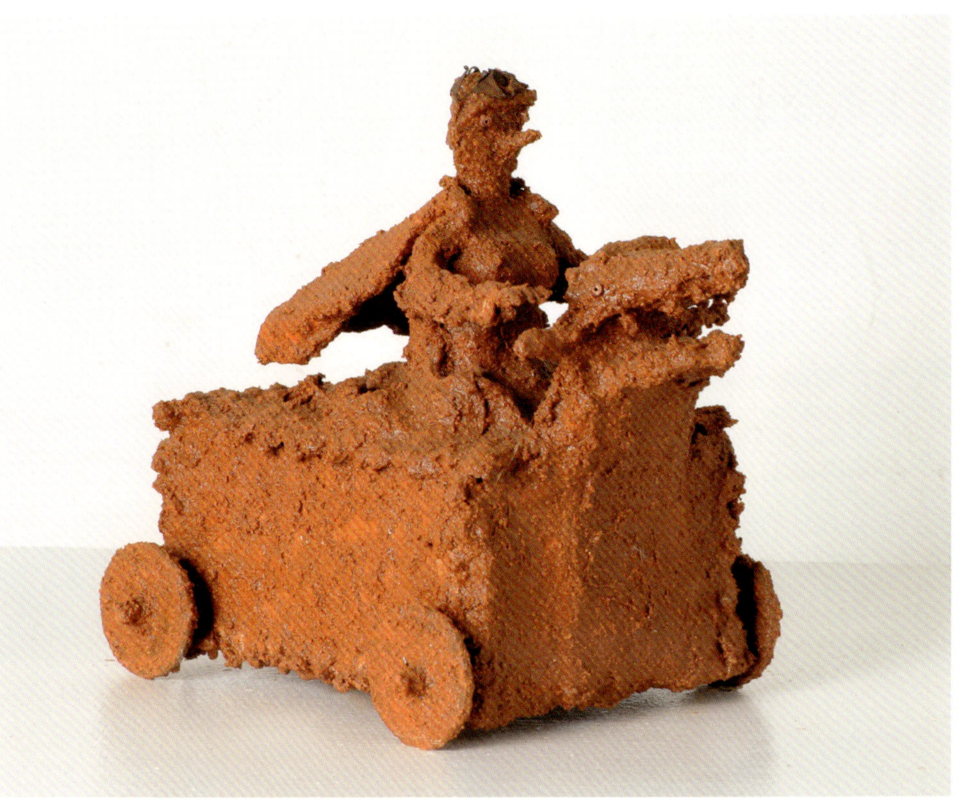

Kathleen Curtis, *The Queen's Ride.* Earth sculpture; 7 x 10 x 10 in.

and healed earth in the only way that felt right—through making earth sculpture. She experimented with resins and combined them with the earth she'd been collecting over the years. She designed armatures for figures that would, when completed, tell stories that resonated with myths and whimsical tales she'd read about or invented after studying ancient cultures and rituals of Australia, New Guinea, South America, and Native America.

"When I gather earth for my work," she says, "I always leave a gift, whether I collect it from the track of a bear or deer in the woods, near my home, or from Nevada's rich black earth used to dye bracken fern roots for Washoe baskets. I use earth in my work with great reverence."

She joined a dream circle and began to identify the wild, potent night dreams that floated through her head. First, she created life-size mummy bundles after reading about Peruvian work, using earth, acrylic resins, and burlap (coffee bean bags) over armatures. And that was the beginning. She rented a small studio, then moved it into a larger space in Truckee, California. Hundreds of sculptures followed, such as *Spiritual Synthesis* and *The Queen's Ride*. Curtis secured the services of a professional photographer and sent slides out of her work; she found shows and galleries in other states, and it was the beginning of a long and fruitful career. "Of course there were rejections," she tells me. "But getting rejected made me stronger. I knew I was an artist."

The third life-changing event happened when Curtis joined a new group of professional artists, the Wild Women.

Eventually, her husband retired. Their son, Matt, had moved to New York, and later to Seattle, Washington, and the Curtises decided to seek a climate that didn't involve shoveling mountains of snow. That place was a solar home and studio on six acres in Pilot Hill, California. Curtis delights in deer that come down from the forest to drink from the pond, and lizards, bees, bullfrogs, and other creatures who have found homes among her earth sculptures that are placed in hillocks and cubbies, near trees and gardens, greeting human and animal visitors alike. Her son, Matt, visits family frequently, and grandchildren Clementine and Clyde delight in artmaking projects at the studio/barn.

And Curtis, now at an age when wisdom counts, observes that youth is the only thing that matters on television. She's proud of her gray hair and face of expressive hills and valleys. She earned it. She continues sifting the earth, creating her mythical figures, and enjoying her secluded piece of heaven. She has indeed fulfilled Markova's suggestion: she explored all those conversations that made her more alive.

Notes

1. Native baskets are called *cradleboards* in many parts of the United States. However, those in the Great Basin are made of willow, the same material utilized in the majority of the baskets. Hence, Great Basin tribes—Northern and Southern Paiute, Western Shoshone, and Washo—refer to their baby baskets as *cradlebaskets.*
2. The basket dance is a blessing dance, blessing the materials and the basket as a sacred gift to the Paiute people. When they dance the basket dance, the women are praying for abundant food for the coming year. They carry handmade willow baskets used to gather, prepare, and store food. The Stone Mother is a tufa formation at Pyramid Lake. She has engendered creation stories and it is said her tears formed Pyramid Lake. The area around her is sacred to the Northern Paiute.
3. Fowler, a research associate for the Nevada State Museum and the Smithsonian Institution National Museum of Natural History, is an anthropologist whose work has focused on preserving the cultures of the Native People of the Great Basin. She is professor emerita of UNR.
4. This process is described in Fulkerson and Curtis, *Weavers of Tradition and Beauty*.
5. To be enrolled in a tribe, you must prove your lineage or descent. Rebecca's mother's family is from Pyramid Lake.
6. Casinos are open twenty-four hours a day; swing shift goes from 8 P.M. to 4 A.M. This is the most sought-after shift, because there's more activity and a much larger tip pool. In those days, casino work paid women better than they were paid in other fields of work.
7. Reno's Coral Academy of Science is a public charter school sponsored by the Washoe County School District. It was established in 2000 by a handful of University of Nevada, Reno, science professors who were concerned with the lack of science and technology being taught in Nevada schools. They have evolved from a STEM (science, technology, engineering, and math) to a STEAM school (adding the arts).
8. The vision quest is a rite of passage, a universal and ancient means to seek deep understanding of life's purpose.
9. The term *pyrography* means "writing with fire." Flores says it's a traditional art of using a heated tip to burn or scorch designs onto natural materials such as wood, leather, and gourds. A vast range of natural tones and shades are achieved by using various tips and temperatures.
10. Many languages translate the word *tia* as *aunt*.
11. The State Organization on Arts and Disability provides quality arts opportunities for all, focusing on children and adults who have a disability, are disadvantaged, at risk, or underserved by the arts.
12. GTAW is generally defined as an arc-welding process that uses a nonconsumable tungsten electrode to produce an arc to melt filler wire and to fuse metal to the welded target material. Tungsten inert gas (TIG) welding is the same process as GTAW.
13. This type of education is a broad study of liberal arts and sciences.
14. A purchase award is a pledge from businesses and individuals to buy art.
15. According to publisher and ghost town expert Rich Moreno, a shadow town is "still more than a memory but less than what it was once" (2010). Wescott's revered grandparents once lived in Wabuska, where her grandfather worked at the railroad depot.
16. The eight mountain ranges are the Pine Nuts, Buckskin, Singatse, Pine Grove, Wassuk, Sweetwaters, Wellington Hills, and the Sierra Nevada in the distance.
17. Boys State and Girls State are summer leadership and citizenship programs sponsored by the American Legion and the American Legion Auxiliary for high school juniors.
18. "Old dumps are part of our Great Basin past," Wescott tells me.
19. Artist Cheryln Bennett was northern Nevada's first gourd instructor and is a mover and shaker in the Reno Artists' Co-op and helped start the Nevada Rock Art Society.
20. From Mara R. Witzling, *Voicing Our Visions:* Writings by Women Artists, New York: Universe, 1991, page 11.
21. Fulkerson and Curtis, *Weavers of Tradition and Beauty*.
22. Clarissa Pinkola Estes, in her book *Women Who Run with the Wolves (1992)*, calls them small facsimiles of self.
23. This land will remain protected following its sale to the Nature Conservancy by owner NV Energy.
24. Los Angeles, California, artist Betye Saar collected images of African American figures from folk culture and advertising and incorporated them into collages and assemblages; later she combined shamanistic fetishes with images to evoke the magical and mystical. She was part of the black arts movement, challenging myths and stereotypes. O'Keefe and Nevelson persevered with their art into old age.

STAGING

Author and art professor Dave Hickey (1993) said, "The vernacular of beauty, in its democratic appeal, remains a potent instrument for change in this civilization." And from the standpoint of those who value democratic culture, this is all to the good.

Wearable Art refers to individually designed pieces of handmade clothing, purses, and jewelry created as fine or expressive art. While the making of any such article requires aesthetic considerations, the term *wearable art* implies that the work's intention is a serious and unique artistic creation or statement. It transforms the wearer into a dynamic, performative artwork.

Like all art, it communicates ideas on a visual level. It often employs symbolism to infer abstract concepts. An examination of all of it requires a consideration of the social, cultural, and political climates in which they exist.

Wearable art was the first true women's art form, and it is high time to give this form of sculpture the acknowledgement and credibility it deserves.

This chapter features two jewelers, Barbara Uriu and Gail Rappa; two wearable artists, Jimmie Benedict and Jill Altmann; and a maker of sculptural purses, Jill Atkins.

BARBARA URIU • BORN 1950

The Japanese word *shibui* describes an aesthetic of subtle, unobtrusive beauty. *Shibui* objects seem simple at first glance, but a closer inspection reveals understated details—textures, planned imperfections, shadowy lines—that balance simplicity with complexity. *Shibui* jewelry might offer contrasts—elegant and rough, for example.

The gemstone jewelry of Verdi, Nevada, artist Barbara Uriu embraces *shibui* sensibility. No wonder her work is presented in galleries and magazines around the West. The Japanese American National Museum is one of her exhibitors, and collectors from Hawaii to Washington, DC, wait years for their name to reach the top of the list to purchase her one-of-a-kind pieces. Uriu (pronounced "yer you") pins, bracelets, and pendants offer *shibui* balance, and their highly engineered subtlety ensures that, because no frills are added, her pieces instantly draw the eye as they radiate strength and invite a deeper look.

One piece designed to be either a pendant or a brooch might have been influenced by nature. Shaped like a leaf, the piece is a druzy stone, a nontraditional stone that occurs in nature in the interior of a geode. The bright pink color is natural in color and sparkle. Uriu loves combining unusual stones. The bracelet illustrates this sensibility, as well as her basic principles of color, texture, and balance.

A lifelong collector of rocks, Uriu designs and fabricates her extensive collection of gem art—from boulder opals and Tahitian pearls to diamonds, cobalt, tourmaline, and hundreds more—with 14-carat and 18-carat gold and sterling silver sheet and wire. The artist has worked with ammonites from Russia and fossilized tortoise shell. She has used white turquoise from Tonopah, Nevada, and a cabochon stone (shaped and polished but not faceted) cut from silver mined in Nevada.

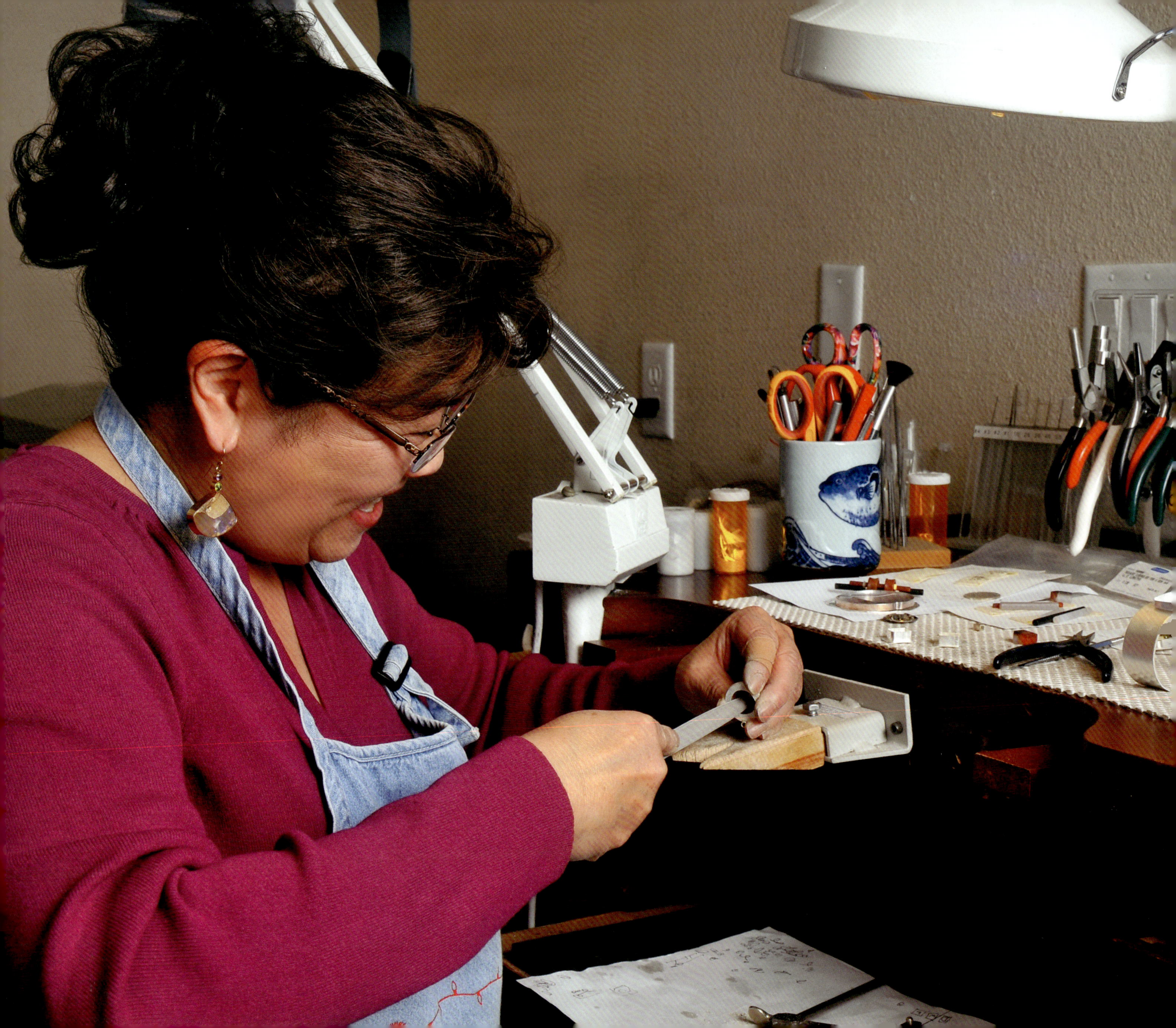

Today, January 14, 2014, Susan Mantle and I have followed a path under twittering birds through lush vegetation landscaped by Uriu and her husband, Don. After enjoying tea and snacks in their living room beside a plate of freshly gathered leaves, we tour her studio that is lined on two sides with file drawers containing all the elements needed for her work. Rose-tinted pearl earrings dance against jet-black hair as she looks up after describing a stone composition in progress. "I finally found work where precision is not only important, but required." She has highly regarded perfection all of her working life.

"Half of my job is engineering. I first visualize something that looks beautiful," she holds up a leaf, "but it also has to work." Her ideas always come from nature, and she pulls out boxes, drawers, and papers with stones of various types, colors, and sizes arranged as part of the design process. "I'll wake up in the morning figuring the design and process through, switching from right brain to left." First, she considers dimension, color, proportion, and textures; then she spends "an inordinate amount of time" determining the engineering process before she cuts the first piece of metal. "I never cut a piece of metal without knowing exactly how the piece will be engineered." Next comes the complicated process of determining the metal and preparing it, fitting it around the stone in a tight, perfect fit. Shaping, filing, and soldering involve several steps and many hours before the piece is cleaned and polished. She must use a respirator and surgical gloves through her operations. She writes copious notes with each piece. Her unusual composition of stones from around the world, surprising color combinations, and minimalist designs reflect not only her agricultural background, but also her Japanese American heritage.

Born in Worland, Wyoming, Uriu was the second daughter of Kaz and Toshie Uriu. Kaz had leased a farm, then purchased bare land from the Bureau of Land Management's Desert Land Entries program, and went on to make the desert bloom. "My dad was very forward thinking. With an engineering background, he revolutionized sprinkler systems in the Rocky Mountain West, and his financial and technical success was highly regarded." But the road to Kaz's success was paved with tears—tears his daughter didn't shed until later, when she learned his dark secret.

Meanwhile, the young artist relished farm life. Uriu enjoyed following her grandmother, Seki, who lived with the family, up and down hills, picking wild asparagus and chokecherries and hunting for stone treasures. "Born in Japan, my grandmother was a great inspiration to me, because of her skill in making handmade items, her pride of workmanship, and her reverence for nature." Barbara joined the 4-H Club program at the age of eight and learned to sew. Like Seki, she'd always loved working with her hands, and now she made clothing from beautiful fabrics.

But her worldview was about to have a makeover. One day when she was nine, Uriu sat on the front porch chattering and cleaning wild asparagus with Seki, wondering if she'd be a pharmacist as her grandmother had been long ago in Japan. The girl ran inside and pulled an old, dented colander from the kitchen shelf, then dashed to the porch and handed it to her grandmother. Seki hugged the colander to her body and began to sob, her shoulders shaking, and the green asparagus spears scattered over the porch like so many pick-up sticks.

Shocked, Uriu ran to her mother, and that's when she heard the story. "I couldn't believe it." On December 7, 1941, life changed for Japanese Americans when Japan's attack on Pearl Harbor set off World War II and a wave of fear and suspicion against the Issei and Nisei.[1] President Roosevelt authorized the military to conduct forced removal of 120,000 persons of Japanese ancestry. Groups along the West Coast wanted to rid the region of Japanese. "My dad was taking engineering at a college in their hometown of Los Angeles, and he was evacuated, along with his parents

Barbara Uriu has a tool for every step in the jewelry design process.

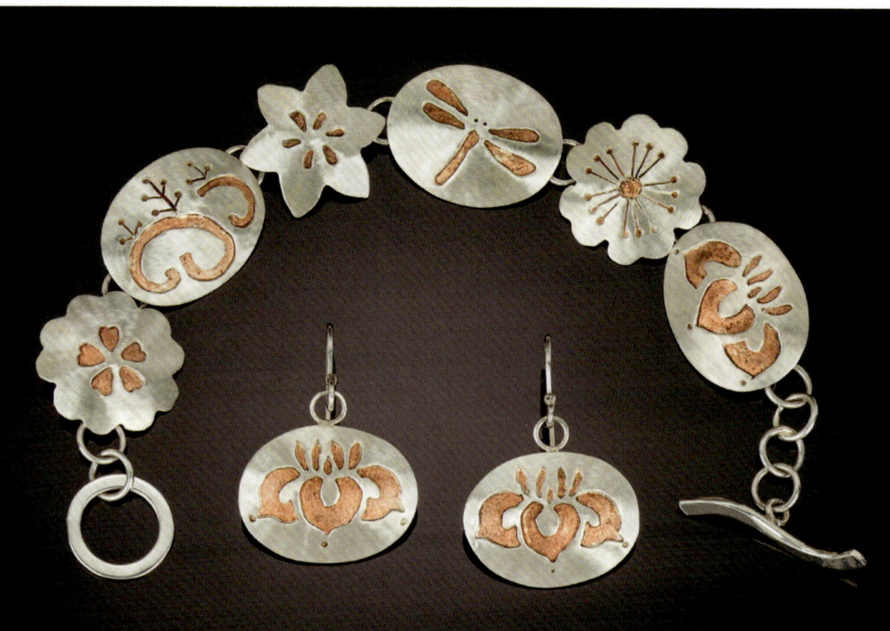

Barbara Uriu. Japanese "Mon" Bracelet and Earrings. Sterling silver, copper; 1 x 7¼ x ½ in. Reproduced by permission from David Orr Photography.

and nearly 15,000 other Japanese, to Heart Mountain," a hastily set up internment camp in the desert near Cody, Wyoming, and there they lived through scorching summers and bitter winters until 1945.

Uriu was shocked. "My dad never talked about it. No one had said a word to me. My mother then told me that Grandma carried that colander all the way on the train from California." The colander was one of the few items she chose, as each Japanese American could take with them only what they could carry. Many things became clear to Uriu after that revelation. She knew she was different. Once, at school, when the girl stood to answer a question, the teacher told her to sit down, and when she asked her mother about it, "Mom said 'because you have dark eyes and dark hair, people are going to see you first,' and that translated to either my advantage or my disadvantage."

Another time Uriu, who had perfect attendance at the Methodist Sunday School, came home in tears. "I told my mom, 'You and Daddy aren't going to heaven because you don't go to church,' and Mom said, 'Oh, honey, daddy's a farmer. He works with God all day.' My mom just made it all okay."

Uriu continues, "Our generation, the Sansei [third generation], were raised to be all-American kids. We were expected to get straight As, do the right thing, and never get caught in a compromising situation. We never learned the Japanese language because of the prejudice. The work ethic, oh, my God, the work ethic! My greatest fear would be that I would become lazy. My parents had to prove themselves and I had to prove it on their behalf. The Japanese mentality is, 'You never want to shame your family.' Shame is the greatest of sins."

Uriu says there was never any bitterness in the family because of the concentration camp experience. "Sometimes law students from the University of Wyoming would come and talk to Dad, and he would say, 'Everyone suffered as a result of the war, and Heart Mountain was my suffering.' But," she says, "he never talked about it and I knew it was inappropriate to ask him."

Later, as an adult, Uriu became a founding member of the Heart Mountain board of directors, dedicated to passing on the Heart Mountain story to future generations (www.heartmountain.org). The Heart Mountain Interpretive Center opened in 2011.[2] Uriu also served a term as a member of the board of governors for the Japanese American National Museum in Los Angeles.

Uriu believes the Japanese internment situation made her more mainstream because she became Americanized. "I may have a face that's different, but I sound like you. All of a sudden you forget I'm different." She continues, "I wish people who suffer prejudice would understand. But if you

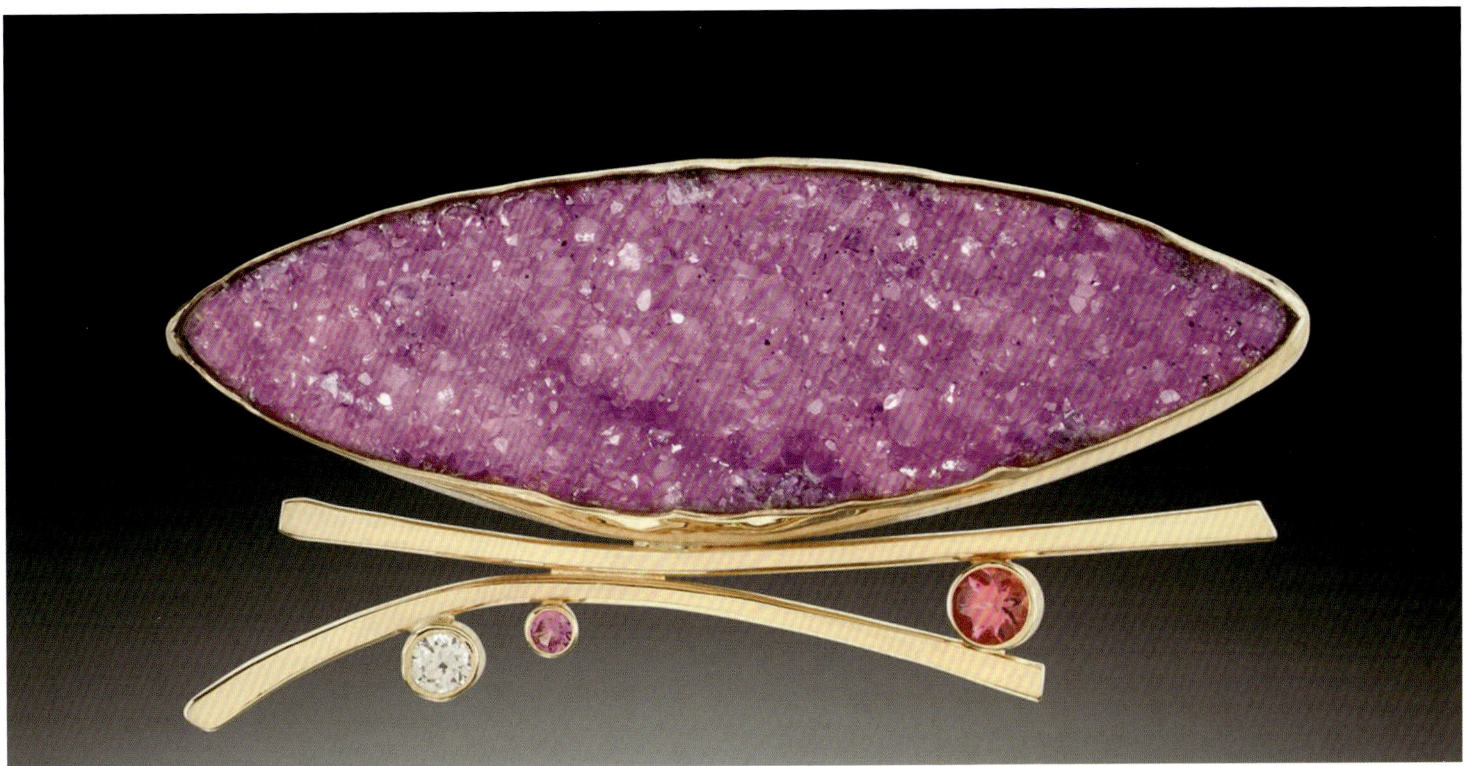

Barbara Uriu. Gold pendant/brooch with stones, 14kt. yellow gold, cobalt calcite drusy (large stone), faceted round pink tourmaline, and 1ct round diamond; 1¼ x 2¼ x 1½ in. Reproduced by permission from Hap Sakwa.

speak your home language, people think you're different and can't get past it." Actually, she says some people can't get past the face. But now that she's matured, "I like being different because it makes me more interesting. Now I like being Japanese."

Part of that pride came from reading Muriel's Barbery's *The Elegance of the Hedgehog (2013).* "The Japanese gentleman in the book exhibited the richness of my culture so eloquently. I was reminded of the importance of taking pride in my work and doing it well." Uriu designed one bracelet of Japanese family crests of Mon.[3] She says, "they are all official Mon, with the exception of my dragonfly design." The flowers are cherry blossom, Paulownia, clematis, and iris. The bracelet was her most labor-intensive work, a homage to her culture, and is not for sale.

Interestingly, her mother remained in Billings, Montana, during the war, staying with her family, who owned a restaurant. "My mom came from a proper family. She got straight A's and took piano lessons; they were well known in the community. She was an evolved person, friendly and gregarious."

By the time Uriu was in high school, she was making most of her clothes, she went on to obtain her bachelor of science at the University of Wyoming and her master of science from Kansas State University in textiles; she became a textiles specialist at the University of Wyoming. Jewelry and gems were still in her future, but she never stopped collecting stones and admiring their beauty. Then came a marriage, which became extremely unhappy and ended in divorce. This sad time, however, was about to turn around, for she met Don Rolston. That meeting eventually led to marriage and, Uriu believes, her rebirth, because her husband gave her all the support she ever needed.

She followed him in his career, joining the faculty of universities where they traveled, and in Flagstaff, Arizona, she was introduced to gemstones. She studied under jewelry Spectrum Award winner and designer Sondra Francis; and when the couple moved to Reno the first time in 1981, Uriu worked with this designer and learned to focus on the movement of the lines of the stone. It was the beginning of her love affair with creating jewelry, and Uriu says, "I reinvented myself. I found Reno and the Great Basin open and receptive to people who are making new beginnings in their lives."

In 2000 Uriu and Rolston moved to Reno for good, where together they built and landscaped their home in Verdi at the base of the Sierra Nevada. "Don said now it was my turn. He was important in Wyoming and could have stayed there, but he came with me. He drives me to the Tucson show, schlepps my cases up and down stairs, and takes me to shows. We've now been married a wonderful thirty-two years."

How does she continue to reinvent such original, coveted work? At each year's end, she meets a long-time friend, Susan, in Tucson, and they perform a ceremony. It's based on a Native New Mexico tradition, where the people take all the beliefs and objects they want to let go of and stuff them in a big puppet, a *Zozobra,* and then they have a big celebration and burn the paper. "Susan and I meet and review the previous year's life goals and discuss them. Then we take the things we no longer want and write them on pieces of paper. We go to a parking lot and burn them. Then we talk about what we're looking at for the coming year." Uriu meets each year with a fresh page in her life, happy to be alive and creating.

Since childhood, nature has been her motivator, her inspiration, her solace. "As I work in my studio, I watch the changing of the seasons, my garden grow, deer, mountain lions, hummingbirds, hawks, and falling stars. I collect rocks, leaves, twigs, and weeds. I have lived my happiest years in this environment."

GAIL RAPPA • BORN 1969

A growing number of artists have moved out of the box of tradition to develop jewelry's mythic, spiritual, or symbolic element. Gail Rappa of Tuscarora, Nevada, is one of them. During the hot August 21 day of our interview in 2013, we're chatting in Rappa's studio, a remodeled former assay mill she shares with her husband, landscape-painter Ron Arthaud. (The couple also transformed a 1870s brick-assay office, only steps away, into a comfortable family home.)

Rappa points to a silver pendant embedded with a small bone, then a bracelet of small silver shadowboxes whose linking squares each contain a tiny, shrine-like diorama. "I often stamp special inspirational reminders on the backs of my pieces," she says. "Sometimes it's a quote from a favorite poet or author, or a poem or thought of my own." She turns over both items so I can read the messages stamped on the back.[4] "The relationship between the person who wears one of my pieces and myself is really an intimate one because there's the public part of it and the private part. It's an opportunity for the person that only they know about." And, absorbing this explanation, I begin to view Rappa's jewelry as installation art that is fully complete only after it has been incorporated into the aesthetic of its wearer.

A bright summer sun pierces the studio windows and floods two compact work areas—a workbench for soldering, piercing, hammering, and so on, and a table for the finish work of refining and polishing. A bevy of doll figures from all parts of the world (some created by Rappa herself)

Gail Rappa at work in her studio.

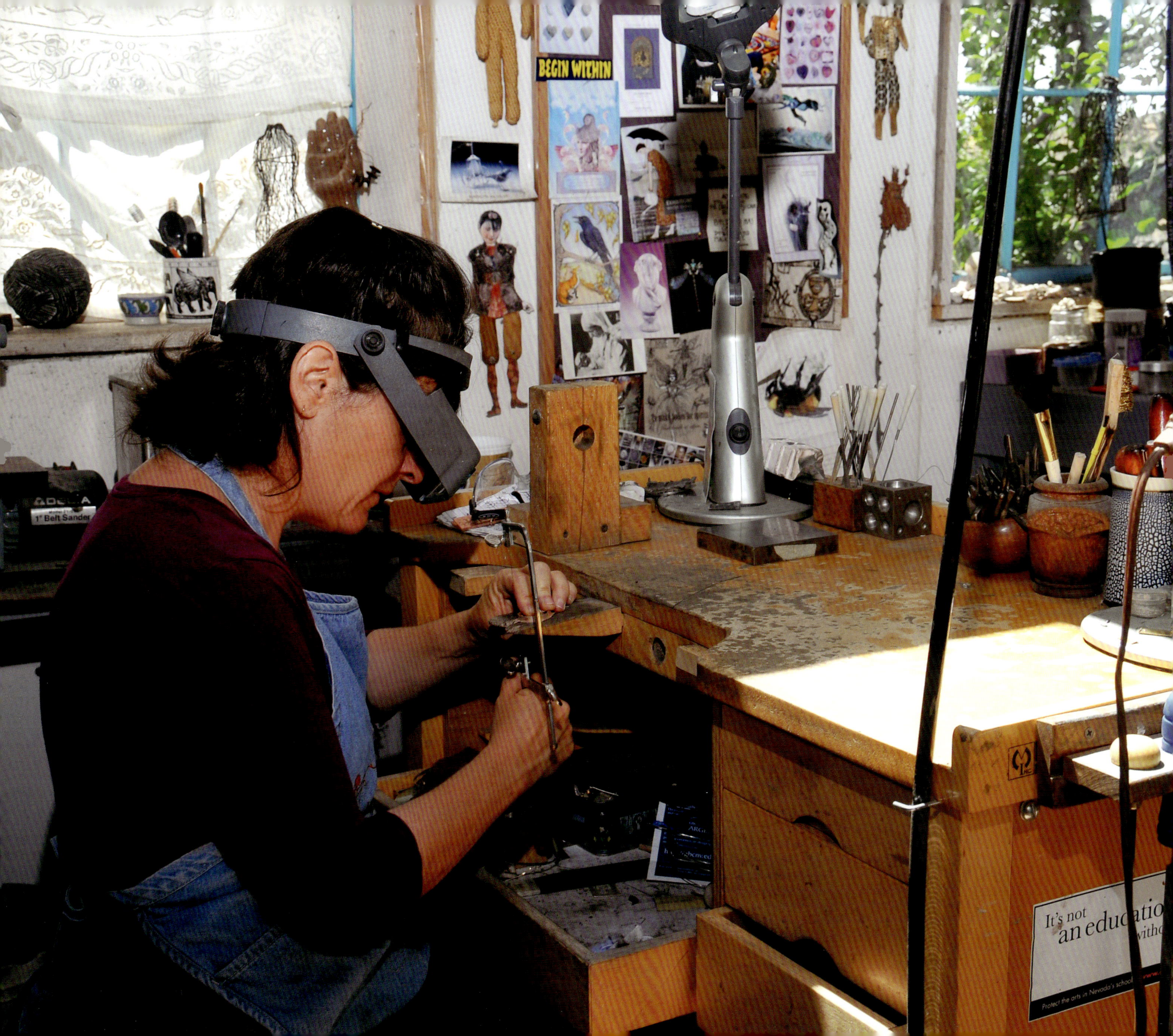
BEGIN WITHIN
1" Belt Sander
It's not

gaze down from the ancient plank walls, happy companions to the artist at work. Windows to the natural outdoors line three sides of the studio, while halfway up the wall of the fourth a hollowed cavity holds soft blankets, pillows, books, and a journal. Here Rappa does her art imaginings. Below this inspiration cubbyhole, a compact professional display stand filled with some of Rappa's jewelry sits center stage, for this is the big weekend, Tuscarora Open Studios, where hundreds of art lovers and curiosity seekers like me converge. A former mining town in Elko County and now a haven for artists, Tuscarora overlooks the sage-covered hills of the vibrant ranching community of the Independence Valley.[5]

Photographer Mantle snaps shots, and Rappa glances out a window. This is an important day for her—the grand opening of the Tuscarora Society Hall, a project she and her husband initiated more than a decade ago. It started when Rappa formed the nonprofit Friends of Tuscarora and Independence Valley. She not only wanted to preserve the town's rich history but also sought a deeper sense of community. The group raised $20,000 to purchase the old stone tavern and partnered with Elko County to get the building restored. It now serves as a community gathering place as well as a venue for displays about the colorful history of this once-flourishing town. Rappa worked hard to meet today's opening deadline, and it seems like the world has come to Tuscarora this weekend.[6] The Independence Valley 4-H Club is firing up a barbecue and a steady stream of cars and pickups crawls up the road, headed for the festivities. Rappa apologizes; she is needed elsewhere.

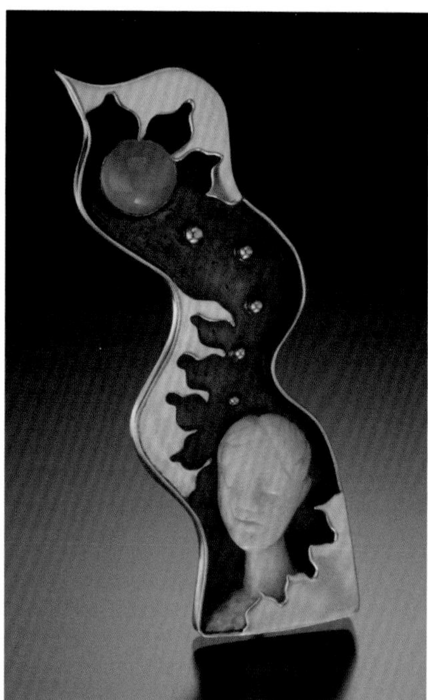

Gail Rappa, *Moon Dreams*, pin/pendant. Sterling Silver, 14kt gold, moonstone, carved bone; 1 x 3 in. Reproduced by permission from Hap Sakwa.

We set a date for a future interview. Before heading out, we admire Arthaud's plein-air work in the adjacent studio, then trip along the stone path to the house to say hello and to meet Theo, eight, and Serafina, two and a half. Rappa had said that both she and Arthaud are equal participants in childrearing and home upkeep. "There's no way I could have done any of this if it weren't for Ron."

"Any of what," I wonder? And several days later, from inside the Great Basin College Art Gallery forty-five miles away in Elko, I learn the answer.

Amazingly, tending to family, her art, and the Society Hall isn't all she does; Rappa is also curator of 130 linear feet of gallery (plus six display cases). That's a lot of space to fill. She finds the artists, hangs the work, does the labeling and the press, and throws an artist reception. Rappa is off to the races, for the show must be in place before school starts the following day. Once again, we reschedule our interview.

Our third and final interview happens on a perfect day in late summer. Arthaud and the children have dropped off Rappa at the college near an outdoor table, where we sip water and chat. We look out over brick buildings planted in acres of perfectly clipped grass. A slight breeze rustles the leaves of the maple tree hovering over us, and this idyllic scene belies the story unfolding from her lips. I hear it and understand so much more about what makes this artist tick.

"My dad was a pragmatic guy and I emulated him a lot," she says. "Mom was the passionate and creative one. I ended up having both sides." Born in Poughkeepsie, New York, the youngest of two boys and two girls, Rappa was

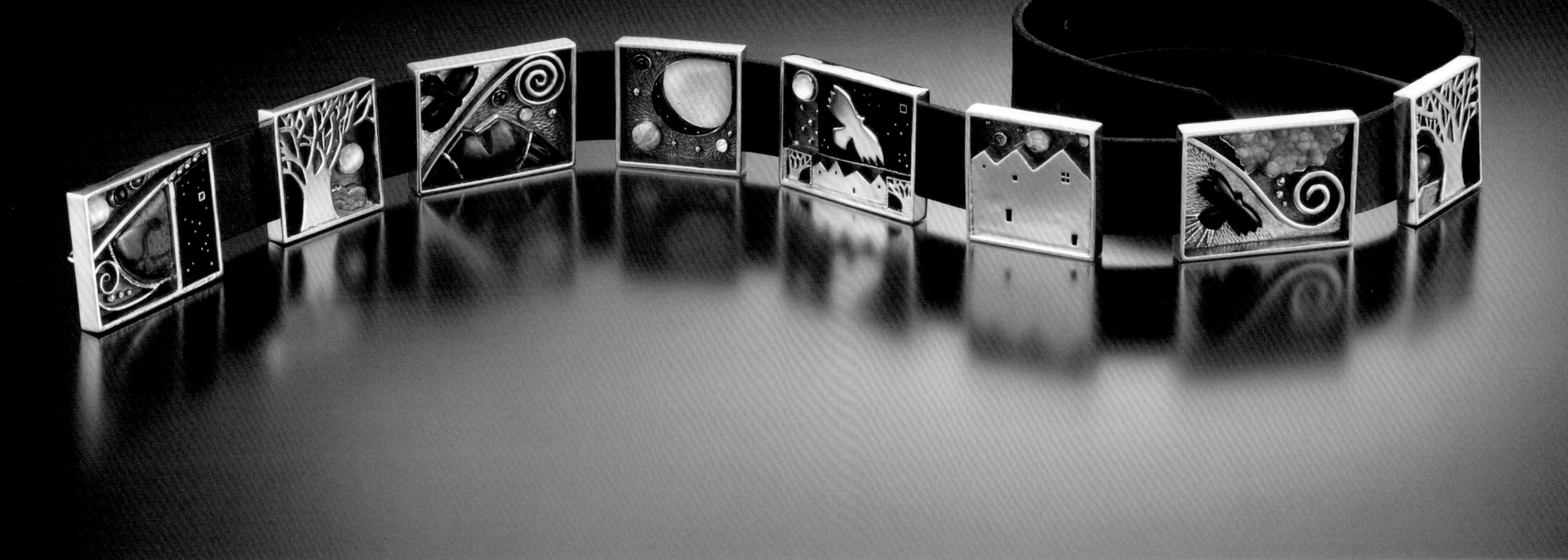

Gail Rappa, *Raven Finds Home,* shadow box concho belt; one buckle, seven conchos, sterling Silver, 14kt gold, carved jet, sugelite, moonstone, amethyst, opal, iolite, purple chalcedony, drusy quartz, leather, copper slides. Reproduced by permission from Hap Sakwa.

four when the family moved across country to San Jose, California, where her father was a computer engineer. Her grandparents followed, and when her grandmother, an accomplished Sicilian lacemaker, taught her to sew, Rappa became aware of making things by hand. "She had this big bureau and would pull out the drawers and then she'd pull out jewelry, cameos, handkerchiefs, and keepsakes from her childhood, and would tell me the story of each one. It gave jewelry and objects a history and an importance to me."

Three years later, her parents divorced and the family was split—their father kept the boys in San Jose and their mother took Rappa and her sister to Palo Alto. As a seven year old, she thought, "At least I'm not a little kid; I can handle this." But she would have a lot more to handle in the coming years—her dad remarried and the readjustment was a challenge for the whole family. When she was ten and her dear brother, Tommy, was sixteen, he developed leukemia and died three years later, leaving a devastated family.

Fortunately for her, there was art. In those days, Rappa says, art funding for schools was abundant and art was popular. She painted, built pottery, and wrote poetry in her elementary school classes, and artmaking took her thoughts to another realm above the difficulties of her everyday world. In high school, she signed up for more art classes, and her teacher, John Robinson, was a great influence and support; they've stayed in contact over the years. "He'd take a group of art students to the Museum of Modern Art in San Francisco, and we not only got to learn about contemporary art, but we also got to take the train home all by ourselves!" Robinson encouraged Rappa to enroll in a summer program through the Academy of Art University in San Francisco, which offered her a scholarship. She did that, making the drive daily with another art student from her high school. A yearning to attend the famous Rhode Island School of Design was quashed because of lack of the necessary funds. After finishing high school, the plucky graduate headed for Santa Fe, New Mexico, knowing not what she sought, only that she didn't have it yet. She stayed with an aunt temporarily, and eventually, amid struggles with personal and career issues, found an apartment as well as a job at a folk art import store. She advanced rapidly from waiting on customers, to designing all the store displays, to becoming the buyer. In that capacity, she traveled to surrounding reservations purchasing items for the store. "I will never forget the day I walked into a room completely jammed with concha belts," she says, describing the glitter and the feeling of beautiful excess in that room.

Still seeking that "something," she entered therapy and enrolled in a variety of classes at the local community college. Then one day in 1994 she spontaneously put her dog, Mavis, in the car and headed to the northern California coastal town of Mendocino, where she fell into an arts residency in ceramics. While there she also took some jewelry classes, but "I distinctly thought it was way too labor intensive compared to clay."

However, that opinion was about to change.

At year's end, she returned to Santa Fe and began working with jewelry designer Victoria Maase Stoll, and later with Susan Green. To keep up with the high cost of living in Santa Fe, Rappa began making and selling her own jewelry. In 1996 she met Arthaud, and in what she calls a "crazy roundabout story," they eventually ended in Tuscarora. Rappa's jewelry designs developed rapidly and with distinction; by the time of her relocation, her work was being sold in a handful of prestigious galleries.

"When I got to Tuscarora, our house wasn't livable yet. We were house-sitting for other folks in town and Ron set up a studio for me right away. I needed to produce quickly to keep up with the demands of the galleries. Sarah Sweetwater heard about me and asked me to teach at the college; I started right away and have been teaching ever since." She rushes to explain, "I was experimenting with new techniques and doing my best to hone my craftsmanship while supporting myself along the way." Teaching provided a necessary social component; at the time, Tuscarora had twelve full-time residents, none her age, and she knew almost no one in the nearby town of Elko. Rappa says her students kept her on her toes and helped her to seriously invest in herself as a jewelry artist.

And take it seriously she certainly did, attending workshops to learn new techniques, studying with well-known designers in Arizona, North Carolina, back at the Mendocino Art Center, and at the Revere Academy of Jewelry Arts in San Francisco. As her career grew, so did her name and reputation. Her work has been featured in books in magazines.[7] She was selected to create the Governor's Arts Commission Award for the Nevada Arts Council, and that body awarded her an honorable mention in the Artist Fellowship program. She exhibits at various venues with the professional Great Basin Wild Women Artists, and has shown her one-of-a-kind pieces in galleries across the country.

Her journal bursts with new ideas, but before she begins work, she relaxes in her work space and fills some artist pages "to clean the slate of the minutia in my head."[8] She quietly says a little prayer, one she has created as a beginning ritual to her creative work. Then it's time for her to begin.

Almost all her work is hand fabricated. She begins with raw materials—sterling silver and 14-carat gold in various forms. She saws, pierces, hammers, stamps, and solders to get the sculptural shapes she seeks, then she refers to the journal ideas. Rappa is drawn to the shadowbox shape, and she creates small sheltered containers for the semiprecious stones, elements she has carved out of jet, or bone, and found objects.

Story has always been a part of Rappa's approach. In New Mexico she became enamored with clay sculptor Melissa Zinc, who created small figurative vignettes of emotional experiences made manifest in figures. "I was enchanted," she says. "My interest continues to be in creating wearable sculpture that tells a story." Her story in jewelry is sometimes literal, as in the words embedded in silver; sometimes the story is implicit in the piece, as in *Show (Don't) Tell* and *Moon Dreams,* where title and a code-like design in silver dots against jet imply a message. Sometimes, she says, a story is too large to interpret inside a small jewel. In that case, she will work on a larger scale such as in her eight-buckle-long concho belt, *Raven Finds Home.* When an idea does not fit within the limitations of wearability, she will create a wall piece or fashion a figure in fiber and clay.

Rappa continues to experiment, exploring new concepts to satisfy an unshakable yearning to touch nature, beauty, and memory in a way that feels authentic. She is deeply connected to the wildness of Tuscarora, which gives her room to breathe with the solitude she finds necessary to create, and to be with her family. With two children, she spends less time in the studio, and, she says, "I wouldn't be the woman or the artist I am today if it weren't for Ron."

I ask her for final thoughts, and she is silent for a moment, and then says, "I wish everyone who wants to would give themselves permission to create in some way. I think of the idea of permission a lot, especially as I get older. It seems as [with] women there's less permission to express the gritty part of ourselves because it's not seen as attractive. I say give yourself permission to express all aspects of yourself, even if it doesn't fit the general idea of what is acceptable or pretty, because there is an intrinsic beauty in honesty."

Rappa's ritual prayer ends with these words: "Help me to know that I create magic when I trust my inherent gifts and talents. In gratitude, love, and patience. Gail."

JIMMIE BENEDICT • BORN 1944

Jimmie Benedict has been in motion most of her life, and the Great Basin was fortunate to lasso her for twenty-one years. Benedict says she was the lucky one, however, because the muted colors of Nevada are perfect backdrops for the dips and swirls of color she injects into her wearable art, the likes of which have awed collectors for more than thirty years. Her pieced, quilted, and distinctively designed clothing won purchase awards from the Southern Highland Craft Guild, North Georgia College, and the Tennessee Arts Commission, and it's no wonder because her work is indeed unique. When Benedict entered the colorful world in the genre known as art quilts, she began reinventing and combining such techniques as Seminole patchwork with thread painting, stump work, and various embroidery and quilting skills, to create garments. She treats cloth as if it was paint, then moves, slashes, and stitches it into one-of-a-kind fabrications; she will sometimes top everything with beads and a jangle or two. To see Benedict's creations come alive on the body is to understand why her work has entered the realm of art.

At our interview on May 21, 2013, we sit at the dining room table piled with samples of her creations, while Benedict pushes an orange-threaded needle in and out of a length of purple hand-woven Guatemalan cloth. She begins to tell me her story, and the turquoise ornaments at her ears shake as she affirms her reason for designing in cloth to create sculpture for the body.

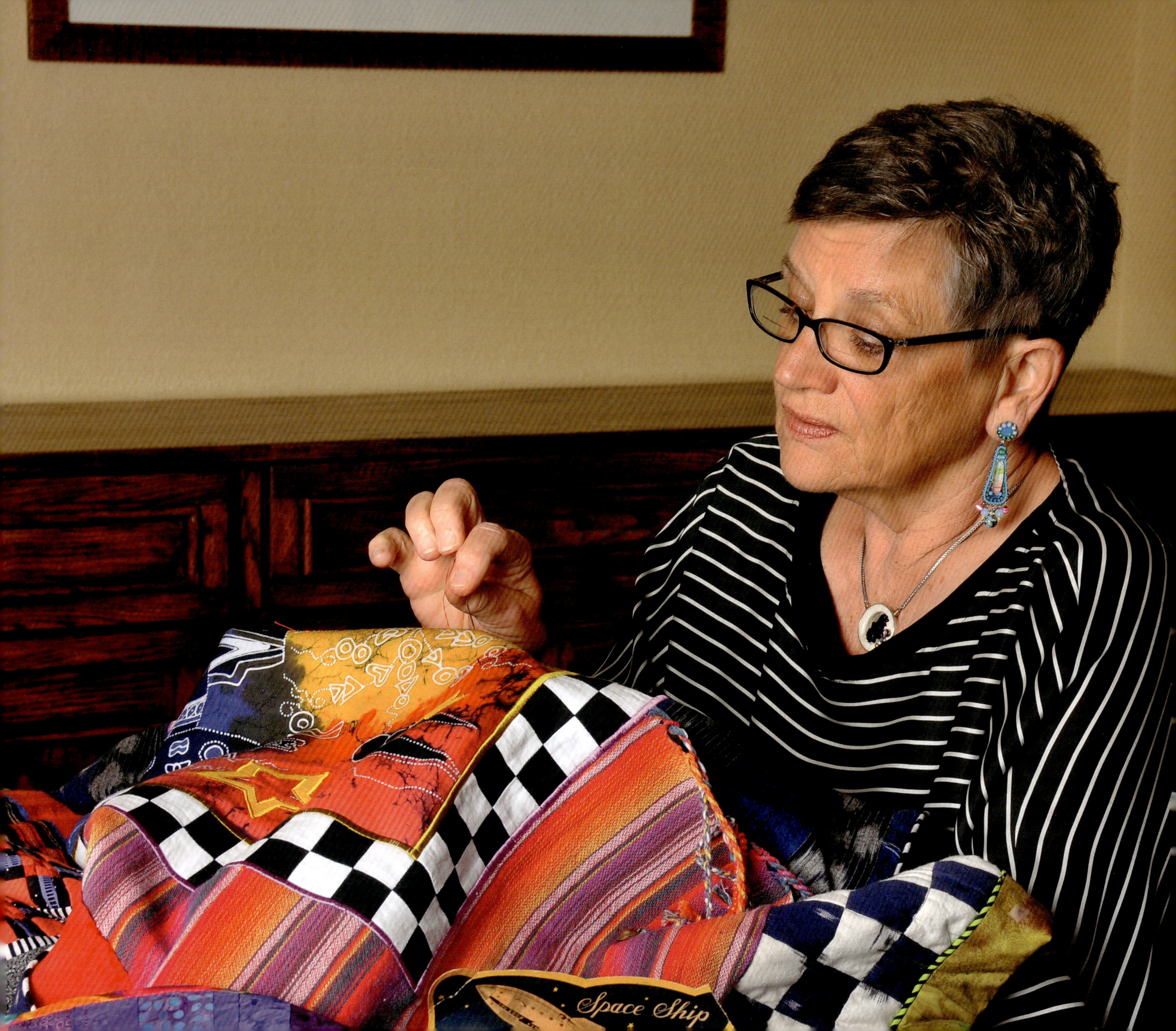
Space Ship

"Why wouldn't I? My mother and both grandmothers sewed."

Benedict was born in Craig Air Force Base in Selma, Alabama, in 1944, where her father, Sam McNatt, was a World War II pilot trainer. At war's end, Sam found work with an oil company, and this new career took the family to various Kansas locations. Along with her brother and two sisters, Benedict rode bikes all over, so her motion began when she was young. She attended Kansas State University where she studied design, with a major in fashion, and that's when art and sewing took center stage. At that time, the 1960s, Benedict recalls that most women students majored in home economics, nursing, or education.

She married William and lived in Manhattan, Kansas, while he was still attending college. She became pregnant and they didn't have much money. At first she worked selling calculators and slide rules, and remembers it being funny because she didn't know how to use them. When her son, Shane, was born, she started modeling in Kansas State University's art department. She continued modeling until she was pregnant with her second son, Peter. She stopped then because it was hard for her to sit still, and she noticed the students were distracted by her belly moving around.

Next, the family moved to Knoxville, Tennessee, where Peter was born, and she subsequently modeled in the art department at the University of Tennessee. At this time, Benedict learned to macramé and met Ellen Sherbourne Jones who encouraged her to apply for membership into the prestigious Southern Highland Craft Guild (www.southernhighlandguild.org), and in 1971 the guild accepted her.[9] After her initial exposure to macramé, she went to Arrowmont School of Art and Craft in Gatlinburg, Tennessee, for a workshop with Joan Michaels Pacque. It was there that her sculptural bent started.[10]

Benedict's large sculptural macramé installations gained distinction throughout the Southeast and found their way into exhibitions and private homes. Corporate collections of her wall pieces include Opryland, USA; the Tennessee Valley Authority; and Radisson Hotels. Unfortunately, the constant knotting motion brought stresses to her neck.

Benedict turned to the Unitarian Universalist Church. She became active in the women's group, where the average age was sixty, and at the age of twenty-three she was elected president. The women created fine crafts and mounted bazaars, and Benedict participated, with Sherbourne Jones's encouragement. "She was a real mother figure to me back then," Benedict says.

But once again it was time to move—and this time the change was drastic. A group of professional couples at the church had been discussing the idea of a commune, and in 1972 five families pooled their money, purchased a large house, and moved in together. Household duties were shared, and the experiment succeeded for everyone but Benedict, who worked from home. She had daily care of eight children and their dogs and saw to all the home maintenance and repairs. "I had no control over my environment," she said.

One rainy afternoon, her hands hurried through knot manipulations as she bent over a macramé wall piece in a race to meet a show deadline, when several tired and grumpy children tumbled into her box of beads. As she watched masses of tiny beads roll across the expanse of floor, the realization struck— she was finished with the grand commune experiment.

Benedict was thirty-two when she left. William remained behind with their children, and while she saw the boys regularly, she never did live with them again. "But," she says, "the communal system brought a sense of fairness to kids growing up in that environment. They're [her sons] much more forgiving than I am."

She moved into a small apartment and began her work. Her celebration was to put a small bowl of beads on the floor, go out, and when she returned the beads were where she placed them. She had gone straight from being a kid to a

Jimmie Benedict at work.

mom, and she played pretty hard during this part of her life. She knew that knotting was hard on her body, and when she found an alternative medium to work with, she jumped at it. Today, she considers her work to be pieced, quilted, and embroidered.

Benedict visited her parents in Oklahoma, and at a Tulsa museum she discovered the art of Seminole work and was transfixed. When she returned to her home, her mother, Ella, mailed her a book on the subject. Benedict was hooked. "The color in that book was fabulous after all my muted macramé," she says, "and I decided to work completely in color."

She met Ron, a professor of atomic physics, and they married in 1980. The following year Benedict participated in her first show with fabric. Her many skirts, clothes pinned to a rope strung around her booth, blew in the summer breeze, swirling a myriad of checks, stripes, weaves, images, and the entire color wheel. Agnes Fort Moore purchased Benedict's skirts at that first show, and she went on to become a major collector; when she died thirty years later, she owned 140 pieces that Benedict had made, some of which became part of the Southern Highland Craft Guild permanent collection.

"Agnes's mentorship was the main stimulus for much of my recent work," Benedict recalls. "She'd say, 'try this, try that,' or 'do this' or 'add this.' Or she'd send me a bolt of fabric and I'd have to figure out how to put it together."

Benedict always benefitted from networking, and, after taking Libby Platus's workshop on making money with one's art, she invited some women artist friends to her home.[11] They met each week and encouraged one another to embrace Platus's ideas, and ultimately decided to organize their own shows. They needed a name that would catch media's attention, so they came up with "The Amazing and Astounding Women Artists Breakfast Club." The women succeeded beyond their wildest dreams.

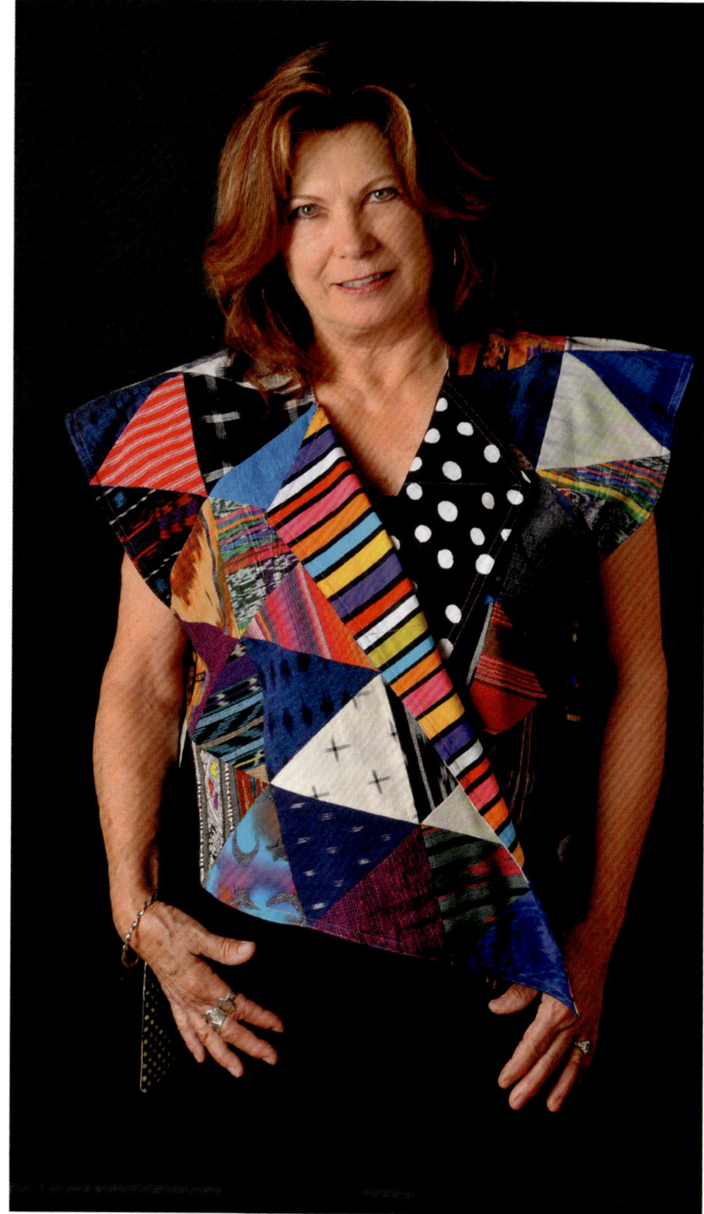

Jimmie Benedict, *Triangle Vest.* Cotton; triangle assemblage using ikat-woven fabrics.

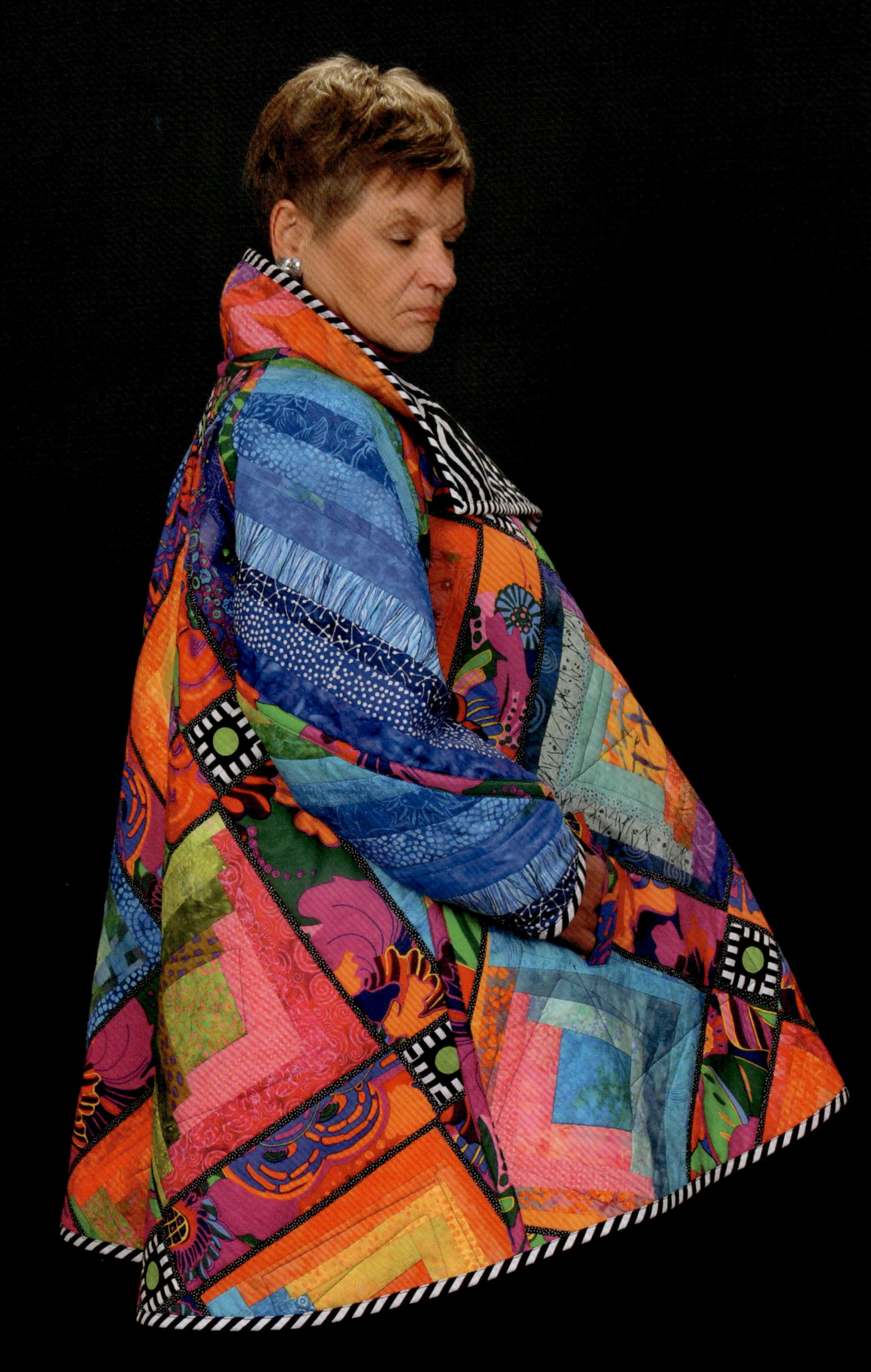

In 1992 Ron accepted a job at UNR, and again Benedict started over, this time in the wilds of Nevada. Once here, she yearned for the lush flowers, trees, and green, green grass of Tennessee. And where were the artists? She could find no support base but kept digging, and through Reno's Sierra Arts Foundation and word of mouth, she located a few professional women artists. The group, Wild Women, met at Benedict's home to discuss their work and aspirations, and after meeting for several months, they decided to take their art seriously. The group has grown and changed over the years as members come and go, guest artists make appearances, and art in every medium imaginable appears in their shows. The Wild Women, whose mailing list reaches into the thousands, recently passed its twentieth year of existence.

Benedict had always been impressed with the work and determination of American artists Georgia O'Keeffe and Louise Nevelson, but when she traveled to Austria and saw the creations of Friedensreich Hundertwasser, she returned to Reno with new color and design ideas. She was always in demand as a teacher both locally and nationally; quilters wanted the scoop on her design techniques and color secrets, but her skills went way beyond quilting. She became author/designer with Pyramid Jacket Pattern Books.

Benedict came to love Nevada. An early bus trip led by Nevada Women's History Project founder Jean Ford and friend Janet Carson on the subject of water issues took her from Lake Tahoe to Pyramid Lake, with farm towns and ranches along the way, and Benedict became acquainted with the Western landscape. She and her husband found rubies at Great Basin National Park and camped at Lye Creek in the Santa Rosa range. Against the quiet colors of sagebrush and piñon, which gave way to a big blue sky, Benedict became aware of the open spaces and remarkable

Jimmie Benedict, *Reversible Swing Coat,* one side. Cotton, machine quilted.

light that skimmed mountain and desert. Color burst forth in her fabric designs, a contrast to a muted landscape and bright as the neon along any Nevada main street. Buyers flocked to her studio and show venues.

"We ended up knowing ranchers and true Nevadans," she says. "We got to see a whole different and wonderful culture."

And now, true to her style, Benedict is again moving on, this time to Colorado, as Ron retires and they set up housekeeping near grandchildren Otter, Tucker, and Wren. She acknowledges the sculptural aspect of her work, but at times she is discouraged over the direction or inspiration of it. Her life experiences of getting ready to move and relocating took a lot out of her, and she is now just starting to think in a creative way. The new home has a large studio, of course, and it will once again be time for Jimmie Benedict to reinvent herself. And there is no doubt that she will.

JILL ALTMANN • BORN 1947

Although the left-brained, right-brained myth of logic versus creativity has been discredited, researchers believe that some abilities are actually strongest when both brain halves work together. That concept certainly applies to textile artist Jill Altmann.

In bringing a new wearable sculpture or three-dimensional wall hanging to life, Altmann first invokes her intuition and imagination to envision form, design, and emotional impression. Her vision becomes real only by using a skill set of technology, tool and media choice, and plenty of mental arithmetic. The two sides of her brain work together in perfect harmony to create a body of work so unusual and dramatic that it is collected by women the world over.

Shortly after Altmann's move to Reno, Nevada, in 1985, the late Chelsea Miller Goin, curator at the Nevada Museum of Art, encouraged the accomplished loom weaver to design and create a body of wearable art based on Navajo rugs. Altmann says, "It's important to keep the human sculpture in mind," because she believes a handmade garment draped over a human body completes the sculpture. She did just that and mounted her first one-woman show of wearable art at the museum.

Later, impressed with Native use of natural material in the Great Basin, Altmann developed a Washoe Bark Clothing series. She gathered natural materials, including cottonwood, sagebrush, and willow barks, from around western Nevada, rehydrated them in the studio bathtub, mellowed them in heavy damp towels, and wove them on an eight-shaft floor loom into oversize clothing shapes that alluded to and honored historic Native wear. These framed pieces exhibited in various venues and inspired massive woven wall hangings, with weeds, barks, and bamboo added to the array of plant materials.

Altmann's tools and techniques are many. In addition to computers and looms both large and small, she employs a knitting machine. "I use that machine to create form," she says, "just as a metal sculptor might use a welding torch." In addition to various weaving and knitting manipulations, she does felting, dyeing, discharge (i.e., color removal), surface design, silkscreen, spinning, and other related fiber techniques.

During the interview on March 18, 2014, Altmann walks me around her studio, fingering dramatic vests, capes, elongated coats, and dimensional sweaters, and pointing out various wall hangings. Her green eyes flash as we weave around looms and equipment, worktables, and mannequins. Her gray-streaked hair is feathered short, and she resembles a stalwart pixie dressed in black under a vest streaked with color. Her earrings match the vest, and they swing in cadence with the wearer, who doesn't seem as if she ever stands still. The studio is attached to her home, which Altmann and her husband, Fred, built. It's a *green* home, with solar and wind power. You can see outside the massive window bits of green shoots from a vegetable garden poking

Jill Altmann at the loom. She is wearing a handwoven shibori vest.

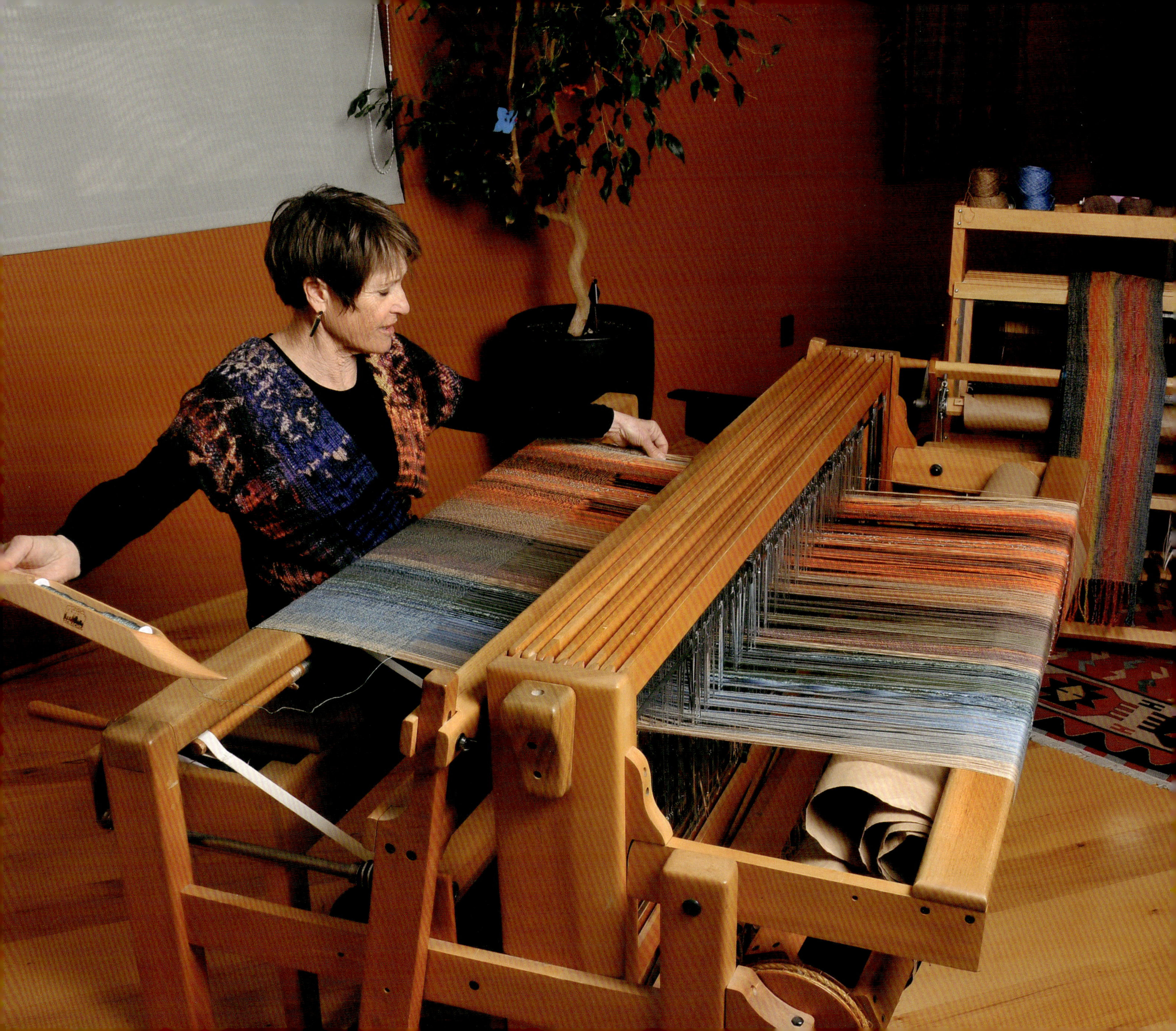

through the soil. From high atop these foothills at the edge of town, I look beyond stone and sage, past small ranches below, and upward to two mountains that watch over the Truckee Meadows—Mount Rose and Slide Mountain. The view to the north shows Peavine, the third defining mountain.

"The Great Basin has been my inspiration since I moved here," she says, "from monochromatic winters to dramatic sunrises and sunsets." She's added the construction techniques of previous cultures, as well as art forms and cultural icons from around the world. These all play into her textile artistry.

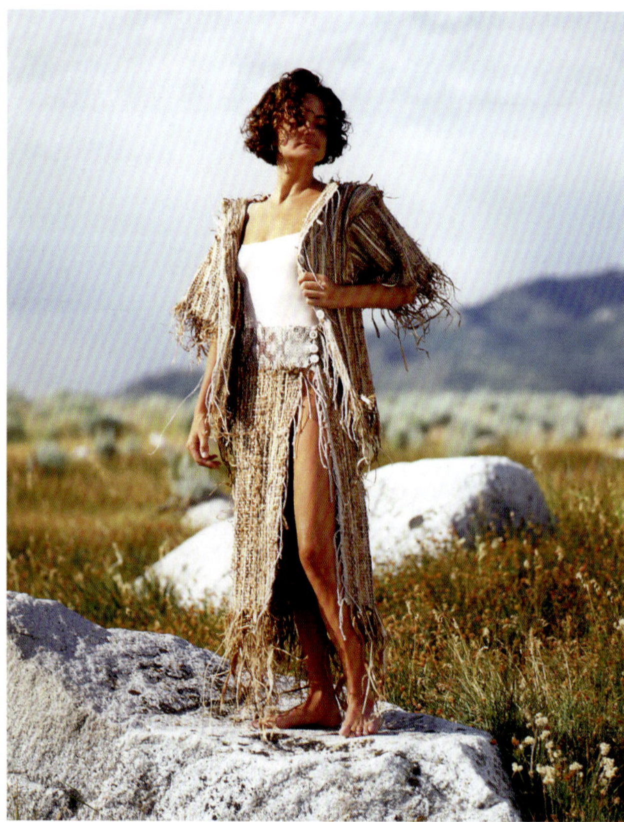

Jill Altmann, *Washoe Bark Clothing.* Handwoven linen warp; "found weft"-sagebrush bark, bitterbrush bark, cottonwood inner core, split willow bark, wild grasses, more. Reproduced by permission from Jill Altmann.

Early on, Altmann's innovative apparel was juried into the prestigious American Craft Council shows in San Francisco and Baltimore. Her work was discovered by Sandra Sakata, owner of San Francisco's Obiko, the first Western U.S. retailer to sell exclusive art clothing. Sakata's boutique in New York City's Bergdorf Goodman store selected Altmann's work for their collection, a distinction offered to few.

She continued to exhibit in museums and other venues throughout the West. In San Diego she twice won Best of Show awards and was a finalist in the Nevada Governor's Arts Awards. Her work can be found in numerous private and corporate collections.

Altmann was a founding member of the Wild Women, and she has served as guest speaker, mentor, and store-owner. Altmann has also been a working partner with her husband, Fred, at DF Altmann Construction Inc.

The oldest of four children, she was born Jill Cecilia Jackson in Oakland, California, to Mary (a dietitian), and Bill (a World War II Navy veteran). Altmann grew up in Castro Valley, where she spent a great deal of time with her grandmother, Lillian Reading. "She taught me to sew and crochet, and I loved it. She was a great role model. "I'm trying to be like her with my grandchildren now."

At age five Altmann began accompanying Lillian to church sewing circles. She joined 4-H Club and immediately entered the county fair. "You got ribbons and money if you won!" She also enjoyed art and home economics in both middle school and high school. Her father worked in the family business, Red's Early California Foods, and she worked there during summer college break, gaining practical business experience.

The year of 1964 was a time of great social change in California. Her parents promoted college, but definitely not the nearby University of California, Berkeley. They

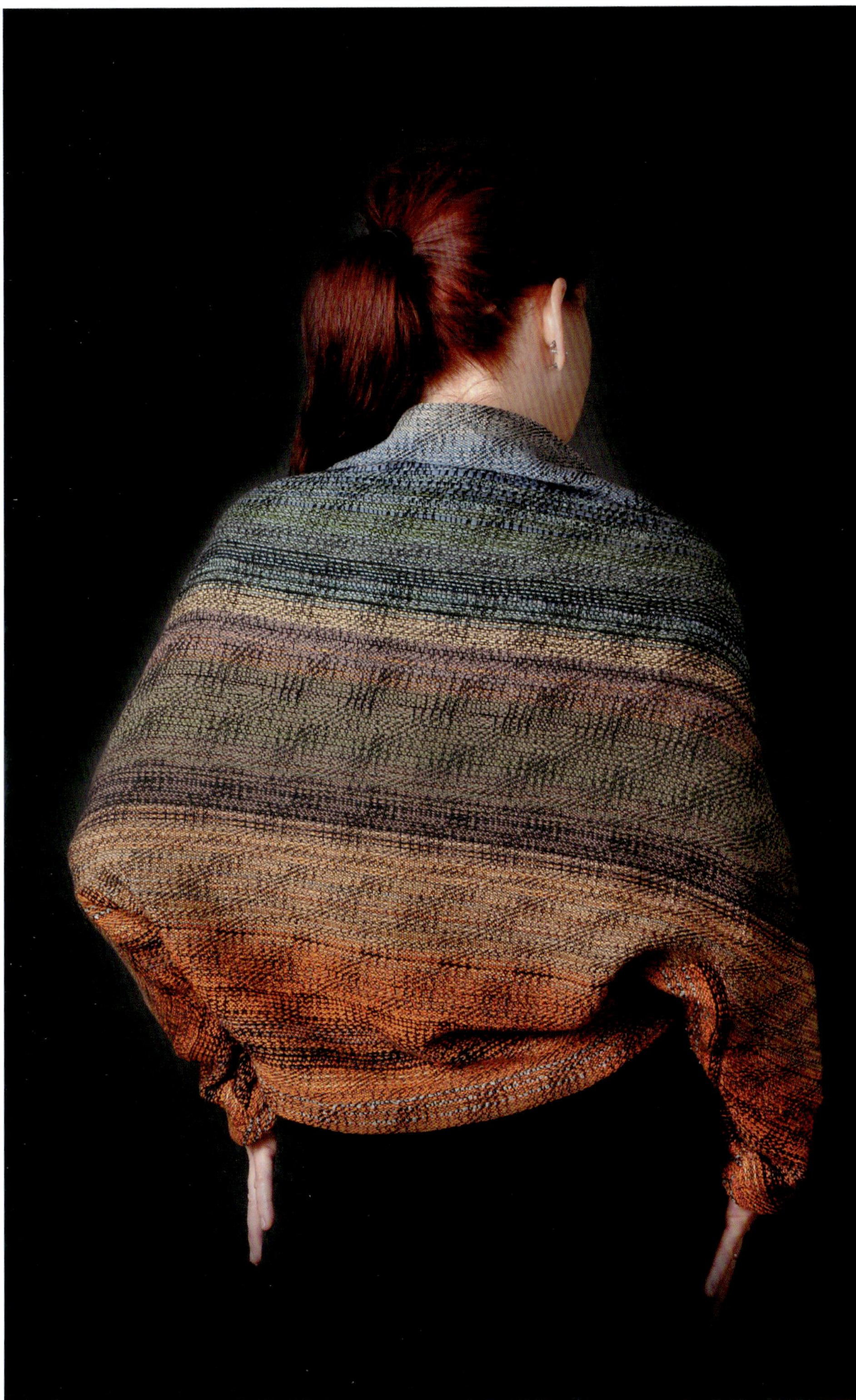

worried about the Berkeley riots and political protests. It was also home to hippies and the drug culture. Instead, Altmann attended University of California, Davis, majoring in home economics, and took design classes from Katherine Westphal and Professor Shapiro; she enrolled in as many design classes as she could without changing her major—her parents wanted her to finish quickly. "There are three other kids behind you," they warned. Altmann worked at the family business and taught sewing during summers. "I had to have a job," she says. "I had to pay for tuition and books."

She and her husband-to-be, Fred Altmann, had crossed paths in high school and reconnected one summer; they married right out of college and both commenced teaching. Altmann also took adult education classes in backstrap weaving, natural dyeing, and spinning. "And I taught design. We made backstrap looms out of Popsicle sticks. It was fabulous!"[12]

The couple traveled to Europe as chaperones/teachers through a foreign study program; after her return, Altmann took her first formal weaving classes with Professor Marsha Chamberlain at San Jose State University's art department, and she became hooked on weaving from that time forward.

In the early 1970s Bay Area artists began exploring the work of hand-weaving, glassblowing, woodworking, and more. The craft art movement emerged in response to mass production and plastic goods of the 1950s and 1960s. This new work eventually changed the perception and definition of what art could be. Altmann was part of that change and the new art-to-wear movement.

After teaching home economics and physical education for four years, the Altmanns began a journey of exploration that knitted all their dreams together into one big cloak—skiing and building their first house in Los Gatos, California; traveling throughout Europe; and buying a van

Jill Altmann, *Origami Fold Jacket.* Cotton; handwoven 8-shaft network.

and spending four months on the road. Her connections in Greece, Denmark, Sweden, and Finland would provide inventory for her new store, Mountain Weaver, which she opened upon their return to Los Gatos in 1974. Altmann was also pregnant at the time, and her son, Peter, was born Christmas Eve. Daughter Niki was born four years later. For twelve years, Altmann offered weaving materials, looms, hand-woven items, workshops, and lectures.

But the couple sought a slower lifestyle, a quieter place to raise their children, as well as access to ski slopes. Reno was the perfect solution. They collaborated with some Reno developers and an architect and, with Fred's background in construction, developed their first houses.

"It was always the two of us. I was a designer with the architect, Fred, the builder. And," she adds with a grin, "I cook."

Altmann shared a studio with weaver Toni Lowden and joined the Reno Fiber Guild. She was soon designing, weaving, and exhibiting. Her work was photographed professionally and juried into the American Craft Council shows. For a time her cottage industry employed thirteen people. She learned how to use a knitting machine and she has "never stopped."

She established a local market for her one-of-a-kind art wearables. Her assistants along the way have been Priscilla Streng, Ryrie Valdez, and Serena Robb, who each helped sell her work, and Sandra Sakata, mentioned earlier. She also works with others to produce shows in her studio.

At our interview, Altmann speaks of her life's turning points. Some are small, like the weaving class at San Jose State, others large, like the move to Reno. One was huge. In 2009 a skiing accident shattered her right arm—her working arm—and she was unable to create for nine months. During that time, she discovered Hands Along the Nile (www.handsalongthenile.org), the Egyptian school for underprivileged girls, and donated yarns and materials. The result was an invitation to travel to the school, where she taught in Cairo and became part of its teaching team. The next year, the Egyptian director was invited to Reno's Nevada Museum of Art Bazaar, where they sold products made by the girls.

"Talk about life-changing!" she says. "That ranks up there with moving to Reno. And all because of a stupid ski fall!"

This artist isn't slowing down. She still creates new designs on her computer that are sent to the knitting machine for execution. She continues to find inspiration in travel, study, and collaboration. She has become an expert at natural dyeing, and her shows draw crowds. She gardens. And most importantly, she enjoys having her four grandchildren in the studio. Recently, she gave her eight-year-old grandchild a sewing machine for her birthday, remembering her grandmother's lasting influence.

At our interview, Altmann perches on the edge of a chair and says, "I chose clothing because I look to the human body as my roots. And with my networking and travel, I feel I'm part of a circle of all the hands of all the women and men back through time." She gazes out the window toward Mount Rose, her fingers touching a piece of golden fabric on her work table, and adds, "And the circle goes on."

JILL ATKINS • BORN 1946

On March 11, 2014, Jill Atkins gazes out the window of her Red Rock, Nevada, studio, and repeats her favorite quote, by Alfred Camus: "In the midst of winter, I found there was within me an invincible summer." She recites this after describing personal life challenges during our interview that might have shot a lesser woman down in flames.

"The trick is to find summer," the artist says, her golden bear-claw earrings flashing against chestnut hair. "And we need to make sure our self-talk isn't destructive. We get enough of that from the outside world."

Atkins has indeed transformed a life of lost hopes into one of pleasure and satisfaction. As she describes her particular art form—sculptural purses—I notice the frames of her glasses are the same royal blue as her shirt. I look

Jill Atkins in her studio developing a design.

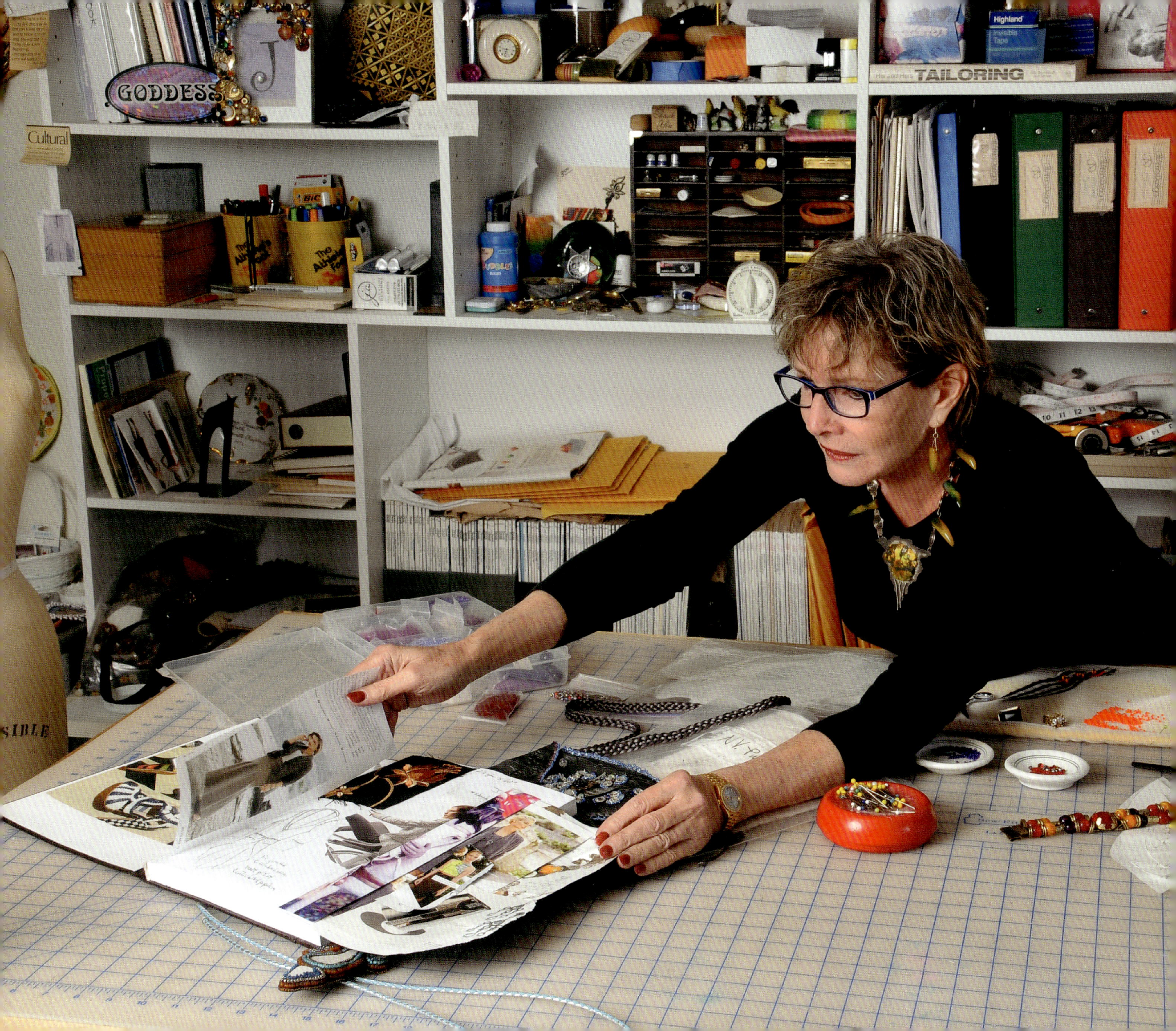
GODDESS
Cultural
Highland
Invisible Tape
TAILORING
BIC
SIBLE

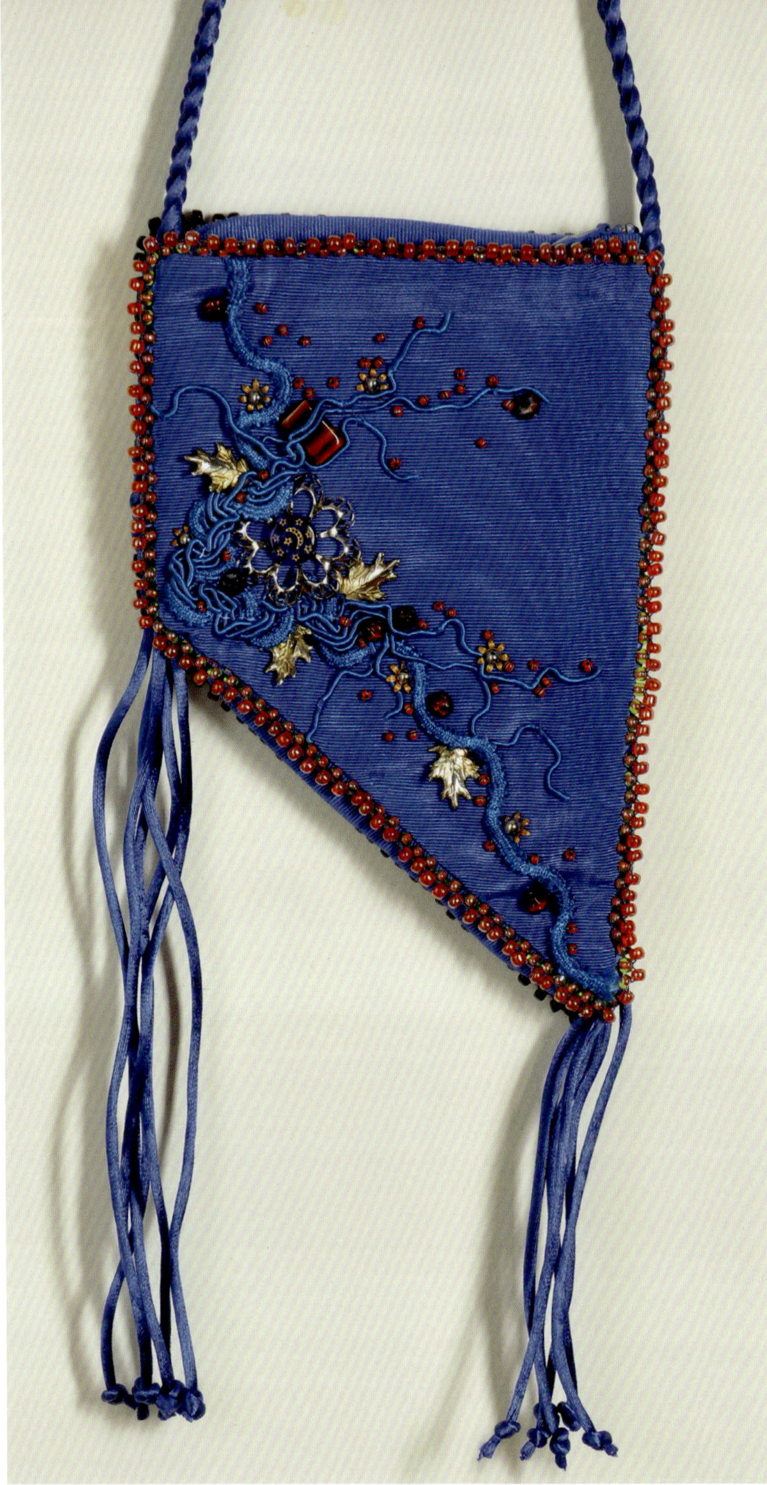

past her studio worktable covered with sewing tools and brightly colored fabrics, past walls splashed with calendars, poetry, measuring devices, thread spools, and books, past the mannequin and three sewing machines, past cases and cases of beads, past the music and display corners, to the large window overlooking Stead Valley and the Granite Mountains rising in the far distance, and I realize all over again that I have written this book to highlight women like Atkins—women who have walked through adversity to create art that changes our perceptions of the world because they do it their way.

That's a lot to expect from a purse, the palette over which Atkins explores stories of the Great Basin in beads, threads, fabric, and more. "I use plastic, leather, electrical components, old gun parts . . . anything is fair game," she explains. You might have guessed that hers aren't just any old purses. Atkins's creations are sculptural studies in cloth, where ends and sides and openings are never found where you'd expect them to be.

To build a piece, she creates or finds a distinctive frame, and from there dreams up a subject, explores a human condition, or expounds on a societal view, like *Sunset at Tahoe,* or *Urban Cowboot*, or *Julia Bulette*. Once she created a purse in the shape of a piano. After a day or maybe a month, a three-dimensional shape forms in her mind, and she begins to design and engineer a piece that will transform this idea into a bold and imaginative work of art. Colorful fabrics and threads, shiny beads in various shapes and sizes, extra additions like charms, sequins, bells, or rhinestones are tossed randomly across the worktable, playing against each other until a plan is formulated. Even as the piece begins to take form, the design will change, for Atkins's techniques (beading, layering, embroidery, applique, sculpting with stitches,

Jill Atkins, *The Power of a Sunset at Tahoe,* from the Wedding Train series. Mixed media with card case included; 36 x 7 in.

and more) are highly improvisational. She simply picks a bead and begins. "Then I add another bead and another until I have finished." Hands flashing with needle and thread, she might decide to add a wraparound tail, or a side opening, or extra flaps that, when lifted, reveal a special image or secret message.

From a distance, Atkins's work seems painted, but a closer look will reveal meticulous layering of fabric, thread, beads, and more. Color is almost everything. She considers value, tone, intensity and emotional qualities in her color choices. She also deliberates on the relationship of one hue to the next, and she works to convey beauty, drama, and vulnerability with her use of dimension and texture. She seems to call on the impressionists of the late 1800s, who used bright colors and captured light qualities. The neo-impressionists pushed these experiments farther, using strokes or dots of pure color, letting the eye of the beholder mix the ingredients. Atkins walks a line between these two movements, achieving a dramatic edginess. Each work captures a moment of stillness in the midst of change.

The artist has been widely recognized for her skill and originality. Her award-winning sculptural work has exhibited in galleries and museums throughout Nevada and elsewhere and has appeared in such publications as *Belle Armoire, Beadwork,* and the DIY Network's publication *Dazzling Beaded Jewelry*. In 2004 she was featured in the DIY TV show "Jewelry Making," and in 2008 she was a featured artist on the HGTV Network's "That's Clever." One artwork piece is a part of the Nevada State Museum's permanent collection, and twice her beaded sculpture was juried into the White House Christmas collection in Washington, DC. Her original purses are in private collections around the country, and she teaches beadwork on the local and national level. She has worked with the Marjorie Russell Clothing

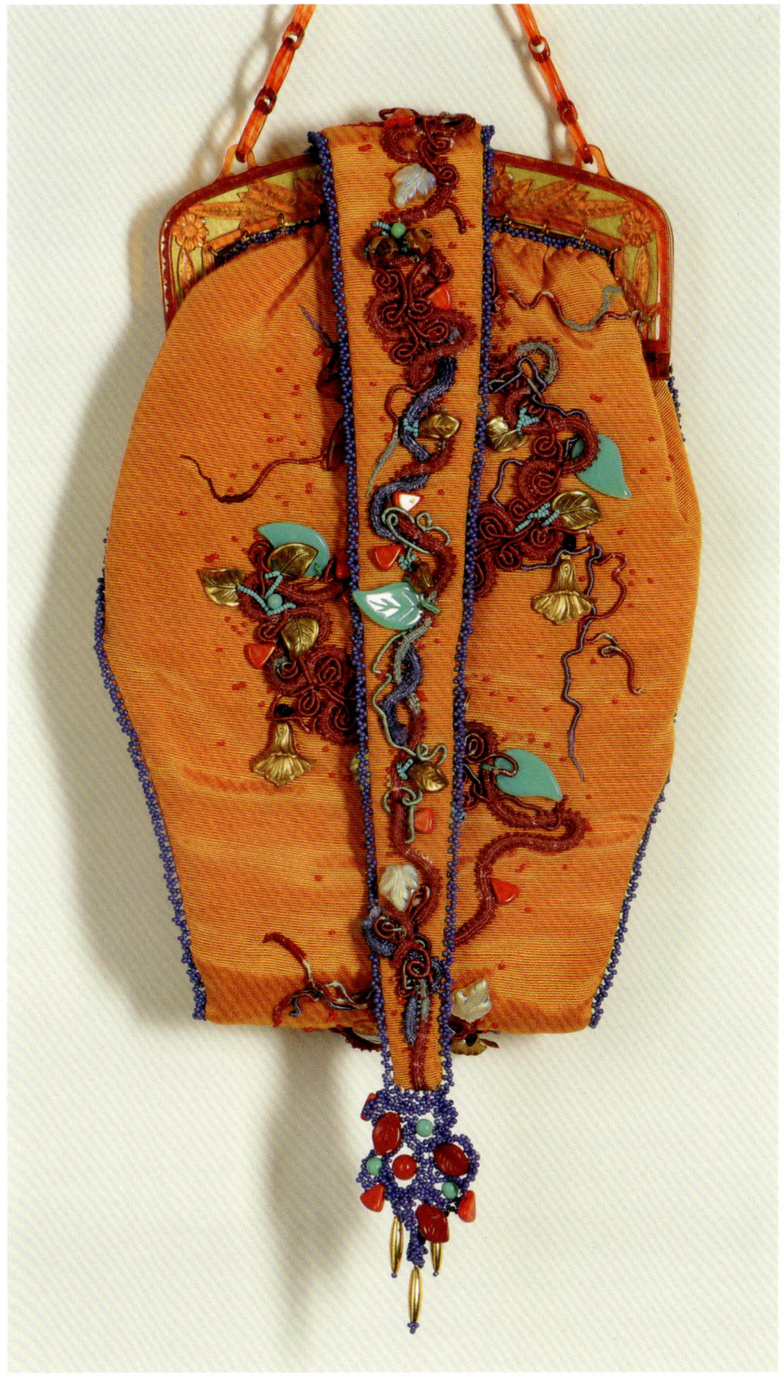

Jill Atkins, *Ruby Mountains.* Fabric, dyed-to-match braid; beads, metal findings, silk-lined; 9 x 5 x 1 in.

and Textile Research Center in Carson City, Nevada, and, like many artists in this book, she donates intricate works to help raise funds for nonprofit organizations such as Arts for All Nevada, Soroptimist International, and the Wounded Warriors Project. She has recently taken up the art of silversmithing, and her one-of-a-kind silver necklaces, bracelets, and earrings are frequently subjects of bidding wars at these nonprofit events.

This life of a successful artist wasn't always hers. Born Jill Anne Langworthy in Buffalo, New York, she was the oldest child of a World War II disabled army veteran—her mother, Theresa—and a career army father. The family traveled frequently with her father's military assignments. Moving through six different elementary schools wasn't easy, especially when home was not a happy place. A younger brother, Jack, and sister, Susie, came along, and Atkins and her sister were the sad victims of their father's abuse. Remembering that terrible time, Atkins says, "I sucked my thumb until I was thirteen; then my parents divorced and my father left." Her mother found a low-paying job while Atkins cared for her siblings. The youngsters were on their own during summer months. Then Atkins found work caring for two children—the oldest girl was eleven and had Down syndrome—up to eighteen hours a day. "I didn't know what to do when the girl started her period because I hadn't started mine yet!" At summer's end, Atkins received $100, which was money for school clothes.

She learned to sew in junior high and then high school. California always offered art classes in schools, and after making an enormous canvas mural she was hooked. "I knew then that I wanted to be an artist." During a class outing to the San Francisco opera, she discovered Rembrandt in two small gift shop reproductions and bought them; they were the beginning of an extensive art collection.

Atkins's jobs were many and varied following high school and included becoming a flight attendant, where she learned "how to dress," a bank clerk, and, after enrolling at UNR, a full-time cocktail waitress at the Primadonna Casino. She obtained a five-year baccalaureate (majoring in elementary special education) in three years and became the special education coordinator at Stewart Indian School. She married and had two children, all the while trying to make the marriage work and commuting to a full-time job that ended when the Stewart School closed. A difficult situation arose when Atkins and her husband divorced. Unable to financially care for her children, and remembering her own childhood of poverty and neglect, she reluctantly agreed to cede custody of her young children, John and Jenia, to their father. "It was," she recalls, "the biggest mistake of my life. I thought it was the best thing, but all these years later I keep coming back to terms with it."

She found work as a parole officer but was discontented. She then seized an opportunity to fulfill one of her life dreams: enroll in the Sethna School of Fashion Design in San Francisco. For two years she learned the secrets of couture sewing and developed methods to create one-of-a-kind artworks with fabric.

The artist experienced many turning points in her life, the Sethna School being one of them. Losing her children was certainly another. A third was experiencing the healing power of long-term therapy, where she could put old memories to rest and develop a path to personal power through understanding and forgiveness. Then she met and married Gary Atkins.

"I could never be without him. I talk with him, he talks with me. We are down for the long haul."

Atkins experienced a new direction with a beading workshop sponsored by Reno's Sierra Arts Foundation. Author and bead artist Robin Atkins (no relation) said, "You can be like a child in a castle, every room filled with unique, challenging, and beautiful toys, and hours to play with them." The instructor went beyond technique to empower students to reach into their own creative capacity, to let go of fear of failure, and to produce something with heart and soul.

"That was my medium, my big turning point," Atkins remembers. "I couldn't get enough beads, time, ideas on paper fast enough. "From design school I had the ability to work in three dimensions. I could figure out what I wanted to do and I did it!"

Great Basin people and places frequently serve as her subject. "I came for college, but I stayed for the climate, the people. They're very complex. On a summer night we look out and see stars in the sky and hear the coyotes sing. There's sagebrush all over the place. It's energizing to have peace where you live and work."

I tell Atkins she has used traditional "women's work" to create art that is important, that she presents a new vision of what art is and can be. She owes much of this vision to her adversities. She responds, "The best steel is that which is hammered and fired and plunged into ice cold water. All the experiences that I've had led me to where I am now."

Notes

1. Issei were first-generation Japanese, and Nisei were the American-born children of the Issei.
2. Uriu says, "They actually built the irrigation system that is still used in Powell. My father was a superintendent." Interestingly, the Heart Mountain Boy Scout troop went to a Cody Jamboree, where internee Norm Mineta and Wyoming resident Alan Simpson were tent mates. They became lifelong friends; later Congressman Mineta and Senator Alan Simpson would travel and speak about the Heart Mountain experience. Uriu is currently trying to bring them to the University of Nevada through the Distinguished Speakers Series.
3. According to the Encyclopedia Japan (doyouknowjapan.com), "Kamon," or simply "Mon," is a crest that indicates a person's origins, such as family lineage and bloodline.
4. One silver back reads, "Let go of fear[,] and trust." The other says "Courage."
5. There is a description of this fascinating quasi-ghost town in chapter 11.
6. The Society Hall is open to the public on weekends Memorial Day through November 1; it is also open to the public by appointment.
7. The books featuring Rappa's work are Snyder (2008, 2011), *Celebrating 70* (2010), Meilach (2005), and Cox (1999). Her work has been featured in "Trends" (2008), "Woman of the Wild" (2006), "Step by Step" (2006), and "Gallery" (2001).
8. Artist pages are suggested in Cameron (1992).
9. Founded by Frances Goodrich in 1908 and chartered in 1930, the Southern Highland Craft Guild would grow to become one of the strongest craft organizations in the country, with a focus on encouragement of excellence. It represents more than nine hundred craftspeople, and Benedict would eventually become president of the organization.
10. Macramé is a handmade lace-like webbing of knotted yarn or cord. Benedict would continue working with macramé at the corporate level until 1980.
11. Los Angeles sculptor Libby Platus traveled the country presenting workshops that addressed the business of art. Artists learned about pricing, finding buyers, printing business cards and brochures, professional photography, and more.
12. Backstrap looms are ancient weaving tools consisting of sticks, rope, and a strap worn around the weavers' waists.

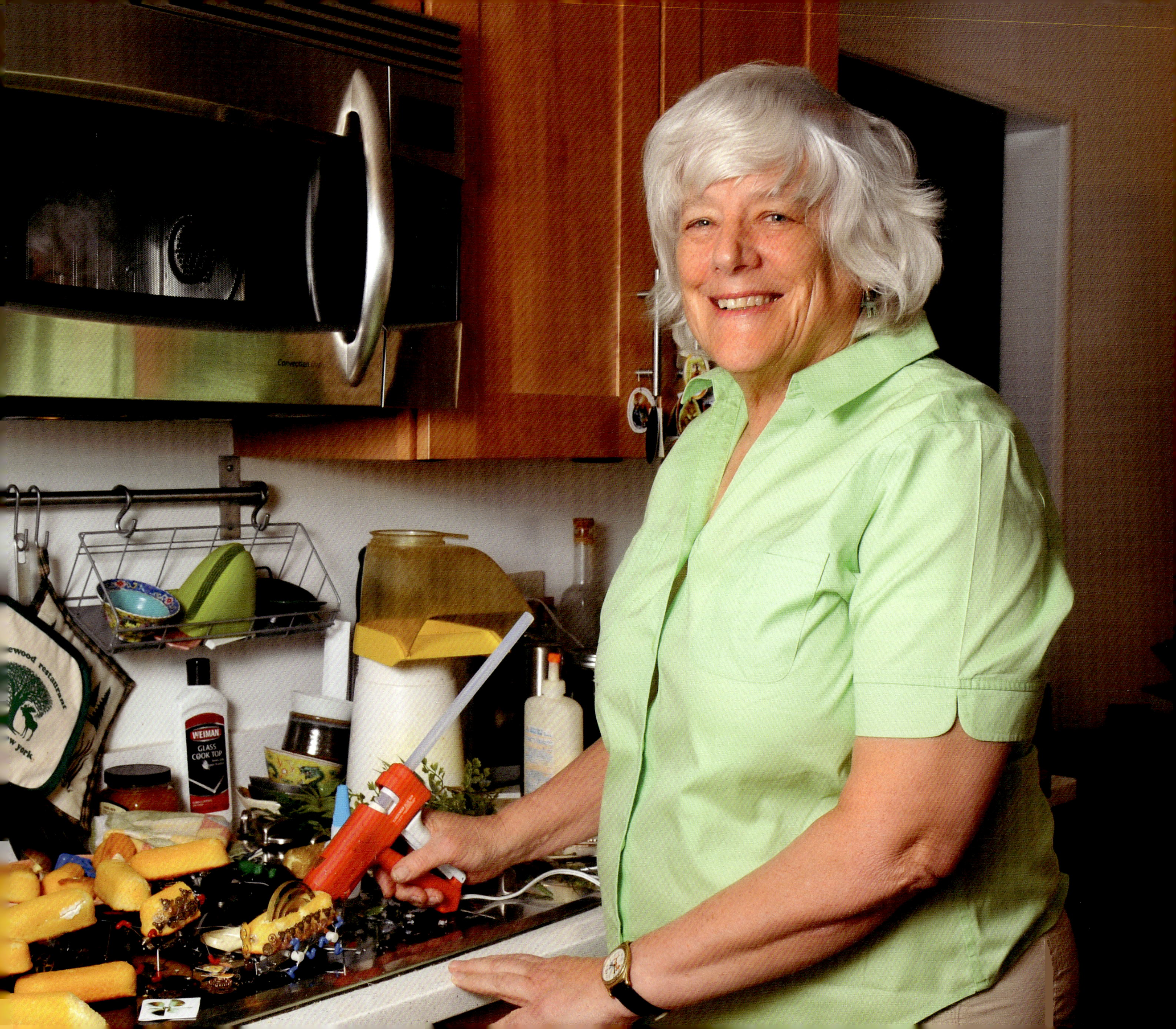
WEIMAN
GLASS COOK TOP
Convection
restaurant

CHEERING

Previous chapters have highlighted artists whose work touched others because of either its process or its subject matter. This chapter looks at the ways in which artists create art to inspire joy and to restore hope and cheerfulness and sometimes a hearty guffaw or two. Author and storyteller Rob White says that "laughter is an expression of the soul dancing."

Cheerfulness opens one's life to joy. It can push away our worries for a little while, awaken us to new possibilities, remind us of our own freedom to let go and just have fun. Like the art mentioned previously, joyful art can help us see things differently, give us an opportunity to bring forth a fresh view. It's such a relief!

Nancy Peppin, Kathleen Durham, Claudia Knous, and Christine Shively-Benjamin have provided artistic fodder for all of us, each in her own inimitable panache. Prepare to be delighted!

NANCY PEPPIN • 1945–2015

Nancy Peppin died before she could see to fruition the publication of this book. What follows is the result of the interview.

The first thing I see when Reno artist Nancy Peppin ushers me into her living room/studio on March 21, 2013, is a gigantic moose head above the brick fireplace; the span between its antlers must be five feet. But it's not your ordinary furry animal head, oh, no. Nancy carved the entire piece out of wood.

"Why kill a perfectly happy moose just for its head?"

Nancy Peppin working on a project. The kitchen stove is her workspace.

she muses, reaching to pet Felix Unger, one of three cats who share her living space. That moose was the beginning of thirty years of moose collecting, and today moose of all shapes crowd the mantel and desk. Little ones even swing from the giant moose antlers. I notice her dangly earrings—moose, of course.

My eyes graze the room, unable to rest on anything, wanting to take in the bumper-to-bumper accumulations of this artist's life—a desk not for writing but for holding more moose, as well as books, a cupful of pencils, unfinished artwork, and more. Paintbrushes, paper, magazines, small objects, and works in progress crowd a three-tiered walnut coffee table with moose legs. A massive window overlooks her backyard, where on this spring day purple and yellow pansies tumble over clay pots, and in the vegetable garden lettuce leaves burst through the dark soil to glow in the morning sun. Back inside, shelves climb to the ceiling, stuffed with books of all subjects, from *Stopping Time* to *Thiebaud* to *The Arcimboldo Effect.* Emmylou Harris's "Old Yellow Moon" wafts from a CD player.

Peppin has built all the furniture in the room, sturdy and interesting. Not only does she create individual works of art, but her entire living room (a "mooseum," as she calls it) is a work of art, a window to the life of Nancy Peppin, artist.

At the far end of the bookshelf, I catch my breath. For there, neatly arranged, I discover the real reason for my visit. Stacked carefully, one upon the other, story shrines employing her favorite medium—Twinkies—are finished and waiting for other Twinkie works that will go into a one-woman show at Reno's Sierra Arts Center. The glass-covered dioramas range from eleven by nine inches up to fifteen inches square and are about three inches deep—plenty of room for the stories Peppin has created inside. Stories involving a gondola, hot air balloon, boat, rocket ship, and more, that are told mainly with Twinkies, which she describes as "the ultimate American food icon."

In the past, photorealist watercolor brought her recognition. Then she began forming the painted paper into dimensional landscapes. And finally came the Twinkies, which she has manipulated into hundreds of satirical artworks that have delighted thousands and been discussed on National Public Radio and in publications from the Yiddish *Vos Iz Neias,* across the country to the *Washington Post.* Peppin, who views a serious world with her own brand of wit, was influenced by the late artist Andy Warhol, who proved that even a Campbell's soup can could be a work of art.

An award-winning artist, Peppin has an exhibition history that would put most to shame. She participated in hundreds of one-woman and group gallery, college, university, and museum shows from UNR, to Reno's Sheppard Contemporary Gallery, to the Nevada Museum of Art, to Reno's Sierra Arts Foundation Gallery, and to the Freehand Gallery in Los Angeles, California, to name a few. Her selected exhibition list fills two pages, single-spaced. She donates to deserving causes, and *Marie Twinkoinette* was a hit at a recentUNR art department fundraiser.

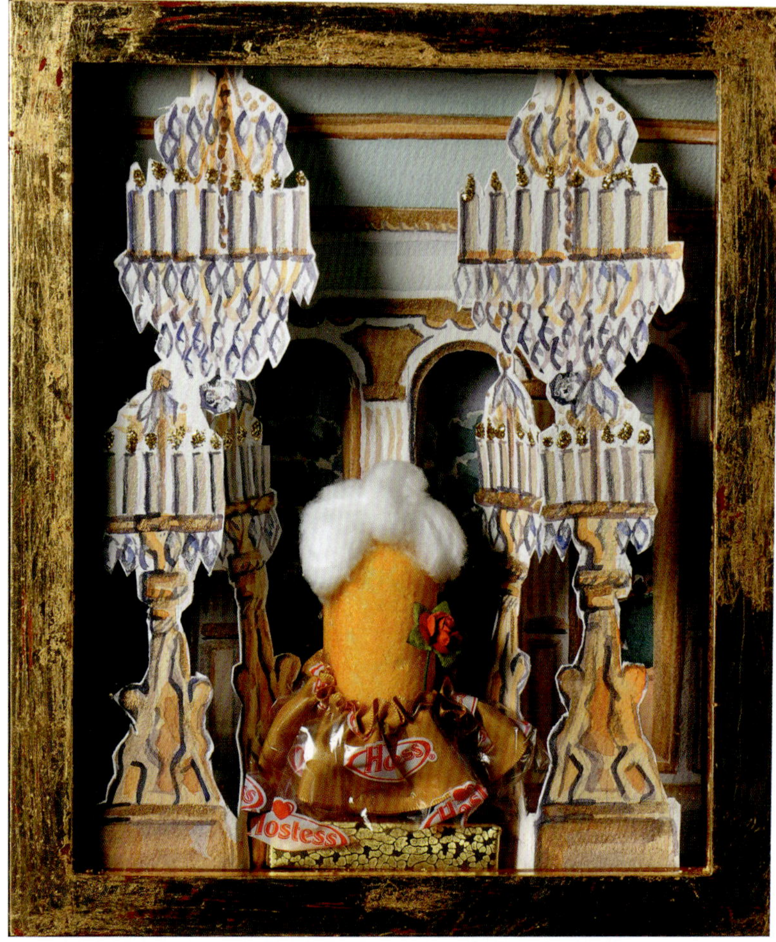

Nancy Peppin, *Marie Twinkoinette.* Watercolor and mixed media of real Twinkie on paper; 14 x 10 x 2 in. Collection of Robert Morrison.

Where did it all begin? A native of Oakland, California, she was interested in anthropology and attended the University of California, Davis, in the 1960s, where she studied with sculptor Tio Giambruni, and where such artists as Wayne Thiebaud, William T. Wiley, and Peter Voulkos were building their reputations. She received her bachelor of art degree in anthropology at University of California, Berkeley, and specialized (no surprise here) in folklore. She worked in graphic arts and book production, then married, and immersed herself in art at the College of San Mateo before moving to Reno, where husband Bill joined the faculty at UNR. There, Peppin received a second bachelor's degree in art, specializing in watercolor and printmaking. For nearly twenty-five years she enrolled in woodworking courses at Truckee Meadows Community College, learning furniture

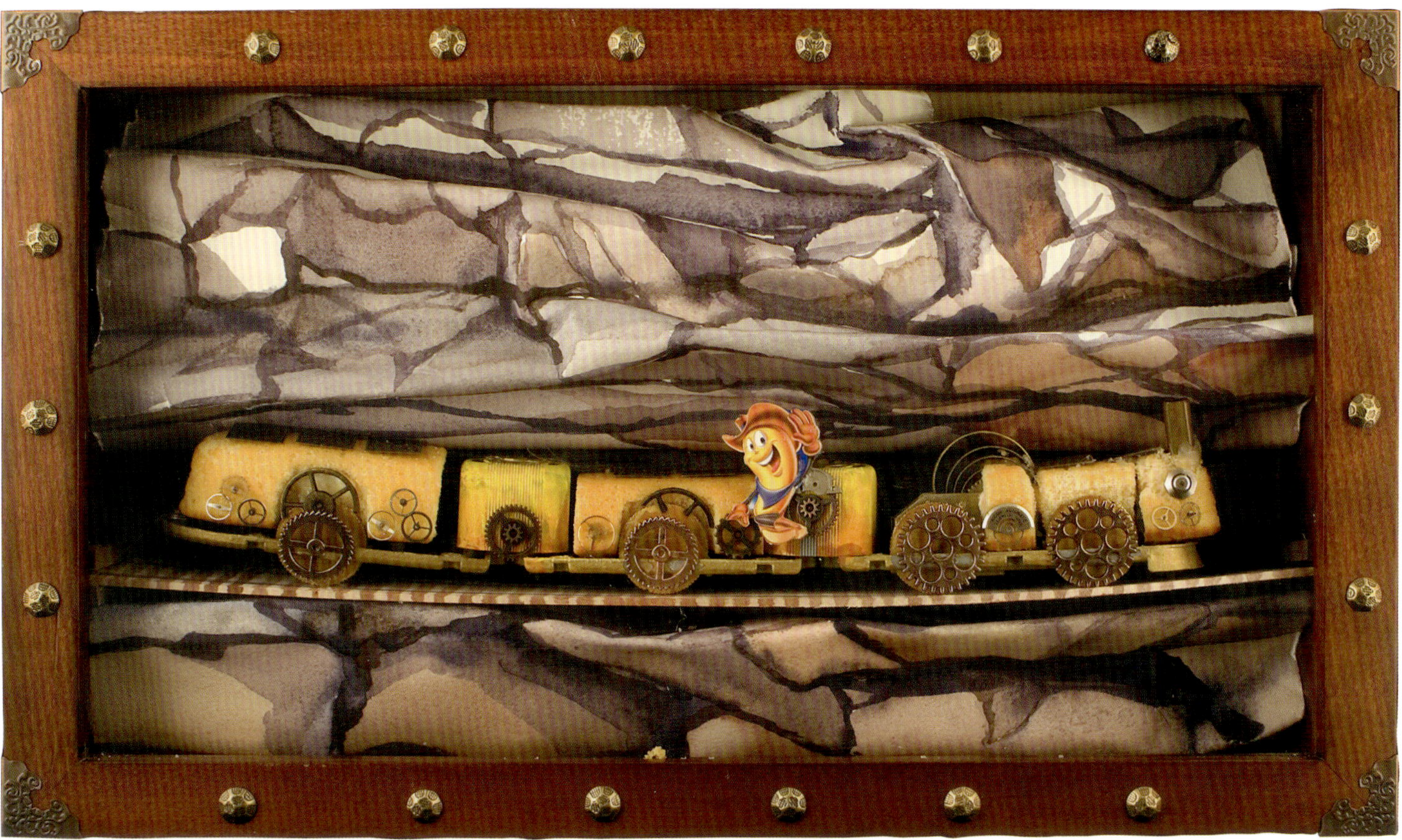

Nancy Peppin, *Cmdr. T. T. Kidd's Steam Subway Train.* Watercolor and mixed media of real Twinkies on paper; 9 x 14 x 2½ in. Photographed by Pete Slingland.

and structure design, and I'm sitting on one of her creations, a sturdy chair of walnut, as I conduct the interview.

Typical of her style of taking on multiple ventures, Peppin taught at UNR, managed the Truckee Meadows Community College Gallery, did contract work for the Nevada Humanities committee, and opened her home business, Nancy Peppin Graphic Arts. In spite of all these projects, she never stopped making her own art, although in the early 1990s exhibition opportunities in Reno were few.[1]

Her marriage dissolved, and because UNR wouldn't hire her to teach more than six units, she didn't qualify for benefits. But she soldiered on, growing her graphic arts business, completing mural projects, and doing her contract work. She began making little moose ornaments and decided to begin a mass production business with the animals, but she says, "It was part of the failure of being female." Banks would not make loans to a woman with a home-based business, and when she called folks in South Korea about mass-producing they wouldn't talk to a woman.

But like many who have undergone loss, this artist rose from the depths. She applied to and was hired by Reno's International Game Technology for twenty years.

Her professional life is a bit like her house—jam-packed with a variety of different interests, each one requiring deep insight and attention. She continues to operate her graphic arts business. She designs and produces history and photography books as well as logos, posters, brochures, and the like. She volunteers for such nonprofit agencies as the Artemisia Movie Home and the Audubon Society. She's a lifetime member of the Sierra Club. And of course, she never ever stopped creating art.

"You just make your own energy," she says, as if that explains everything.

Early on, she decided that Hostess Cakes were the epitome of American culture. She created watercolors of Hostess Cakes, an etching first of Twinkies, and serigraph of the cakes. She still does cupcakes from time to time, but has never left the Twinkies. After Hostess Brands, manufacturer of these cakes, announced closure, Peppin painted *The Last Snack*, a takeoff of da Vinci's *The Last Supper* featuring Twinkies, Ding Dongs, Ho Hos, and other Hostess products gathered at a table.

Why Twinkies? I wonder. She mentions the Warhol idea of making everyday objects into art as an influence, then adds with a smile, "I'm definitely not in the 'in crowd.'"

Thankfully, she's not, for to see the work in progress for her upcoming show is to wonder at this artist's brain and wish for one like it.

An earlier work in a California *Food as Medium* show, her *Dia de los Muertos Nicho* included *milagros*, worry dolls, and skeletons. But nowhere is Peppin's offbeat sense of humor more evident than in the title of her upcoming show, *The Steampunk Machines of Cmdr. T. T. Kidd: Steam Twink*. The dioramas described earlier (gondola, hot air balloon, boat, rocket ship) play large parts in the show, and to call the media "mixed" is to make an understatement. For this show she has created a variety of tiny objects of transportation, using everything from handmade paper to plastic palms, dinosaurs, balls, paper cutouts, mushrooms, little wheels, paint, and more. Peppin was, of course, responding to the retro-futuristic aesthetic called Steampunk, which draws inspiration from nineteenth-century steam-powered technology.

Her description on the show announcement declares, "Following the successful exhibition of Charles Darwin's notes from the 1835 Search for the Darwin Twinkie—a scientific study that has never been equaled—this group of artworks attempts to explain what happened to the Twinkie in the years of the industrial revolution in the world of the later 19th century. Commander T. T. Kidd demonstrates the use of the Twinkie in a full range of 19th-century futurist mechanisms, each presented in context before a representative watercolor of its environment."

I ask Peppin about her process. She takes long walks up the hills and canyons around Reno and says she switches into her right brain. Or she will lie in bed and let her mind wander where it wants. She doesn't check the flow of ideas, but accepts them all until she comes up with a theme. Then she makes a list of possibilities under that theme, or, as she says, "What cool things could be made out of Twinkies." She makes pencil sketches of everything, and then transfers the sketches to watercolor paper. She paints the paper in grisaille and adds glazes for depth and three-dimensionality.[2] She adds paper to the box, wet or dry, depending on the subject. And then the fun of creating Twinkie objects begins. The artist uses actual cream-filled Twinkies, which are preserved to last. She takes them out of the package and goes to work. The shrines she builds are labor intensive and will take several months to complete.

Earlier exhibitions include her Twinkies in History series that portrays how scientists such as John James Audubon, Charles Darwin, and Leonardo da Vinci would have sketched and written about Twinkies in journals or books. Her Audubon series on the "South American Twinkie (twinkopus galapagoensis hostus)" includes illustrations of three "important subspecies—Cream-bellied Twinkie,

Strawberry-throated Twinkie, Golden-backed Twinkie," along with writings describing the so-called birds. She updated this series after Hostess Brands shut down operations: "It went from being the most popular snack cake in the world to sudden extinction due to consumption by raptors—capitalist vultures (cathartes wallstreetidae)."

Viewers and buyers flock to Peppin's exhibitions, and they come prepared to smile a lot and sometimes laugh out loud, while Peppin watches the show, no doubt dreaming up ideas for her next series.

Hostess Brands were out of stock for nine months. Peppin was undaunted. With many potential buyers lined up, she knew that Twinkies would survive into the future.

"It'll become a mutation of the species, but it'll perpetuate the species," she says. "There are all sorts of history applications to explore, like Twinkies being found in the ruins at Pompeii."

As I reluctantly stack my papers and prepare to say goodbye, I notice a sticky note in the artist's hallway, pushed among little statues and a jar of pencils. It reads, "You have to get rid of the life that you planned in order to get the life that is waiting."[3]

■ CLAUDIA KNOUS • BORN 1946

An artist fishes for the visual language that will communicate her unique insights into life and how it works, and Claudia Knous of Carson City, Nevada, chose feltmaking. Years ago, she discovered it could be soaped, pressed, and pushed into any shape she could dream up, and this magical process sent her on a path of delightful exploration that has nourished her creative fire for many years.

Knous's designs might be referred to as "realism in the abstract" because she has brought forth a diverse body of sculpture, some of which allude to the human form; others are as abstract as a Mule's Ear leaf crossing a willow branch. As she leads us to her studio for our interview on May 23, 2013, I pass blazes of color expressed in her felted work—sculptural masterpieces on the walls, in corners, and rising from the floor. Some pieces combine felt with metal in larger-than-life abstractions, while others build on themselves in a mysterious approach that I can't decipher. All are saturated with color; all radiate a sense of delight. This substantial body of felted sculpture, meticulously executed, is the first of its kind in the region.

Felt, for those who who aren't familiar with the term, is a nonwoven textile. To prepare it, Knous adds warm, soapy water to loose fibers, and these fibers then swell, revealing tiny scales. When agitated by rolling, these scales open and entangle with each other, producing the textile. The result can be soft and pliable or tough enough to become construction material. Knous has the ability to create both kinds and frequently does in a progression that is time-consuming and extremely physical. The critical step of pushing a heavy tube over soapy wet wool to trap the design requires her to roll at least one hundred times in each direction as she pushes firmly against the table—much like rolling out a piecrust, except on a larger scale. Her metal work stand is approximately the size of a Ping-Pong table, and some projects require her to press fibers over the entire length and width of this table.

Knous's top physical condition makes her fit for the task. She and husband Ward slice out time hiking, biking, and skiing in the Nevada outback. Carson City is Nevada's capital, and the Knous's home lies smack in the middle of Eagle Valley, on the eastern edge of the Carson Range.

At the time of our interview, Knous is preparing for a four-hundred-mile hike over the Pyrenees Mountains across Spain, along the Camino de Santiago.[4] Her goal is to walk twelve miles each day. "I'm up to nine right now," she says, her dangly earrings bouncing to the nod of her head. "I've got to push myself."

Knous has "pushed herself" from the beginning. She is just four years older than her brother, K.C., a quadriplegic with cerebral palsy. Her home life was different from

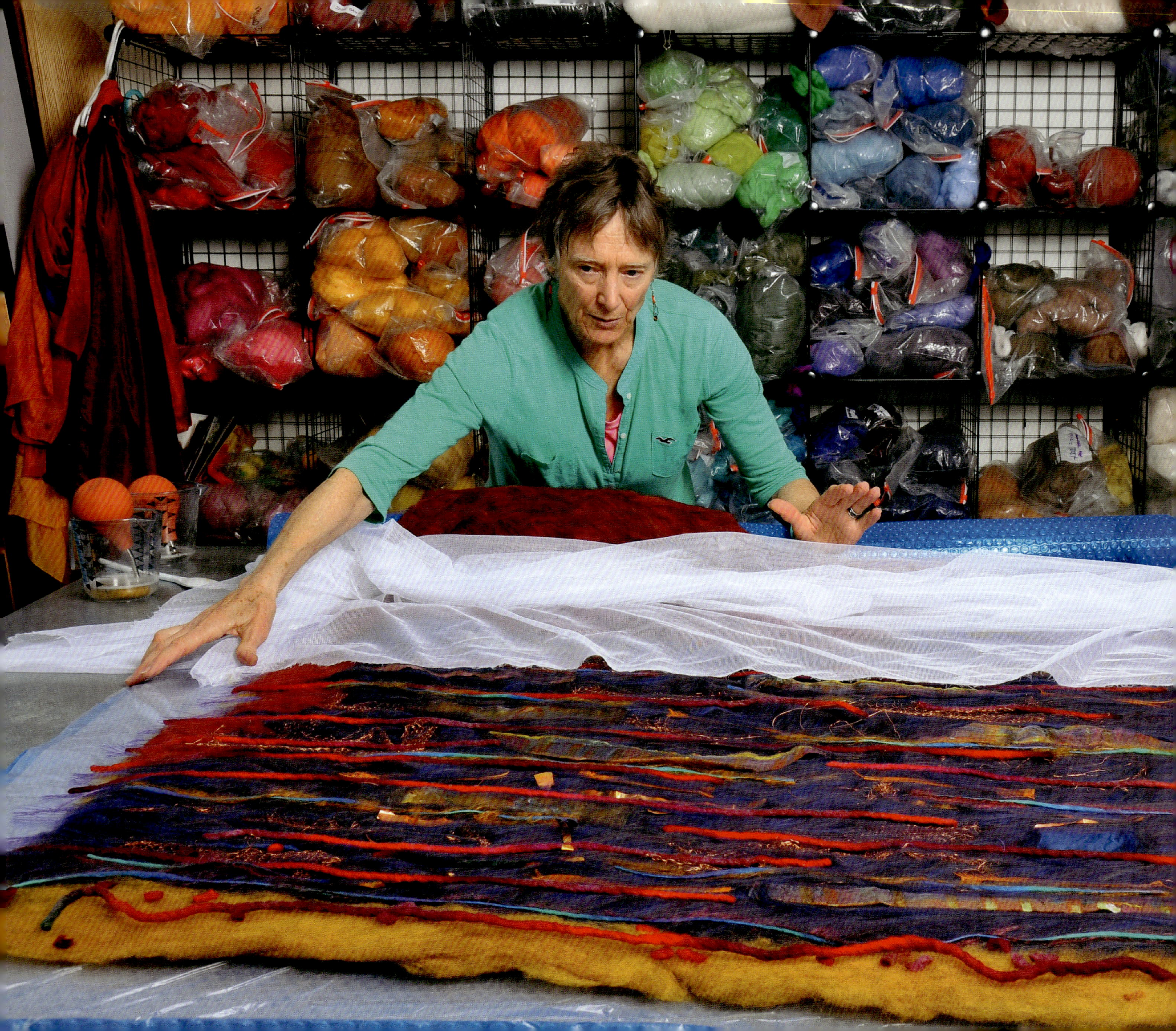

that of most children when growing up. She helped with K.C.'s needs and no doubt was left to her own devices when the family needed to focus on him. Still, the Fresno, California, native says that she was given many choices and even attended eighth grade in Switzerland, then returned to Santa Catalina to attend high school.[5] At Fresno State College, she earned a bachelor of science degree and became a registered nurse and, as usual, she pushed herself to do the most difficult things: she chose critical care nursing.

Knous worked at the Stanford Medical Center in intensive care with open heart and heart transplant patients, but the job eventually became so stressful that she realized a life change was critical to her sanity. She yearned for new adventure, and in 1975 she left California and hospital traumas behind and headed for Mt. Alyeska, a ski resort in Girdwood, Alaska. She found a job with the ski patrol, where she not only returned to her former exuberant self, but also met her future husband, Ward. The two moved to Anchorage and she worked in intensive care unit and emergency room nursing for ten more years.

In 1996 Knous became an elementary school nurse. She enrolled in a feltmaking class and was instantly attracted to the touch and feel of the wet wool, as well as to its sculptural, textural, and color possibilities. More classes followed and she decided to use this newfound art form to create puppets. She used these perky, colorful dolls to teach health and hygiene habits to the schoolchildren. "I made health puppets that sneezed germs," she laughs. "And then there was the head louse puppet with pipe cleaner hair. The kids loved them and could easily visualize how germs and critters [nits] could be spread."

When the couple retired and moved to Carson City in 2002, she began felting in earnest, enrolling in workshops around the country, and discovering new techniques and ways to combine felt with other materials and methods to create sculpture—much of it whimsical and all of it flooded with color.

Claudia Knous preparing to roll the fibers in the felting process.

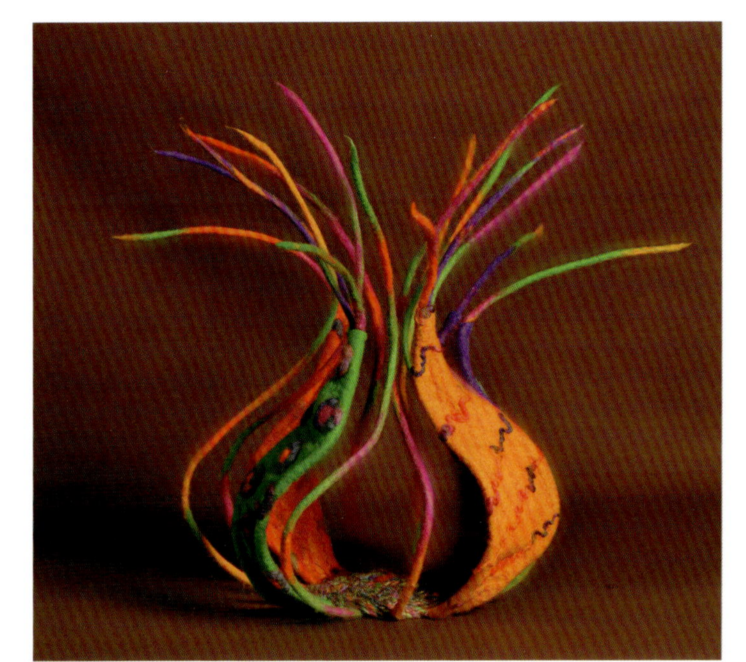

Claudia Knous, *Tendril Basket*, mixed media of felt making with wire and yarns; 1 ft. 6 in. x 1 ft. 6 in. x 1 ft.

"My mom is responsible for that risky manipulation of color," she says, as we munch on one of her warm homemade scones and sip lattes. "Mom was ahead of her time. She once even made a fluorescent Christmas tree! She went back to college when I did, took art, and made a little studio in back of the house. She was such an influence." Claudia went on, "When I started making felt infused with color, Mom said 'Good! You won't be limited to the rules they teach in school.'" She smiled. "Now I fiddle with the color until it feels good."

Much of her inspiration comes during long hikes, and there she remembers the Spanish Catalan architect Antoni Gaudí's belief that "Nothing is invented, for it is discovered in nature first." Knous adds to that thought, "Each outing supplies a wealth of creative ideas for an art piece, not to mention inner peace." Knous revels in a red Indian

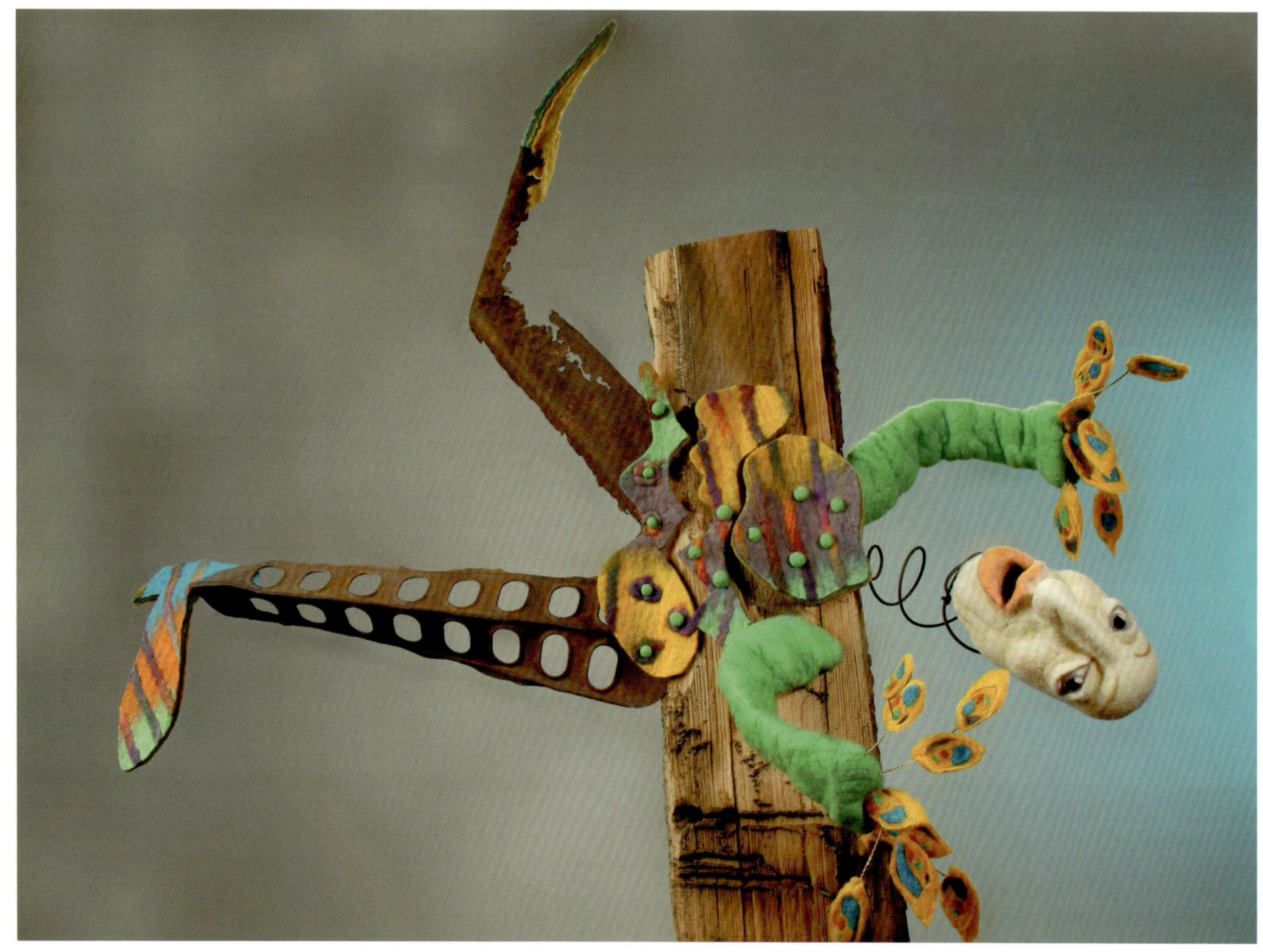

Claudia Knous, *Acrobat*. Mixed media of felt making assembled with found metal and cedar wood; 4 x 4 x 1 ft.

paintbrush, blue lupine peeking out from behind a stone, a snow plant against the high desert sand, or a blazing sunset streaking across the evening sky. She's aware of long, tall shadows of juniper and pine, the lacy texture of a dried Mule's Ear leaf, snow on branches backlit by sun, and the texture and multiple colors of the peeling bark on old aspen trunks. "There is so much beauty in the desert."

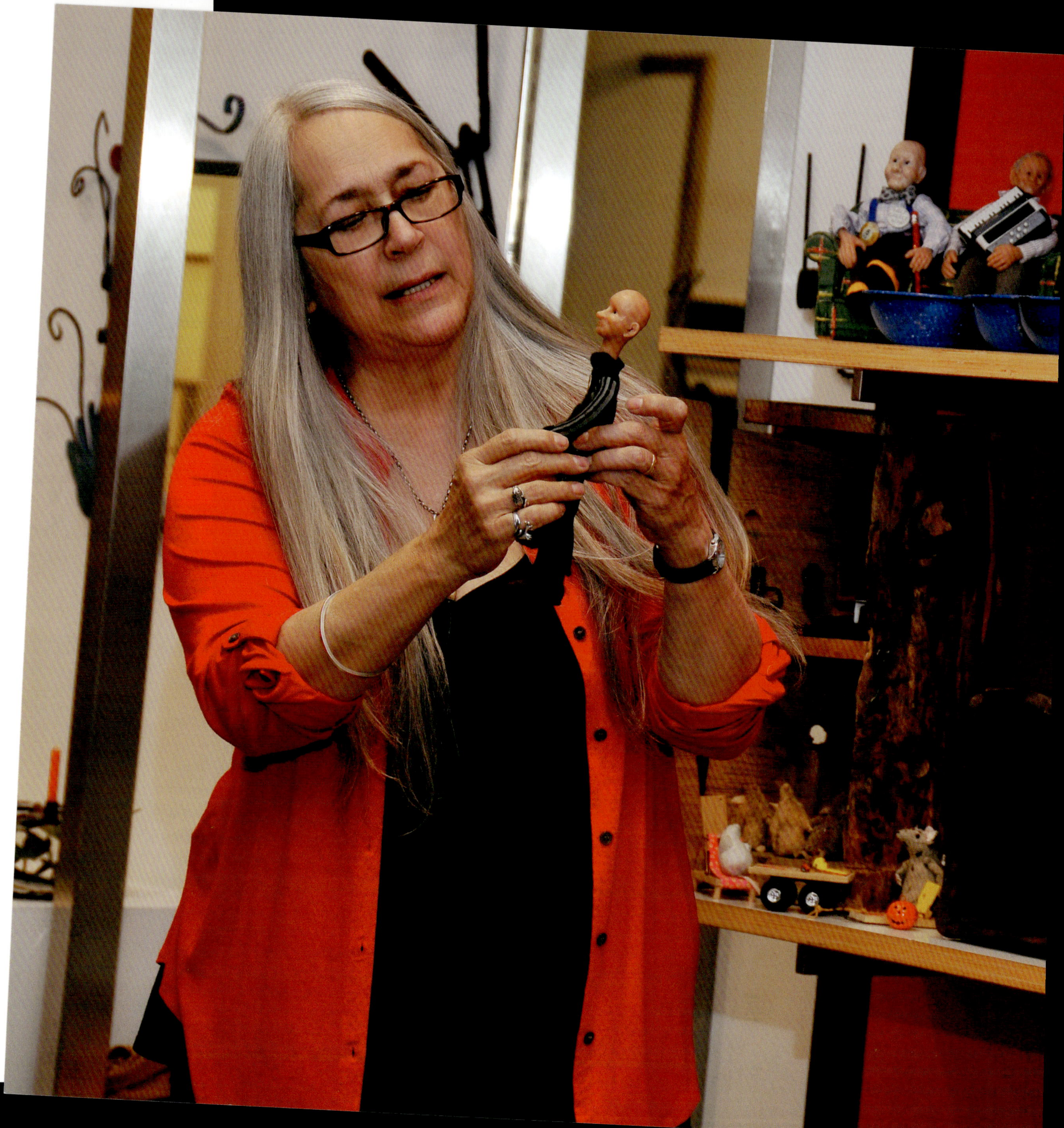

Most Great Basin artists do not have the luxury of living near other professionals in their field. In Knous's case, the dearth is greater, because felters are scarce, if not completely

on stilts—he's too scared to take a step away from the wall. There will be a flying pig, and of course Onion Ed will be there, weeping, and the Sock Guy with all his socks. There will be an art gallery and library, run by Fred Mouse, who is trying to distance himself from this tawdry circus.

That's all for now, because I am in the midst of making nurse uniforms for some mouse girls who will work in the infirmary at the circus. The infirmary is right next to the place where Mario Gorgonzola will be holding a cheese-eating contest. That's why we have to have an infirmary—mice really don't know their limits when it comes to cheese!

Thank you so much, dear Mary Lee, for this invitation. The Underfolk and I will work out some method of equal representation so no one feels left out.

Love, Kathleen

During the interview on February 21, 2014, I pull a chair up to her kitchen table, arrange my notepad and recorder on the blue-and-white checked cloth, and take in the scene. Durham faces me, her back to the cooking area, filled with hanging pots and spoon jars; plants peek out from crocks on the windowsill. A pie cools on the sideboard and atop the stove a lid bounces in the steam rising from its pan. Our small table expands, she tells me, to serve twelve easily. Relaxing against the wall side of the table, a crowd of eight-inch-high Underfolk, each with its own unique coloring and outfits, oversees our interview, their eyes following our every word. Durham explains why she developed this art form while I glance at the little dolls and fully expect them to smile and nod their heads.

"Children are enthralled by stories. Sometimes it's a burden to be a grownup, asking, 'Is this true?' But it really doesn't matter." She straightens a jacket on Onion Ed and continues, "What I do may appear silly, but I take it very seriously. I feel stories are hugely important in our lives—and not just for children!"

Indeed, stories are how we make sense of ourselves and our world. It's likely that oral storytelling has been around as long as human language. Our ancestors probably hunkered around night fires and voiced their fears, beliefs, enchantments, and heroics through story. Today, this type of spoken communication is truly an art form in three dimensions. And Durham, who constructs and outfits small whimsical clay figures that give shape to her stories, has extended her wordsmithing into the realm of sculpture. As she says, "Words are the colors in my storytelling palette."

Small figures have a long history, too. For centuries, humans have felt that dolls emanate a sort of holiness. In her book *Women Who Run with the Wolves* (1992, 89), author Clarissa Pinkola Estes says the doll is the symbol of what lies buried in humans that is a glowing facsimile of the original Self. "Superficially, it is just a doll," she says. "But inversely, there is a little piece of soul that carries all the knowledge of the larger soul self." And so the word *doll* loses its characterization as being childish and takes on deeper significance.

Once informed by a high school art teacher that she had no talent, Durham has taken her stories and little people—Underfolk, as she calls them—to exhibition venues in northern Nevada and California, including galleries, museums, art centers, doll shows, and colleges. She's a museum docent and a participant in Artown, Reno's annual July celebration of the arts. Cultural and civic groups invite her to present the Underfolk and their tales at various gatherings, and her stories are in great demand at shows sponsored by the Wild Women, of which Durham is a longtime member.

The Wild Women shows present some difficulty, as eager adults arrive early and grab the front-row chairs. Durham has solved that problem by inviting the children to sit on the floor very near the Underfolk village. She sets the stage to pick up an Underfolk character for her story with Earl Grey and Jasmine settled in their antique teapot house,

Kathleen Weymouth Durham in the midst of a storytelling event, *Here Is Bobby Pin*.

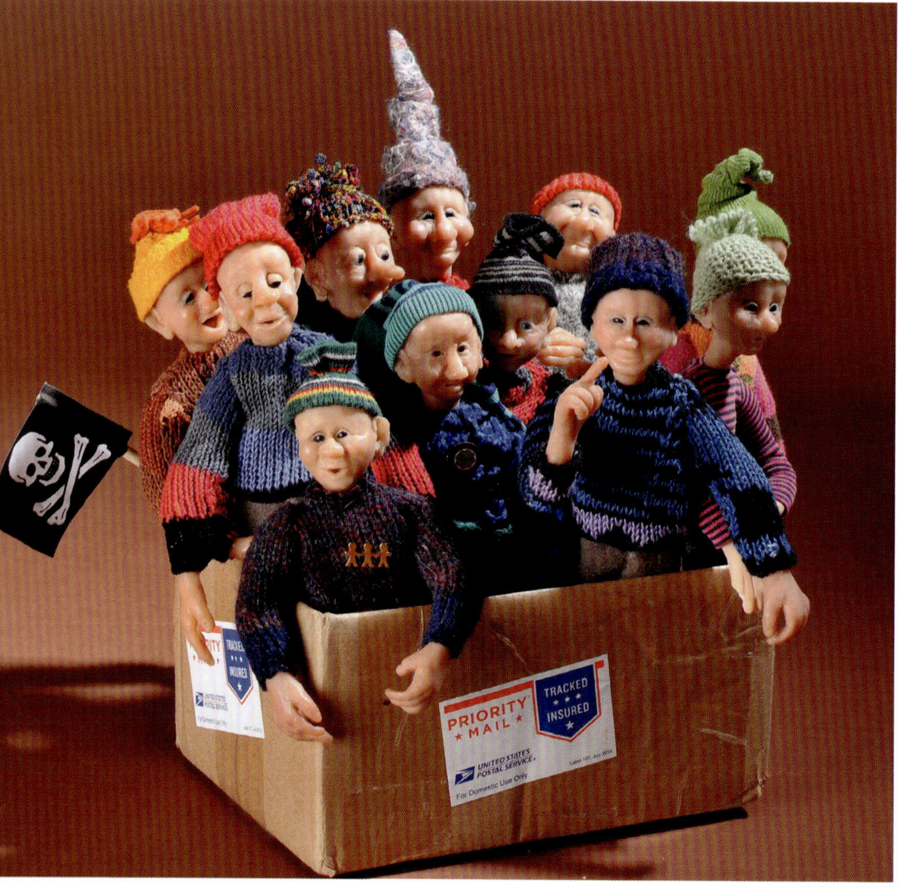

Kathleen Weymouth Durham, *The Thirteen Icelandic Brothers Ready to Launch Their Pirate Ship*. Mixed media of polymer, wire, wool, and more; variable dimensions.

the mice riding the Ferris wheel, several Underfolk busy in the dollhouse while others are in residence in the large stump of a tree, and still others are hanging around with their various props (a zucchini, onion, or Christmas ornament hanger) and watching the pig and goose fly overhead. Grandmothers and two-year-olds lean in, so as not to miss a word. Oldsters chuckle while children frown to hear of Fred Mouse, who "fell in love but didn't realize it was a red silk tassel he saw hanging from the draperies. He thought

she was just very quiet." At program's end, children sign the birthday book and volunteer to pass miniature cookies, which the Underfolk are said to have baked earlier.

Durham explains her motivations. "It was my grandmother, Mary, who lived with us and taught me to sew," she says. "I made tiny things then. I remember her always when I sew. She's the one who shaped my love of fabric. And it was my mother who taught me that in our house everything was alive—the toaster and vacuum, they all had names and personalities—so I think she was the one who made me a storyteller."

It seemed Durham, daughter of Margaret (an elementary school teacher) and Al (a highway engineer father), was destined for an idyllic life in San Francisco, the city of her birth. But on Christmas day when she was five, everything changed. Her eight-year-old brother, Bill, was diagnosed with infantile paralysis (or polio as the disease was called). The doctor hammered a quarantine sign on the front door, packed Bill in blankets, and took him away. Two weeks later, Durham stumbled and fell. She, too, had contracted this dangerous illness, which became a national epidemic where many children lost their lives. All the San Francisco hospitals were full. Bill returned home to share a room with his sister, and the doctor taught Margaret to exercise the children's limbs and make hot packs to continually press over them, in accordance with the new Sister Kenney therapy treatment. Margaret moved a wringer washing machine into the kitchen and made hot packs all day, grandmother Mary prepared meals, and the family soldiered on.

As they recovered, the children heard stories and followed the San Francisco Seals baseball team on radio. Durham learned to read. Their parents obtained a great dollhouse, placed it under the big living room window, and Durham concocted stories about the little creatures that lived there. Both children eventually recovered and returned to public school, but Durham never regained complete control of one leg. "Polio changed me," she says, her long, gray-streaked hair falling forward as she leans in. "I couldn't jump rope. I was never good enough at any sport—I was always the last one chosen."

Tragedy struck again. Father Al suffered a stroke and died at the young age of fifty-three, and grandmother Mary passed away the same year. In high school Durham, who had always loved sewing and making things, signed up for drawing and painting. "But the teacher told me I had no talent." She believed the man's pronouncement, and "I never made anything after that until I had my sons. Then I made things for them."

She met future husband Griff in high school and they reconnected at the University of California, Berkeley. "President Kennedy spoke at Cal Berkeley about the Peace Corps and Sargent Shriver, its first director, was with him. As soon as Mr. Shriver talked, we knew we were going. There were so many service-oriented things going on. Hundreds of kids were registering black voters in the south." She gazes out the window, "Those were idealistic times. We believed in serving."

The Durhams went to Brazil, where the artist taught sewing and worked with midwives, and Griff, an agriculturalist, helped develop a hog-breeding project. Since they were among the first Peace Corps members, the couple next traveled to Wisconsin, where they taught other volunteers and helped to instill the fledgling organization with the knowledge, compassion, and credibility that remains fundamental to the Peace Corps.

Next, the couple headed to the University of California, Los Angeles, where Griff worked on his master's degree and Durham fell in love with the art department, majoring in art history. When she became pregnant, the couple realized they didn't want to raise children in Hollywood. Griff was hired as an anthropology teaching assistant at UNR, and in 1969 they headed north and east, stopping for a few weeks with her mother in San Francisco, where Matthew was born. Griff maintained his interest in agriculture and the family always had horses; in fact, a visitor to their rambling southeast Reno home today might stretch out in the living room beside a fine big saddle.

Son Will was born in 1973 and soon Kathleen began her creative endeavors. "Grandpa Troll was the first one I made. When I had his little head in my hands, I realized I actually made something out of clay—it was amazing!" And Durham's clay people with whimsical and captivating histories took shape.

When she begins a story, the baffle of sound that surrounds her seems to part, and a silence moves right through it. No feet shuffling or distant traffic or people talking; we hear only Durham's smooth, custardy voice rising and falling, as the newest Underwood (home to the Underfolk) drama streams like liquid honey from her lips. Her serious expression affirms the story will be true; yet behind the solemnity, a great smile of light blazes, and in this glow we lean forward so as not to miss a single word:

> Maybe some of you remember when the Undermice came to live with us in Underwood. They had been evicted from their ancestral home, and had staged several dramatic protests, which nobody saw, and had a Million Mouse March, which nobody saw. So they moved right in here, and things have never been the same. That was almost ten years ago, and apparently they long for those good old days of political activism. We've become aware of lots of mouse meetings, and placards being produced, and speeches being rehearsed. I truly do not know what their cause is, because I think they have it pretty easy here—free room and board, a dollhouse, an art gallery, a library, and access to my fridge. Plans for a large Underwood library are underway, and tweets have been sent out (by bird) advertising for a librarian. And in the meantime, Mr. Punch has been busy getting the books catalogued. He isn't very efficient. He reads and reads, but I haven't seen much organizing going on.

As far as the creative process, sometimes Durham begins with an idea, such as thinking how nice it would be not to cry (Onion Ed). Other times, she'll see an object, like an antique teapot, which inspires an entire story (in this case it was Earl Grey and his wife Jasmine). Every figure is hand sculpted, down to tiny fingers and toes, using wire, paper, clay, and more. After the pieces are fired, she finds appropriate fabrics and stitches intricate pieces of clothing.

Durham's artistic trajectory was inspired by family—mother, mother-in-law, and grandmother—as well as fabric artist and designer Jean Ray Laury, and various folk art and artists. Other role models include local artists Sue Morrison, Joan Arrizabalaga, and Pam Hatzenbiler, and a stream of well-known women: Beatrix Potter, Mother Teresa, Tina Fey, Rosalind Carter, Michelle Obama. Children's literature, "from Pooh to Babar to Peter Rabbit," have played center stage since her childhood polio days, and now she reads her treasured stories to granddaughter Eleanor, who often makes up stories of her own. Durham says Griff "has been a rock. He schlepps everything for me—Will and Matt, too. My family is very supportive."

As for her Great Basin influence, Durham says, "Griff and I came to Nevada forty-three years ago and I have never regretted it for a minute. I could never live in a place that doesn't have a sky like this. I love this big blue sky—it's empowering and exhilarating. I love the inclusiveness of Nevada—everybody fits in. I thought I would miss the ocean. I didn't know that I would replace it with something more complex and wonderful and subtle. Living between the amazing Sierras and the desert is always new, always exciting. And Reno is just the right size."

Offering advice, Durham picks up one little man to illustrate a point. "Onion Ed here cries for you. If you bump your knee you just go to him and he'll do it. He's not sad, he just is good at crying." She adds, "Every artist has a guy on her shoulder at one time or another who says you're not good enough." She pauses. "You have to knock him off."

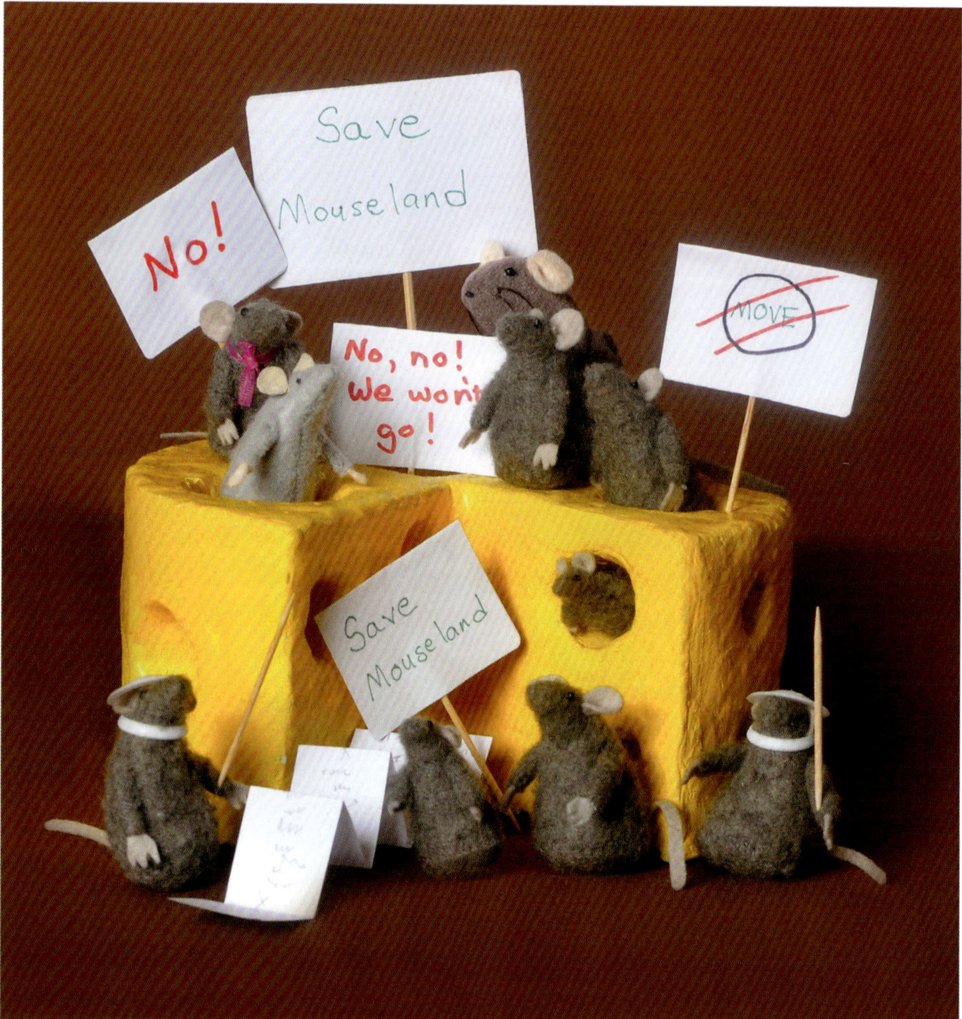

Kathleen Weymouth Durham, *Getting Ready for the Million Mouse March*. Mixed media, variable dimensions.

This artist manages to address issues of the day with spontaneity, using the age-old tradition of story, while telling it through her inventive, wistful, or playful characters. In this way, we sense a freshness not seen in any other art form. But Durham explains it much more simply. She mentioned a quote from *Crow and Weasel* (1998), a book about self-discovery by Barry Lopez and Tom Pohrt, one that has had a lasting influence on her determination to keep her stories and figures alive: "The stories people tell have a way of taking care of them. If stories come to you, you care for them. And learn to give them away where they are needed. Sometimes a person needs a story more than food to stay alive."

She continues with her own philosophy: "The whole thing about storytelling is wanting to pass on Fairy Gold. If you hoard it, it disappears. But if you tell a story, the people will give it away and away, and it passes on."

CHRISTINE SHIVELY-BENJAMIN • BORN 1952

Small inanimate people—in other words, dolls—offer collectors and viewers an opportunity to recreate their own early lives, and they can remember and celebrate their youthful worlds. The therapeutic value can't be overlooked either, for dolls often soothe a psychological need or an emotional void. Immediately, then, the word *doll* loses its characterization as being childish and assumes a status of significance and credibility.

Christine Shively-Benjamin, of Carson City, Nevada, calls upon her art background to create dolls that have exhibited in shows and fairs around the country. When I interviewed her on May 23, 2013, she was preparing to leave for the United Federation of Doll Clubs conference in Kansas City, and recently stepped down as its national president.[6] A member of the Original Doll Artist Council of America, she teaches and shows at various venues nationally and never stops learning, enrolling in classes whenever possible.

"Everything I create has to be an illusion," she says. "I want to evoke some kind of response that challenges your perception." She adds that her work continues to change, sometimes in ways that surprise even her.

For Shively-Benjamin, exploring the possibilities of creating a character with fabric is the result of a lifetime fascination with dimensional forms. She grew up in Denver, Colorado, and was the second of six children with plenty of opportunity to play dress-up, read and tell stories, stage neighborhood theater productions, and watch movies. "I loved *The King and I* and *Gone with the Wind*," she says, "and I bookmarked pages and pages from a book series we had called Lands and People." She received a Barbie doll the first year Barbies came out. All these influences gave her a background of period costuming with a contemporary edge and a love of story and possibility.

Her art degree from Kansas Wesleyan University in Salina prepared her for options. Although she also obtained a teaching certificate and taught school at the secondary level in Salina, she tells me, "I always wanted to make a living with my imagination."

The drawing and painting, sculpture, and art history classes were the preparation for a doll maker just waiting to emerge. It was always tucked away in the back of her mind that a doll could encompass storytelling and costuming into a dimensional figure.

Her new husband, Lou Lyda, a light-hearted teacher, was supportive and encouraging as she explored this unusual art form. And because she loved the theatricality of costuming, Shively-Benjamin wanted dolls that expressed the drama of theater and the stories of her childhood delights.

"There was just one problem," she says, smiling. "I couldn't sew. Back in high school Home Ec, I got a D minus in sewing." But she called upon her art background and, she adds, nodding, as her silver-white hair springs around her head in coils much like those of her dolls, "this allowed me to play. I examined all the possibilities." She actually learned to sew by replaying the movie *Cinderella*, and used the same technique as the little mice characters when they threaded a needle and sewed Cinderella's gown.

A connection to the ancient arts of doll making and storytelling, as well as historical and cultural traditions, all

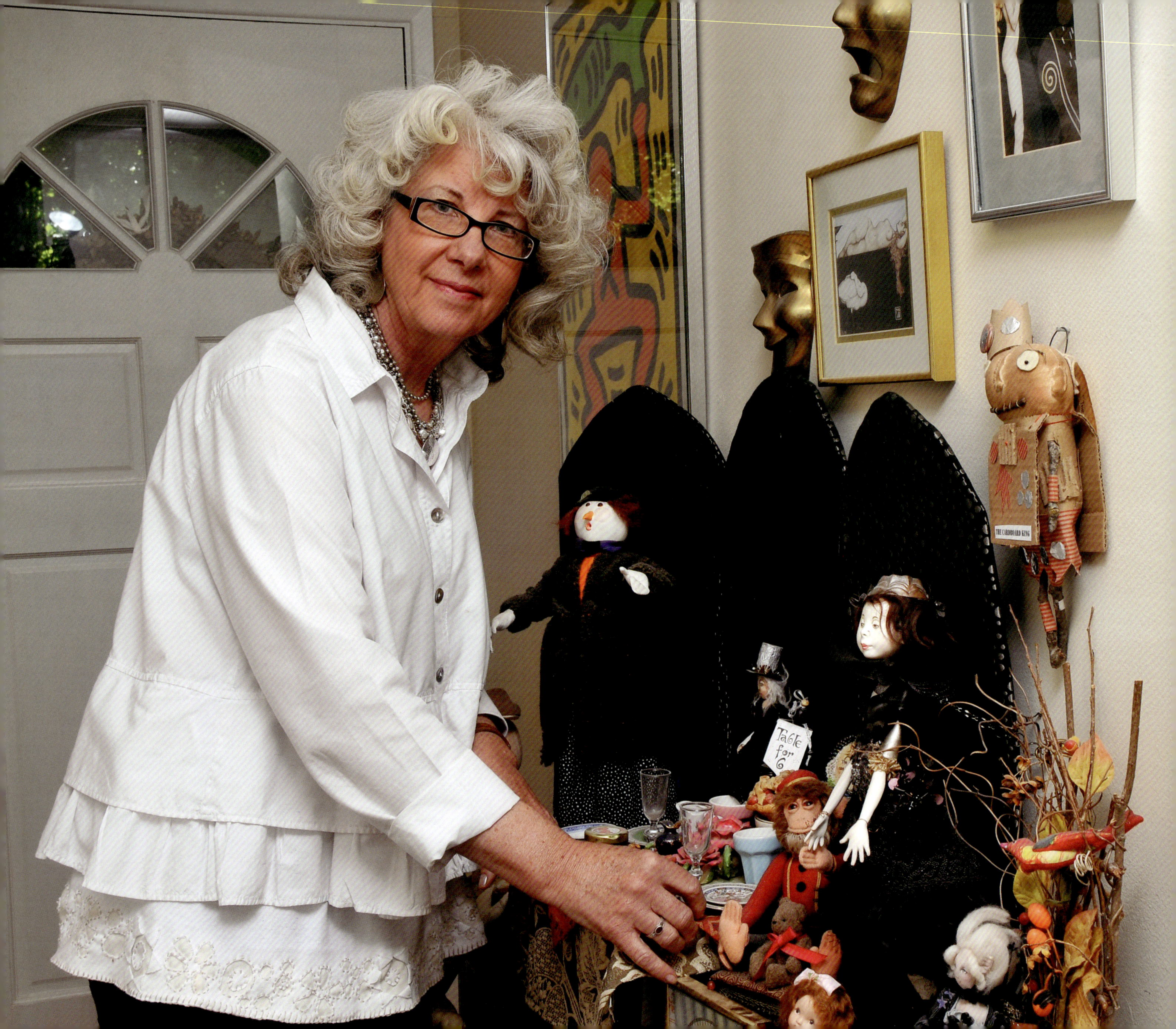
THE CARDBOARD KING
Table for 6

play into her designs that have evolved over the years from simple to innovative. She likes to quote Misaru Ibuka, who said, "Creating comes from looking at the unexpected and stepping outside your own experience."[7] One series might revolve around a trend, such as Steampunk, or a ceremony, or even an emotion. (Currently, she's working around a theme of royalty.) She draws inspiration from a variety of media—Peggy J. Parks's *Impressionism*, the Bravo channel program "Inside the Actor's Studio," and all of the Alabama Chanin books.

After coming up with a subject, she draws the body shape and structure she plans to use for her fabric figures, which range from ten to twenty inches high. She transfers this drawing to the fabric and breaks down the parts into simple shapes—cylinders, squares, and triangles. "It appears complicated, but it's really not," she says. "I want the piece to be simple but clever."

She then sews, incorporating other materials as well—beads, papier mâché, recycled wires, and so on. A used file folder might transform into a fairy-tale book, a baby shoe might become a girdle. The costuming and embellishment are key elements in expressing her theme, and colored pencil and acrylic paint add features, contours, and depth. Each doll has a purpose; each has a name.

When photographer Susan Mantle and I arrive at Shively-Benjamin's home, the first thing to greet us is a ceremonial diorama of a tea party. Alice's rabbit stands at the front to welcome us, and behind him smiles a carrot-nose storyteller, a storybook doll, and a red-capped monkey holding hands with a princess, while a silver-hatted magician presides over the well-appointed tea table. Shively-Benjamin is preparing for a show, and every available space in her living room holds a figure. There are no two dolls alike—there are never any two alike because they are created one at a time. Her entire house is filled with art—wall pieces, handmade books, rugs, and, in the corner, a hay cart

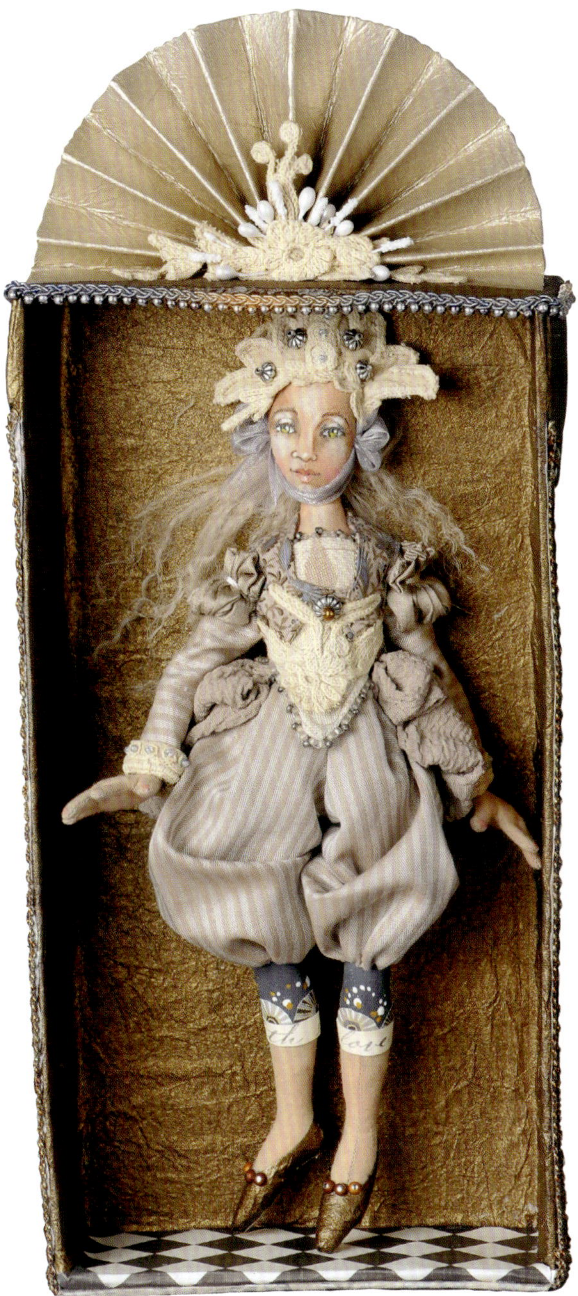

Christine Shively-Benjamin, *Altered Ego*. Mixed media; 15½ x 4½ in.

Christine Shively-Benjamin arranging a diorama.

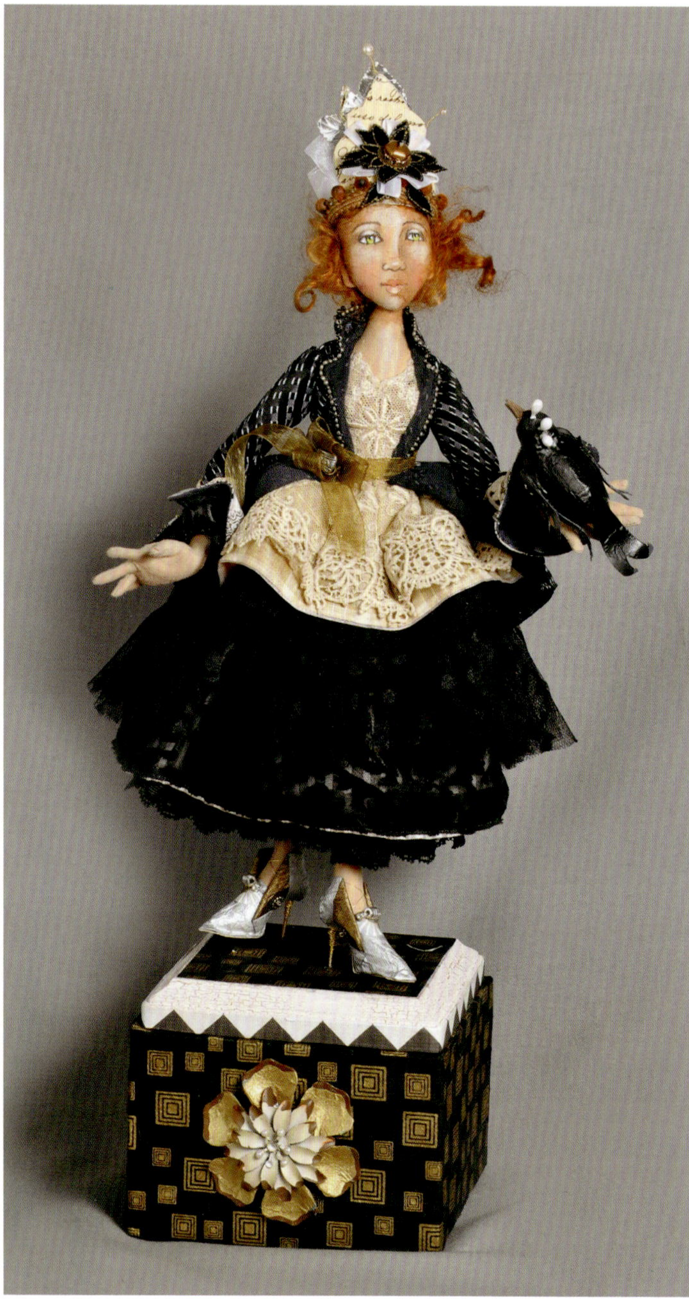

Christine Shively-Benjamin, *Return to Me II*. Mixed media; 15½ x 4½ in.

piled with baskets. I realize I have entered a realm presided over by an illusionist.

In the beginning, her constructions were simply a hobby. Back in 1980, when she and husband Lou were teachers, their summers were free, and they traveled around various cities, where Shively-Benjamin began showing and selling at art fairs. Then in 1983 she donated a doll to a charity auction, and the unbelievable happened: her doll received one of the top bids. It was time to get serious. She participated in the big Kansas City Renaissance Festival, a fall tradition and major event in the Midwest.[8] With the help of her sisters, whom she costumed, Shively-Benjamin was part of that festival for the next seven years.

Life was good, and then, suddenly, it was not. Husband Lou passed away in 2001, and Shively-Benjamin grieved terribly. She says, "Like millions of women who lose spouses, I had to navigate the grieving process while still trying to make a living. The difference is that I had to be able to tap into my imagination to create dolls that my buyers would like to purchase [while] at the same time I felt the loss of my husband and supportive partner. I did not have the luxury of tinkering with sketches." She met her second husband while they were dropping off newspapers, bottles, and cans at the Walmart Recycling Center in Lawrence, Kansas. An attorney, Charles's environmental work brought them to Carson City in 2007, and the couple purchased a home. For Shively-Benjamin, being once again surrounded by mountains brought back childhood memories of Colorado, and she settled in easily. Her cheery home had room for a studio, and the fabric characters developed cousins—the *Queen of Hearts* and the *Jewel of Experience* seemed to gaze out with sad eyes, but they, and their cousins that followed, began to enter shows and to find new homes.

Charles developed cancer and, after a valiant struggle, passed away in 2010. Once more, Shively-Benjamin was set adrift by a loss that was compounded by the first one. One year passed, then two, and three. She finally rose again from despair and began the long, lonesome trek back to reality—the reality of living alone.

Except, she wasn't really alone, because her people—her dolls, her characters in fabric, and her creations—waited patiently. They occupied her studio, living room, kitchen, bedroom, and even the bathroom. As she says, "the fabric and paper speak to me in many voices. The combination of these voices gives life and harmony to the finished figures." Strangely enough, as I settle in to the interview, I realize the figures do seem alive and, as Shively-Benjamin reports, they do exist in harmony with one another. "All art is autobiographical," she tells me.

And with the deepening of her emotions came thoughtful new figures—*The Gift, Beyond Your Own Experience, Return to Me*. She recalls, "Throughout the tough transitions of rebuilding my life from loss, the one constant that I could always count on is my imagination and desire to create art. It is the one thing that will be with me till the day I die. And it has never let me down. It still amazes me that I was able to make a living creating beautiful dolls."

She feels rooted in Carson City, surrounded by mountains that lie on the eastern edge of the Sierra Nevada. "There's a sense of home when you live in the mountains," she tells me. "Carson City feels like a hometown." It seems like this artist has settled in to stay, working and creating little inanimate people only she can.

The introduction to her website, www.fancifulclothimages.com, begins with this quote: "Imagination takes flight on the wings of Dreams."

Notes

1. Reno's oldest gallery, the Artists Co-Op Gallery Reno, limited exhibition to members only. Galleries within UNR campus were restricted to student art and art with intellectual, or teaching, content. Stremmel Gallery primarily showcased artists from outside the Truckee Meadows. Sierra Arts Foundation—a nonprofit organization created in 1977 by Carol Mousel, Fran Harvey, and Barbara Feltner to serve Reno and Northern Nevada—developed and supported local artists. It did not offer a gallery until later, when Reno attorney William C. Thornton, a longtime supporter of local arts and artists, opened one in the basement of his office building, located on the corner of Sierra and First Streets, site of the earlier Montgomery Ward store and the present-day Reno Parking Garage. Sue Clark managed the gallery, and at last local artists had a show venue.
2. Grisaille is a term for painting entirely in monochrome, in shades of gray.
3. Joseph Campbell (1904–1987), author of this adage, was an American mythologist, writer and lecturer. His philosophy is often summarized by his phrase, "Follow your bliss."
4. Known as The Way of St. James in English, this is an ancient pilgrimage route where tradition has it that the remains of the apostle Saint James are buried.
5. Established by the Dominican Sisters, the Santa Catalina upper school for girls is a boarding and day school in Monterey, California.
6. The organization was originally named the Doll Owners of America.
7. The late electronics industrialist Masaru Ibuka cofounded what is now Sony. He authored the book *Kindergarten Is Too Late* (1971), claiming that the most significant human learning occurs from birth to three years old.
8. A longtime popular event in the Midwest, this fair, held in Bonner City, with its 165 booths, 150 shops and vendors, and thirteen stages, entertains 180,000 visitors annually. It begins on Labor Day weekend and continues for seven weekends.

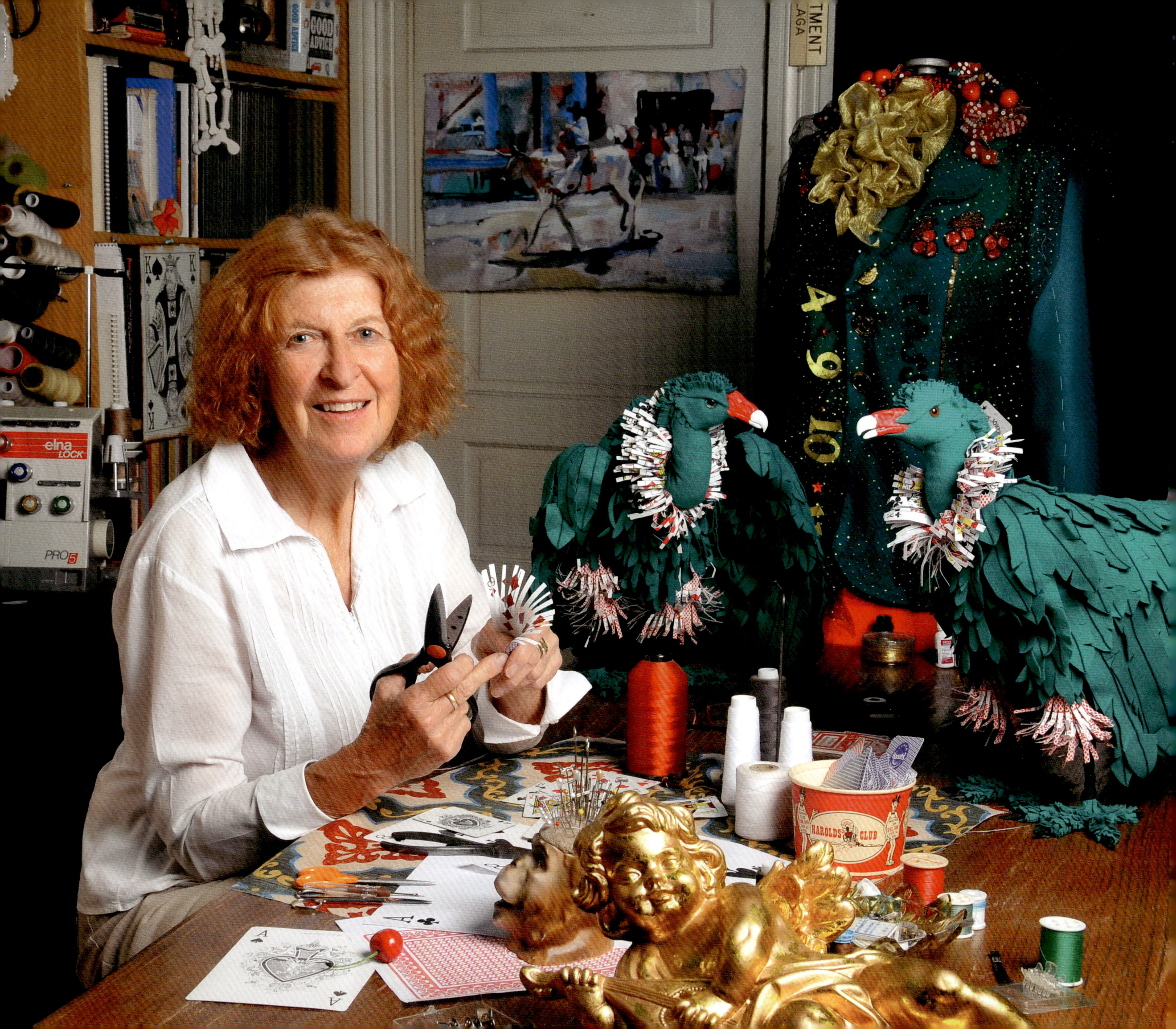
GOOD ADVICE
elna LOCK
PRO5
HAROLDS CLUB

HONORING

It's not unusual to attend a ceremony to celebrate someone's accomplishments, character, or high moral standards. But it is rare to see an artist who spends her career paying tribute to just one chosen topic, profession, or culture. Three artists in this book have diligently and persistently paid tribute to single subjects that have occupied their thoughts and work over many years.

Joan Arrizibalaga has focused on gaming and all the themes it engenders, including its historic beginnings. Pam Bowman's work pays tribute to the seemingly ordinary domestic pursuits of the homemaker. Demetrice Dalton broadens her scope to honor the stories and activities of non-white cultures.

JOAN ARRIZABALAGA • BORN 1939

Artist Joan Arrizabalaga's gaming themes of compulsion, luck, temptation, winning, and chance are ideas explored by many of us. Her grandparents, Ramon Arrizabalaga and his wife, Tomasa Erquiaga, who lived in the Spanish Basque province of Alava (today, referred to in its Basque orthography of Araba), exercised those very themes when, in 1909, they abandoned their village and took a chance to follow their dreams in America. They left family, home, and friends behind, crossed the ocean, and headed to Austin, Nevada. Ramon began herding sheep, and over their lifetime the couple won happiness and prosperity beyond their wildest dreams.

Little did they know that decades later their granddaughter would explore the same passionate issues that had powered her grandparents. The difference is that she articulates them in two- and three-dimensional art forms that reveal some of the deeper elements of the state's primary industry—gambling (or *gaming*, as it's referred to these days).

"There's the psychological part of it," she tells me as she attaches a green felt feather (cut from a blackjack table cover) to a papier mâché vulture, part of a sculpture in progress she calls *Dead Man's Hand.* "Temptation, risk, and winning—everything can be a gamble." Arrizabalaga's contemporary artworks like *Easy Money, Midas Well, You Betcha, Felt Alive, The Roll of the Dice,* and *The Luck of the Draw* are metaphors for our own expectations—not only in gambling, but also in everyday life. Her sculptures and wall works have exhibited in numerous group and one-woman exhibitions at the regional and national level, including Los Angeles, San Francisco, and New York. Her gaming-related art can be seen in numerous private, corporate, and public collections, and she received the Nevada Arts Council's Artist of the Year award.

At our interview Arrizabalaga arranges playing cards for *Dead Man's Hand* on a work table scattered with spools of thread, scissors, green felt, and fabric in vivid designs of red, yellow, blue, purple.[1] Her Bernina sewing machine is at the ready. Straight pins with yellow and white heads stick out from a blue dish next to a plastic cherry and a screwdriver. A red and white Harolds Club cardboard change cup, now holding pencils and pens, is decorated with cartoony male figures in top hats and gloves, their bare legs

Joan Arrizabalaga working on *Dead Man's Hand*. The vultures' necklaces are stripped playing cards; their bodies, gaming felt.

protruding from a barrel in an obvious allusion to losing all their money. The slogan on the barrel says, "Harold's Club or Bust!"[2]

I'd arrived minutes earlier on August 29, 2013, and she flung open the door, where my eyes instantly fell on a frowsy-haired woman decked out in red plaid blouse and black skirt stationed against a wall behind her. I almost said hello before I realized I was looking at a life-size mannequin, strategically placed to greet visitors. Various adjoining rooms open to this entry area and all contain talisman-like objects—a collection of crystal balls, two antique slot machines plus one in clay that the artist created, a piano, spectacular chandelier (commissioned in Venice, Italy), an old black dial telephone, variety of large and small art pieces, a Russian samovar, a green felt jacket with gambling adornments, and hundreds of other items of mystery and surprise. Books are stuffed onto shelves, and on an end table a stack of papers is held down by a golden cherub. It feels like an enchanted castle, and I'm not surprised when Arrizabalaga reveals that decades earlier when she bought the house (built in 1902), a neighbor told her a lot of singing always emanated from it. "I like that feeling," Arrizabalaga says. "This house is part of the luck I've had."

Her work area, where our interview is conducted, sits center stage. She sews and builds here, but paints in a third-floor studio, and does her clay and woodwork in the backyard area, where she keeps a kiln for firing clay. As we chat, I can just see her rosy cheeks, hazel eyes, and wavy auburn hair over the top of the yellow Bernina. Occasionally, she reaches for a bobbin from the rack behind her, and I notice a silver snake ring curled around her finger.

Arrizabalaga is between projects. She'd recently curated an exhibition at UNR's Knowledge Center, titled *The Art of Gaming +*.[3] The following week would see her traveling to Turkey, one of many trips she makes to various countries around the world. "I like to be out of my comfort zone," she explains, "although I don't know if I've ever had a comfort zone." To fulfill that quest, she once lived in Florence for a month in order to learn Italian, and kept her journal in that language. "Nobody spoke English, and it was perfect."

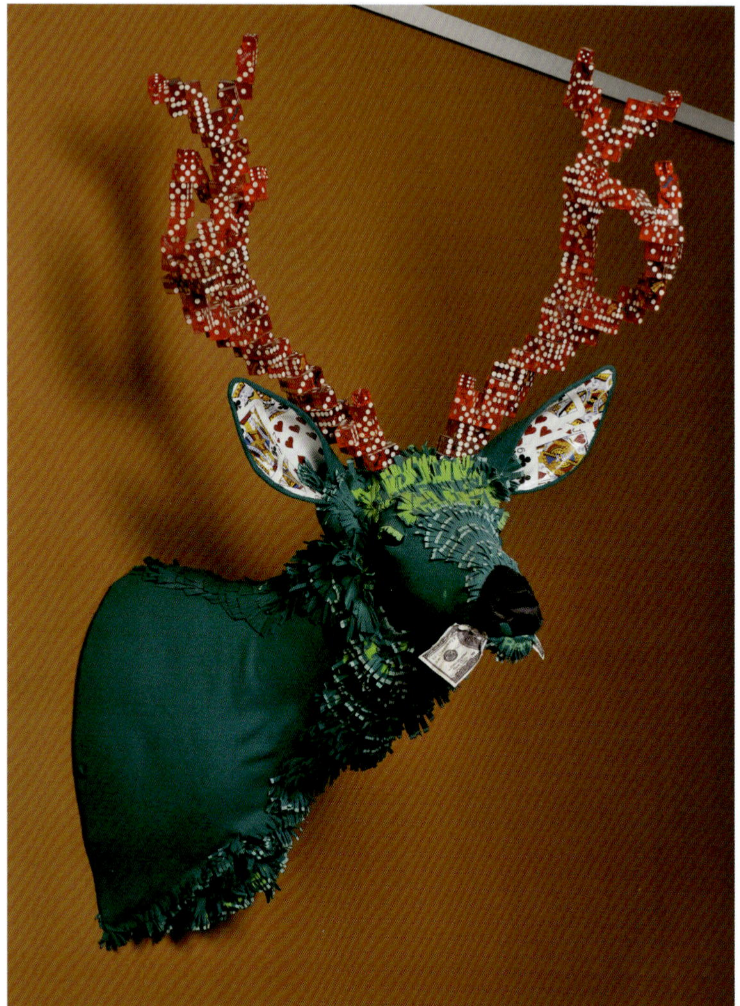

Joan Arrizabalaga, *Nevada Deer*. Gaming felt and dice; 42 x 20 x 25 in.

Born in Ely, Nevada, Arrizabalaga's early years found her in the small town of Fallon climbing trees, running through alfalfa fields at the edge of town, or playing at Consumer

Supply Co., the hardware store owned by her dad, Ramon, and his brother-in-law, Lewis Moiola. The store was adjacent to the Grand Hotel, a Basque hotel and gathering place owned by none other than her grandparents, Ramon Sr. and Tomasa.

"They were constantly fixing washing machines and even built houses. My brother (Ramon III) and I were always in there, watching. Today, I like to walk through Ace Hardware on Virginia Street, looking at the bins of nails, and walking over the creaky wood floors." She developed an interest in what made things work. "I always liked machinery. I loved the insides of slot machines, or funny mechanical things, like clocks."

She continues, "Things looked like other things to me. It's not *just* a lamp: it's a shade made up of various elements." She'd find pieces of old metal, "crazy string," bottle caps, and so on, and bring them home. "It made my mother crazy, of course." The girl always loved artmaking. In grammar school, when her teacher, Laura Mills, received the gift of a ceramics wheel, she stored it in a little closet, and it was there that Arrizabalaga learned to throw pots.

She tells me, "My father was in World War II, where he was in the Fifth Army, CIC [Counterintelligence Corps] in Morocco and Italy, catching spies." Her mother, Frances, moved the family to live with her maternal grandparents, the Gibsons, in Carson City, where Frances worked for the state. "My grandmother taught me to sew [there], and I took to it, because I was tall and nothing ever fit me." A gifted painter, Frances never got the hang of sewing, so Arrizabalaga assumed all duties of mending and dressmaking.

She made her way through the University of Nevada, as it was then called, majoring in art with a focus on ceramics and sculpture. Under the tutelage of legendary department chair Craig Sheppard and professors Ed Yates and Bob Hartman, students created art in makeshift Quonset huts, where they walked down a series of campus stairs to the area affectionately known as Skunk Hollow.

Life moved quickly after graduation, when Arrizabalaga married and began a family. She established a ceramics studio and kiln and thought about recreating slot machines in clay. "Slot machines were everywhere and no one seemed to notice," she says. "When you're used to it, you don't think of it. One day, I thought about making a mold of one of them and doing a series." She also used her sewing skills to experiment with fabric collage. Two daughters were born during this time of growth and change.

The 1960s came along. Arrizabalaga was part of a generation that was going to change the world, and in many ways it did. By the 1970s the movement was full steam ahead, and women and men who came to their power in that time period were ripe for new experiences. Arrizabalaga sought a larger slice of the world; she felt a longing to leave her comfort zone and once again to come alive. She and her husband divorced, and the split was amicable. She moved to England with her daughters, Danielle, four, and Adrienne, six, where she sewed for friends who owned a vintage clothing shop. Inspired by the life and times, the glitter and glitz, and the art of the British rock-and-roll world, she began experimenting with fabrics, using flash and rhinestones. As she thought of home, she began to fashion fabric slot machines. "I now could make fabric do things I never saw done before."

Back in Reno three years later, Arrizabalaga became wardrobe mistress for the largest casino in town, Harrah's Club. She started in the Cabaret and then went to the famous Headliner Room, where she costumed showgirls.[4] Between the two venues, she worked with some of the biggest stars in the country—Ray Charles, Loretta Lynn, Phyllis Diller, the Righteous Brothers, and Paul Revere and the Raiders. And she had the time of her life. "The enthusiasm of the entertainers was really fun. I saw all the mechanics of it, the insides of the entertainment business. It takes so

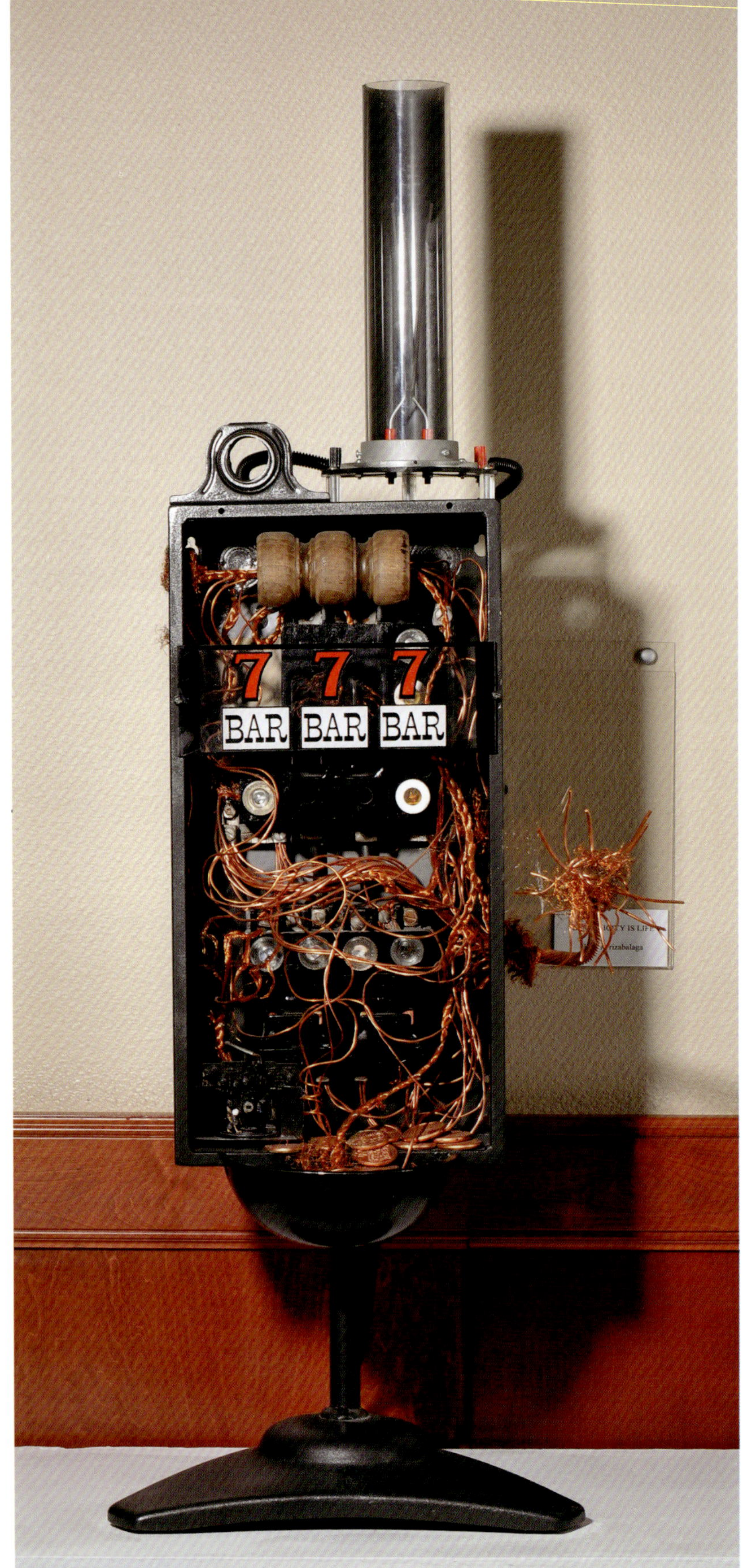

many people to put a show together: there was Mistinguett, the costume designer who started out as a potter. Then she became a dancer, then a choreographer, and finally was producing shows. She drew all those costumes."

Arrizabalaga's hands move and her eyes light up at the memories flashing through her head. "There's a lot of art that goes into all these things, and a lot of drama, too. Add all the various personalities. The technique of producing a show becomes very precise to make it look so easy. That show was a gift to the gamblers. People came here and were entertained. It was the entertainment business." She quiets, and says,

> I think it's changing quite a bit. I don't understand it anymore. Harrah's is a corporation now. A casino needs to be personally owned by someone who really cares about it. Once it becomes a corporation, it's soulless. You don't want to give the customer a great show. Back then it was supposed to be a gift. Bill Harrah used to change the light bulbs. Pappy Smith handed out silver dollars randomly to customers. The cartoons on the change cups—all those little touches—they were perfect! The customer was entertained. I'm not saying good or bad about it; it all leads to art.

Arrizabalaga picks up the change cup and gazes at it. "I liked the cherries and lemons and all the clanking. And these designs—it used to be people didn't make them on a computer; they had to draw these concepts." After a moment, she exclaims, "There has to be a gaming museum. It all started here!"

Where most gamblers and casino goers experience gaming from the casino floor, Arrizabalaga functioned behind the scenes, on the inside, understanding what made things work, just as she learned at her father's hardware store so many years earlier.

Joan Arrizabalaga, *Electricity Is Life*. Mixed-media; 35 in. high.

And all the while during those delightful working years, Arrizabalaga created art, the art of gaming, using such mechanisms as slot handles and wheels, and paraphernalia like felt, cards, and dice, putting things together like one of her idols, Rube Goldberg, or mixing scale and subject like another favorite artist, Marcel Duchamp. She often used classical references in unexpected and humorous ways, like her *Mona Casino*, to juxtapose the old with the new. She might use the familiar faces on playing cards, such as the Queen of Hearts, for her characters. A favorite character is the Joker, who can be like the Trickster in Native American lore. She started doing take-offs on Italian objects. "The latest joker I made has wings. Now I'm seeing the cherubs as the joker." She added, "This whole thing about religion comes into play, too. All of the good luck symbols and talismans—this is endless. Everything can be a gamble and I see everywhere the use of the magical world to gain success, help us win, or keep us safe."

"I'm still feeling that intensity, and I used it in the [*Art of Gaming+*] show. We tried to gather as many artists as we knew who had gambling-related items and also people who were involved with all the other artistic pursuits, including Turkey Stremmel and Marsh Fey. We needed facets of the whole industry. The old slot machines were beautifully designed pieces of sculpture, which is what got me going on all of this anyway."[5]

And she's still making art. She enjoys making what she calls Game Animals. "People hunt in this state." She points to the vulture in progress. "Vultures are fabulous. I thought I would tie this piece in with "Wild Bill" Hickock and the *Dead Man's Hand* because vultures were all over the West." She's also made *Card Shark, A Good Bet* (deer with horns) and more.

Myths of all kinds, Western and historical references, and personal experiences blend together in her fascination for what we worship, or superstitions, and the never-ending search for luck.

She smiles. "It's one of the privileges that artists have—to keep doing and going in all kinds of directions and putting all the experiences of a lifetime into your artwork, and you can do it 'til your dying day."

PAM BOWMAN • BORN 1953

For many years, Pam Bowman's flame smoldered as she went about the everyday, repetitive activities required of a mother, wife, basket weaver, churchgoer, and homemaker. Nothing wrong with that: really, her life was full. But when, many years later, she decided to leap into the mystical, magical world of art, that smoldering flame began to blaze and sparkle. The Utah artist came to view those ordinary domestic pursuits as treasures, and today, a master's degree in sculpture behind her, she celebrates those everyday activities in massive installations that fill a gallery room in silent tribute to the grandeur of the small and seemingly ordinary.

Bowman elaborates, "There are many endless loops in our lives—personal grooming, sleeping, cooking, doing dishes, going to a job day after day." We chat at the dining room table in her Provo home that sits at the base of the massive Mount Timpanogos in the mighty Wasatch Range. It was September 25, 2013, photographer Susan Mantle and I have arrived amid a late-afternoon downpour, and I'm trying not to drip on the white carpet as we listen to Bowman, who explains her work. "I'm interested in those rhythms, routines, and rituals of life." Her labor-intensive creations demonstrate how small everyday acts build to create the whole of a person, much like her dramatic architectural installations are built up from single, un-noble elements.[6] (Bowman purposely uses fibers and fiber techniques in her creations because of their association with women's work.)

Later, I view her exhibit, *Becoming*, at BYU Museum of Art as part of a four-woman show titled *Work to Do*.[7] Suddenly, I understand what she's talking about. As I enter the gallery, a wall out of which hang one thousand pieces of string in regulated layers confronts me. String falls and curls to the ground in a loopy mass, much like an Eva Hesse sculpture. As I walk around the wall, I can see that these same strings are pulled taut in a dramatic diagonal, going into and forming a mountain-like rope structure. The strings symbolize the many tasks associated with repetitive ritual and service. Bowman says, "Such tasks could include activities as varied as daily devotionals, a father regularly reading to his children and tucking them into bed, parents consistently providing the means to feed their family, an individual strengthening him/herself with the constant work of overcoming a weakness or addiction—any small acts that over time help to build strength, build character, and over time result in the 'becoming' of a greater, even more holy, person."

For Bowman, this mountain or temple-like form represents the accumulated, complex, magnificent aggregate of memory and experience, an allegory transforming the mundane into the sacred. Collectively, each small strand builds the nest, the artwork. Yet as the strings wrap around the form, they are not neat and tidy. Since we are complex beings, and since our lives are complex, the strings and rope do not line up in an orderly way—they are also complex. Yet the higher you look on the sculpture, the more ordered it becomes. As we "become" better people, as we learn and progress, we become more perfected.

Becoming is a favorite of BYU Museum of Art curator Jeff Lambson, who wrote, "Everything on the outside is orderly, but it's tangled on the inside. It's just one of many meanings of a sculpture that explores how the daily, sometimes monotonous, work of women comes together to create something beautiful." He went on to say this artist's work "is somewhat of a mission statement and a rigorous and serious reclamation of the marginalized and dismissed domestic life of so many women."

Bowman's second piece in the show, *Watercourse,* is a gray loopy ribbon of vinyl streaming across the walls. The artist's family likes to run rivers, and she says that camping on the river brings out the most basic routines of life. Eating, sleeping, setting up and breaking camp, and the rhythm of the river all become part of a daily repetition. Both pieces relate to our life paths. "There are certainly many ups and downs, and our progression never happens in the most efficient way."

Bowman is in love with the Utah deserts, mountains, and rivers. "It's important to me that things are beautiful. In the art world, beauty is seen as problematic. But I want to embrace it, give it a positive feeling." Like other contemporary Great Basin artists, she is part of a movement in the western United States that sees the reemergence of beauty as a coveted value.[8] "Sometimes I feel my work is not hip enough, cutting edge enough to be selected for contemporary art exhibits. At the same time, it is too out there for traditional venues." She worked to find exhibit opportunities, and find them she did. She has exhibited in more than thirty art-related locations from California to all over Utah; to Philadelphia, Pennsylvania; to Nanjing, China; eleven events were solo exhibitions. Additionally, she has won "Best" and "Juror's Choice" awards and appeared in several museum catalogs and publications. And all this happened after being a stay-at-home mom until she returned to college in her mid-forties. But by then, she says, she had a lot to say. It's no wonder she works large. Bowman's ideas, seeded in the ordinary, incubated for many years until she elevated them into monumental structures.

Her ties to Utah are old and strong; both sides of her family show pioneer Mormon ancestors. Born in Salt Lake City, the middle child of two brothers and three sisters, her family moved to Nebraska when she was one year old with her father's employment. Bowman grew up on the plains, riding horses, and spending much time out of doors. Indoors, she made puppets and mounted her own puppet shows, figuring out how to build them. "I do that with my art now: I figure out things as I go." She learned to play the

Pam Bowman working on *Ebb and Wax* project.

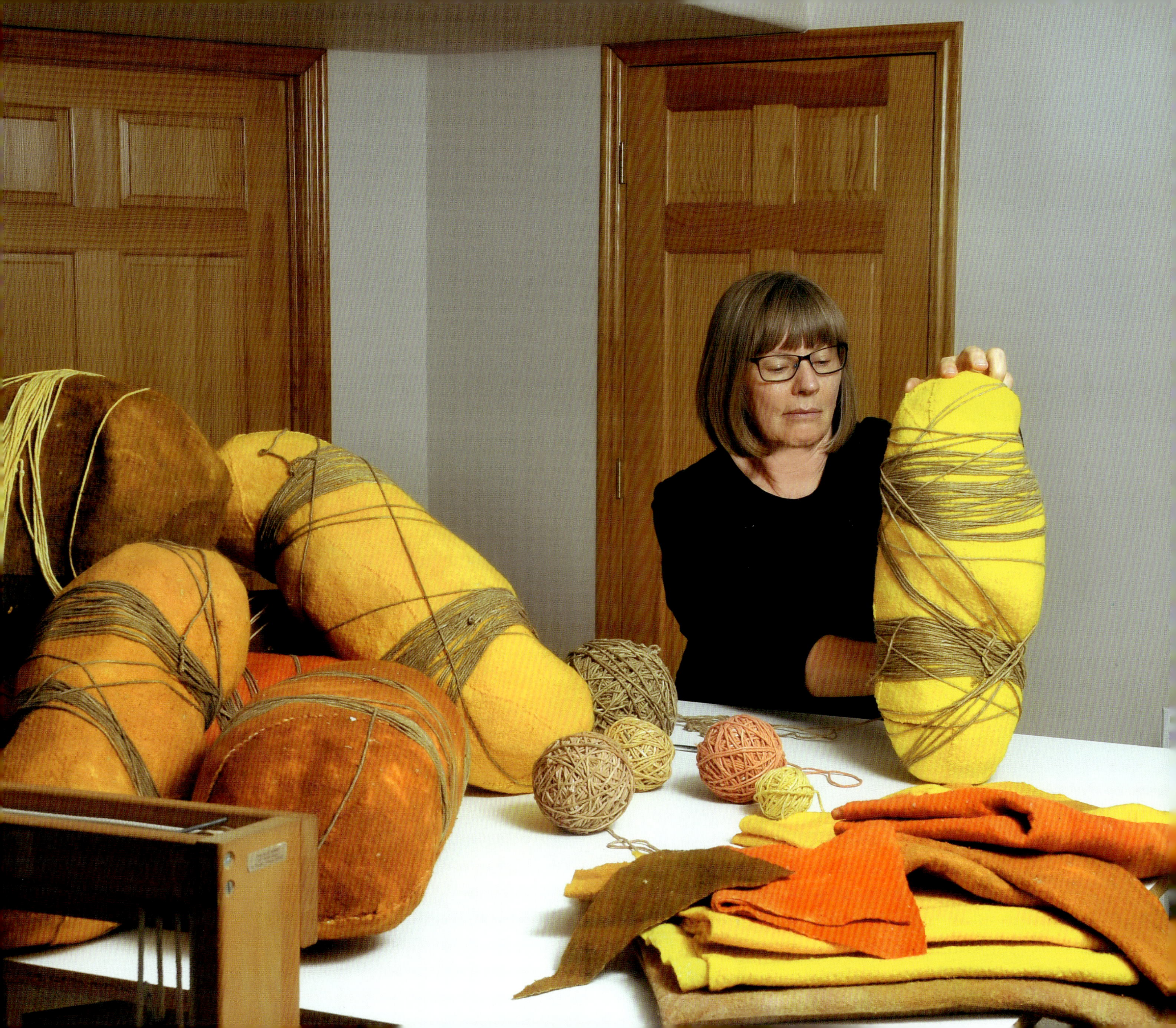

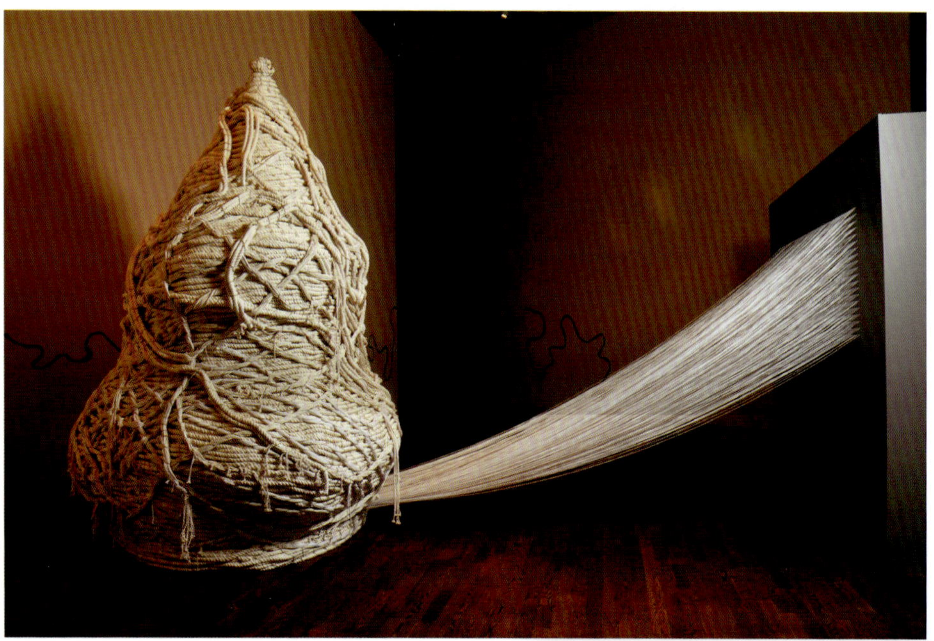

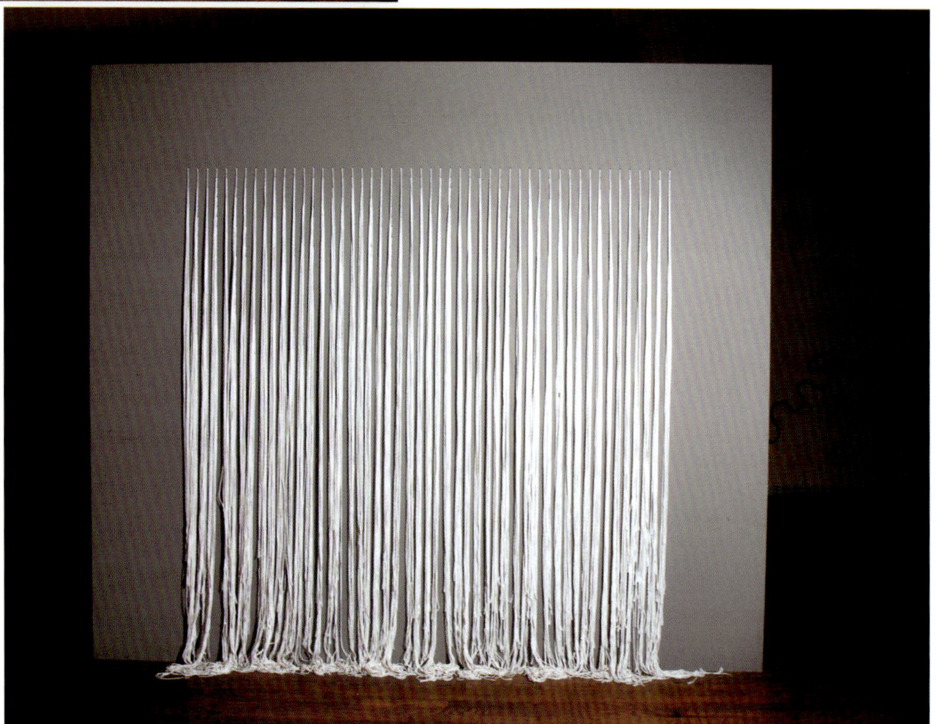

Pam Bowman, two views of *Becoming*, a temple-like form representing the aggregate of memory and experience. Mixed media of cotton rope, string, steel, wool, paint caulking cotton; 20 x 10 x 12 ft., entire piece.

piano and music became her first love. Summers saw her back in Utah visiting family, and she enrolled at BYU to major in music. However, her parents, worried about her ability to support herself, convinced her to change majors to medical technology, like her older sister before her. After more than a year, she was in distress. She withdrew from school and moved home. Her mother, remembering the puppet phase, advised her to do something creative, and Bowman returned to college and received her undergraduate degree in interior design.

It was at BYU where she met, and soon married, Jerry, the brother of her roommate. Jerry pursued a career in the Air Force, and Bowman, who eventually gave birth to sons Corey, Eric, and Trent, made the choice to be a stay-at-home mom. Encouraged in that role by her Mormon faith and the military culture, it also felt to her to be the best choice as she struggled with health issues (both fibromyalgia and chronic fatigue) that frequently required rest. In addition, the family moved, as military career families do, and they lived in Florida, Ohio, and Colorado. Looking for a creative outlet, Bowman explored weaving and basketry. She was primarily self-taught; over a period of fifteen years she joined the elite class of basket artists, entering shows and winning awards. At the annual Ohio basket conferences, she met guest instructors who had master of fine arts degrees and she could see the difference between their mind-set and approach to their work when compared to the traditional basket makers that follow time-tested patterns. She was drawn to the nontraditional styles, and that's when she developed a yearning to study art.

After twenty years in the military, her husband was offered a teaching position at BYU, so he retired from the Air Force. As a faculty spouse, Bowman decided to use her tuition benefit and seek a master's degree in sculpture. She enrolled in undergraduate classes in order to build a portfolio, and then applied to and was accepted into the master of fine arts program. She arranged her classes to be home when the boys returned from school, and between that schedule and health issues, the entire university coursework commitment stretched to eight years. Eight stimulating years. She received her degree in 2005. "I was determined," she says, "and my professors were really open to whatever path I wanted to take. My most inspirational teachers were Brian Christenson, Bryon Draper, and Von Allen, the full-time 3-D professors. 'You want to work with fiber? Fine.' They were open to letting me express myself with whatever processes or materials I wanted to use. They were my mentors."

The process of obtaining her master's degree was powerful. She explored the ambiguities of male/female labor. She researched feminist theory and gender studies to build an academic foundation. She created artwork to emphasize domesticity by using labor-intensive processes—weaving and stitching—and also gathered and prepared her materials. And she found herself elevating the domestic role with beauty and reverence.

"As I developed my artistic voice I needed to overcome an assumption that my voice was not important. . . . I had been a stay-at-home mom during a time period when it was frowned upon. A career was seen as more worthwhile and more intelligent. But I knew working at home was the right choice for me, and being careful with money I was able do it economically." Nevertheless, the flame within her yearned to burn brighter, and "at times I felt discontent. That's why I had so much to express when I eventually started making art, and I had to learn that that expression had value."

She explains, "So my path was design, then craft, then art. And when I do installation, I use it all. All that background comes into play."

We are all influenced somehow by what we read, and when Bowman mentions author and art critic Suzi Gablik as a deep influence on her work, I get it. In her book, *The*

Reenchantment of Art (1992), Gablik denounces overproduction and excess and expresses hope for a new art that embraces a sense of community.

Bowman does indeed return meaning to her work, as Gablik proposes. And as far as the excess that Gablik disdains, Bowman deftly handles that problem: her installation eventually returns to its original material. The strings in *Becoming* might have come from a previous installation, the four-foot diameter *A Big Ball of String,* perhaps. Or the rope will lie in coils, waiting for the next regeneration. Viewers will have a memory of only this mammoth sculpture, which will be gone forever when the show closes. Her undulating gray *Watercourse Artwork* will be removed and discarded.

And as far as Gablik's push for community, Bowman calls on friends, family, neighbors, and museum staff to help mount her installations. Their response is generous. Husband Jerry, an engineer, solves the structural and mechanical challenges of all of her difficult creations. The Bowman couple collaborates extensively about structure and installation difficulties during the planning stage of each installation. Bowman frequently enlists people from all walks of life to participate in her art pieces. In one component of *A Big Ball of String*, for example, she sent letters to fifty people who had accomplished a great deal and asked them to send some sort of *string* that related to their lives. The manipulated responses became part of the exhibit. Another project, *Kinetic Melodies*, was the result of living in China for a year. She compared routines and rituals with those in the United States. She asked her students in China and also family and friends in the United States to "tell me about an everyday routine important in your life." Each American response was made into a panel and incorporated into a quilt. Each Chinese response was incorporated into collages on traditional silk and rice paper scrolls. The exhibit included a thirty-minute video comparing routines in the two countries, and a book with the written responses from the quilts and scrolls.

This artist, who has interpreted eloquence in her massive abstract installations, continues, as all great artists do, to question herself, and at times she feels like giving up. Her *Becoming* at the BYU show might also be an allegory to the artist's life—at times orderly as she tends to family, home, and church, whereas at other times a jumble. Materials are expensive and she receives little or no pay for her work. Then there are the health issues. The large installations take a toll.

But the compulsion to create won't go away. And the responses from curators, other artists, and viewers have led Bowman to realize that her work is an influence for good. "It is my way of having a voice, and I hope my voice is somehow helpful to other women. For now, my mission is to create art."

You might say Bowman's path has followed the inspiration from a children's book she once read to her young sons. In Marion Holland's 1958 book, *A Big Ball of String* (which inspired her exhibition), there's a page that says, "With a big ball of string I could do ANYTHING, anything, anything, ANYTHING AT ALL. . . . I CAN DO ANYTHING WITH A BIG BALL OF STRING."

And she certainly has.

DEMETRICE P. DALTON • BORN 1960

One summer day back in 1967, a man carrying a briefcase climbed the wood steps of Demetrice Dalton's northeast Reno, Nevada, home and knocked on the door. When her mother, Ceola Davis, answered, the salesman asked to speak to the artist who had mailed in the well-executed drawing, because, he explained, this artist had been accepted into the Famous Artists Correspondence School. He pulled a file from his briefcase and studied it.

"I'm looking for Demetrice."

Mrs. Davis was shocked. "But . . . but . . . ," she sputtered. "Demetrice is only seven years old!"

That incident became a family legend, and Davis

Demetrice P. Dalton in her studio.

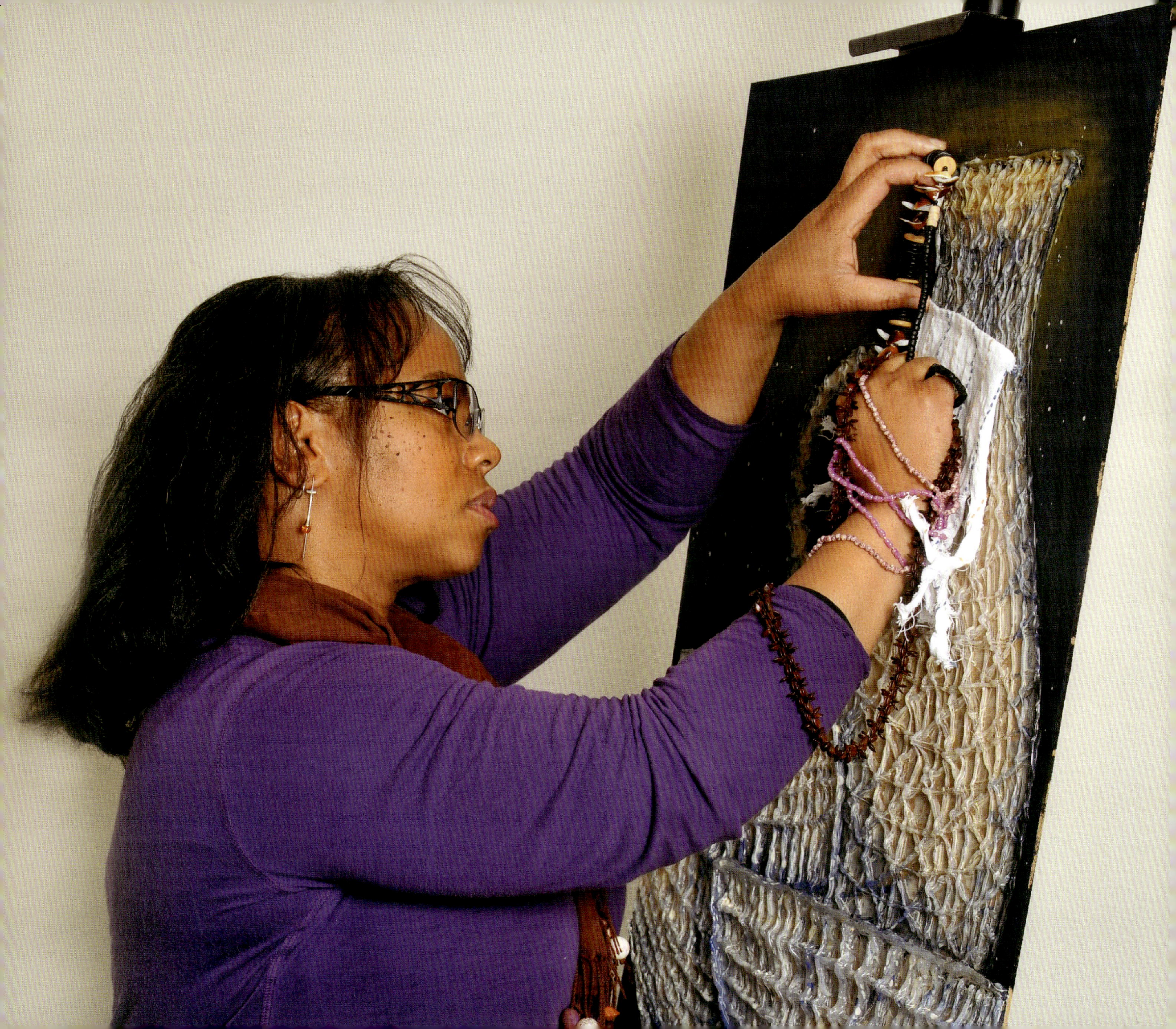

probably wasn't too surprised, because her daughter by this age already thought of herself as an artist. After all, the little girl had been drawing since she was able to hold a pencil.

Today, a visitor to her seasonal gallery, the Fourth Street gallery, observing the beads and netting, the rattan and even fabric spilling from a frame, might be moved to think of her as an art maverick. Dalton views many of her paintings as three-dimensional objects rather than surface images. Her goal is to create sculptures out of raw or repurposed materials. And her personal mission is to work from her own sense of what is authentic, whether sourced from her own African American background or another culture that might be underserved or overlooked. Born in Odessa, Texas, Dalton lived with her grandmother, Johnny Mea Luster, until the age of three. After Davis found a job in Reno, she sent for her little girl, and mother and daughter have been great friends ever since.

Dalton shows her work seasonally in a traveling gallery style. At the time of our interview on March 3, 2013, she called her Reno show space the Gallery at EnSoul, because it was connected to her mother's adjacent hair styling/photography studio, Ensoul. Both businesses are situated in a contemporary brick office building. Salon clients frequented the gallery, and Dalton's patrons are known to make appointments with Davis, too. Her compact studio is crowded with four easels that hold canvases in varying stages of completion. Tubes of acrylic paint fill the easel lips. Her stool, placed before a work in progress, is topped with a modified tractor seat. Dalton rises, smiles her welcome, and drops her paintbrush into a wide-necked jar of water, and I watch the clear liquid turn soft blue. Hunks of foam core, a hot glue gun, and a serrated knife occupy a tabletop, poised to create the dimensionality that is a signature of Dalton's work. Netting, containers of beads in many colors, fabrics, glue sticks, rope, and twigs pile on shelves along one wall, and tacked here and there are history articles and reference images. Rolls of textured papers hold up a corner, and as I scribble my notes, the flute strains from her CD player of Carlos Nakai ebb to a soft finish and a moment later, the energetic music of a gospel choir fills the room.

Dalton can get an idea anywhere, she says. "I might see a rock pattern, a poem, a moment, a car driving by, and in my mind it's done." Then she figures out how to execute the inspiration.

I step out the studio door into her gallery and survey the artist's paintings, sculptures, and assemblage.[9] Rich, brightly colored images explode with acrylic paint, pen and ink, and stippling. Vibrant faces show contour lines like topography maps. As she works, I see netting, heavily folded fabric, twine, beaded jewelry, and other materials I can't identify but that lend her work an interesting dimension. Texture spills outward from a piece and over a section of its frame. It is obvious that Dalton experiments with media. She points to one assemblage with a black background. "Be careful of that one," she warns with a smile as she points to the background. "That's not paint, it's black pepper." She removes the artwork and turns it to the back, where I see a bulletin board instead of the artist canvas I expected. Maverick indeed.

It wasn't until she was a student at Reno's Traner Middle School that her vocation took hold, when she enrolled in art classes taught by well-known Great Basin sculptor Larry Williamson. "He really opened it up for me," Dalton recalls, her small hoop earrings glittering contrasts against raven hair. "The techniques he taught were amazing and very cool." Not only did Williamson teach everything from ceramics, to drawing and painting, jewelry making, silk screening, and batik, but he was also brave enough and passionate enough about art to lead students on a field trip to art museums in San Francisco.

Dalton's brown eyes gaze out from under her bangs and into the distance as she remembers her former teacher. "Mr. Williamson opened up the door to what was possible."

In the coming years, through high school graduation,

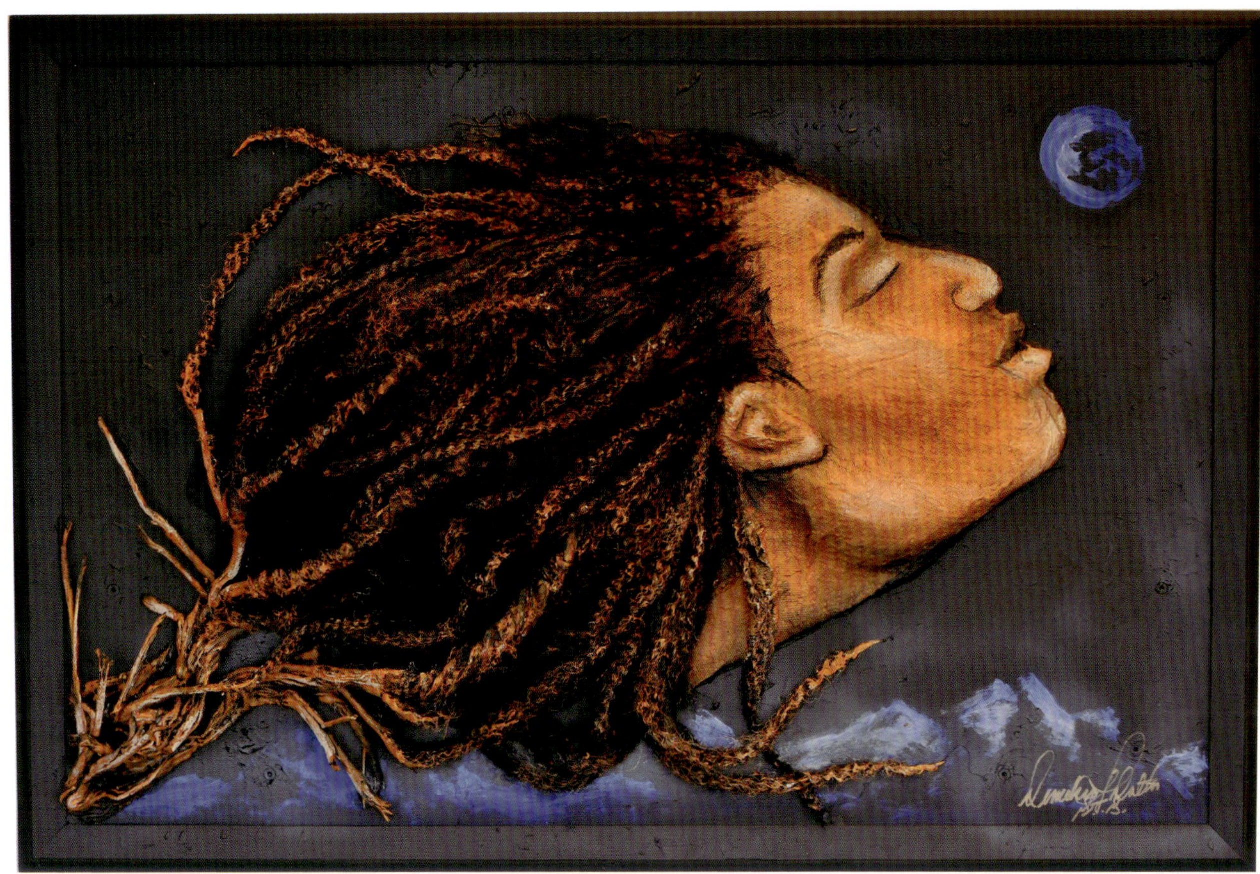

Demetrice P. Dalton, *Untitled*. Mixed media on bulletin board; 36 x 24 x 3 in.

an early marriage, and a move to Sacramento, California, Dalton never forgot the skills and zest for art that Williamson gave her. She started her family, which eventually grew to four children, and continued to produce drawings and collages for people. "Whatever people wanted, I figured out how to do it," she said.

When her children became teenagers, she enrolled in the California Academy of Design (now the International Academy of Design & Technology), where drawing, painting, printmaking, and sculpture filled her days. Her sculptures were of the nontraditional variety—no bronze or marble here—and she began working "outside the box," as she calls it, with wire, cloth, anything that worked, in order to interest her free-spirited teachers. She remembers challenging boundaries with an experimental painting on venetian blinds that altered images when the blinds were manipulated. Dalton attended the academy for two and a half years and received her associate of arts degree and, she says now, "I wouldn't mind going back."

The family moved to the Bay Area, and Dalton continued her art while supporting her husband's ministry, and, as she had learned to do, made any art that buyers and friends requested—program covers, murals in children's rooms, a website, one time even a special toilet seat.

And then her world transformed with an overwhelming loss she didn't see coming and never expected—divorce. Discouraged, Dalton returned to Reno, where her mother provided a place to heal and regroup. The divorce was a miserable transition time, when money was scarce and her professional life seemed to be over. She underwent some difficult years, but weathered the storm, and she never stopped creating art.

To this day, her subjects tend to be women. "Women are the ones who work, who set the mood for the home, who make something from nothing," she explains. "I relate to that."

She, too, was gradually making something—a new life—from nothing. Looking back from the present, Dalton realizes that her marriage failure actually made her stronger. "When you have lost what you think is everything and find that you are still standing, you no longer have that paralyzing fear. You tell yourself there's nothing to lose so you might as well try new and different things."

About this time, as she was metamorphosing from victim to empowered woman, an interesting event occurred, one that became her second transformative experience. She met Ken Dalton, the man who would become her husband.

"Ken played a huge part in my change," she explains. "Before I knew it, I was meeting new people and visiting new places. It's reflected in all parts of my life, including my art."

Dalton discovered the world with fresh eyes. Colors were brighter, and she embarked on new adventures. When she returned to her art, she became looser, more experimental. She changed from the woman who was what she called "a conservative thinker" to one who is outgoing and adventuresome.

"Thinking back on it [the divorce], I see that the worst thing that happened to me was actually the best thing," she says.

Today, she creates art, curates art shows, counsels artists, and manages art galleries in between travels. Dalton has also taught art at the secondary level, and during that time became aware of young Washoe County students who were being given their last chance to be educated in the school district. She began teaching at a charter high school that specializes in helping troubled young people.

"One of the reasons why I became a strong supporter of the arts and its benefits to society is that, early in the years when I taught at this particular school, some of my students would only attend school on the days they were scheduled to have art. But it's a funny thing about sitting and talking while doing art. It is a great balancer of the psyche. And in turn [these discussions] made it easier for me to convince them to attend all of their classes and complete their secondary education."

In many ways she feels rooted in her place, Nevada's Great Basin, referring to it as a "hidden treasure" full of resilient people. She identifies with the little town of Goldfield, where she and her husband frequently rest and refresh on their 450-mile drive to Las Vegas.[10] "I love Goldfield," she says. "It hangs in there despite all its rough edges. It's full of stories and culture and history, and if you talk to people, they'll tell you. You can zoom through the town like many travelers do. But if you take time to learn about it, you'll find it's pretty rich. It would be a great place for an art community as well."

Dalton has done just that with her work—learned about the subjects and found them rich and rewarding. Her techniques and style vary with each piece, but one element stands out—movement. An Asian couple dances, the African woman holds a basket to her head, Mayan women twist and hug their highly designed *huipils* (loose-fitting tunic), a black elder bends to explain an adage to an eager child, a Native American mother tends her cradled baby, a ruddy-skinned woman with dark braids flying gazes upward.[11] She's beginning a Bride Culture series because "I consider the concept of the bride to be a culture." She points to a just-completed piece. "This one shows the beauty and absolute perfection experienced by women being prepared for marriage, while emotional struggles, pain, fears, and imperfections are ceremoniously and aesthetically covered in order to show the perfect woman and wife."

She continues, "I want to record the fabric of life. The things people use, the relationships they build—I love how history affects culture." Dalton feels a connection with people from various cultures. She relates to their stories of survival, history, traditions, design patterns, and textures, and she sees a sense of honesty in the way they lead their lives. And she creates art that reflects this authenticity. She feels it is vital that we as individuals do not forget the history and contribution of all cultures to our world.

This artist might have been following the plea of Coretta Scott King, who said, "Women, if the soul of the nation is to be saved, I believe that you must become its soul."

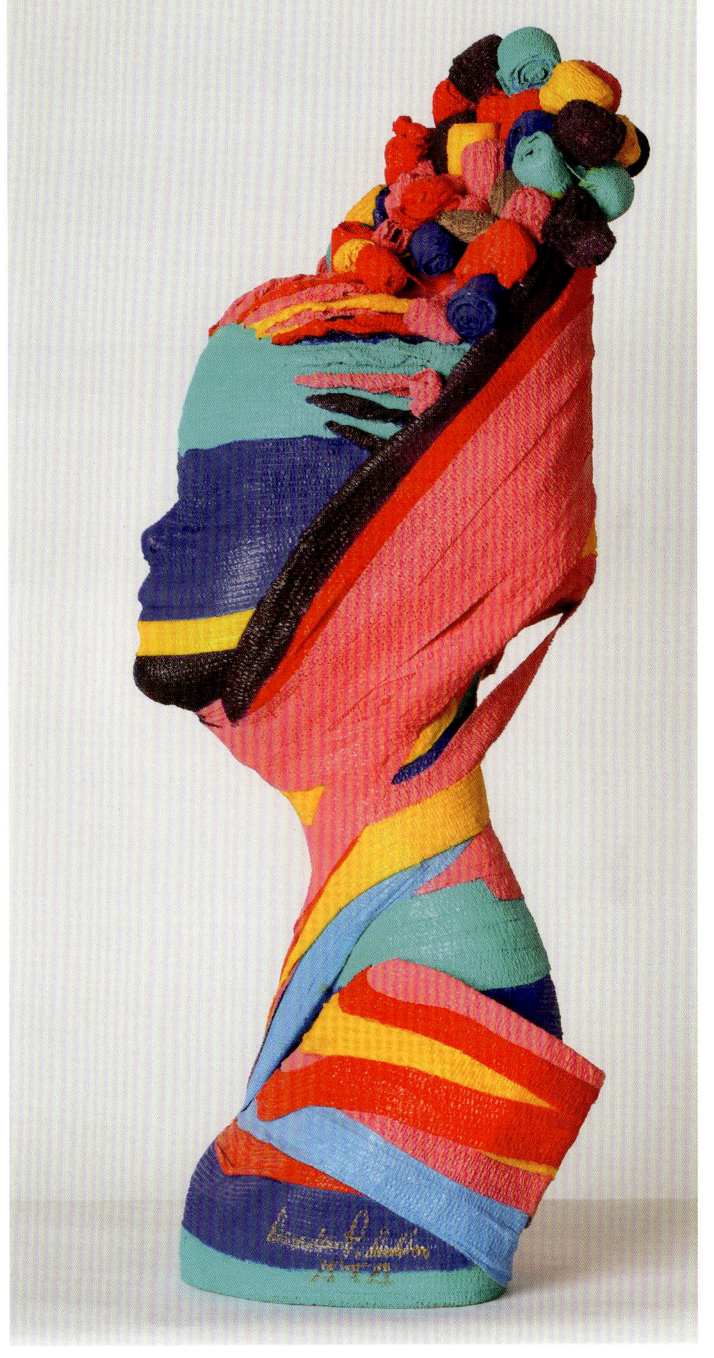

Demetrice P. Dalton, *The Bride*. Mixed media; 28 x 15 x 24 in.

Notes

1. *Dead Man's Hand* is a reference to Old West folk hero, lawman, and gunfighter "Wild Bill" Hickok when he was murdered.
2. Reno's Harolds Club, established in 1935 by Raymond I. (Pappy) Smith and his son, Harold, was world famous. "Harold's Club or Bust" signs could be spotted anywhere in the world, including at the North Pole. Smith was a pioneer gaming operator, both for his operational innovations and for his broad-based marketing. The club closed in 1995.
3. This was the first show in the country to detail the history, art, and culture of gaming, which began in Reno when Nevada legalized it in 1931.
4. The Cabaret offered such varied acts as reviews, singers, bands, and other entertainers. The Headliner Room featured important stars of the time. Its name was later changed to Sammy's Showroom in tribute to Sammy Davis Jr.
5. Along with Michele Basta, Arrizabalaga curated the first and only comprehensive exhibition of gaming; it all began in northern Nevada. The show covered five floors of the University of Nevada Knowledge Center. Turkey Stremmel, co owner with husband Peter of Stremmel Gallery, nurtures artists to greatness. In cooperation with Harrah's, she curated Reno's first Art of Gaming show. Marshall Fey and his brother, Frank, opened the Liberty Belle Restaurant in Reno in 1958 with a few antique slot machines, including father Charles's first three-reel slot machine. Serious collecting continued until 2006. The Liberty Belle is now closed.
6. The noble elements in sculpture are generally considered to be bronze and marble.
7. The Brigham Young University Museum of Art is the highest-attended University art museum in North America, according to curator Jeff Lambson, who came from the Hirshorn Museum and Sculpture Garden in Washington, DC. The Brigham Young University Museum of Art hosts national and international shows.
8. Professor and art critic Dave Hickey, in his book *The Invisible Dragon* (1993), states, "The vernacular of beauty, in its democratic appeal, remains a potent instrument for change in this civilization." In his revised book (2009, 119), he says that beauty in art is about freedom in a shrinking unfree world—"blue skies and open highways." Sounds like he spent some time in the Great Basin. And he has, when he was professor of art at the University of Nevada Las Vegas.
9. Assemblage consists of making artistic compositions by putting together found objects. The art form dates to Cubist constructions of Pablo Picasso, and before him, in the ritual and tribal objects from Africa where Picasso found his inspiration.
10. The county seat of Esmeralda County, Nevada, Goldfield has a resident population of 268 at the 2010 census. It is located along U.S. Route 95.
11. The *huipil,* a loose-fitting tunic, is the most common traditional garment worn by indigenous women from central Mexico to Central America.

EXPLORING

Explorers are the women and men who range over unfamiliar territory in order to discover something new and remarkable. This process has consequences, however: the path to the unfamiliar can just as easily lead to a dead end. True explorers are willing to take that chance, and they are the ones who will make great discoveries.

Many contemporary and historic visual artists achieved fame by exploring new techniques, processes, or media and by investigating the "what ifs." Curious and imaginative artists are the ones who conceived the art movements like impressionism, Pop Art, and minimalism. Others then jumped on the bandwagon, and this exploration process created the many art movements that are now discussed in art history classes.

Three women are not interested in kicking off new movements, but they're always ready to leave their most recent creations, successful though they might be, and move forward. Rebekah Bogard, Sue Cotter, and Elaine Parks continue exploring. They will come up with a new idea, develop it fully, and then move on to the next new idea in some kind of magical process that continues to lead to new territory and work that remains fresh year after year.

REBEKAH BOGARD • BORN 1971

Rebekah Bogard pushes her dark hair back with the bend of her wrist (her hands are white with clay powder) and flashes a conspiratorial grin.

"I've got that renegade spirit, I guess."

And, halfway through my August 27, 2013, interview with this ceramic artist, I'm beginning to agree with that "renegade" handle she gives herself. For one thing, her inspiration comes not from the great masters of history or even the art stars of today, but from Disney cartoons. Her larger-than-life ceramic sculptures reject conventional art movements like abstraction, minimalism, postmodernism, and others, and instead explode with a rare beauty and female iconography such as butterflies and flowers in pastel colors—pink, soft purple, powder blue. But even with that, the graceful, flowing, and beautiful sculpture challenges the viewers, because as we look closer, we are likely to be shocked with some sly eroticism among the sweet-looking caricature beasts Bogard likes to create.

"I like to flirt with the viewer," she says laughing. "That's a feminine thing too. Being a female, people like to contain you and box you; they don't necessarily like you to flirt." She recalls a time in 2008 when Hillary Clinton was running for president "and a little bit of cleavage was showing. People didn't like that. What's wrong with dressing nice? That's another thing about femininity: flirting can be a source of power and confidence."

Bogard's rebellious spirit comes naturally, and she describes her wild Wyoming roots. Her grandfather was a trapper. Her great great grandfather, "Uncle Nick" Wilson, rode the Pony Express, but before that he became what she calls a "white Indian." According to Bogard, the Shoshone mother of Chief Washakie had a vision that she was going to have a white boy. One day, tribal hunters came upon the young boy Nick, who was working hard on his family ranch.

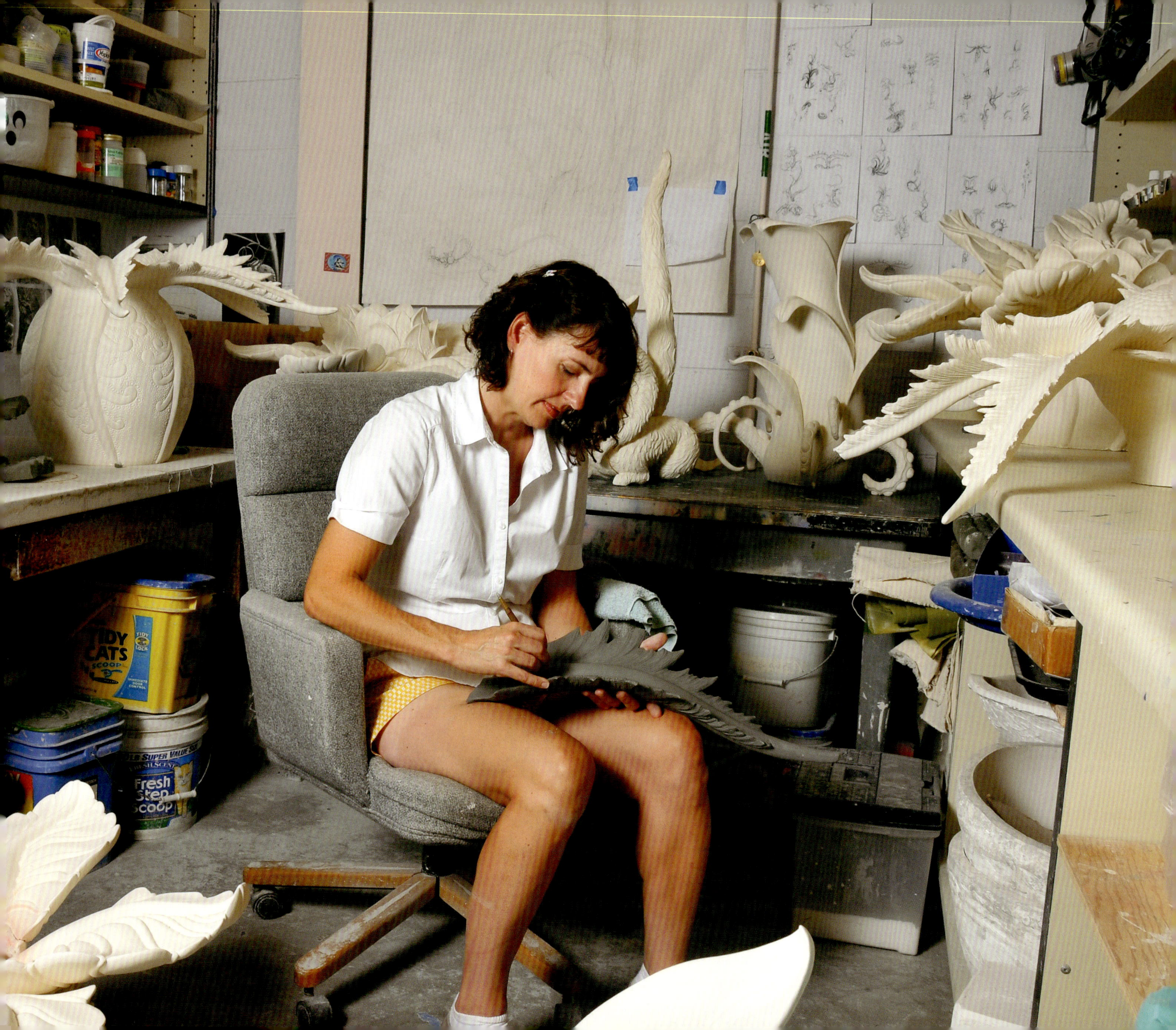
TIDY CATS
Fresh Step Scoop

They led a pony forward and said, "If you run away with us, we'll give you this pony." And the boy decided life with Indians sounded pretty good, so he agreed. He lived with the Indians for two years before returning home. He had many adventures afterward, living off the land, trapping on Indian reservations, and, most notably, forging the Teton Pass.[1] He wrote a book about his experiences and formed the town of Wilson, Wyoming. Although born and raised in Casper, Wyoming, "Wilson" is Bogard's maiden name.

We're talking in her basement work area adjacent to a large classroom at UNR, where Bogard is associate professor in ceramics. It's after hours and most state employees have left for the day. But she's working hard, preparing for a new show and creating labor-intensive sculptures that require, among other techniques, mold making, casting, hand building, and oil painting. Right now she's bent over a wing-like shape, pressing a tool over the surface to create texture. Texture in clay? Of course. Why be normal when you're a renegade? Curvaceous white clay forms in various sizes and stages of completion crowd desktop, shelves, and the slip-spattered floor.[2]

The youngest of two sisters and two brothers, Bogard says, "We were all feral children." They ran freely through Casper and the high plains of Wyoming, hiking on Casper Mountain and boating in Alcova Lake Reservoir. "Our parents said I could get good grades or not; it was up to me. I grew up working class my whole life, and I was always a tomboy. My dad, Stark, who had his own audio/visual repair business, always said, 'Do it yourself,' and I would figure it out. It taught me self-reliance and determination." As a child, her parents took her to work with them every day and gave her a desk and all the paper, tape, and glue she wanted. And she loved it. The family spent summer vacations in Yellowstone National Park, where Bogard, always shy and introverted, ran around looking for animals to draw and paint. Stark was a fisherman who loved the outdoors and took her to beautiful wild places all summer long. She commented, "It wasn't summer if we weren't camping!" Today, her love and awe of animals and nature are indispensable parts of her work.

When she was a high school senior, her mother, Darlene, enrolled her in an art class at the local community college, and that experience led her to enroll at Casper College where she majored in fine art. "I found my voice naturally with ceramics." She asked a counselor to give her an aptitude test, and he replied, "You already know your destiny, Rebekah. You are going to be an artist." And that confirmed her artistic future.

But after an early marriage, six years of college, and three diplomas, in true renegade spirit Bogard abruptly quit school and began work at the local flower shop. As she says, "I was a little confused about what I was to do for a profession as an artist. I hated it—the flower shop work." She drops her hands and her brown eyes seem glassy. "I was on a path to regret." After two miserable years arranging flowers, she connected with former college professors and they encouraged her to give the University of Wyoming, Laramie, 150 miles from home, a try.

She plunged right in, and although her husband would have no part of the move, they saw each other most weekends. At the university, Bogard worked hard. A special teacher and artist, Phyllis Kloda, showered her with encouragement. "She helped me grow artistically in ways I was not able to do on my own." Kloda encouraged Bogard to enter competitions listed in the back of *Ceramics Monthly* magazine.

Then there were the animals. "Animals were always my favorite subjects. But college doesn't think animals are a legitimate subject matter, so I quit doing them. There are rules to art." Still, animals started popping out of her clay vessels, but in a more abstract nature. "Phyllis was great. She not only appreciated the animals, but helped

Rebekah Bogard making marks on wax.

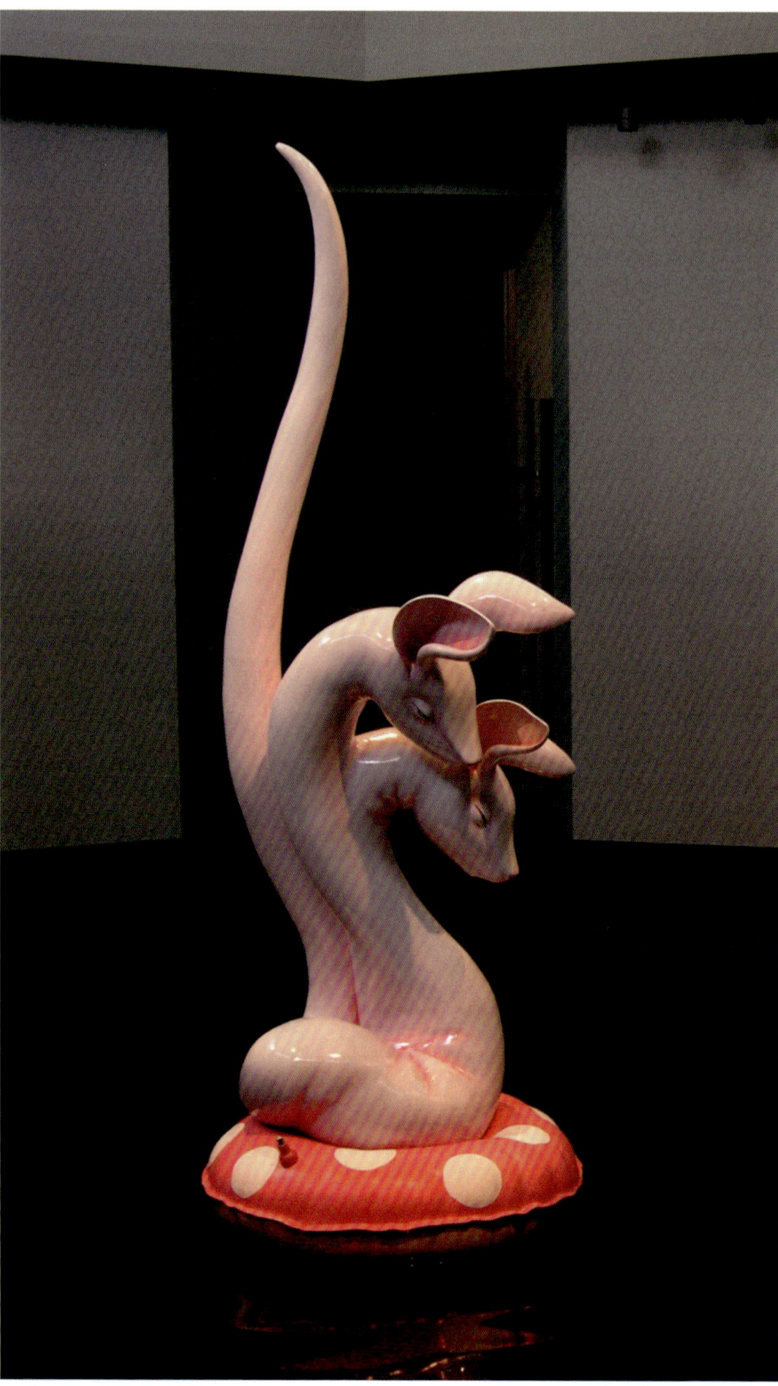

and encouraged me." She flashes another Bogard grin and gestures to the new work surrounding her. "It's the same thing as now. How do you make feminine art and make it relevant?"

Bogard received her bachelor of fine arts and applied to the University of Nevada, Las Vegas, where she was accepted into the master's program. She was fortunate to receive mentorship and advice from Professor Mark Burns, who, she says, opened her eyes to the difference between craft and fine art. Her work there involved a great deal of flora and scientific theories, but she extended those ideas to include her beloved animals. And, renegade that she is, she never stopped believing in the idea of injecting beauty into her art. "That honed my ideas of narrative and what it is I wanted to say."

Her open mind, rebel spirit, and hard work were paying off. Curators and reviewers admired her spunky explorations, skillfully executed and cleverly original. But her marriage couldn't survive these life changes and a divorce cut to the bone, where failure and doubt ruled. It was, Bogard says, the right decision, but "painful and difficult." She turned to the only thing that mattered—her ceramic work. She took big risks, blended the beautiful with the sad, fantasy with reality, idealism with truth, and the sexual with the innocent. Her work, in a way, told a coded story of her life. She created animals—fantasy-like squirrels and bambis—that could be read simultaneously as happy-go-lucky as well as melancholic and out of place. "Without that strife, we don't really go down to our depths. For me, I'm a spiritual person. I don't talk about that very much, but it was one of the things that pulled me through. You always have God."

Realizing it was her chance to build a reputation, she entered competitions. "The first time I was published, I was shocked. Since then, I've figured out how to do it."

Rebekah Bogard, *Crush*. Earthenware; oil paint; 68½ x 21 x 23 in. Reproduced by permission from Rebekah Bogard.

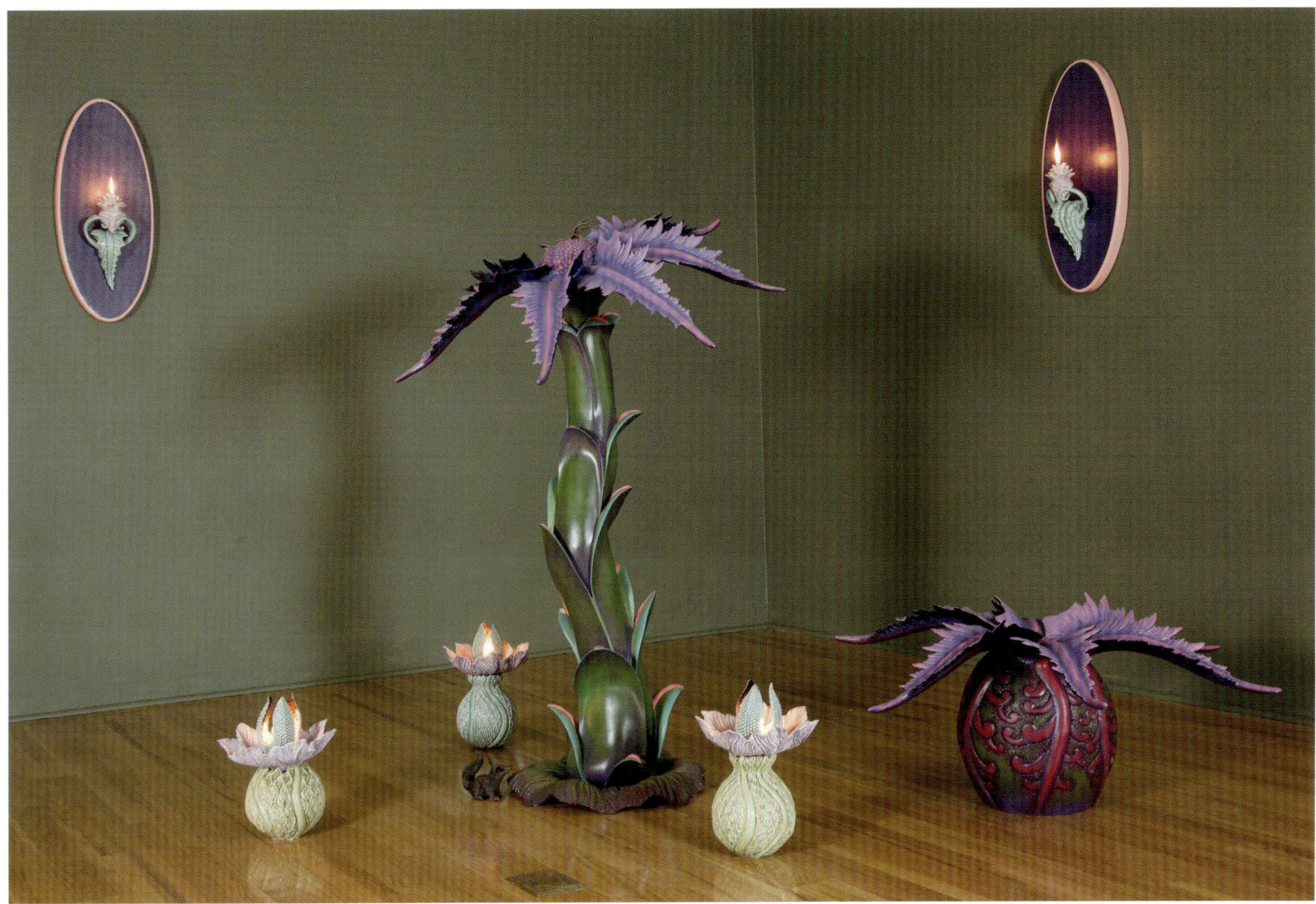

Rebekah Bogard, scene from the *Heaven* installation. Earthenware; oil paint, glaze, fire; variable dimensions. Reproduced by permission from Rebekah Bogard.

Bogard's work has shown in solo and group exhibitions nationwide and received several Best of Show awards. She was named an "emerging artist" by both the National Council on Education for the Ceramic Arts and *Ceramics Monthly* magazine, and was awarded residencies at the Bemis Center for Contemporary Arts in Omaha, Nebraska, and at the Watershed Center for the Ceramic Arts in Newcastle, Maine. Her work has appeared in numerous publications and brought her several fellowships and grants, and she's been a visiting lecturer in universities and art centers around the West. She received her master of fine arts in 2003 and came to teach at UNR in 2004.

Much of her work is larger than life-size. It involves a magical playland of bubbly flora, curvy fauna, and cute animals that at first glance seem engaged in harmless poses; I warn you, though, be prepared to blush when you approach them, for there's an erotic surprise in store. As University of Nevada professor Joanna Frueh (2008, 173) wrote in an *Art in America* review, "Whether munching rose petals or poised belly to belly, these creatures clearly know the meaning of happily ever after."

She came to UNR thinking it would be her starter job. But now she's thinking this is the place for her. The facilities and outstanding bachelor of fine arts program are conducive to a great teaching experience, and she does her best to inspire her students. "I absolutely think it's working. In beginning ceramics we realize the power we all have and how we choose to use it. Every little thing matters. I like telling beginning students that art connects you to your heart. I get to work with their heart and figure out what really matters to them and how they want to live. It's working, because my advanced classes are doing the best work I've ever seen. I love to hear my philosophy coming out of them. They are getting ready to go out and do amazing things."

Bogard feels the hum of the Great Basin. "The people are really real here—rugged, embracing the natural." She loves the Western landscape; she grew up in it and feels at home. The wide-open terrain, big skies, and subtlety of color seem to encourage her own use of color. "I love color and love pulling out all the stops; color is another way to pull the viewer in." She adds, "I don't want it to be garish, but sophisticated, smart, elegant, likeable."

This artist has no worries about being copied. In fact, her entire process is described and illustrated in several pages of her website, www.rebekahbogard.com. "Process is really important. You realize if you're not enjoying the process it's going to reflect in your work. You better find a process you enjoy, and it's about the same as life. It's not [about] the destination: it's about the journey. I do my very best to enjoy that moment in time and that's the way I teach."

And now, fresh layers are growing in Bogard's life. A new relationship is developing, and also a new show, a solo show, will be mounted at the American Museum Of Ceramic Art in Pomona, California. It's to be called "Heaven," and is actually about fire. This body of work reflects the painful decision of divorce and the idea of fire lighting the whole show from within. "That's the way I felt about finding my own happiness and being single, and now I'm lit within." She continues, "The idea is looking from within and finding your own happiness, or heaven, like a Phoenix rising." Bogard will rent a U-Haul trailer and drive it herself to Pomona. The volume of work created for her installations is tremendous and this self-transportation is the safest and most economical way to transport it.

Bogard says that artists, because they are visionaries, have a responsibility to the world. "We are agents of change. Artists have the power to change the world with their artwork and the dialog that follows." And she always goes back to the theme that drives her—beauty. "Beauty is so important to the way we live our lives," she says. "We are hungry for it. And I think if we don't like that part of ourselves, we restrict our own pleasure. Pleasures help us live a happy, productive life." She adds, "Creativity is the language of the twenty-first century and if you don't teach that, I don't know what we're going to do to our society."

SUE COTTER • BORN 1955

Our childhood dreams change and shift as we mature into the real world. So I can imagine the then-six-year-old Sue Cotter's parents chuckling the day they took her to see a Van Gogh exhibition in Buffalo, New York, where her dad lifted her high for a clear view of the artist's famous painting, *Wheatfield with Crows.* "I saw how he [Van Gogh] painted birds the same way I did, like little black M's in the sky! I realized I could be an artist, too!" That's when Mr. and Mrs. Cotter no doubt nodded and smiled, reminding her that

Sue Cotter working in her studio.

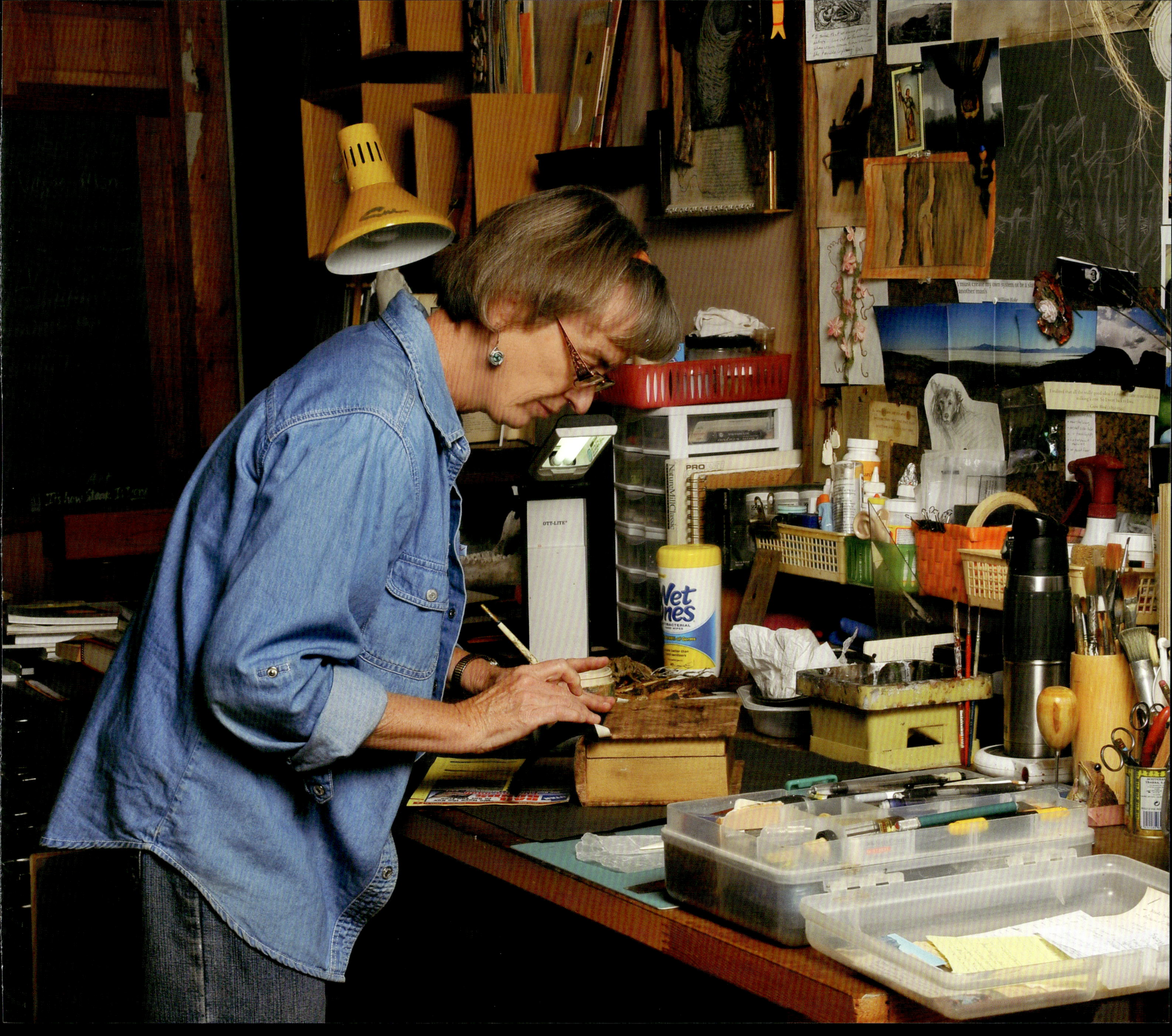
OTT-LITE
Wet Ones

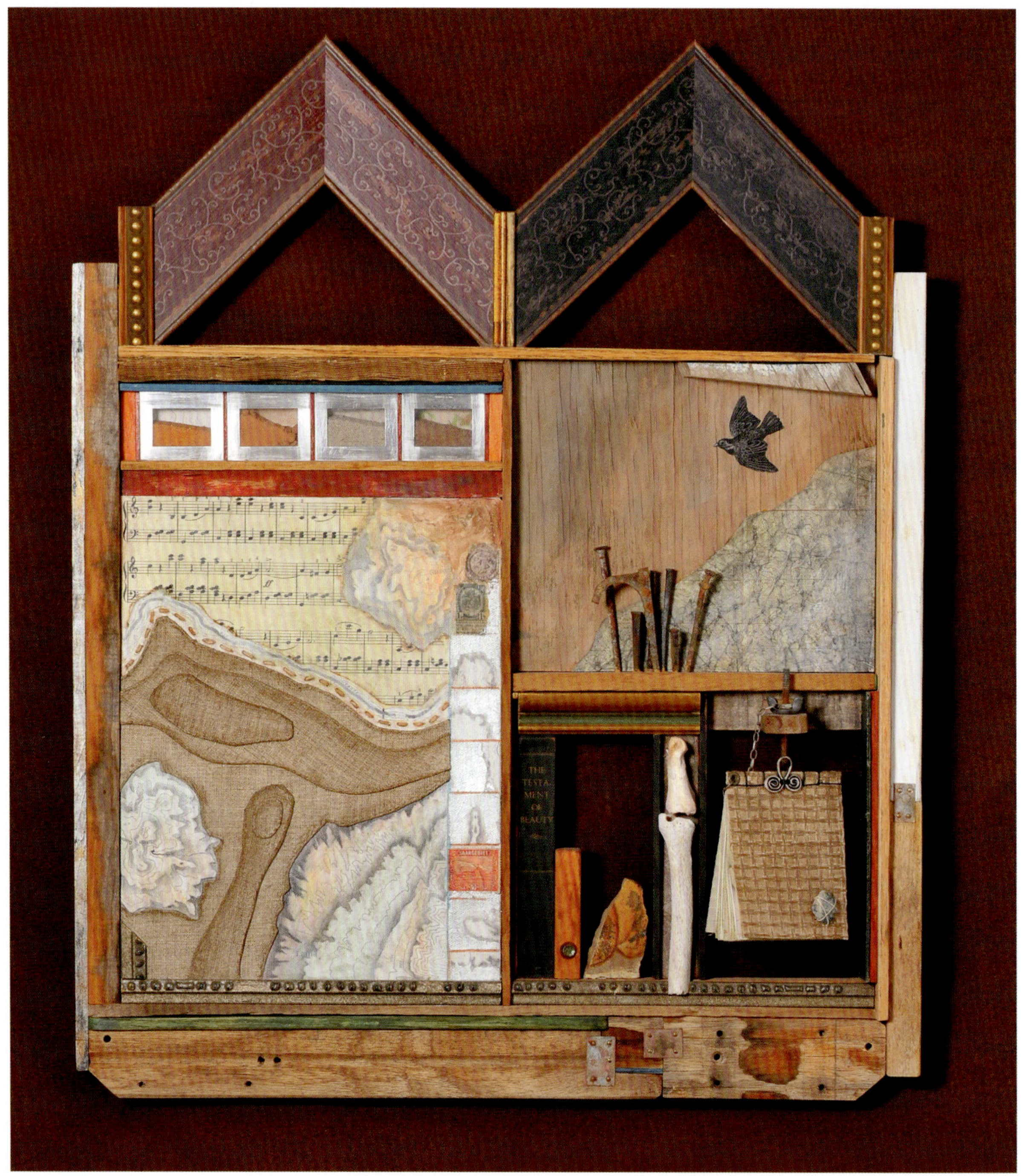

Sue Cotter, *Testament of Beauty*. Mixed-media assemblage with book; 26 x 16 x 3 in.

girls grew up to be nurses, Mommies, or teachers. But at that moment, Cotter decided she was going to be an artist. "And I never changed my mind."

Any professional artist knows that the path to success is congested with obstacles, and those barriers multiply if the artist is a woman. Cotter's career trajectory took many a detour. She experienced poverty, displacement, and feelings of failure, but, like a river, she eddied around the rocky obstructions to pursue a career in art. And not just any art, but her art, the kind she was determined to make, whether or not it met conventional definitions.

"I did anything to survive," the Parowan, Utah, artist recalls during our interview on September 25, 2013. Her journey demanded resourcefulness and vision, and she crossed personal and artistic boundaries to become one of the West's foremost contemporary book artists. Today her resume lists more than fifty solo and group exhibitions in museums, art centers, and galleries in Utah, New Mexico, California, Colorado, Idaho, and Nevada. She has received artist grants, jurors' awards, and a fellowship. Cotter curates exhibitions, conducts workshops, and has appeared in numerous catalogs and publications. Her Artists' Books and shadow-box assemblages are part of major museum and university collections and private collections across the country.[3] In one review of a Cotter show at Las Vegas's Charleston Heights Arts Center, the writer Chuck Twardy said, "Cotter's books, her poems, her assemblages, come across as prescriptions for living—how-to manuals with a metaphysical edge."[4]

The books Twardy refers to are Artists' Books. From papyrus scrolls of the Egyptians, to illuminated manuscripts of medieval monasteries, to pulp novels of the twentieth century, the book has had a monumental role in the creation of civilization. Because of this historical and cultural context, the book offers a wealth of possibilities to the artist. Cotter has explored those possibilities in depth, creating uncommon shapes in a variety of media like bones, sticks, and stones and, within them, unfolding story in letterpress, reviving Gutenberg's fifteenth-century printing technique. Later she added shadow-box assemblages and introduced the power of narrative without words. Cotter's ability to preserve the essential quality of story has brought her recognition throughout the West.

But success didn't come easily, as photographer Susan Mantle and I are about to learn. We'd driven 540 miles from Reno to the tree-lined streets of Parowan, and now we head for Cotter's home and studio where she lives with her longtime partner, Spike Ress, a highly regarded landscape painter of the Southwest. I pull up behind a 1955 Airstream trailer, the couple's home when they're on the road.

These two make their living as artists. The couple built their home on an acre of land, adding rooms as art income allowed. A kitchen separates a studio for each, and the couple is currently finishing a great room complete with high ceilings, stucco walls, and tall log beams. They recently completed a two-person show, *For the Love of Art and Travel,* at Utah's St. George Art Museum, and currently they're preparing for an upcoming show in Zion National Park. This area suits them. "Parowan is right smack between the Colorado Plateau, which Spikes loves, and the Great Basin, which I love," Cotter says. "This was our compromise."

She didn't always love the Great Basin. Born in Kalispell, Montana, the second of three children, Cotter moved to upstate New York when she was six weeks old. Her father, Jim, a civil engineer, traveled where the work called, and the family lived first in Massena, then Youngstown, New York, until Cotter was seven, then on to Idaho Falls, Idaho, and finally to Las Vegas. Accordingly, she grew up with a feeling of not being from anywhere, a continual displacement. The landscape unsettled her as she went from lush forests of upstate New York to the hay fields and bare foothills of southern Idaho. "But far worse," she says, "was the move to Las Vegas, where, in my ten-year-old perception, it was nothing but hot, dusty, treeless, and colorless." They lived at the edge of town with an alkali-crusted yard that popped up one tamarack tree and one thorny mesquite. The well water was undrinkable. "I truly thought I had traveled from heaven to purgatory to hell, and this was hell."

It was while living in Youngstown that she awakened to artmaking and visiting museums. Her mother, Phyllis, found a woman teaching oil painting to adults and talked the woman into accepting her six-year-old into the class. Cotter painted her way across the country, but Las Vegas was still hell. "The kids seemed mean. Having just come from the Mormon-dominated culture of southern Idaho where being nice was the rule, I was unprepared to deal with bullying, rudeness, and snobbery. I never adapted to that and made a vow to leave Vegas as soon as possible." She heard about Henry David Thoreau and Walden Pond, and found a paperback copy of his collected writings; it became her bible. "I found solace and guidance in his philosophy and deep love of the natural world. I still do."

At age nineteen she married a man who shared her ideals, or so she thought. The couple converted an old delivery truck into a camper and headed for West Virginia to live off the land. But she had forgotten about mosquitoes and cockroaches, humidity, claustrophobic-dense forests, drenching rains, and people everywhere. "No great vistas, no open space, no place to pull off the road and camp." One day the end of the fantasy came when Cotter happened upon "the biggest spider I'd ever seen. I freaked out." Back to Las Vegas they went, and "I saw Nevada through fresh eyes. I had a new appreciation for open spaces, dry heat, subtle colors, delicate and varied flora and fauna." She spent time camping, hiking, meditating in the desert, away from the city. "I noticed the special smells after a quick rain. I learned some botany, took up weaving, and made natural dyes from local plants, and learned about Nevada geology, earth pigments, the drama of plate tectonics and erosion." She pushes back a strand of tawny curl. "I learned to love it."

Cotter's husband refused to pay for her to attend college. "After high school, I didn't know you could go to college just to study art, but when I found out I applied for financial aid, and when I didn't get it I cried my eyes out. Then I learned there were scholarships available in different categories. There was no category of art, so I checked 'other' and wrote 'art' in the blank space. A few days later, I was notified to bring a portfolio. I didn't know what a portfolio was, so I just brought in everything I had." She got the scholarship. That first year, her drawing instructor commented that her style resembled O'Keeffe's. "I had never heard of her and he sent me directly to the library. I fell in love with her work and came to be inspired by her life's path." But after three years, Cotter became disillusioned, with pressure from her husband that she was wasting her time. She buckled, dropped out of college, and within a year she obtained a divorce.

In 1980 she made the move to Reno. "I fell in love with it. I loved the river running through the city and the setting. I became even more enamored of the beauty of the Great Basin region of Nevada." She enrolled at UNR, receiving Pell grants and work-study. "I lived on $80 a week, barely surviving. I moved all over, sometimes with roommates, one time in an old rooming house on 9th Street with a bathroom down the hall. I fantasized I was an artist in my garret. I needed more room to work and rented a commercial place on 4th Street and showered at the gym on campus. I did anything to survive." Cotter always intended to be a painter, but wanted her work to be a narrative in some way. "At both UNLV [the University of Nevada, Las Vegas] and UNR, it was all about abstract expressionism. I didn't fit in and struggled with feelings of failure. When I first saw David Hockney's work, it was liberating![5] I could put narrative images and even text in a painting. But I couldn't get a grasp on my own direction."

However, change was coming. One of her housemates had geology textbooks and topographic maps of sections of Nevada, and Cotter was enthralled with the shapes of the contours. "The patterns of the land were beautiful. They

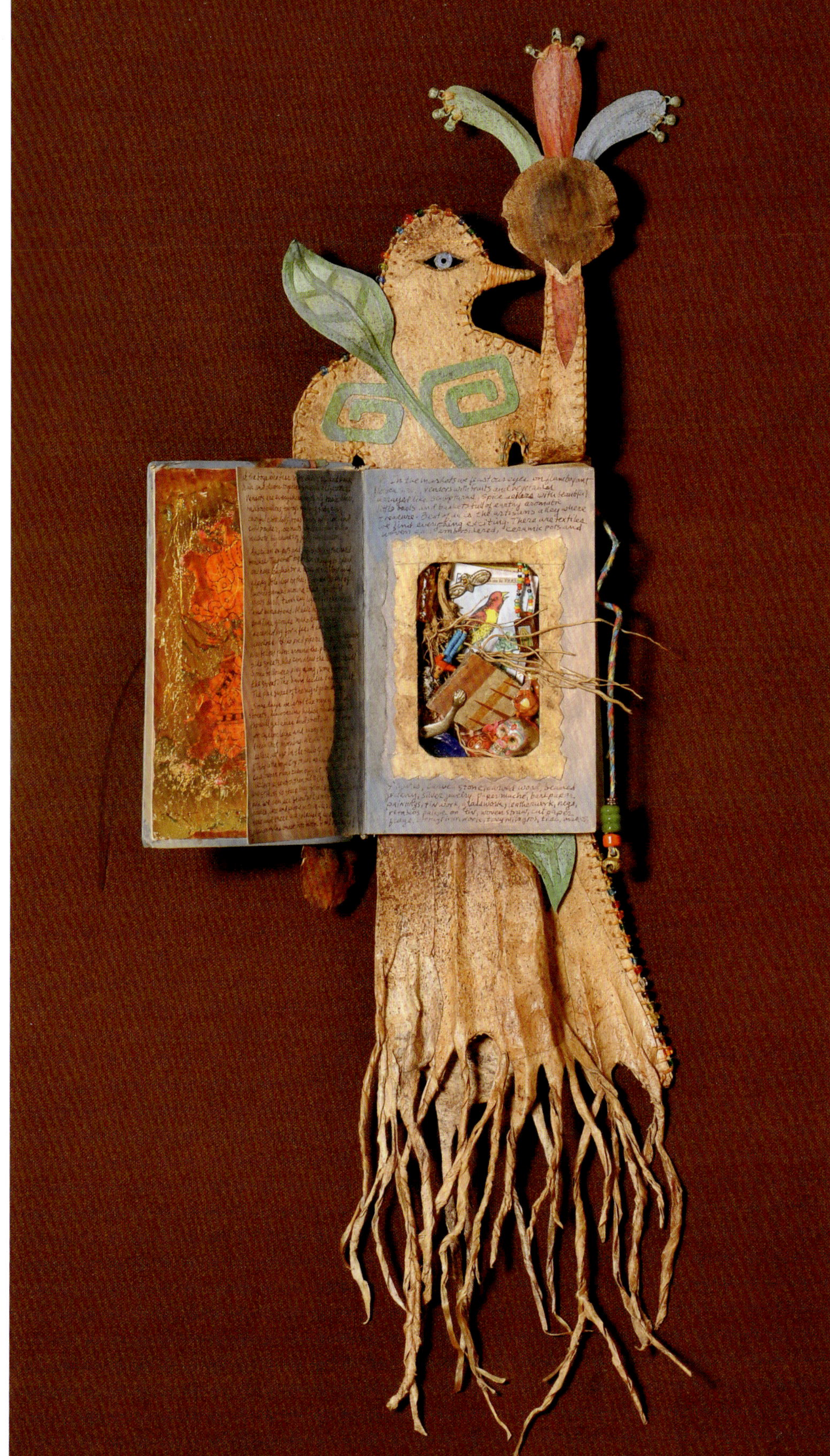

seemed like a mystical calligraphy, a secret language. I began to incorporate topo-maps into my artwork."

She sensed a connection among map grids, topographic shapes, alphabets, illuminated manuscripts, and anthro- and zoomorphic (human and animal forms) images, which seemed to be another kind of story text.[6] What emerged in her art was landscape-based mythology, which Cotter calls "topographic mythology." She explains, "Just as we earth-bound humans developed mythology while looking up at star constellations, I imagined flying creatures looking down at Earth and developing a mythology of landforms."

Meanwhile, Cotter still had to fund her education, even though she hadn't quite found a way to express her ideas. She succeeded at both painting and sculpture, but something was still missing. One work-study job led her to the-ater, where she built props, sets, and costumes, including all of the mouse heads for the *Nutcracker* ballet ("I think they're still using them!"). She was moved by the immediate audience responses and thought about how art in galleries never received such feedback. "I wondered how you could make art that engages people, make art that could be touched, read, explored."

She received a degree in painting, went to work at Macy's display department, and then saw in the University of Nevada catalog a description of a class on the historic practice of printing at the Black Rock Press.[7] It fascinated Cotter, a reader who was still trying to find ways to combine text and art. Director Bob Blesse gave her a tour. "He showed me examples of fine press, hand-printed, and hand-bound books. He then showed me a few very unusual books called 'Artists' Books.' I was so jazzed and wanted to take the class immediately. This might be the way to bring together images and text, to tell the stories I felt an urge to tell."

Sue Cotter, *Un Amor de Mexico*. Altered book. Bird figure is made of Mexican bark paper; 25 x 7 x 1½ in.

Prior to her introduction to the Black Rock Press, Cotter was the victim of a car accident when a drunk driver slammed into her Toyota and not only caused long-term injuries, but also totaled her car. It took two years for her lawyer to extract compensation; when the settlement came, Cotter quit her job, lived on that money the entire year, and took Blesse's class. "I loved it. They couldn't get rid of me. I worked with Bob and he found ways to pay me here and there. I found part-time jobs and did my projects. It was meditative and satisfying, with a bit of magic thrown in. I discovered the myriad approaches to book design and construction, pushing the envelope of what a book can be. Not only does the Artists' Book genre let me bring together imagery and text, these books include the element of audience engagement and participation I was looking for."

Cotter didn't realize it at the time, but she was part of a larger movement that questioned the accepted conventions of what art should be. As Artists' Books evolved into experimental sculpture, they created a forum and venue that exploded into the art scene, including galleries and museums. Cotter began exhibiting her Artists' Books in both Reno and Las Vegas.

She met and connected with Ress, and in 1990 the two of them headed to southern Utah. A $5,000 Utah Arts Council Fellowship underwrote costs of a press, type, cabinets, and all the equipment necessary for her own letterpress studio. She continued exhibiting, selling, and teaching, and after the couple's move to Parowan, she cast a wider net as her work found venues around the West.

During a stay in Mexico, Cotter became fascinated with the variety of decorative doors she saw in cities and villages. She liked to imagine what dramas were taking place behind these doors, in the hidden halls and courtyards. This led to the creation of visual stories inside boxes. "I don't remember when I first saw Joseph Cornell's work. Simple yet powerful, it instantly resonated. He conveys story and mystery with just the right touch. He is the master of assemblage and always the one whose work I turn to, to remind myself to trust intuitive impulses." Cotter refers to her small shadow boxes as "stage sets for stories."

As reviewer Twardy noted, "And so Cotter's work is at once loftily philosophic and refreshingly commonplace—head in clouds, feet on dirt."[8] She likes to collect things, and the shelves in her studio sag with the detritus of her gatherings, apt media for the next piece. She begins with a concept that grows out of something she might have come across by chance, such as the piece *Tufa Woman*. Other times, she might work with smooth sticks, or a rock that nature has already split. (One rock that was shaped like a skull became a *Day of the Dead* book.) The sticks became *Sticktionary* and, piled in a box, contained phrases from a dictionary. Recently, she created a second stick piece, *Tangle of Language*. An idea will light up, and she has to figure out the mechanics of creating the finished piece. She might press russet dirt into her paper, or stitch bone and rock onto pages of her handmade books. Rocks, words, and dirt work together to invoke reverence. If a viewer looks intently at several of her sculptures, she will discover a crow, an echo of that first bird she drew when she was six years old and decided to become an artist.

Cotter is, like that long-ago little girl, determined to continue her art journey, following examples of "all the women artists who struggled to keep at their work in a time of little support for women artists—Camille Claudel, Frida Kahlo, the women surrealists, Judy Chicago, to name a few. I still look west toward the desert I love most. I love the underdog, the land that is so often overlooked, written off, considered a good place to dump toxic waste. The Basin makes you stop, be still, then move slow, explore carefully, sit down in silence, and absorb an indefinable presence. This is the challenge I continue to embrace and pursue. I know I will never grow tired of exploring the nooks and crannies of the Great Basin and turning my experiences into art."

ELAINE PARKS • BORN 1959

"Watch out for the snake!" Elaine Parks cautions. We hesitate, and then step gingerly inside the door of her studio, our eyes darting back and forth across the floor. Her warning is our introduction to the life of an artist who lives and works in Tuscarora, Nevada, surrounded by open spaces and a variety of life forms, including snakes.

On this hot morning of August 21, 2013, photographer Mantle and I finished our Elko-style beignets at Mattie's and drove north on the Mountain City Highway, bound for the tiny artists' community and former mining town and our interview with Elaine Parks. The road was deserted, with no traffic coming or going; we drove across Independence Valley, smack in the middle of the Nevada outback. The undulating waves of sage-covered hills might have been the inspiration for Stephen Trimble's book *The Sagebrush Ocean* (1999). A string of willows in the distance marked one of the little creeks that sustain the animals and rural dwellers out here. Three craggy cottonwoods and a pile of old timbers signaled a ranch that once flourished, and back against the distant mountain a couple of working ranches nestle, their cattle grazing in a pasture so green it seems fake, a lush Irish meadow dropped into the muted colors of sage and sand.

After about forty-five miles a small arrow marked "Tuscarora" pointed west, and we followed it, passing an ancient cemetery where cars lined the road and people strolled among weathered wood and granite headstones, gleaning pieces of this ghost town's fascinating history. It was Open Studios weekend and the grand opening of the Society Hall; the town was alive with tourists, historians, and art lovers like us.

On a little rise (I later learn locals called it "Nob Hill"), I expected to see a sign, "Welcome to Tuscarora," nailed to the rusted and dented body of a pickup, its tires and windows missing. No sign, but the truck rose from the brush as if it had always been there, while behind it towered a couple of lone chimneys. The double chimneys on Nob Hill would be from a house, and the stamp mills were north of town. I am told the Nob Hill homes were the fancy houses.[9]

We drove past a throng of 4-H Club members firing up a barbecue made from a cutoff oil barrel, stacking hot dog and hamburger buns on a card table—good eats in a town with no store, café, or saloon. (We even had to borrow people's bathrooms.) We inched past cars and people crowding the Society Hall's front entrance, in search of Elaine Parks. Wild patches of poppies and rhubarb punctuated the rugged, dry terrain; lilac bushes and gnarly apple trees grew on lots where homes stood long ago. Caved-in buildings lay in splintered heaps with tatters of old wallpaper dangling here and there. Things considered as trash elsewhere were part of the scene, like glass bottlenecks and rusted bedsprings strung on fences, where they took on a different kind of aesthetic here.

Artists' studios were designated with arrows painted on rusty can lids and nailed to a fencepost or tree. We passed homes ranging from brand new to rehabbed to ramshackle, took a wrong turn, and pulled up at the edge of a great pond where a woman and a child bobbed in the water. With my Camry's thermostat reading 103 degrees, I contemplated joining the swimmers, but, remembering our mission, I turned and headed up another likely road. This time it led to Parks.

The snake turns out to be a harmless bull snake that sought the comfort of Parks's studio, which is a welcome respite from the summer heat for human and reptile alike. Snake dozes comfortably behind a pedestal while photographer Mantle sets up her equipment. Parks and I settle down in cushioned chairs in her light-flooded studio to discuss her intriguing sculptures, which include crickets, bones, and various abstract forms in clay and other media. In one corner clay and wire crickets attack a fencepost. Another piece is a precursor to the crickets. It's a large insect form,

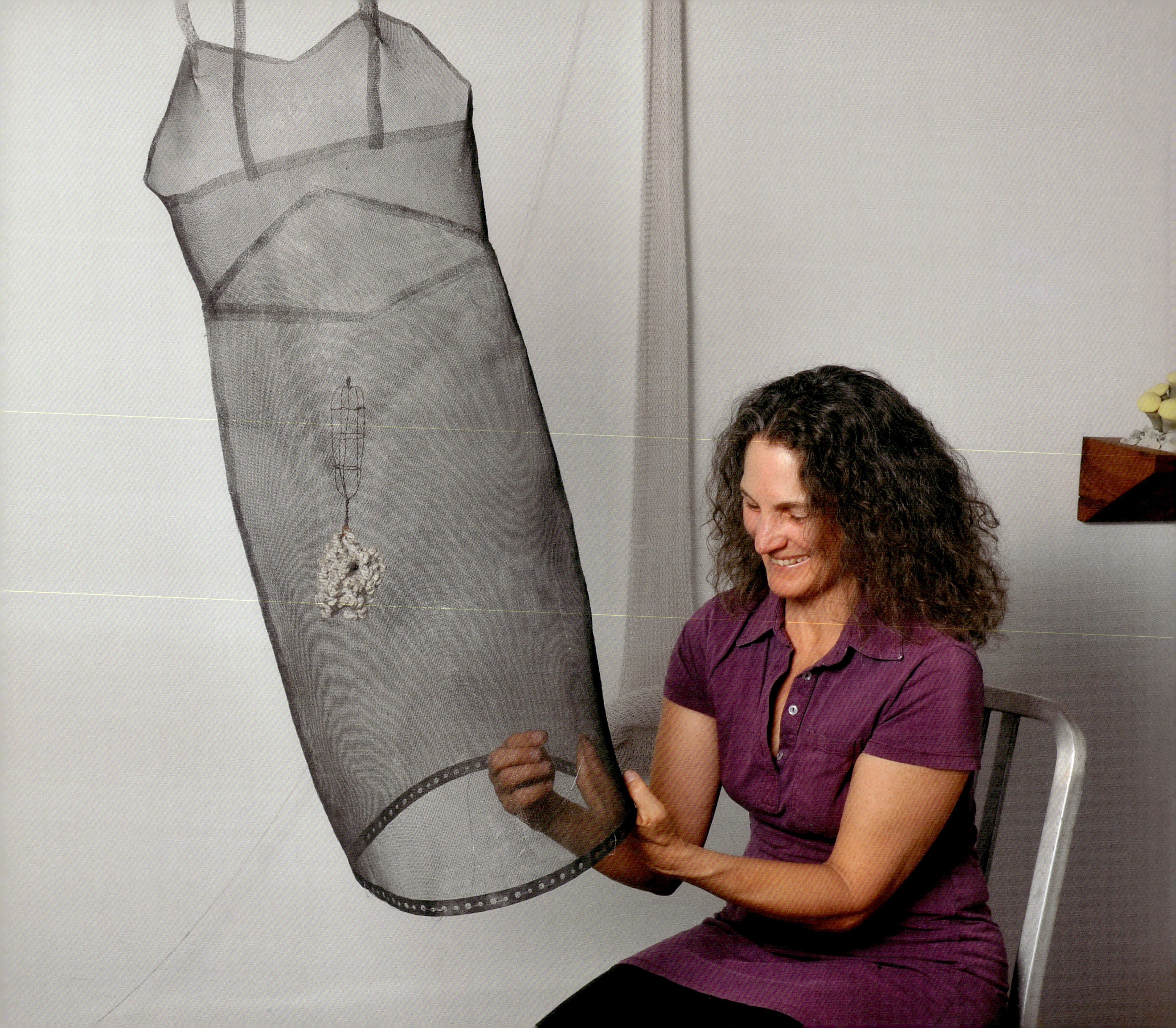

made in the manner of papier mâché but with cloth instead of paper and it stretches along one floor area. Elsewhere, several pedestals hold pillow-like forms the color of soft rust and sand, their bumpy, dimply protrusions arranged in some kind of inexact rhythm that seem alive and growing. A dress shape sewn from window screening waves gently, hanging from the ceiling. One wall holds square, thick panels on which a series of bones are arranged in some kind of mysterious order, embedded in a black textured background that I later learn is tar.

Parks, who works primarily in clay, is interested in abstraction as a strategy to seek answers. Except for the crickets, she doesn't often create realistic forms to reflect a theme; instead she rolls ideas around in her head and begins to create textures and marks in clay (and sometimes tar), a sculptural equivalent to recording words in a journal. Then she abstracts those forms. They might allude to objects such as pillows for dreaming or stylized chimneys or a star-studded sky, rather than realistic representations. "I want to see where an idea takes me. I want to be surprised," she says. To see her work is to want to know more—about the world in general and about Parks in particular.

Gallery and museum curators have wanted to know more, too. Parks has exhibited in Germany and China, and extensively in Southern California and Nevada. A former group show, Museum of Alternative History, at the RNG Gallery in Omaha, Nebraska, was a provocative and alternative take on political ideals and think tanks. She was awarded several significant grants from the Nevada Arts Council, including two Governor's Arts Award commissions and two Artist Fellowships in the visual arts. Her work has appeared in catalogs including *The Ceramic Design Book: A Gallery of Contemporary Work* (1998), and *Ceramics Monthly* magazine, to name a few, and she's completed two major collaborative projects—one in Los Angeles and the other at the Bonneville Salt Flats in Utah. She has also taught and lectured extensively about her work.

Elaine Parks constructing the window screen *Slip* in her Tuscarora studio.

"Ceramics is the ultimate chameleon material," she says. "Clay takes on the quality of other materials while maintaining its malleability."

Parks is an important name in Tuscarora; the famous Tuscarora Pottery School was founded by Dennis Parks, and student flocked there. Elaine was once married to Dennis's son, Ben, a highly recognized artist himself, and she was a permanent resident for ten-plus years. Now divorced, however, she travels back and forth from Tuscarora to Los Angeles, the city of her birth. Parks and daughter Aurora make their home in Los Angeles during the school year, but summers and school holidays will find them back in Tuscarora, where Aurora connects with her father, Ben. Then mother and daughter circle back to Los Angeles, where Aurora is immersed in various activities and Parks watches over her ninety-seven-year-old father while developing her sculpture as time allows. "Women have to do it all," she says. "If you want to make art, that's fine. But you also have to keep the house going."

But how in the world does she do it? By "it," I mean how does this woman transition from a town with a population of 20 in winter and 148 in summer, where she walks down empty roads for miles without seeing another human, to the teeming, brawling, musical, kitschy, noisy, busy city of Los Angeles, the second-largest city in the United States? To answer that question is to study Elaine Parks's background.

Born Elaine Elenore Fuess in Los Angeles, she was the only child of older parents, who were delighted at last to have a child. (Parks comments, "The two names are both from Helen, meaning light. It's partly why Aurora, meaning dawn, got her name.") She adds, "Every man in my family on my father's side has something to do with carpentry or contracting." Parks's mother, Marie, director of nursing for the Red Cross, and father, Wayne, a general contractor, didn't want her to get caught up in the wild events of the 1960s and 1970s, and were very protective.

Growing up, she did not attend public schools and

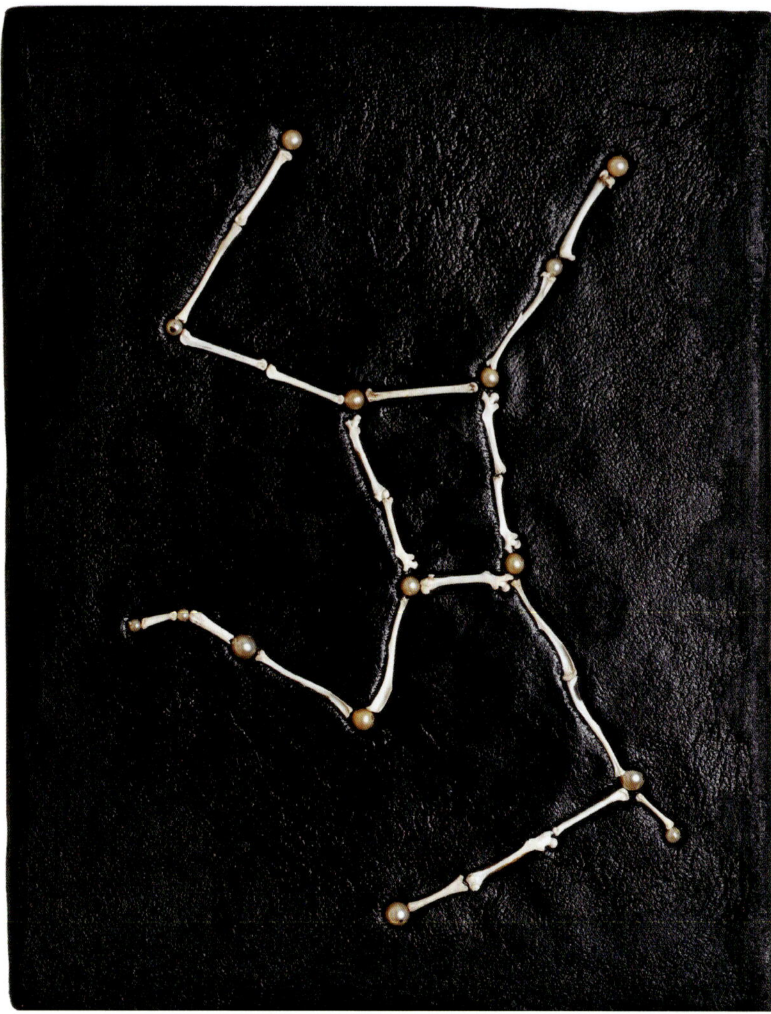

Elaine Parks, *Hercules*. Mixed media of tar, bones, pearls on wood; 12 x 9 x 1½ in.

spent a great deal of time by herself. She says, "Any fun I had, I just had to make up." The family frequently traveled to remote high desert areas in California and Oregon, and Parks developed a love of nature early in life. She studied the contours of stones and made mud cities in the dirt, which might have seeded her love affair with clay. Later, when she enrolled at Glendale Community College in California, she majored in art. There was and still is an excellent ceramics program that inspired her "I got turned on to ceramics," she says. She and fellow students mounted little sales and shows together. She learned about the need for a resume and began to enter juried shows. She eventually obtained her bachelor of arts degree in ceramics from California State University, Northridge, and her master of fine arts in ceramics from California State University, Los Angeles. She managed the California State University, Los Angeles, art gallery during the school year for two years, worked as a lab assistant firing kilns and maintaining the studio, and also taught a beginning ceramic class. The program at California State University, Los Angeles, was a mentoring program, which is why they had so many hands-on opportunities. While there, her art department chair, Joe Soldate, told her about Tuscarora. Soldate moved to Tuscarora and did art work there that was then recognized and shown in the Los Angeles area. He assured Parks she would love it.

"I'd wanted to leave L.A. for twenty years," she says, sliding a hand down her thick, wavy hair, "so I came to visit." Tuscarora, with its natural surrounds, reminded her of her childhood family trips to the desert, and in 1999 Parks made the decision to stay. She met Ben and fell in love; the two married in short order. Today, even though divorced, they remain good friends. The next ten years were a time of great growth. She hiked the fire roads and cattle trails, discovering streams, springs, and abandoned mines. She collected things—animal bones, shards, bits of discarded plastic, and rusted tin, and turned them into sculpture, balancing the roughness of the materials with refined shapes. She says, "My clay forms took on the patterns and organization of the desert, a combination of order and randomness; empty, yet full and always the imprint of humankind on the landscape. Even though few people live there now, you can see traces everywhere." Without city lights and distractions, the vast dome of sky began to seem accessible. She elaborates:

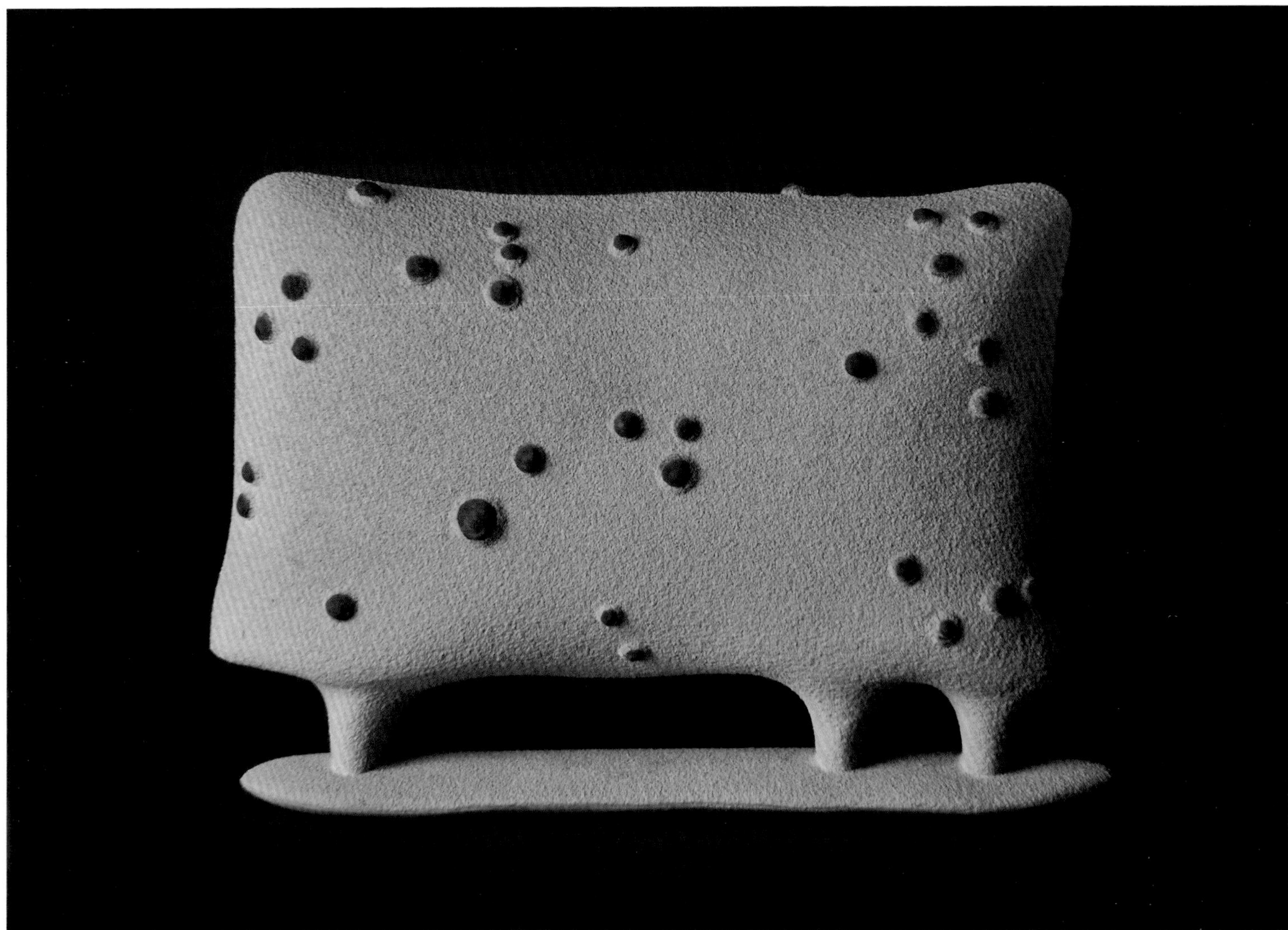

Elaine Parks, *Night Sky Reversed*. Glazed-earthenware ceramic; 8 x 11 x 2½ in.

People used to just look at the night sky, and there's still something profound and primal, the looking at night sky connects us with our ancestors. This view hasn't really changed. The stories are represented as drawings, and I choose the most interesting drawings to express in bones, pearls, and tar. Not only do I always have tar around, but also it is such a deep black and will accept the embedding of the bones and pearls, making it like a fossil. Just as you can think of the starlight as fossil light, since many of these stars no longer exist as we see them, my rendering is like an in situ fossil carved from a deposit.

This is where Parks pressed the small rodent bones, along with fake pearls from a discarded necklace, into warm tar, creating her own constellation. "I always have a bucket of tar around to fix the roof," she explains.

Ideas on randomness came from the desert. Foxtails, for example: "They're so beautiful dancing in the wind." Then she continues, "A lot of people see nothing here, but there's so much. It's random, but it's organized in a way. I develop my own organized system and it all comes from walking around in the desert. There is such freedom to have all this space compared to the city."

As she was developing her own abstracted vocabulary, Parks also participated in the rich, diverse art life of the Great Basin, and for seven years taught ceramics, sculpture, and art history at Great Basin College in Elko, networked with folks at the Nevada Arts Council, exhibited in group shows around the country and in Germany, and gave lectures and workshops in Utah and at the Churchill Arts Center in Nevada, where she eventually mounted a one-woman show, complete with catalog.

A four-year cricket invasion, where the creatures assaulted every inch of Tuscarora, including her house and even her bed, was pivotal. "If we were different people, we'd think of them as food and be happy." She smiled. "But these guys overran us." The invasion happened at a time when she was driving back to Los Angeles every three weeks to help her parents. "The rug was pulled out from under my life." When Valerie Sherpa of the Churchill Arts Council asked for Christmas ornaments, all Parks could think of were crickets. So she made a few. And then she thought about a swarm of clay crickets, which led to a show at Reno's Nevada Museum of art, called *Swarm*. She made over 2,000 crickets. She studied the creatures as she was working and picked out certain features to reproduce; she decided to make them white ("white made them more beautiful") and, not being a mold person, she made them all by hand and installed them at the museum's small works gallery according to how they behaved in life and where they would most likely be situated.

Parks admires artists Louise Bourgeois and Eva Hesse, because "they were women working in a man's field. She is most indebted to Japanese/Brazilian artist Kenzi Shiokava, who advised her about selling. "You don't want to sell until you know how you feel about a piece, and whether it's good or not," Shiokava advised her, "and don't sell your work, or if you do, put a real price on it. Some of what you make is valuable and you need to honor it."

Where is she going from here? "I'm starting to process some of my family things. My mother's mother crocheted handmade lace; I've formed it into a little structure; the lace has become a tent. I won't show it with the constellations, they are a different body of work, but I am working with antique handkerchiefs from my family and doing some embroidery on them, developing another body of work. I have several things going on at once. It's all a bit more clear to me now than when we spoke." She gazes inward, thinking and planning in tiny Tuscarora of a show to be mounted in Los Angeles. "I've learned that one success doesn't necessarily lead to other successes, but you can't stop trying." She hesitates, and then adds, "But I'll always come back to Tuscarora."[10]

Notes

1. This high mountain pass is located at the southern end of the Teton Mountain range of Wyoming.
2. Slip is a watered-down clay, and is used to hold pieces together and lessen chance of cracking.
3. As Cotter puts it, "Book Art is a creative work that uses the form or function of a book as inspiration, but in the hands of an artist it can take any shape. A book conceived and produced wholly by an artist becomes an artwork in itself" (*Spectrum* 2015).
4. Citation details unavailable.
5. Born in 1937, David Hockney—painter, draftsman, printmaker, photographer, and designer—is one of the best-known British artists of his generation.
6. Illuminated manuscripts, often very old, are decorated with gold, silver, brilliant colors, other elaborate designs, or miniature pictures.
7. Located at UNR, the Black Rock Press teaches the arts and crafts associated with the creation of finely printed books and broadsides.
8. Citation details unavailable.
9. Starting in the late 1860s this town was a mecca for gold and,later, silver mining. The camp of three thousand to four thousand boasted saloons, restaurants, stores, churches, lodges, and newspapers. The nearby Chinatown enjoyed gambling dens and a richly colored joss house. As each generation of miners, mavericks, retirees,and artists moved in, they set up lives among the deteriorating holdovers. The town's summer recreation area, dubbed the Glory Hole,is an open mining pit filled with clear blue (nontoxic) water.
10. Recently, since our last interview, she wrote,

    I have a whole show of work based on the constellations and night sky phenomena. They are the single constellations, which you saw, also larger pieces of just pearls representing the sky, in all its vastness. Some of these are a usual rectangular format and some are made on shaped wooden forms. One like a keyhole or coffin and another shaped like an eye. I also have a group of round pieces, some with a grouping of constellations and others with celestial clouds, made with metallic powders in tar. I also made a series of bone shapes from clay, with constellations made from seeds and an incised line. These are based on a seventh-century star chart. So they are the same stars with different stories and drawings. With this work, I want to keep tying the celestial to the earth, because we have long looked to the sky for answers to the questions we have.

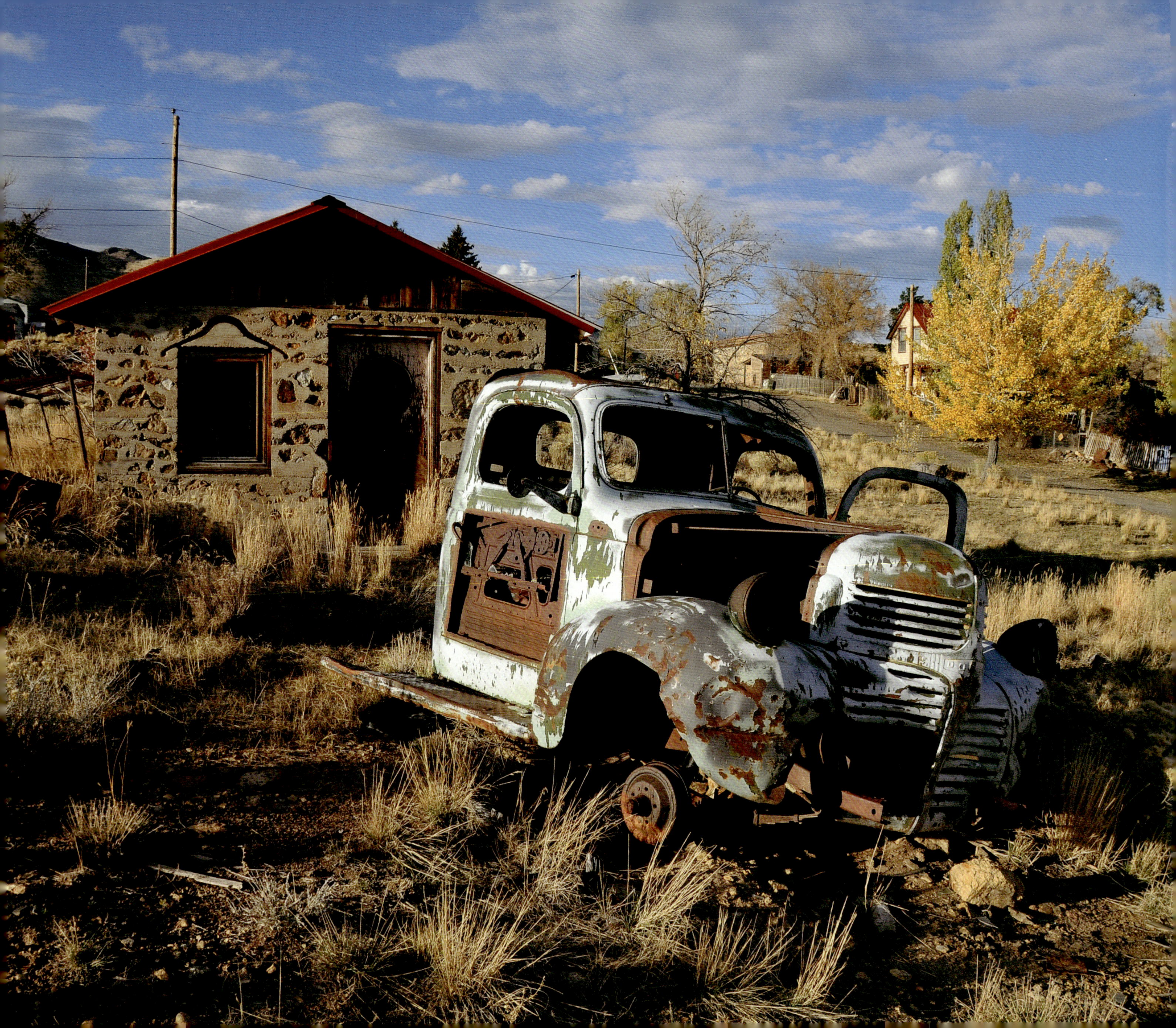

DREAMING

First Lady Michelle Obama, speaking at the opening of New York City's Whitney Museum of American Art in 2015, inspired the title of this chapter when she said a museum is a place for "dreaming, witnessing, and making things possible."[1] The artists in this book have dreamed big and produced visionary work. As I said earlier, their creative rivers flow deep; they and their contemporaries are the standard-bearers for generations to come.

These artists face drawbacks, however, the first of which is also their greatest inspiration—the vast Great Basin itself. Many of the women live distances away from the handful of cities and towns that dot this vast region, and those who dwell in populated areas find few outlets for their work. And being female doesn't help the situation.

What do I mean by that? Author and curator Maura Reilly, in a May 2015 essay in *ARTnews,* said that art-world statistics make it glaringly obvious that "the majority (of artists) continues to be defined as white, Euro-American, heterosexual, privileged, and, above all, male. Sexism is still so insidiously woven into the institutional fabric, language, and logic of the mainstream art world that it often goes undetected."[2]

She summarized some of the statistics:

1. "Female art-museum directors earn substantially less than their male counterparts, and upper-level positions are most often occupied by men."[3]
2. Women have considerably fewer solo exhibitions than men, although the Whitney, which Mrs. Obama lauded, led the numbers, with a disappointing 22 percent of solo exhibitions by women in 2014. Other museums had much lower numbers.
3. Women receive less coverage than men in magazine articles and reviews. "In the December issue of ARTnews, for example, of the 29 reviews, 17 were devoted to solo shows of men artists and 4 to solo shows of women artists."[4]
4. "In 2014 Artnet.com revealed a list of the 'Top 100 Living Artists, 2011–14,' examining the last five years of the market, with five women listed."[5]

As Kathrine Lemke Waste wrote, "When we venture into our museums and public parks, notable galleries, or high-end auction halls, it's rarely our [women's] work that we see. . . . According to numbers released in 2014 by the National Museum of Women in the Arts in Washington, DC [https://nmwa.org], women make up more than half of the working artists in the country today, but virtually disappear when it comes to representation in the repositories of American culture."[6] "Only 27 women are represented in the current edition of H.W. Janson's survey, History of Art—up from zero in the 1980s."[7]

The National Museum of Women in the Arts injected this quote: "This is so good you wouldn't know it was done by a woman." This was artist-instructor Hans Hofmann's "compliment" to Lee Krasner.[8]

Are there solutions to this inequity? In her *ARTnews* essay, Reilly suggests there are:

Truck in landscape, Tuscarora.

> We can hold collectors accountable. If one encounters a private collection with few women in it, one might consider sending a Guerrilla Girls "Dearest Art Collector" postcard, which reads, "It has come to our attention that your collection, like most, does not contain enough art by women. We know that you feel terrible about this and will rectify the situation immediately." Art collectors have the power to demand a broader selection than what they're being offered by most gallerists. . . . Boards have acquisition committees to whom curators present objects for possible purchase. . . . If museum collection policies were modified to attend to gender discrepancies, then perhaps acquisitions could be more justly made. . . . [Russell Storer, senior curator at the National Gallery in Singapore, said,] "Curators need to become aware of what women are doing, how women are working, the kind of ideas and interests that women are dealing with, and that can be quite different to what male artists are doing." This is not affirmative-action curating, it's smart curating.[9]

The Guerrilla Girls, who visited Utah from New York in the summer of 2014 to speak about discrimination against women artists, offered a different perspective. In a presentation in Salt Lake City, they announced that Western women experience greater art opportunities and freedoms than those living in the East.

Why has this come about? How is it that women artists in the West have explored their own frontiers with such pioneer-like vitality?

Once again, the answer might lie with the region where they live and work. The women circle outside the conventional art world of galleries, museums, and art publications, all rarities in the Great Basin, and explore diverse options. Two of the artists in this book have had wealthy benefactors who encouraged out-of-the-box artistic creations and then purchased the results, while several have gained reputations through creative marketing strategies and now have collectors waiting in line. Others present workshops and lectures in conjunction with their exhibits. Three have no problems entering their work in prestigious exhibitions outside the Great Basin, and two women are so well known that the world comes to them. Many women own and operate their own art businesses, while two aren't remotely interested in the traditional exhibition/gallery scene.

The networking process offers an important avenue where women can come together from across the miles. Local, regional, and national clubs and guilds support members' professional growth through idea exchanges and local exhibition venues. While living in the remote town of Caliente, Nevada, Kristen Frantzen Orr joined the Creative Artists of Lincoln County and found the support she needed. Later she joined the newly formed Society of Glass Beadmakers (that became International Society of Glass Beadmakers), and this group helped her career thrive.

Tuscarora is internationally famous as a haven for artists, and some of them are better known in Los Angeles, San Francisco, and New York City than in the Great Basin. We've been told the population is down to a little more than a dozen who winter through, plus more who return for the summer. When Dennis and Julie Parks, inspired to move here by Utah artist Lee Deffebach, established the Tuscarora Pottery School in 1966, students flocked here from around the world, and an artist colony was born.[10] Today Tuscarora artists have resurrected some of the old houses to live in, paint, create imaginative jewelry and pottery, write, and sculpt, inspired by the space, silence, soft color, and sensuous hills and mountains. Hundreds of people from all over the Great Basin gather at the biennial Tuscarora Days, where artists offer their highly professional work for sale in gallery-like settings. The newly opened Society Hall is an added attraction.

The recently formed Great Basin Native Artists collective is the first of its kind in the Great Basin. Members have gained some recognition within and outside the area and come together to share ideas and discover exhibition sites. Their reach is far; they are determined to show non-Native viewers the high degree of Native talent that exists in this region.

Salt Lake City, Utah, artists formed a nonprofit organization called Artists of Utah (www.artistsofutah.org) with, they note, the largest directory of Utah artists in the world. Their online magazine, *15 Bytes* (http://artistsofutah.org/15Bytes/about), announces exhibitions, reviews, and events to bring "artists, art professionals, and art lovers together."

And then there is the group Wild Women Artists. Formed in 1995 by Jimmie Benedict and others to nurture artistic growth and provide sales venues, their members are professional artists who work in a variety of media and live in various regions of the Great Basin. They invite guests, bringing diversity and change with each show. The Wild Women exhibit twice yearly in October and January in a variety of venues in Reno and Elko, and the group has struck a chord for hundreds (and sometimes thousands) of buyers, and collectors flock to the three-day exhibit shows.

The group's name (designed to attract publicity) was inspired by a passage on the book's cover in Clarissa Pinkola Estes's *Women Who Run with the Wolves* (1992): "Within every woman there is a wild and natural creature, a powerful force filled with good instincts, passionate creativity, and ageless knowing. Her name is Wild Woman, but she is an endangered species." The group donates a portion of their raffle sales to a nonprofit arts organization of their choosing. Every year brings a theme, and each artist creates a work around it. Recently, the art focused on breast cancer awareness themes to honor members, friends, and family members who have been stricken with the disease.

The artists in this book have dreamed up a variety of solutions to introduce their work to a broader audience and find a degree of support. They couldn't succeed, however, without private collectors. And if public institutions would step forward to promote women's art, the problem of obscurity would no longer be an issue.

Collectors are the engines that drive artists' careers, and this line of action is evident when one sees the Wild Women Artists' success. Sales at these shows can support an artist for nearly the entire year.

Wally Cuchine, who moved to Eureka, Nevada, in the 1970s, has amassed "Wally's World," what is believed to be the largest art collection in the state of Nevada, with an estimate of 1,500 to 2,000 works mostly created by Great Basin artists, with an equal representation of women's art. UNR professor emeritus James McCormick noted that Cuchine "has been a relentless and generous patron of Nevada artists."[11]

Cuchine's collection, which has traveled to exhibit sites around the Great Basin, is famous not only for the large number of works, but also for the variety of unconventional creations. "I buy what I like," he said.[12]

Sheryl Sandberg, Facebook CEO and founder of LeanIn.org, and Professor Adam Grant, author of *Give and Take* (2014), cowrote four essays in the *New York Times* opinion column "Women at Work." In their fourth essay, published on March 5, 2015, "How Men Can Succeed in the Boardroom and the Bedroom," they assert that women bring new knowledge, skills, and networks to the table and state, "Equality is not a zero-sum game. . . . The risk is in not including women. Teams that fail to leverage the skills of a diverse work force fall behind. . . . And when we make headway toward gender equality, entire societies prosper. . . . We need to go further and articulate why equality is not just the right thing to do for women but the desirable thing for us all."

These conclusions could be directed at any business, including galleries, museums, art centers, and other art-related enterprises. Institutions that step up their exhibitions of women's art, and add more art by women to their collections, bring more women buyers, members, and supporters through their doors.

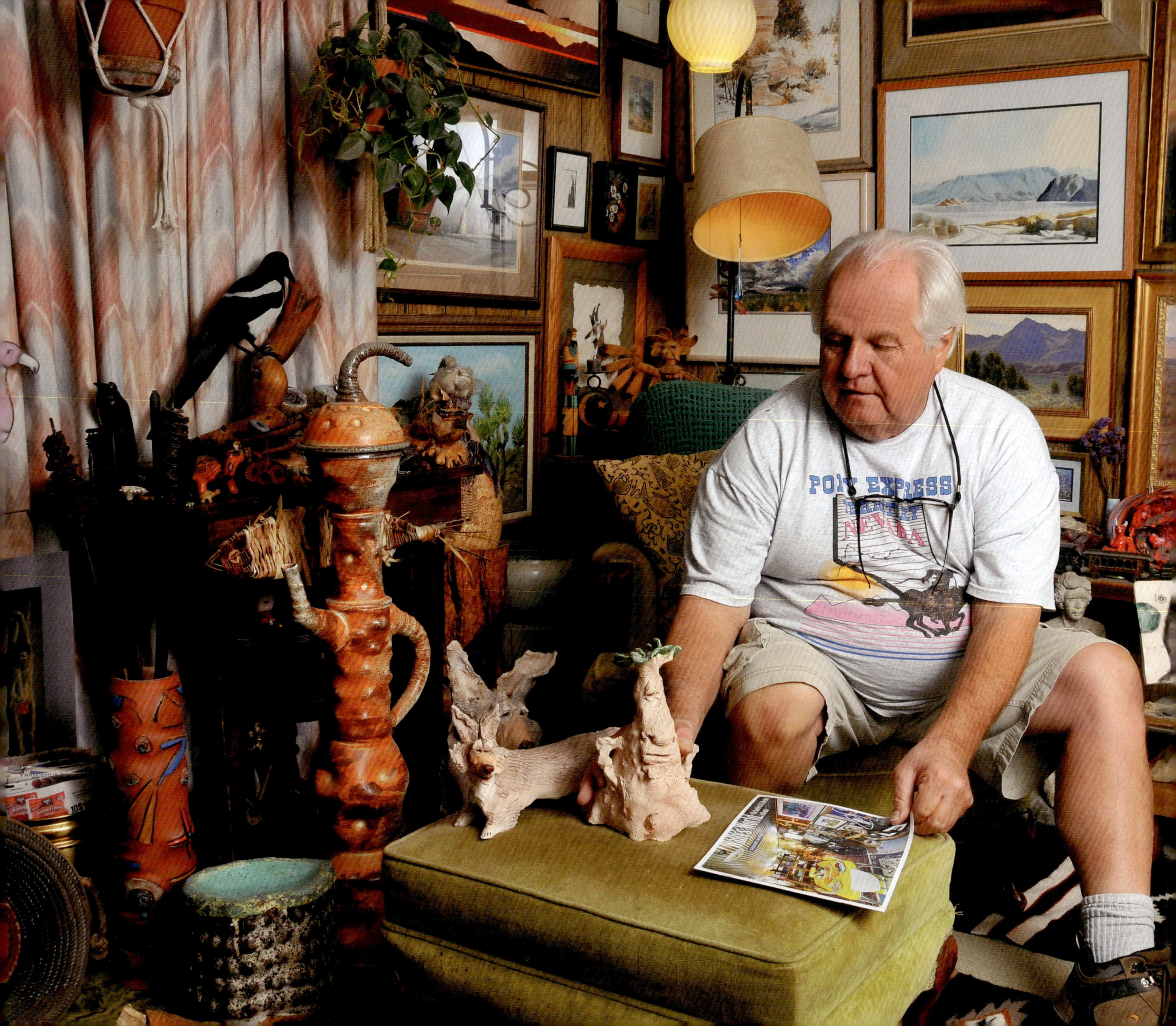
EXPRESS

The women whose stories appear in this work are pioneers. They stand on the shoulders of the many unknown Great Basin women before them who created art in obscurity. They kept their dreams alive and struggled long, hard, and mostly alone to imagine and to produce work of significance. They represent the Great Basin well. It could very well be true, as Jann Haworth proclaimed, "There is a different blood here."

I dream of a world where their world-class sculpture will be publicized, exhibited, collected, and purchased for what it is—world class. The journey of Great Basin women artists is on an upward spiral. May it ever be so.

Art collector Wally Cuchine in his Eureka, Nevada, home.

Notes

1. Saltz (2015).
2. "Taking the Measure of Sexism" (2015).
3. Ibid.
4. Ibid.
5. Ibid.
6. Waste (2015).
7. National Museum of Women in the Arts (n.d.)
8. Ibid.
9. "Taking the Measure of Sexism" (2015).
10. Lee Deffebach (1928–2005) was one of Utah's leading abstract painters and sculptors, and some have called her "the most significant female artist in Utah." She lived summers in Tuscarora, enjoying the solitude. "When some people tell me there's nothing going on in Nevada, I say, 'Good, keep on driving,'" she told Salt Lake City's *Deseret Morning News* (Gagon 2003). "I think you can find more going on in a one-foot square of the desert than almost anywhere." She convinced Parks.
11. Quoted from text describing Wally's World exhibition, Eureka, NV, July 2014. McCormick and his wife, Loretta Terlizzi, are art collectors.
12. Interview with author, September 24, 2013.

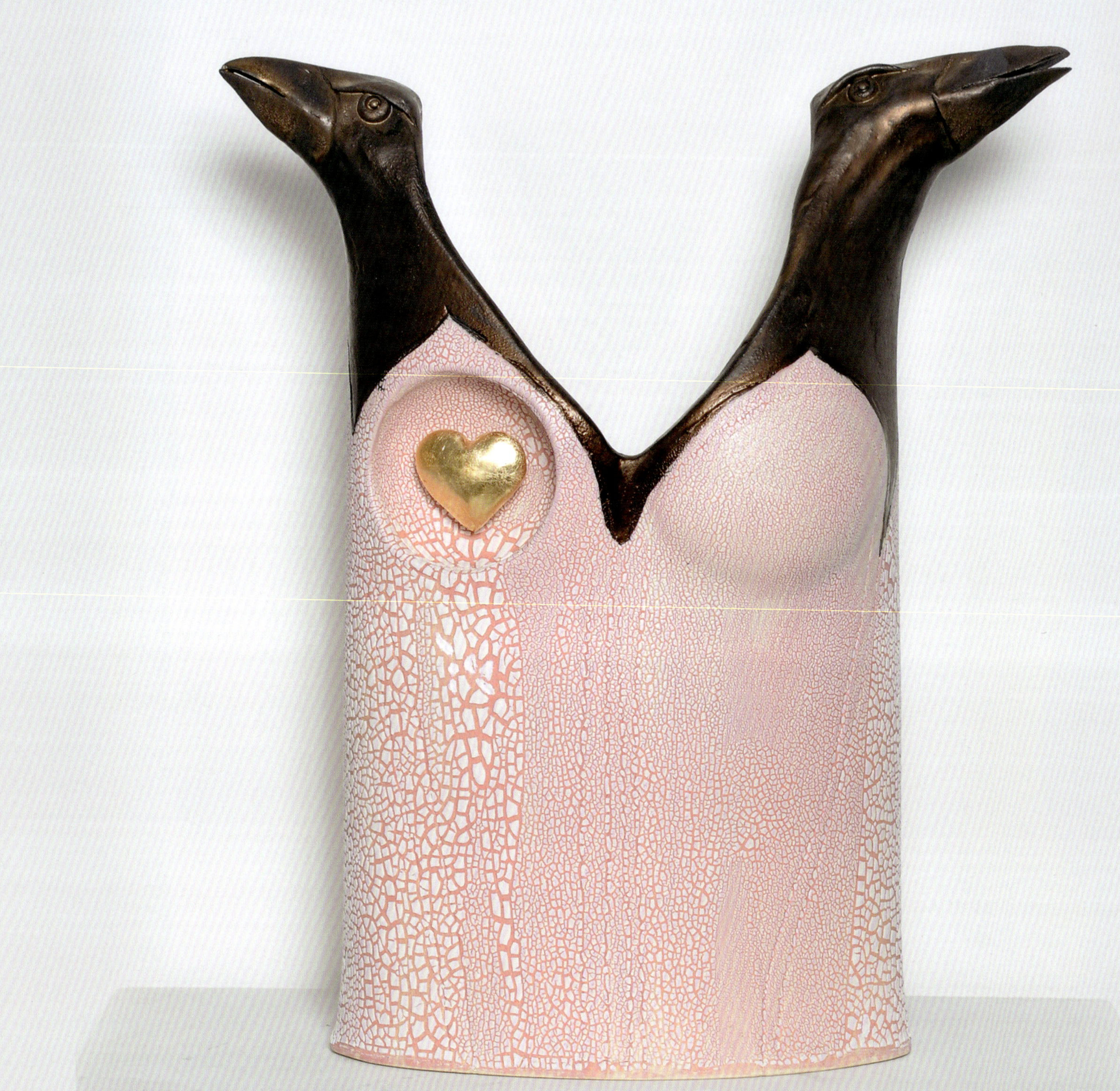

ABOUT THE AUTHOR

Mary Lee Fulkerson is a fourth-generation Nevadan whose ancestors came West even before the Gold Rush. She is immersed in stories—the mystical ones her father spun, the folktales her mother read from their Book House books, and later, histories and legends Native elders whispered around a smoky fire.

She became a military wife, traveling the country and world, but never forgot the power of home, and, with her family, returned to Reno, her birthplace. She obtained her bachelor of arts degree from the University of Nevada, Reno, and apprenticed with California Living Treasure Lillian Elliot and Nevada folk artist Rolling Mountain Thunder. As a counselor-advocate with Reno's Committee to Aid Abused Women, Mary Lee championed women's issues. In making her living as an artist, she chose a women's art form, the basket, to express ideas of story and women and the Great Basin landscape.

Her baskets were exhibited and collected in Europe and around the United States, including in the White House in Washington, DC. She curated and organized local and traveling exhibitions, taught workshops, lectured, and served on several founding boards, such as Nevada Women's Fund, Committee to Aid Abused Women, and Note-Ables Music Therapy Services. She founded the Great Basin Basketmakers and cofounded Connections Artists and Wild Women Artists. She has been featured on public television and in books and publications, including *Nevada Women's Legacy: 150 Years of Excellence.* In 1999 she was named one of twenty "top artists, authors, and entertainers of the century" by the *Reno Gazette-Journal.*[1]

With photographer Kathleen Curtis, she wrote *Weavers of Tradition and Beauty* and a perpetual calendar, *A Basket of Blessings*.

With her late husband, three children, and eventually their spouses and five grandchildren, she has enjoyed many years of bumping over Nevada backroads, discovering fertile valleys and wild horses, flipping pancakes over a cookfire, and camping under the stars.

Notes

1. Delaplane (1999); Skorupa (1999).

Barbara Glynn Prodaniuk, *Untitled,* Breast Cancer Series. White Stoneware; 16 x 8 x 3 in.

ABOUT THE PHOTOGRAPHER

SUSAN MANTLE has photographed Nevada for nearly thirty years, twenty of them as lead photographer at Susan Mantle Photography, located in Reno's midtown historic district. Her passion emerged at age twenty-two, when she saw a copy of *Life* magazine with a cover story of W. Eugene Smith's beautiful black-and-white portraits of a country doctor. With a four by five graphic camera she began making images, hands deep in darkroom chemistry at a community lab. She made images as a single working mom, from San Francisco to Nevada City and then to Reno, working nights as a waitress and bartender until she could enroll in college.

She received a bachelor of arts degree in photography from the University of Nevada, Reno. While there, she studied conceptual photography under Professor Peter Goin and printed for his book, *Stopping Time*. She was fortunate to assist professional photographers Mary Ellen Mark and Marsha Burns. Museum quality was the norm, as was detail in the darks and lights with focus on the concept.

She taught photography classes at the University of Nevada, Reno, for two years. She shot several book projects, including two Italian cookbooks for Biba Caggiano, one of them with Leo Buscaglia. She also worked with food stylist Bunny Martin, believing she learned from the best. She served as intern and junior partner in *Stopping Time: A Rephotographic Survey of Lake Tahoe*.

She has exhibited at Reno's Wilbur May Museum, McNamara Gallery, and Sheppard Fine Art Gallery at the University of Nevada, Reno, and at Western Nevada College. Her videography projects include *Survivors* and *Self Esteem by Maybelline*.

Her list of clients includes artists, entertainers, nonprofit organizations, political leaders, Nevada mining associates, and the United States Navy. She is known for her ability to capture the spirit of an individual.

BIBLIOGRAPHY

Ashley, Clifford W. *The Ashley Book of Knots.* New York: Doubleday, 1944.

Austin, Mary. *Land of Little Rain.* New York: Penguin Books, 1997.

Barbery, Muriel. *The Elegance of the Hedgehog.* London: Gallic Books, 2013.

Barnhill, David Landis, ed. *At Home on the Earth: Becoming Native to Our Place: A Multicultural Anthology.* Berkeley: University of California Press, 1999.

Bender, Sue. *Everyday Sacred: A Women's Journey Home.* New York: Harper Collins, 1996.

Berlo, Janet C., and Ruth B. Phillips. *Native North American Art.* Oxford, New York: Oxford University Press, 1998.

Cain, Susan. *Quiet: The Power of Introverts in a World that Can't Stop Talking.* New York: Broadway Paperbacks, 2013.

Cameron, Julia. *The Artist's Way: A Spiritual Path to Creativity.* New York: Tarcher/Putnam, 1992.

Celebrating 70. Atglen, PA: Facere Gallery, 2010.

Chadwick, Whitney. *Women, Art, and Society.* London: Thames and Hudson, 1990.

Cox, Ron. *Stories from the Sagebrush.* Reno, NV: Nevada Humanities Committee, 1999.

Cozzolino, Robert, ed. *The Female Gaze: Women Artists Making Their World.* Philadelphia, PA: Pennsylvania Academy of Fine Arts, 2012.

Cushing, Val M., and Chris Rich (eds.). The Ceramic Design Book: A Gallery of Contemporary Work. New York: Lark Books. 1998.

Delaplane, Gaye. "A Century of Arts, Authors, and Entertainers." *Reno Gazette-Journal*, November 21, 1999.

Eaton, Evelyn. *The Shaman and the Medicine Wheel.* Wheatob, IL: Theosophical Publishing House, 1982.

Ehrlich, Gretel. *The Solace of Open Spaces.* New York: Penguin Books, 1985.

Estes, Clarissa Pinkola. *Women Who Run with the Wolves: Myths and Stories of the Wild Women Archetype.* New York: Ballantine Books, 1992.

Fiero, Bill. *Geology of the Great Basin.* Reno: University of Nevada Press, 1986.

Fowler, Catherine S., and Don D. Fowler, eds. *The Great Basin: People and Place in Ancient Times.* Santa Fe, NM: School for Advanced Research Press, 2008.

Francaviglia, Richard V. *Believing in Place: A Spiritual Geography of the Great Basin.* Reno: University of Nevada Press, 2003.

Frederickson, Kristen, and Sarah E. Webb, eds. *Singular Women: Writing the Artist.* Berkeley: University of California Press, 2003.

Frueh, Joanna. "Rebekah Bogard at the Sheppard Fine Arts Gallery, Univ. of Nevada." *Art in America* (April 2008): 173.

Fulkerson, Mary Lee, and Kathleen Curtis, *Weavers of Tradition and Beauty: Basketmakers of the Great Basin.* Reno: University of Nevada Press, 1995.

Gablik, Suzi. *Has Modernism Failed?* London: Thames & Hudson, 1984, 2004

———. *The Reenchantment of Art.* London: Thames & Hudson, 1992.

Gagon, Dave. "Artist's Studio: Desert Painter Responds with Color." *Deseret Morning News,* June 15, 2003.

"Gallery." *American Craft* 61 (1, Feb/Mar 2001).

Giannecchini, Joan. "Ecotourism, New Partners, New Relationships." *Conservation Biology* 7 (2): 429–32.

Grant, Adam. *Give and Take: Why Helping Others Drives Our Success.* London: Penguin, 2014.

Greene, Brian. *The Elegant Universe: Superstrings, Hidden Dimensions, and the Quest for the Ultimate Theory.* New York: W. W. Norton, 2003.

Gross, Terry. "Terry Gross and the Art of Opening Up." *New York Times Magazine.* October 25, 2015.

Harney, Corbin. *The Way It Is.* Nevada City: Blue Dolphin Press, 1995.

Hay, Louise. *Heal Your Body: The Mental Causes for Physical Illness and the Metaphysical Way to Overcome Them.* Santa Monica, CA: Hay House, 1982.

Hickey, Dave. "Enter the Dragon: On the Vernacular of Beauty." In *The Invisible Dragon: Four Essays in Beauty,* 15–24. Los Angeles: Art Issues Press, 1993.

———. *The Invisible Dragon: Four Essays in Beauty.* Chicago: University of Chicago Press, 2009.

Holland, Marion. *A Big Ball of String.* New York: Random House of Books, 1958.

Hopper, Kippra, and Laurie J. Churchill. *Art of West Texas Women: A Celebration.* Lubbock: Texas Tech University Press, 2010.

Hussa, Linda. *Blood Sister, I Am to These Fields.* Reno, NV: Black Rock Press, 2001.

Ibuka, Masaru. *Kindergarten Is Too Late.* Tokyo, Japan: Gomma-shobou Publisher, 1971.

Jenkins, Cindy. *Beads of Glass, the Art and the Artists.* Pyro Press, a division of Jenkins Crafts, Inc. USA, 2003.

Kirkham, Pat, ed. *Women Designers in the USA, 1900–2000: Diversity and Difference.* New Haven, CT: Yale University Press, 2002.

Konigsburg, E. L. *From the Mixed-up Files of Mrs. Basil E. Frankweller.* New York: Simon & Schuster, 1967.

Koren, Leonard. *Wabi-Sabi for Artists, Designers, Poets and Philosophers.* Point Reyes, CA: Imperfect, 2008.

Laird, Charlton Grant, ed. *Walter Van Tilburg Clark Critiques.* Reno: University of Nevada Press, 1983.

Lark Books. *Masters Glass Beads: Major Works by Leading Artists.* New York: Lark Books, 2008.

Lippard, Lucy. *Mixed Blessings.* New York: Pantheon Books, 1990.

———. *The Pink Glass Swan: Selected Essays on Feminist Art.* New York: New Press, 1995.

Logan, Kristina. *1000 Beads.* New York: Lark Crafts, 2014.

Lopez, Barry, and Tom Pohrt. *Crow and Weasel.* New York: Farrar, Straus and Giroux, 1998.

Malchiodi, Cathy A. *The Soul's Palette: Drawing on Art's Transformative Powers.* Boston: Shambhala, 2002.

Markova, Dawna. "From Rut to River: Co-creating a Possible Future." In *The Fabric of the Future: Women Visionaries of Today Illuminate the Path to Tomorrow,* edited by M. J. Ryan, 285–99. Berkeley, CA: Conari Press, 1998.

Martin, Courtney. "An Ego of One's Own: Why Gender Parity Is Still So Elusive in the Art World." *American Prospect Magazine* (May 13, 2011). http://prospect.org/article/ego-ones-own.

McPee, John. *Basin and Range.* New York: Noonday Press, 1981.

Meilach, Dona. *Teapots: Makers and Collectors.* Atglen, PA: Schiffer, 2005.

Moreno, Rich. "Backyard Traveler by Rich Moreno." August 17, 2010. http://backyardtraveler.blogspot.com/2010_08_01_archive.html

Munro, Eleanor. *Originals: American Women Artists.* New York: Touchstone/Simon and Shuster, 1979.

National Museum of Women in the Arts. "Get the Facts." n.d. https://nmwa.org/advocate/get-facts

Norwoood, Verea, and Janice Monk, eds. *The Desert Is No Lady: Southwestern Landscapes in Women's Writing and Art.* New Haven, CT: Yale University Press, 1987.

Ostwald, Tanja. *Inspiration in Glass: Learn from Leading Glass Artisans Around the World.* Frankfurt, Germany: CreateSpace, 2015.

Ronald, Ann. *Oh, Give Me A Home: Western Contemplations.* Norman: University of Oklahoma Press, 2006.Index

INDEX

abstractions in clay, 181, 183
activism, 4, 67–72, 74
advocacy (defined), 55
African Americans: in art, 104, 106n24; as artists, 100, 164; communities, 12; encounters with, 63
African culture, 13
Aiken, Kirk, 32
Alcatraz Island, occupation of, 70
alchemy, 15, 19
Allen, Von, 161
"Alpha Awareness," 92, 94
alternative healing, 94
Alternatives to Violence Project, 77
Altmann, Fred, 125
Altmann, Jill, 107, 122–26
Amazing and Astounding Women Artists Breakfast Club, 120
American Craft Council shows, 31
American Legion, 97
American Studio Glass Movement, 17, 35n2
American textiles, 59
animal medicine, 87
animals: in art, 40, 42, 43, 45, 171–72, 173–74; in shamanism, 43
annealing, 21
Antelope Woman (sculpture), 31, 34
antinuclear activism, 74
arc welding, 27, 35n10
Arrizabalaga, Joan, 4, 146, 153–57
Arrizabalaga, Ramon, 153
art (defined), xii, 3, 62
art activism, 4
art brut (term), 52
art career, challenges of, 83, 86, 177
art collections and collecting, 191
art education, 85. *See also* teachers, artists as
art fairs, 60
art gallery, changing role of, 60
Arthaud, Ron, 112
artist colonies, 190
artist opportunities, gender impact on, 7, 9n3, 189
artist residencies, 16
Artists' Books, 177, 179, 180
Artists Co-Op Gallery Reno, 135, 151n1
Artists of Utah, 191
The Artist's Way (Cameron), 95
The Art of Engagement (Selz), 69
The Art of Gaming (exhibition), 154
art quilts, 117
Arts for All Nevada, 88, 130
Art Shack Studios, 59, 60
art *versus* craft debate, 5–6
Ashley, Clifford, 46
The Ashley Book of Knots (Ashley), 46
Asian culture, 13
Asians, 63
assemblage (defined), 164, 168n9
At Home on the Earth (Barnhill), 11
Atkins, Gary, 130
Atkins, Jill, 7, 107, 126–31
author background, xi
authors, artists as, 58
autobiographical nature of art, 151
backstrap looms, 125
Bamboo Prayer Spirit (art figure), 95, 97, 99
Barbery, Muriel, 111
Barnhill, David Landis, 11
basket dance, 79
basketry: artists, xi, 71–72, 79–80, 81–82, 83, 104; baskets defined, 46; experimenting in, 50; instruction in, 49; overview of, xi; pine needle use in, 48; works on, 104
Basques, 12, 13, 64, 153, 155
Bauer, Inge, 141
beaded baskets, 79–80, 81, 82, 83
bead release (defined), 21, 35n5
beadwork: glass beads and beadmaking, 19, 21, 22–23, 190; learning, 80, 81
Beatles, 57, 58
beauty as value, 158, 174
Becoming (art exhibit), 158
Believing in Place (Francaviglia), 11
Benedick, Jimmie, 107, 117–22, 191
Benedict, Ron, 120, 121, 122
benefactors, 83, 190
Bennett, Cheryln, 87, 99
Bennett-Miller, Danaë, 4, 6, 37, 40–46
Berkeley Folklore Program, 64
A Big Ball of String (art exhibit), 162
A Big Ball of String (Holland), 162
birds in art, 45, 136–37, 174
black arts movement, 104, 106n24
Blackie (cowboy), 64
Black Panther Party, 75
Black Rock Press, 179
blacksmithing, 27–28, 33
Blake, Peter, 57, 58
Blesse, Bob, 179, 180
Bodine, Danielle, 141
body-mind-spirit complex, 43, 54n3
Bogard, Rebekah, 15, 100, 169–74
book art, 177
Boulet, Susan Seddon, 104
Bourgeois, Louise, 39, 186
Bowman, Jerry, 161, 162
Bowman, Pam, 4, 153, 157–62
box assemblages, 71–72
breast cancer, 7, 29, 40, 94
Bride Culture series, 167
Brigham Young University, 161
Brigham Young University Museum of Art, 157–58
bristlecone pine, 12
bronze, 45
building, 37
Burning Man event, 12–13, 15
Burns, Mark, 172
business aspects of art, 120

Cabaret, 155
Cain, Susan, 49
Calder, Alexander, 26, 141
California Academy of Design, 165
California Institute of the Arts, 38
Cameron, Julia, 95
Camino de Santiago, Spain, 137
Campbell, Joseph, 137, 151n3

Campsey, Leland, 63
Camus, Albert, 126
cancer, 7, 60
Cannon, Hal, 64
Caples, Robert, 52–53
Card Shark (sculpture), 157
caregivers, 7
Carosne, Paolo, 71
Carson, David, 87
Carter, Rosalind, 146
casino culture, 4
casinos, work in, 86, 106n6
casting processes, 42, 45
Catholics, 63
Catlett, Elizabeth, 100
Cat Woman (art figure), 97
ceramics: abstract forms in, 181, 183; clay people, 145; on display, 33; earning living at, 32; experiments in, 172; as fine art, 75; narrative sculptures, 31; opportunities in, 184; pottery, 31, 32, 50, 52, 53; practical applications, 48; residencies in, 116; study and instruction in, 155, 171, 174
Chadwick, Whitney, 3
Chamberlain, Marsha, 125
Chapman, Tim, 87
Charles, Ray, 155
cheerfulness, art to restore, 133
Chicago, Judy, 180
childhood: abuse, 130; caregiver role during, 86, 97, 130; challenges of, 6–7, 16–17, 37–38; death and loss in, 80, 83, 115; homelessness in, 15; illnesses, 60, 62–63, 144–45; solitary, 46, 48
child support, 6–7
China, 162
Chinese people, 12, 64, 74, 75, 162
Chinese symbols, 42, 88
Chouinard Art Institute, 38
Christenson, Brian, 161
Church, Susan Glaser, 15, 23–30
citizen activism, 70
Clark, Walter, 11, 13n1
Claudel, Camille, 180
clay, work with. *See* ceramics
Clinton, Hillary, 169
clothing design, 117
Cohn, Abe, 72
Cohn, Amy, 72
Colescott, Warrington, 71
colors: in ceramics, 174; changing, 13; in feltmaking, 139; in glass beadmaking, 21; purses, 129; toilet tissue holders, 62; use of, 4
communities, artist role in, 7
computer technology, 48–49
Comstock, 52
Comstock Mine, 54
constellations, artistic creation of, 186
copper, 15
Coral Academy of Science, 86, 88
Cornell, Joseph, 52, 180
costume design, 155
Cotter, Sue, 13, 169, 174–80
cowboys: in art, 64–65, 66; as artists, 64; in modern times, 60; stories and poetry, 12, 13, 60, 64, 65
cradlebaskets (term), 79, 106n1
cradleboards (term), 79, 106n1
craft, 6, 75, 172
craft art movement, 125
craft traditions, 4
creation stories, 34, 35n18, 46, 79, 106n2
Creative Artists of Lincoln County, 22
creativity, teaching, 174
Crete, 43
crickets in art, 181, 183, 186
crocheting, 97
Crow and Weasel, 146–47
Cuchine, Wally, 191
culture, lost memory of, 11–12
Curtis, Dick, 103
Curtis, Edward, 82
Curtis, Kathleen, xi, 4, 79, 100–105

Dalton, Demetrice, 153, 162–67
Dalton, Ken, 166
Darwin, Charles, 136
Dat-So-La-Lee, 71–72, 82, 83
Davis, Ceola, 162, 164
Dawsey, Jill, 55, 77n1
Dead Man's Hand (sculpture), 153, 157
death as art theme, 34
Deffebach, Lee, 190
DeLorme, Bernie, 80, 81, 82
DeLorme, Norm, 80, 81, 82
Dentures Art Club, 72, 74
De Staebler, Stephen, 75
Diffeye, Kenneth, 11
dilemmas, universal nature of, 6
Diller, Phyllis, 155
dioramas, 57, 70
discrimination, fight against, 67, 70
Disney cartoons, 169
divorce, 39, 40, 43, 54, 58, 63, 92, 94, 112, 130, 135, 155, 166, 172, 178, 183, 184; parental, 16, 38, 85, 115
dog art, 22
doll clothes, designing, 103, 147
Doll Owners of America, 147, 151n6
dolls, 102–103, 112, 114, 141, 143–44, 145–46, 147, 149, 150, 151
domestic role, elevating, 161
domestic violence, 39
doodling, 99
Drake, Sir Francis, 70
Draper, Bryon, 161
Dubuffet, Jean, 52
Duchamp, Marcel, 157
Durham, Kathleen, 133, 141–47

Eagle, Harvey, 80
Eagle, Rebecca, 4, 79–83
earth, healing, 103
Earth Day projects, 104
earth sculpture, 105
Easy Money (sculpture), 153
ecotourism, 72, 76
Egypt, 126
Ehrlich, Gretel, 11–12
Einstein, Albert, 49
The Elegance of the Hedgehog (Barbery), 111
The Elegant Universe (Greene), 95
The Elephant Man (movie), 75
entertainment business, 155–56
Ericson, Gretchen, 37, 46–50
eroticism in art, 169, 174
Erquiaga, Tomasa, 153
escape, art as, 7
Estes, Clarissa Pinkola, 143, 191
exhibition as art requirement, 3
experience, allegory of, 158
experimenting, 49, 50
exploring, 169

families, raising, 7
Famous Artists Correspondence School, 162
Felt Alive (sculpture), 153
feltmaking, 137, 139, 140–41
feminist art, 3
Fey, Marsh, 146
Fey, Tina, 146
fiber sculptures, 46, 49–50
Fibonacci sequence, 49–50
Fiero, Bill, 11
fine art, craft *versus,* 75, 172
fire, 15
fish in art, 52
flamework technique, 19, 21
Fletcher, Curly, 64
Flores, Tia L., 79, 83–90
Food as Medium show, 136
force (defined), xi
forging, 28, 35n12
Fowler, Catherine S., 80
Francaviglia, Richard, 11
Francis, Sandra, 112
freedom, sense of, 3

Friel, Jonda, 103
Friis, Rosalie, 49, 50
From the Mixed-up Files of Mrs. Basil E. Frankweller (Konigsburg), 85
Frueh, Joanna, 174
Fulkerson, Mary Lee, xi

Gablik, Suzi, 55, 161–62
Game Animals, 157
gaming industry, 155–57
gaming-related art, 153–54, 157
gas tungsten arc welding (GTAW), 90, 92, 94
Gates, Bill, 49
Gaudi, Antoni, 139
gender equality, 191
Gene Quintana Fine Arts, 83
generations, future, standard-bearers for, 9
geography, 4
Geology of the Great Basin (Fiero), 11
Geotourism project, 90
Giambruni, Tio, 134
Giannecchini, Joan, 4, 55, 72–77
Girls State, 97
Give and Take (Grant), 191
Glaser family stories, 28, 35n13
glass: beads and beadmaking, 19, 21, 22–23, 190; casting, 45; sculpting, 19, 45; working with, 15, 17, 18, 34
Glenn-Lawson, June, 71
glory hole, 15
Glynn, Agnes, 33
Goin, Chelsea Miller, 39, 122
Goldberg, Rube, 157
Goldfield, 166
Gold Hill, 50, 52, 54
Goldsworthy, Andy, 34
González, Julio, 141
A Good Bet (sculpture), 157
gourd art, 85, 87, 88
Grabowski, Kerr, 141
Grant, Adam, 191
Great Basin, inspiration from, 4
Great Basin Basketmakers, xi, 46, 49, 99
Great Basin description and overview, 11–13
Great Basin Native Artists collective, 72, 190–91
Greece, 43
Green, Susan, 116
Greene, Brian, 95
Greeter (sculpture), 90
grisaille, 136
Gross, Terry, 6
GTAW welding, 90, 92, 94
Guerilla Girls, 13, 57, 190
Guernica (antiwar painting), 60, 77n5

Hands Along the Nile, 126
hands-on experiences, 55, 57
Harney, Corbin, 11, 12, 104
Harolds Club, 153–54
Harrah's Club, 155, 156
Has Modernism Failed? (Gablik), 55
Hattori, Eugene, 82
Hatzanbiler, Pam, 146
Hauck, Dennis, 15
Haworth, Jann, 4, 12, 55–60, 193
Hay, Louise, 95
Headliner Room, 155
Heal Your Body (Hay), 95
Heart Mountain internment camp (*later* Heart Mountain Interpretive Center), 110
Hesse, Eva, 186
Hickey, Dave, 107, 158, 168n8
Hickok, "Wild Bill," 153, 157, 168n1
Hines, Ken, 39
hippie movement, 16
hippies, 75
Hockney, David, 178
Hodge, Gillian, 4–5
Hoffmann, Hans, 189
Hoke, Monte, 92
Holland, Marion, 162
homemaker, honoring, 153
hope, art to restore, 133
horses: in art, 42, 44; raising, 43; wild, 12, 13, 60
hospitalization, 40, 43, 62–63
Hostess Brands, 137
Hostess Cakes, 136
Hugo, Victor, 31
Humboldt River, 23
Hundertwasser, Friedensreich, 121, 141
Hunter, Lissa, 50
Hyde, Doug, 66

Iacavelli, John, 53
illuminated manuscripts, 179
Imagine Peace (calabaza sculpture), 88
impressionism, 169
Impressionism (Parks), 149
Independence Lake, land near, 104
Indian Relocation Act of 1956, 70
individualism, xi–xii
infantile paralysis, 7
infinity, discovering, 37–38
insects in art, 181, 183
International Academy of Design & Technology, 165
International Game Technology, 135
International Society of Glass Beadmakers, 22, 190
International Union for Conservation of Nature (IUCN), 72
introverts, artists as, 49
Invasion of the Body Snatchers (movie), 57
The Invisible Dragon (Hickey), 158, 168n8
Issei, 109
Italy, 66

Japan, 23
Japanese Americans, internment of, 109–10
Japanese family crests, 111
Jason, Elaine, 4, 37–40
Jeremiah Johnson (movie), 57
jewelry, 107, 109, 111–12, 114, 115, 116, 117
Jones, Ellen Sherbourne, 119
joy, art to inspire, 133
Julia Bulette (purse), 128
junk, creating art out of, 26, 28, 29

Kahlo, Frida, 180
Kansas City Renaissance Festival, 150
Kaplan, Stan, 76
Kasten, Karl, 103
Keddy ranch, 25, 29
Kelly, Helen, 33
Kennedy, John F., 145
Kinetic Melodies (art exhibit), 162
King, Coretta Scott, 167
King, Martin Luther, Jr., 57
Kloda, Phyllis, 171–72
knitting, 97
knots and knotting, 46, 119, 120
Knous, Claudia, 133, 137–41
Knous, Ward, 137, 139
Konigsburg, E. L., 85
Krasner, Lee, 189
Kwansee (Great Serpent) (mythical creature), 12

Lake Pyramid baskets, 82
Lake Tahoe baskets, 79–80
Lake Tahoe/Pyramid basket, 82
LaMarr, Jean, 55, 67–72
Lambson, Jeff, 158
lampworking (term), 19, 21
land, protecting, 104
landscape-based mythology, 179
language, art as, 92
The Last Snack (painting), 136
The Last Supper (painting), 136
Las Vegas, 177–78
Latinos, 12, 13, 63
Laury, Jean Ray, 146

lava rock, 90, 92, 94
Laxalt family, 12
Leonardo da Vinci, 63, 136
Leonardo Museum (Salt Lake City), 55, 60
life, art and, 37
light, 4, 13, 19, 23
Lipovsky, Martin, 17
Lippard, Lucy R., 9, 69, 104
lives, examination of, 6
Lobo, Susan, 71
The Long, Long Trailer (movie), 76
Los Angeles Knotters Collective show, 46
The Luck of the Draw (sculpture), 153
Luster, Johnny Mea, 164
Lynn, Loretta, 155

macramé, 46, 119, 120
Malchiodi, Cathy A., 79, 83, 85
Mallea, Sara Vélez, xii
Malotte, Jack, 67
Mama Casino (sculpture), 157
mandrel (defined), 21, 35n5
mannequins, 154
Mantle, Susan, xii, 3, 45, 52, 57, 100, 109, 114, 149, 157, 177, 181
maps in artwork, 179
marble, work with, 63, 66
Marcova, Dawna, 100
Marisol (Maria Sol Escobar), 39
Markova, Dawna, 100, 105
Martin, Courtney, 7
Martini, Pasquale, 66
Masserrella, Frank, 32
mathematics, art connection to, 88
Maya (sculpture), 63, 66–67
McCormick, James, 39, 191
McKnight, Joe, 64
media, mapping, 4–6
Medicine Cards, 87
memory, allegory of, 158
Men Explain Things to Me (Solnit), 3
Merrick, John, 75
metal use in sculpture, 25–26, 28, 92
Mexican Day of the Dead themes, 34
Midas Well (sculpture), 153
Miller, Ron, 43
Miller Welding Heroes, 94–95
Million Mouse March, 145
Mills, Laura, 155
minimalism, 169
mining industry, 50, 54
Minto, Kate, 5, 79, 90–95
Minto, Wally, 92
Miró, Joan, 141
Misaru Ibuka, 149
Mixed Blessings (Lippard), 9, 69
mobiles, 26, 35n10
Moon Dreams (jewelry), 117
Moonwalker (art figure), 97
moose in art, 133
Mormon background, 158, 161
Morris, Willilam, 34
Morrison, Robert, 4
Morrison, Sue, 146
mothers and motherhood, 6–7, 34, 66
mud as art medium, 100
mud crack glaze, 4, 34
Mulcahy, John, 92
multicultural art/craft traditions, 4
Munro, Eleanor, 3
murals: with Beatles themes, 57; in Europe, 18; Native American themes in, 67, 69, 70; reach, extent possible through, 67; women depicted in, 60
museum (defined), 55, 77n3
Museum of Alternative History, 183
myths and mythology, 12, 179

Nancy Peppin Graphic Arts, 135
National Cowboy Poetry Gathering, Elko, Nevada, 12, 60, 64, 65
National Geographic's Geotourism project, 90
National Museum of Women in the Arts, 189
Native American Graphic Workshop, 67, 69
Native Americans: activism, 70; basketry, xi, 71–72, 79–80, 81–82, 83, 104; belief systems, 87; encounters with, 63; Great Basin tribes, 12, 13n2, 79, 106n1, 190–191; life with, 169, 171; literature, 50; medicine, 11; in modern times, 60; oral histories, 71; stereotypes, combating, 67, 69; stories and myths, 12, 13, 34, 35n18, 46, 104; tribal enrollment, requirements for, 81, 106n5
natural world, 21–22, 29, 32, 34
Navajo baskets, 83
Navajo creation myth, 46
Navajo rugs, 122
needlepoint, 48
neon, 37, 38, 39, 40
networking, 190–191
Nevada Arts Council, 186
Nevada Buckaroo project, 64
Nevada Clay Arts Guild, 53, 54
Nevada geology, 178, 179
Nevada Rock Art Society, 99, 106n19
Nevelson, Louise, 39, 104, 121
Never/Always (three-dimensional art), 37, 38
New York, 13, 177
night sky, 185, 186
Nike of Mastectomy (sculpture), 94
Nike of Samothrace, 94
Nisei, 109
Nob Hill (Tuscarora), 181
noble media (defined), 4, 9n2, 157, 168n6
nonfunctional objects, art classification for, 5
nonviolent communications, workshops in, 77
non-white cultures, 153, 166–67

Obama, Michelle, 146, 189
occupational therapy, 63
Ohlone Indian murals, 70
O'Keeffe, Georgia, 104, 121, 178
Old Lady (diorama figure), 57, 58
Old Sturbridge Village, 31
Open Studios Weekend, 26
oral histories, 71
Original Doll Artist Council of America, 147
Originals (Munro), 3
Orr, Kristen Frantzen, 15, 19–23
oxy-acetylene welding, 92

Pacque, Joan Michaels, 119
paintings, 67
Paiute Indians, 34, 35n18, 71, 83
Paiute-Pit River artists, 67–72
Paiute-Shoshone artists, 4
Paleolithic cave paintings, Lascaux, France, 43
Palo Alto Clay and Glass Association show, 31
papier maché, 183
Parks, Ben, 183, 184
Parks, Dennis, 183, 190
Parks, Elaine, 4, 169, 181–86
Parks, Julie, 190
Parks, Peggy J., 149
Parks, Rosa, 49, 67
passive experiences, danger of, 55, 57
Patrick, Mimi, 37, 50–54
Paul Revere and the Raiders, 155
peace as art theme, 88
Peace Corps, 145
Pearl Harbor, attack on, 109
pebble, casting into lake, 83, 85
Peppin, Nancy, 4, 39, 133–37
persons with disabilities, arts opportunities for, 88, 99, 106n11

photorealist watercolor, 134
Picasso, Pablo, 60, 77n6
Pioneer Arts and Crafts Folklife Festival, 64
pioneers, migrations and legacy of, 12
place, sense of, 50
Platus, Libby, 120
playing cards, 157
poetry by artists, 63, 85–86
polio, 62–63, 66, 144–45
polio vaccines, 66
Pop Art, 169
posters, Native American themes in, 70
post-traumatic stress disorder, 6
Potter, Beatrix, 146
pottery, 31, 32, 50, 52, 53
poverty, 16
power animals, 43
prayer baskets, 103
prayer sticks, 103
printing, practice of, 179
prints, 67
Prodaniuk, Barbara, 4, 15, 31–35, 141
Prodaniuk, Orest, 32
professional (defined), xii
purchase award, 92, 106n14
Pyramid Jacket Pattern Books, 121
Pyramid Lake, 4, 12, 34, 79, 106n2
pyrography (term defined), 87, 106n9

The Queen's Ride (sculpture), 105
questions for artists, 7, 9
Quiet (Cain), 49
quilting, 121
Quintana, Gene, 83

Rae, Genelle, 53
ranches and ranching, 25, 26–28, 29, 43, 92, 99
Ranger Bob (earth sculpture), 102
Rappa, Gail, 4, 107, 112–17
Raven Finds Home (jewelry), 117
raw material, 100
The Reenchantment of Art (Gablik), 161–62
Reid, Harry, 88
Reilly, Maura, 189–90
Reinhardt, Ad, 4, 9n1
reinventing self, 54
Reno's Coral Academy of Science, 86, 88
The Retrenchment of Art (Gablik), 55
Richards, M. C., 64
Righteous Brothers, 155
Roach, Carola Nan, 4, 15–19
Robb, Serena, 126
rock groups, 72
rocks, 12
Rodriguez, Favianna, 60, 67
Roller Derby Chicks (sculpture), 31, 32, 33–34
The Roll of the Dice (sculpture), 153
Rolston, Don, 112
Rookstool, Carol, 99
Roosevelt, Eleanor, 49
Ruby Mountains, 21, 28
rugged individualism, 3

Saar, Betye, 104
sage, 11
The Sagebrush Ocean (Trimble), 181
Sakata, Sandra, 124
Sampson, Adele Muzina, 80
Sanchez, Lily, 12, 104
Sandberg, Sheryl, 191
Sand Mountain, 12
Sarton, May, 6
Sauer, Jane, 50
Schulps, John, 32
scrip land, 25
sculptural purses, 126, 128–30
sculpture: animal figures, 43–44; clay use in (*see* ceramics); creation process, 99–100; earth sculptures, 102–103; experimental, 50, 52; glass use in, 19, 45; gourd use in, 85, 87, 88; knot use in, 46; mapping, 4; metal use in, 25–26, 28, 92; nontraditional, 165; overview of, 37; raw material use in, 100; redefined, xii; as specialty, 42; wax use in, 6, 40, 42, 45; wood use in, 50, 52
Seale, Bobby, 75
Selz, Peter, 69
Seminole work, 120
Severy, Richard, 58, 60
sewing, 117, 119, 144, 147, 155
sexism, 189
Sgt. Pepper's Lonely Hearts Club Band (album cover), 57, 58
shadow town (defined), 95, 106n15
shamans and shamanism, 43, 79
Shaw, Spencer, 71
shibui (defined), 107
Shiokawa, Kenzi, 186
Shively-Benjamin, Christine, 133, 147–51
Shoshone baskets, 83
Show (Don't) Tell (jewelry), 117
Shriver, Sargent, 145
Sierra Arts Foundation, 130
silver ore, 52, 54n4
single parents, 66
Sisters Rodeo, 43
slip (defined), 171, 187n2
snowman, making, 55, 57
Snyder, Don, 75
socially relevant stage performances, 72
Society of Glass Beadmakers, 22, 190
The Solace of Open Spaces (Ehrlich), 11–12
Soldate, Joe, 184
solitude, 46, 48, 49
Solnit, Rebecca, 3
The Soul's Palette (Malchiodi), 83, 85
Southeast Asia, 18
Southern Highland Craft Guild, 119, 120
space, 37, 44
space technology, 46
Spier, Nadine, 49, 50
The Spiral Dance (Starhawk), 104
spirituality, 172
spiritual practice, art as, 79
Spiritual Synthesis (sculpture), 105
stabiles, 26, 35n10
Starhawk, 104
stars, 185
State Organization on Arts and Disability, 88, 106n11
Statom, Therman, 17
stay-at-home mothers, 66
The Steampunk Machines of Cmdr. T. T. Kidd (art show), 136
Stegner, Wallace, 11
Stoll, Victoria Maase, 116
stone, 66
Stone Mother (mythical being), 12, 79, 82
Stone Mother (place), 34, 79, 106n2
Storer, Russell, 190
stories: art role in conveying, 88; with dolls, 141, 143–44, 145–47; lingering, 12; mapping, 6, 9; of potential, 31; reshaping and retelling, 3
storytelling, 4
Stremmel, Peter, 39
Stremmel, Turkey, 157
Streng, Priscilla, 126
structures, building, 103–104
Sundance Mountain School, 59, 60
Sunset at Tahoe (purse), 128
Suzuki, Mamiko, 64
sweat lodges, 87, 104
Sweetwater, Sarah, 55, 60–67, 116

Tahoe (term), 79–80
Tahoe (Wolfe), 72
Tahoe basket, 79–80, 83
tai chi, 94, 95
Tanning, Dorothea, 39
tar, 183, 185, 186
teachers, artists as, 16, 23, 34, 53,

63, 66, 69, 70, 72, 86, 88, 99, 116, 126, 166, 174, 184, 186
techniques, mapping, 5, 6
technology, arts and, 55
Teresa, Mother, 57, 146
textile artistry, 124
textiles, 59
Thiebaud, Wayne, 134
three bowls, story of, 31
three-dimensional art, 4, 37, 53
tia (term defined), 87–88, 106n10
TIG welding, 90, 92, 106n12
Timpanogos, Mount, 12
toilet tissue holders, 62
topographic mythology, 179
transformative practice, art as, 79
traumatic events, 7
Trimble, Stephen, 181
Truckee, California, 33
Try and Catch the Wind (art piece), 99
tufa, metal, welding to, 5
Tulane University, 17
tungsten inert gas welding (TIG), 90, 92, 106n12
Tuscarora: as artist haven, 190; Chinese people in, 74, 75; description of, 181; impressions of, 184; ties to, 186; Zimbabwe, comparison to, 76
Tuscarora Days, 26, 190
Twardy, Chuck, 177, 180
Twinkies as art medium, 133–134, 136–137
two-dimensional art, 52

Underfolk, 141, 143–44, 145–46
United Federation of Doll Clubs conference, 147
University of Nevada Press, 12
Urban Cowboot (purse), 128
Uriu, Barbara, 107–12
Uriu, Don, 109
Uriu, Kaz, 109
Uriu, Toshie, 109
Utah, wilderness of, 60
utilitarian ware, 50

Valdez, Ryrie, 126
Van Gogh, Vincent, 174
videos, 67
Virginia City, 50
vision quests, 87
Voulkos, Peter, 134
VSA Nevada, 88

Wabuska, 95
Wabuska Woman (art figure), 95, 99
Walt Disney Company, 104
Warhol, Andy, 134, 136
Washoe Bark Clothing series, 122
Washoe baskets, 82, 83
Washo Indian Woman and Papoose (box assemblage), 71–72
Waste, Kathrine Lemke, 189
water, quest for, 11
Watercourse (art exhibit), 158
Watercourse Artwork (art exhibit), 162
wax, sculpture from, 40, 42, 45
wax casting, 6
The Way It Is, 11
wearable art, 107, 122, 125
wearable sculpture, 4, 117
Weavers of Tradition and Beauty (Fulkerson and Curtis), xi
weaving, 63, 66
welding: awards, 94–95; learning, 75; oxy-acetylene, 92; techniques, 5, 90, 92, 94
Wescott, Don, 95
Wescott, Patricia, 79, 95–100
Wesphal, Katherine, 125
Wessels, Glen, 103
West, artistic depiction of, 79
West, myths of, 60
Westbrook, Helen and Ollie, 12, 13n4
White, Bob, 133
White House, xi
Wild Women Artists: founding of, 124, 191; goals and milestones, 121; members, 29, 34, 35, 105; references to, 6; shows and exhibits, 23, 25, 46, 54, 116, 143–44, 191
Wiley, William T., 134
Williams, Terry Tempest, 11
Williamson, Larry, 164–165
willow baskets, 79, 80, 81, 83
willows as art medium, 103–104
Wilson, Nick, 169, 171
Winnemucca, Sarah, 66, 67
Wolfe, Ann M., 72
women: art career challenges for, 7, 9n3, 58, 177, 180, 189–90; art opportunities for, xii, 3, 190–91, 193; as art subjects, 166–67; history, 66; lived experiences as, 3; men's experiences contrasted with those of, 7; roles and responsibilities, 3, 7, 13, 177, 183
Women, Art, and Society (Chadwick), 3
Women Who Run with the Wolves (Estes), 143, 191
wood, carving, 66
wood sculpture, 50, 52
work-life balance, 7
work outside home, 6–7
Work to Do (art exhibit), 157–58
world, making better place, art role in, 7, 174
World War II veterans, daughters of, 6, 19, 31, 75, 103, 124, 130, 155

yarn in artwork, 97
You Becha (sculpture), 153

Zimbabwe, 75
Zinc, Melissa, 117